Dictionary of Education
A Practical Approach

Dictionary of Education

A Practical Approach

P.M. Lohithakshan

KANISHKA PUBLISHERS, DISTRIBUTORS
NEW DELHI 110 002

KANISHKA PUBLISHERS, DISTRIBUTORS
4697/5-21A, Ansari Road, Daryaganj
New Delhi -110 002
Phones : 2327 0497, 2328 8285
Fax : 011-2328 8285
E-mail : kanishka_publishing@yahoo.co.in

Dictionary of Education: A Practical Approach
First Published-2002
Edition-2022

ISBN: 978-81-7391-462-1

PRINTED IN INDIA

Published by Madan Sachdeva for Kanishka Publishers, Distributors, 4697/5-21A, Ansari Road, Daryaganj, New Delhi-110 002, Typeset by Sunshine Graphics, Delhi, and Printed at Rajdhani Printers, Delhi.

Preface

The origin of this book dates back to over three decades, during the time when I had to conduct inservice-training programmes, conferences, seminars and workshops for all categories of personnel of the Education Department of Kerala as an officer of the State Institute of Education, Thiruvananthapuram. The participants were mainly teachers of pre-primary, primary and secondary schools, Inspecting officers, teacher-educators, research workers and also others from outside the department like social workers, staff of voluntary organizations, parents and even lay men. Though most of the participants were from the teaching community, who have had teacher's training and professional experience, they often complained that many terms I used were unfamiliar to them and so should have to be explained. Another reason for their difficulty was that many terms that they had learned during their training period had disappeared from use and a large number had newly found entry into the terminology. The dictionaries of education available were not very helpful for two reasons – one, that they gave only definitions for most of the terms and two, they did not include terms of Indian origin.

This situation led me, first to think about the preparation of a short glossary of educational terms. Further experience taught me that a glossary or simple dictionary with definition of terms would not meet the requirements. So, finally I decided to prepare a hand-book of reference of the present form, a dictionary for the practitioners, that provided, instead of definitions, short self-contained notes for each term. I also decided to avoid the educational vocabulary which were very familiar to teachers and those terms which did not require any explanation.

By scanning a large number of relevant publications in the different fields of education viz. philosophy of education, history of education, comparative education, Indian education, sociology of education, educational administration, finance and planning, educational psychology, psychology of learning, child psychology, abnormal psychology, guidance and counselling, educational statistics and psychometry, educational methodology, curriculum development, evaluation and measurement, methodology of teaching of languages and other subjects, information technology, educational technology, educational research and innovations in education, I prepared a list of about 2500 terms which seemed important. Indexing and preparation of short notes were undertaken at the next stage. For the final form it was necessary to reject again some items in order to keep the size of the book handy for use. Those items which were functionally of very limited significance were rejected. Final notes were prepared at the next stage, keeping the length under each heading to the minimum, without risking clarity and accuracy.

In the publication of this volume I am deeply indebted to a few persons, all of them my relatives. The typescript was carefully scrutinized by my nephew Dr. B. Dharmangadan, Professor and Head of the Department of Psychology, Kerala University. He offered very valuable suggestions for modification and improvement. My daughter Dr. Sumaranjitha Sahadevan, Counsellor, Abhaya Deaddiction Centre, Thiruvananthapuram assisted me in the preparation of the drafts. She also helped me with relevant suggestions. All the work regarding publication, down from the preparation of the final copy and proof-reading to getting the book in print was undertaken by my son Dr. L. Harenduprakash, Principal Scientific Officer, Ministry of Science and Technology, Government of India, New Delhi.

And finally, I owe immensely to my wife Mrs. K. Vydehi who was the inspiration behind the work and who by her encouragement and unspairing support enabled me to complete the project.

I hope the teaching community and others who are actively engaged in the task of education will find this book useful.

I dedicate this book to the memory of my beloved father.

Thiruvananthapuram **P.M. Lohithakshan**

A

ABC MODEL LEARNING: The method based on behaviour science approach to learning (Lindsley). 'A' refers to Antecedents in environment that elicit desired behaviour 'B', which is then strengthened by appropriate consequences 'C'.

To obtain desired results instruction should (1) be focussed on observable learner performance (2) ensure that the learners possess the basic skills that are necessary to acquire the new skills (3) elicit appropriate responses rapidly and (4) use appropriate consequences following performance (use reinforcements prompts, etc. as needed).

ABILITY PROFILE: Graphical representation of scores of tests of maximum performance (like scholastic tests, aptitude tests and other ability tests) of a pupil. It may be in the form of charts, diagrams, line graph, etc. The profiles provide a visual representation of the abilities or characteristics in a particular dimension like academic performance in the various school subjects.

See: Psychograph

ABILITY TESTS: Tests used to measure the capacity of the individual to do specific tasks. The term is usually applied to tests of the so called innate capacities like, intelligence, aptitudes, psychomotor performance, etc. There are two aspects that are typical of such tests (as in the case of achievement tests), speed and power. 'Speed' refers to the rate at which a number of tasks (of usually of medium difficulty) can be performed correctly during a given time and 'power' refers to the difficulty or complexity level of the items and the maximum number of items that can be done correctly without time restrictions.

Ability tests measure the individual's current status with regard to the ability, but most tests of ability can also forecast performance in related tasks.

See: Test. Capacity

ABILITY: Present level of performance in a task. The efficiency with which an individual can carry out a task is the index of his ability. Ability, therefore, is the power to perform a task, as a result of training or not. The term 'mental ability' generally, means intelligence. Ability can be displayed in any area of human activity, physical or mental. All tests of maximum performance (like intelligence tests, aptitude tests, educational achievement tests) are ability tests, because the results in these tests show the maximum performance the individual is capable of, which is the index of his ability in that task.

ABILITY GROUPING: Organization of classes for instructional purposes, based on abilities, like intelligence aptitudes, achievement etc. The assumption is that by grouping children of comparable abilities, heterogeneity can be narrowed down, which will facilitate effective teaching in a class situation. Lessons are planned according to the requirements of the group. As the class is near-homogeneous under this grouping, with regard to the ability required for learning the lessons, a common approach with some individualization is assumed to succeed to a considerable degree in achieving the objectives. The practice of admitting children to a class on the basis of intelligence tests and other entrance tests is based on this assumption.

The practice has been in favour with various school systems, particularly in the schools in U.K. Later it has become unpopular and now mixed-ability grouping is favoured. The method of detention (class repetition) popular in many countries in the world, in effect, is an attempt at ability grouping in a crude manner.

The advantages and disadvantages of ability grouping are still subject to debate.

See: Non-graded Elementary School

ABSOLUTE ZERO: The absolute point of reference on a Ratio scale. It is the real zero which indicates the non-existence of the quality, characteristic or dimension. So, for a physical entity like length, mass and time there is an absolute zero. But the zeros in the Fahrenheit and Centigrade scales of temperature are not absolute zeros, because those temperatures do not signify the total absence of temperature. In scales of measurement, for qualities we usually encounter in education and psychology (like intelligence, achievement, etc.), there is no absolute zero, since there can be nobody with zero intelligence or zero arithmetic ability.

In scales without an absolute zero, for practical purposes, usually the arithmetic mean (average) is taken as the point of reference in measurements.

See: Statistics

ABSTRACT THINKING: Thinking without the aid of concrete or specific things. In abstract thinking, concepts, generalizations, principles, etc. are used for the mental operations. Abstract thinking relies on symbolic language. More intelligent the person, more is the capacity for abstract thinking. Mentally defectives are severely handicapped in abstract thinking.

ABSTRACTION: The mental process of identifying and separating common elements in objects, situations, phenomena, etc. Other elements present in the situation may obliterate or shield the common elements, so that it may not be easy to perceive them. Ability to abstract subtle elements that are related, in a complex situation, depends on the intelligence of the individual.

Charles Darwin could discover those similarities that existed among the vast amount of variations present in the anatomy, physiology and behaviour of the organisms, from the very primitive to the most complex, both extinct and non-extinct. This led him to formulate the 'Theory of Evolution'.

In all types of generalizations, from the very simple to the most complex, viz., concepts, hypotheses, principles, laws and theories, abstraction is the fundamental process involved.

See: Generalization

ABSTRACTION LADDER: Expansion of conceptual experience resulting in the ability for precise linguistic expression. Example: Visual experience of objects (may be pictures or models) helps children to build step by step complex and abstract concepts. The children do this by classifying objects on the basis of similarities in some basic characteristic: eg., Pepper classified as spice, spice classified as cash crop, cash crop classified as 'export commodity' and export commodities as 'international trade', international trade as 'national income', etc. In abstracting the higher concepts, only the basic similarities are reckoned with while dissimilarities are overlooked. The concept become more and more abstract (and complex) as the process of abstraction proceeds. The stages of abstraction are compared to rungs of a ladder. Linguistic concepts at higher levels of abstraction enable the person to use the language precisely.

See: Concept

ABSURDITY ITEM TEST: A test item with some incongruency which the testee has to point out. Absurdity items are usually verbal, nonverbal or pictorial and are used in intelligence tests. There will be some inconsistency or contradiction in the statement or picture presented. The testee has to point out this absurdity. Absurdity items were used by Binet in his original test of intelligence. Subsequently many intelligence tests used these items. It is also used in tests of creativity, reasoning, etc.

See: Binet-Simon Scale

ACADEMIC FREEDOM: The freedom of a university to decide its own courses of studies, to make appointments of staff members, to conduct examinations to award degrees, etc. It implies freedom, in all matters including financial. In appointments there should be no discrimination on the basis of religion, political leanings, etc. The lecturers have the freedom to teach what they believe to be correct. Academic freedom is included in the rights of a university which functions in an autonomous framework, without intervention from any source, governmental or otherwise.

ACADEMIC YEAR: The period between fresh admissions for particular courses, standards, etc. of an educational institution. In many countries, in the northern hemisphere schools and colleges re-open for admission in June each year and close for summer vacation in March-April. The period between June and May is an academic year in such countries. In the countries in the southern hemisphere, the academic year approximately spreads from January to December. The academic year need not coincide with the calendar year. The academic year is divided into two or three terms. It is also called 'school year'.

ACADEMICALLY GIFTED: A child whose scholastic performance is consistently outstanding. Giftedness is used to include both a high degree of potential and manifest proficiency in any area of human endeavour. Academically gifted child possesses a high level of capacity for school work. His intelligence will be necessarily high. His habits of work, interests, etc. are also conducive to produce consistently exemplary results in school tests and examinations. Such children are also called academically talented or academically brilliant.

See: Giftedness

ACCELERATION: Development at a rate faster than normal. If a 7 year old child has the physical growth of a normal 9 year old child he is said to be physically accelerated. If he is able to achieve the score of an average 9 year old child in an intelligence test, he is said to be mentally accelerated.

The old practice of promoting a child to higher classes by skipping intermediate classes was on the basis of acceleration. For example, an academically brilliant child in class 7 was used to be promoted to class 9 instead of 8. But this practice is now extinct.

See: Retardation

ACCOMODATION: In Piageatian psychology, the mental process which results in the assimilation of new information by the existing schema (i.e., the existing network of information in the mind).

See: Assimilation Schema

ACCOMPLISHMENT QUOTIENT: The ratio between 'educational quotient' and 'intelligence quotient'. Educational quotient shows the relationship between educational age and chronological age

$$EQ = \frac{EA}{CA} x100$$

'Educational age' denotes the level of scholastic performance in terms of age. For example, if the Scholastic performance level of a 10 year old boy equals to the average performance level of 10 year old children, his educational age is 10 and his Educational Quotient is (10/10) x 100 = 100. Educational quotient shows whether achievement level of the child is below, same or above the normal for the age group.

Intelligence is considered to be the most powerful single factor directly related to school achievement. So disparity between Educational quotient and Intelligence quotient can indicate whether an individual is working up to capacity (normal achievement) or beyond capacity (over-achievement) or below capacity (under-achievement). Thus an Educational quotient below 100 roughly indicates under achievement.

See: Educational Age, Intelligence Quotient

ACCOUNTABILITY: In education, holding of responsibility by the personnel involved in the management of education, for the efficiency of the system. The teachers and the entire personnel engaged in the management of education of a state are morally answerable to the tax-payer. As it is not easy to assess the work of a school by cost-benefit analysis or other objective methods, even serious lapses are left unquestioned. The school is accountable to the society for which it functions and which supports it. Eventhough this accountability has been recognized, there is little effort to enforce it. Once there was the system of 'payment by results' prevalent in some countries, where teachers' payments were increased or decreased according to the results they produced (pass in the examinations). Good teachers, consider 'accountability' as a part of their professional ethics.

Accountability in school management implies that those who are involved in the delivering of goods (primarily teachers) are accountable to their clients (parents and public) for the outcomes and processes, of the school's activities. It also indicates the responsibility of the teachers and other professionals to adherance to codes of practice and ethics of the profession. The teacher is considered as the unit of account. Political accountability refers to the schools' accountability to the government. It is the professional responsibility of the institution to ask an individual or a group concerned to account for their actions.

ACETYL CHOLINE: A neuro-transmitter produced in the nervous system. In the peripheral nervous system it is released by motor nerves. It exerts control over the action of muscles. Acetyl choline produced in the brain is involved in the control of cognitive and emotional behaviour. Deficit of acetyl choline in the brain is found associated with Alzheimer's disease.

See: Neurotransmitter

ACHIEVEMENT TEST: A test that is designed to measure performance in an activity area, after a period of training. Achievement test (also called attainment tests) is a test of maximum performance i.e., it measures the maximum achievement possible for an individual in an activity. Achievement tests measure the performance of individual after undergoing a course of study. All examinations in schools and colleges make use of achievement tests. In schools, teachers make use of them for assessment of pupils' work and for deciding promotions. Such tests are based on the objectives specified in the curricula. Standardized achievement tests are also available in various subjects. Such tests are used for inter-institutional or inter-regional comparison of performance of students, for selection for jobs and training, etc.

In short, an achievement test measures the change in behaviour of an individual after a period of learning or training. An achievement test is intended to measure the outcome of learning in relation to the objectives of learning the subject. So the test consists of tasks based on the objectives. The individual is expected to answer the tests, usually within a prescribed time. The total number of correct responses (Score) gives an index of his ability. Achievement tests are used for deciding grades, promotions, scholarships, etc. It is also used for diagnosis, guidance, for evaluation of the effectiveness of teaching, etc. Achievement tests are either standardized or informal (teacher made).

Achievement tests are used to measure both cognitive and motor abilities.

A good achievement test has also predictive uses.

All tests used by teachers for deciding students' progress are achievement tests.

Achievement tests are also called 'Attainment tests' and 'Accomplishment tests'.

See: Tests

ACHIEVEMENT MOTIVE: A concept developed by the social psychologist McClelland to denote the strong urge felt by an individual or society for achievements in various aspects like education, culture, money, etc. that satisfies the need of self-esteem. The aspiration or achievement motive (need Achievement–nAch.) is the deciding factor in attaining success in different fields. An achieving society is characterized by the history of a strong and persistent achievement motivation.

ACQUIRED: Characteristics developed as a result of

experience. From the interaction between the individual and the environment, capabilities develop in the individual which help him to make further successful adjustment to the environment. It has been possible to develop these characteristics because of the physiological and psychological pre-disposition that has made him fit for acquiring these characteristics. It is the intelligence, the various aptitudes, psychomotor abilities, etc., that enable the individual to develop the proficiences. These psychological and physiological characteristics are referred to as inherited characteristics. All other characteristics of the persons, outside the inherited characteristics, are acquired, like proficiency in using language, numbers, tools, instrument, etc.

See: Instinct

ACTION RESEARCH: Research conducted by the practitioner (eg. teacher) in the natural setting (i.e. as and when he is engaged in his regular work) with a view to improving his techniques. It is the research carried on along with the normal programmes of the work of the practitioner (teacher) without upsetting any regular activity. The teacher in his day to day work may encounter a lot of problems. In his own way, he may be improvising solutions to these problems. He retains the solution that has succeeded, for future applications. That is how a teacher improves with experience. But such 'try-outs' takes place generally in a haphazard manner. When the teacher sets out to solve his problems in a systematic manner applying the rigours of experimentation to the extent possible in the school situation, he is said to be attempting 'action research'. As the conclusions drawn from action research are generated in the natural school situations, their applicability in the schools are not in question, unlike the conclusions drawn from traditional research (which are generated under controlled conditions which are often dissimilar to class room conditions).

The situation for action research arises from a serious difficulty that the teacher encounters in his endeavour to achieve an objective. The first step towards the solution of the problem is to identify and locate the problem (may be spelling difficulty, a behaviour problem). Then, the probable causes of the difficulty should be explored. This will require a thorough analysis of the problem. It will naturally lead to the formulation of plausible ways in which the difficulty can be eliminated, i.e. the formulation of hypotheses.

Next step is the trying out of the hypotheses, i.e. the trial of the new method. If the hypothesis is found valid in application, the new method can be considered a worthy one. The experiment is replicated a few times to see whether the results are consistent. In applying action research to solve the teacher's problems it is necessary to adopt the scientific method throughout and apply the controls of experimentation as far as possible.

In short, the steps involved in action research are:

1. Identification of the problem and its focus;
2. analyzing the probable causes;
3. formulation of plausible methods of solving the problem (formulation of action hypotheses);
4. trying out the hypothesis (i.c. action programme in which the new procedure are tried out);
5. drawing conclusions;
6. replication (repeating a few times).

Stephen Corey was responsible in popularizing the action research approach in education.

To solve common problems felt by a number of schools, action research can be organized cooperatively. Then it is known as cooperative research. Action research is also known as operational research.

See: Research Experiment

ACTIVE VOCABULARY: The words a person can use in speaking and writing. It is by continued contact with those words that they become part of the linguistic stock of the person. At first all words are unfamiliar, but with frequent contacts the words become somewhat familiar, i.e. they can be recognized and the meaning understood when presented in spoken or written form. This is the 'passive vocabulary' stage. With still more contact, in life situations, the mastery becomes complete, and the words can be used automatically when necessary, for speaking or writing. The required word spontaneously comes to the mind when the occasion demands. This is the active vocabulary stage. Active vocabulary may relapse into passive vocabulary by long disuse.

See: Passive vocabulary

ACTIVE LEARNING: Learning based on student activity, with minimum teacher intervention. The method is applied largely with students of higher age-groups, the main activity being discussion and group work in a free setting. Learning is student-centered. It is an effective method for development of critical thinking.

ACTIVITY METHODS: Teaching methods that emphasize pupil activity. Many of the methods employed in teaching pupils in the schools in vogue depended largely on the passive learning of pupils, i.e., teacher resorting to verbal teaching and pupils simply listening. Activity methods imply learning by doing. Many experiments have proved that learning will be more effective, meaningful and realistic if it takes place as the result of active participation of pupils. Teaching is now considered as the structuring of learning situation that initiates pupil to activity, mental and motor activity, leading to learning. Learning is the process of modifying behaviour on the basis of experience. In school situations, the teachers' role is to provide opportunities for the pupils to undergo the experiences which are expected to produce the desirable behaviour changes. The teacher contrives the situations in such a way that the pupils undergo the experiences (that is, by reading, asking questions, discussing, observing, problem solving, experimenting etc.) which leads to maximum learning. Good learning occurs only if the pupils themselves have the direct experience. In passive learning (like listening lecture) someoneelse's experience is translated into verbal symbols to which the pupils are exposed. Some learning takes place when listening such talks, as there is some experience, but as there is no direct participation, the learning tends to be often imperfect and unrealistic. All activity methods (project methods, assignments, laboratory methods, discussions, etc.) make use of active participation of pupils in varying degrees.

See: Project

ACTIVITY CARD: Card used in project method which shows the day's assignment of activities for the child. The child proceeds to work as indicated in his activity card, at his own speed. There will be clear indications of what the pupil should do: like what observations, or measurements to make, what to record, what should be done after one stage, what should be the culminating activity, etc. The children should have to manipulate objects, explore relationship, find solutions to problems etc. first under the guidance of the teacher, but at later stages independently, solely depending on the directions in the activity card.

See: Assignment

ADAMS, JOHN: British educationist. He was a brilliant teacher and he popularised the application of Herbartian psychology to education. He emphasized that education should focus attention on the pupil, that is, it should be paedeocentric. His book 'The Evolution of Educational Thought' (1912) discusses educational theory under the heads, 'humanism', 'naturalism', 'idealism', and 'materialism'.

ADAPTATION: (1) Modifying behaviour in order to cope with the situation. Education and a balanced personality help one to make proper adaptation in a new environment. Adaptation involves the altering and adjusting of one's views, approaches etc. to make oneself at home with the new environment. The elements of the environment may be unfamiliar, unfriendly or hostile. It involves modification of the person's psychological characteristics so as to establish balance with the environment, which then leads to good adjustment. Good adjustment is characterized by the ability to get on well with any situation or changing circumstances (i.e., adaptation).

(2) (Sensory) adaptation means the characteristic change in experience produced as a result of the experience (stimulus) preceding it. Eg: Things completely invisible in a dark room become visible after the lapse of a few seconds without any additional light.

See: Schema

ADDICTION: Psychological dependence of a person on liquors and drugs. Apart from alcohol, use of a variety of drugs leads to habituation. The drugs are sedatives (like opium and its products, i.e., heroin), hypnotics (like barbiturates), tranquilizers (like Meprobamate), Stimulants (like Cocaine, Nicotine, Amphetamines), hallucinogens (like Marijuana, Mascaline), etc. WHO Committee views 'Drug addition as "state of periodic or chronic intoxication, detrimental to the individual and to society, produced by the repeated consumption of drugs. The characteristics of drug addiction are irresistable dependence to the drug which leads the individual to procure it by any available means, tendency to increase dosage, etc. More and more youth seem to succumb to addiction in most of the countries and so this has added an additional dimension to the problems to the educational planners".

Addiction can be cured medically. But as in any other case, prevention is better than cure.

ADHESIVE DISPLAY: Display materials exhibited directly on a board; type of non-projected display. In adhesive display, the display materials are stuck to the surface of the display board in some way other than by using pins or glue, eg., Felt-display like flannel board, hook and loop board display, magnetic board display.

ADJUSTMENT INVENTORIES: A test (usually standardized) used to measure the individual's capacity to cope with social and environmental situations. Adjustment inventories belong to the group of personality tests. The score obtained by the individual in an adjustment inventory can provide useful information about his characteristic ways of responding in social and physical situations and the nature of his inner emotional feelings.

Adjustment inventories may be unidimensional or multidimensional. Unidimensional adjustment inventory will have items to test only one dimension (non-composite) like sociability or emotional stability or extraversion. Multidimensional tests may have items to test more than one dimension.

In inventories, the items are presented in the form of 'questions' (eg., Do you have difficulty in starting conversation with a stranger?) or 'statements' (I often cross the street to avoid some one). The testee has to check each item and imagine himself in the situation and mark his characteristic response in the situation. (by underlining, Yes, No, Doubtful, etc. given in the questionnaire). The total score obtained by the individual gives a good index of his position with regard to that dimension (say emotional stability). This score is interpreted with the help of the norms obtained for the test. Personality tests of Eysenck, Bell, Allport-Vernon, Wood-worth, Benreauter, etc. are well known adjustment inventories.

See: Inventories

ADLER, ALFRED (1870-1937): The founder of the school of 'Individual psychology', related to psychoanalysis. Along with Jung, Adler was a close associate of Freud. He was born in Vienna.

One of his early studies was that concerning 'organ inferiority' and 'over-compensation'. Gradually he dissociated from Freud, because of the over-emphasis of sex in psychoanalysis. Adler postulated that the characteristic way in which a person's individuality is expressed in the social environment is dependent on his 'style of life'. Life style indicated the individual's effort to attain goals, and everyone's style of life is unique. Early childhood experiences of neglect, oppression and pampering were the major causes for the development of faulty life styles. Psychotherapy according to Adler, therefore, should attempt to rectify the faulty life style.

Adler's theory of 'inferiority complex' had profound influence in psychological thinking. A variety of normal and abnormal behaviour could be explained in terms of 'inferiority complexes.'

See: Individual psychology

ADJUSTMENT: The process of harmonizing behaviour with the physical and social environment. It is the process by which the person achieves satisfying relations with the people and things around him. A well-adjusted person has good relations with the people with whom he has to interact in social situations, i.e., he is socially efficient and happy. When meeting with new situations, he modifies his habitual behaviour to accommodate the changes in the environment. Integrated personality and proper education are the two important prerequisites for the development of adjustment abilities. The aim of education, according to some educationists is to prepare the individual for proper adjustment.

See: Personality

ADVANCED ORGANIZER: In the implementation of a lesson, the facts and materials presented before the lesson in order to prepare the students to receive (prepare the cognitive structure before hand) the new material. 'Objectives' are important components of advanced organizers.

ADVANCED LEVEL EXAMINATION (GCE)—A LEVEL: The examination taken by abler students in U.K. after a two year study following GCSE. A wide range of subjects are offered at A-level. Normally, a candidate chooses 2 or 3 subjects. For university admission a pass in at least two subjects is necessary.

AFFECT: The mental experience one has, when emotions are aroused: feeling. Affects are broadly classified either as pleasant or unpleasant. Fear, disgust, etc. are unpleasant affects while love, joy, etc. are pleasant. 'Affect'. refers to the general mental state of pleasantness or unpleasantness when responding to a situation, thing, person, etc.

See: Emotion. Feeling

AFFECTIVE PROCESS: The mental processes involving feelings and emotions. It is those processes which produce emotional reactions related to the feelings state (i.e., pleasantness and unpleasantness). Arousal of fear, anger, disgust, love, etc. and the behaviour resulting from such arousal are affective processes. Affective processes are also involved in the complex characteristics, like 'attitudes', 'values'.

See: Emotion

AFFECTIVE DOMAIN: The domain of educational objectives concerned with the emotional spects of learning outcomes. The other two major domains are: cognitive (which deals with knowledge) and psychomotor (which deals with overt activity). Affective domain deals with learning which involves emotions and feelings. Interests, attitudes, appreciations and values can be roughly considered as the outcome of learning in the affective domain. Learning in the affective domain is very important, because the person's motivation to act in a particular situation depends more on the affective aspects of his learning (like attitudes and values) rather than his mastery of the ideas and skills. Whether a person will behave in a democratic manner in a social situation is more dependent on the degree of his internationalisation of democratic values rather than his expert knowledge of democracy and democratic systems. It is the domain of feelings and emotions. The educational objectives in this domain according to the 'Taxonomy Group' consisting of D.R. Krathwohl, B.S. Bloom and B.B. Masia are:

1. Receiving (attending)
2. Responding
3. Valuing
4. Organization
5. Characterization

See: Taxonomy

AFFERENT (NERVES): Nerve fibres that carry impulses from the sense organ to the central nervous system. The flow of impulses from the various parts of the body (sensory impulses) to the spinal cord and brain takes place only through the afferent nerves.

See: Efferent

AGE NORMS: Test norms prepared for different age groups. Whenever the dimension to be measured is found to vary with age, i.e., the scores obtained for the tests designed to measure the dimension increase (or decrease) with age, age-norms are obtained. For example, intelligence, height, weight, etc. normally increase with age (up to a certain stage) and so age-norms are computed for these variables.

Age norms show the typical or average performance (or typical level of the trait) of individuals of different age levels on a test. They are also meant as age-equivalents of raw-scores.

The computation of age norms is done by working out the mean score for each age range desired. The mean score for a particular age represents the typical performance of children of that age. The raw scores obtained by other children are compared with the norm for their age groups. Norms are also prepared in the form of derived scores, like centiles, T-score and other types of standard scores to make comparison easier.

See: Grade equivalent

AGE EQUIVALENT: The equivalent in age of a raw-score on a standardized test. For computing age-equivalent of a score, the average score on the test for each age-group is determined (eg.; mean score in an intelligence test for the age group 10-11 years is 20, 11-12 years is 30). Any child (irrespective of chronological age) who gets a score of 20 in the test has an age-equivalent of 10 years, and a child who gets a score of 30 has an age equivalent of 11 years, and so on. The classical example of age equivalent is the 'mental age'. It is calculated thus: The average performance (based on raw scores) of each age-group (chronological) is computed, and these mean scores are the age-equivalents. If the raw score obtained by a boy in an intelligence test is equal to the average of the scores obtained by the 12 year-olds in the test, his age-equivalent (mental age) is 12 irrespective of his chronological age.

See: Grade equivalent

AGGRESSION: The behaviour characterized by the tendency to attack. Aggressive behaviour is aroused when a person's efforts are strongly thwarted. It is the natural reaction to thwarting. Anger or rage is the emotional core of all aggressive behaviour. When a need based (goal-directed) activity of the person is thwarted, anger is aroused. This may lead to aggressive behaviour, physical or verbal. The aggressive behaviour, is a violent reaction against the obstruction, with the intention of removing or destroying it. The aggressive behaviour may or may not lead to success. As it is an impulsive response, many aggressive responses often result in complicating the situation. A person with a well-integrated personality in a similar situation will modify his approach to the situation and try to overcome the difficulty in an appropriate manner, that is least aggressive.

Some children develop aggressive behaviour tendencies as their characteristic mode of meeting any obstruction, real or imaginary, serious or trivial. For no apparent reason they attack others. Such children have learnt this pattern as their normal way of tackling difficulties. The parents in many homes unwittingly promote the development of aggressive behaviour in children by conditioning such responses–(by reinforcing aggressive behaviour i.e. meeting their needs only when they show aggressive behaviour). Children who suffer neglect at home are also likely to develop aggressive behaviour. Children who belong to a peer group comprising gangsters also are likely to develop aggressive tendencies. Some manic patients are aggressive.

Counselling and psychotherapy are useful for treating abnormal aggressive tendencies.

ALGORITHM: A computer program. It is a program by which a complex calculation is reduced to a long series of simple calculations in a form that a digital computer can perform.

It is also used to denote the series of instructions or steps to be undertaken that is necessary to solve a problem or to help reach a decision in the desired area.

AGNOSIA: Inability to experience sensory input. A person having visual agnosia, though receives the visual images on the retina of his eyes, will be unable to interpret them (i.e., there will be no perception). In acoustic agnosia (aphasia or word blindness) the individual hears sounds but will not recognize their semantic significance.

See: Hysteria

AGREED SYLLABUS: The syllabus for religious instruction adopted by the Local Education Authorities in all state-aided schools in the United Kingdom. Religious instruction in all state-aided schools should be carried out only on the basis of the agreed syllabus. The syllabus will not contain any item of instruction which is distinctive of a particular religious denomination. The L.E.A. works out the agreed syllabus in consultation with representatives of all religious denominations, teachers, associations, etc. Sometimes with minor modifications all L.E. As in the country adopt the same agreed syllabus. The agreed syllabus has been implemented on the basis of the 1944 Education act.

AIDED SCHOOLS: Schools which receive regular financial aid from government. Aided schools, managed by private bodies, are recognized institutions receiving regular monetary aid from the government under grant-in-aid rules or other rules. The managers of the schools have to satisfy the conditions laid down by government with regard to school site, buildings, equipment, staffing etc. in order to qualify for the aid. The quantum of assistance vary from country to country. In Kerala (India) for example, the entire salary of teachers and non-teaching staff of aided schools is paid from the government treasury. In addition to that, the managers are given maintenance grant (for repairs, purchase of educational equipment, etc.) on the basis of the number of students on rolls.

In some countries, only a part of the total expenditure incurred for running the school is given as grant-in-aid by the government.

See: Un-aided school

AIM: 'Aim' as used in education, means, the general purpose, the overall desirable outcome of the educational process. 'Harmonious development of all capacities of the individual' is an example generally cited. Though it is comprehensive, it is not clear enough to plan or direct any educational programme to achieve the purpose. So to plan and implement educational activities 'aims' have to be more specific and clear. Vagueness of 'aim' disappears when it is broken down into 'behavioural outcomes' (like, 'the development of ability to formulate hypothesis') that can be identified and measured. Such identifiable outcomes are now called 'objectives'. Still the term 'aim' is preferred when the ideal, ultimate goal of education is what is meant by the speaker.

See: Behavioural objectives

ALAXIA: Inability to read. It is a neurological disorder which needs medical attention.

ALPHA RHYTHM: The brain waves present generally when the person is resting or relaxing. Alpha rhythum wave ranges between 9 Hz to 12 Hz

See: Delta waves

ALPHABETIC METHOD: An old method of teaching reading (English) now practically discarded. The pupils first spell out the individual letters of the word by their conventional names and then names the word. The phonemes of a word are ignored.

See: Phonic method

ALTERNATE TEST FORMS: A test in two equivalent forms. Sometimes a test is produced in two forms (versions) with items similar in qualitative and quantitative characteristics (like objectives, difficulty level, discrimination, etc.). The two forms have almost similar norms and test statistics like means, standard deviations, reliability and validity coefficients, etc. Therefore the measure obtained from one form will be almost close to the measure obtained in the other. The second form can be used for a second testing, if necessary, within a short interval after the first testing, without risking secrecy.

As it is convenient and economical to produce two equivalent forms, simultaneously, in test development, this practice is very often followed. For ascertaining the reliability of both the test forms, this procedure is advantageous. The correlation between the scores obtained for the two forms from the same set of candidates under identical conditions of testing, yields the index of reliability of these tests. This reliability is called the Alternative form (Equivalent) reliability. Alternate test form is also called Equivalent Test forms and parallel test forms.

ALTERNATE RESPONSE TEST: A test with items that give only two response choices. It is a multiple choice test with only two given responses from which the candidate has to choose his answer. These answers are usually given in the forms, True-False, Yes-No, Agree-Disagree, Similar-Dissimilar, etc. This type of question has a wide range of applicability, in achievement, ability and personality tests. Comparatively these test items are easy to construct and score. Though a high degree of objectivity can be maintained in constructing and scoring the test, the chances of guessing and cheating are very large (upto 50%). When used as achievement test items, a correction for guessing is applied by using the correction formula.

See: Multiple-choice item, Open ended question

AMBI-DEXTERITY: Ability to use both right and left hands with equal proficiency. The vast majority of people are right-handed. People prefer to use one hand and use it most of the time. They are 'right-handed' or 'left-handed' according to the hand preferred. But some people are mixed-handed, that is they use both hands equally well and approximately at equal amounts of time. Such people are said to be ambidexterous.

AMBIVALENCE: Possessing opposing attitudes simultaneously, towards a person, object or goal. A person in an ambivalent situation may possess both feelings of love and hate towards the same person at the same time.

AMBIVERT: A person who is neither an extrovert nor an introvert; person who displays both the characteristics of introverts and extroverts moderately.

See: Extroversion, Introversion

AMINO-ACID: Constituents of proteins. The amino-acid molecules can act both as an acid and as base and they join with other molecules to form complex and long chains of proteins. Plants and animals have the same amino-acids in their tissues, and they number only twenty

See: Glutamic acid

AMNESIA: Loss of memory. It may be due to organic (tissue damage or defect of the brain) or functional problems. Functionally it often occurs with traumatic experiences (i.e., strong emotional shock). Amnesia is treated psycho-therapeutically.

See: Hysteria

AMPHETAMINE: A drug that initially causes elevation of mood and energy. They are central nervous system (CNS) stimulatns, with side effects like suppression of appetite, increased heart rate and blood pressure and euphoria (elated feeling of well-being) E.g. Benzedrine, Methedrine.

See: Barbiturates

AMYGDALA: A part of the limbic system, a basal part of the brain. It is found to have involvement in emotional behaviour. Injury to amygdala causes, particularly, changes in aggressive behaviour.

ANALOGUE: An equivalent in a different form. Something consistently and continuously proportional to some variable; a device or system which handles or processes material in analogue form, like sound waves being converted into electrical impulses in a microphone.

ANALOGUE CODING: Transforming the message (signal) from one form to its corresponding form in another energy medium. In telephones, variations in the sound at the mouth piece produce corresponding variations in the current in the telephone wires. In radio transmission sound variations have corresponding electromagnetic wave transformation.

There is an one-to-one correspondence between the value of the original signal and the converted signal ie for every distinct value of the continuous quantity (e.g. speech) there is a distinct value of the signal (e.g. current).

See: Digital coding

ANALOGY ITEM: A type of item used in intelligence tests, for the solving of which the mental operation required is relational thinking. An analogy test item has two parts, the first part with two elements showing a particular relationship (e.g., pencil : write) and a second part in which one element is given and the second is left blank (eg. brush : ......). In a set of plausible answers given, (usually 4) one element bears to the element in the second part (i.e., brush), the same relationship borne between the first and second element in the first part (pencil : write). For solving analogy item, the candidate has to find out the relationship between the first and second element in the first part and choose the correct element from the given alternatives which carries the same relationship with the given element in the second part. Analogy items can be constructed to produce items at high levels of difficulty and complexity.

(e.g. Boy : Girl–Man:? Alternatives child, wife, woman, sister. Ship : Sea–Airplane:? Jet, sky, submarine, rocket.

Analogy items are used in verbal, numerical and performance type intelligence tests.

See: Intelligence test

ANALYSIS OF CO-VARIANCE (ANCOVA): The statistical technique used to control the effects of one or more variables that could not be controlled at the experimental stage, (in an experimental design), involving two or more groups. It is an extension of Analysis of variance (ANOVA). It permits the analyses to be carried out without distorting the results.

ANALYSIS OF VARIANCE: Statistical technique used to test the significance of the difference between the means of different samples, independent or correlated. It is used in research designs in which more than two sets of measurements in the same variable are obtained and the significance of the differences, if any, of the difference between the sets are to be found out.

Example: An experimenter wanted to study the effects of (1) free–and restricted environment and (2) early-late deprivation of food on shape discrimination in pigeons. There are two independent variables in this experiment and each variable has two categories. So four combinations are possible: free-environment and early deprivation; free-environment and late deprivation; restricted environment and early deprivation, and restricted environment and late deprivation. So there are four groups of experimental pigeons. After obtaining data from the experiment an analysis of variance was applied to find out the significance in the difference in the performance of pigeons in the different groups. The significance of the differences are found out by determining the respective F-ratios obtained from the formula

$$F = \frac{S_1^2}{S_2^2}$$

where, S_1^2 is the mean variance between sets and

S_2^2 is the mean variance within sets.

The significance of F-ratios can be read from the Table of F-ratios.

See: Hypothesis Variance

ANALYSIS: The educational objective, according to Bloom's taxonomy, Level 4 of Cognitive domain. Analysis is the cognitive process which involves the breaking down of complex concepts, systems and processes into their component parts and scrutinising the relationship existing among them.

See: Taxonomy

ANCILLARY SERVICES: School services that are not directly related to teaching-learning process, but are accessory services which facilitate it. School health services, noon-feeding programmes, personnel services, etc. are essential components of the schooling programmes. These services are designed as ancillary or auxiliary services.

ANDROGENS: Male sex hormones secreted from the gonads. The most important androgen is testosterone. Testosterone is responsible for the development of secondary sex characteristics during adolescence. It also plays an important role in maintaining sex drive in the male.

See: Estrogen.

ANECDOTAL RECORD: An objective and accurate description of an incident in which the subject was involved. Subjective impressions, opinions, etc. have no place in an anecdotal record. The observer prepares a brief objective record of the incident in detail including the reactions of the individual, eg.,: A boy who normally appears reserved, moves into action to render first aid to a person involved in an accident and to arrange for his hospitalization, when a number of people stay bewildered. The objective report of the incident brings to light some basic nature of his personality which was not at all obvious otherwise.

All incidents are not fit for preparing anecdotal records. Only situations that are apt to throw light on the personality qualities of the individual are to be considered for anecdotal records.

Anecdotal record is a non-testing method of collecting data on behaviour. These records are useful in rendering guidance and counselling to the candidate.

See: Guidance

ANGER: The feeling aroused when an activity is interfered with (i.e., when the individual feels opposed). Anger is aroused by a situation in which rights are denied, injury is inflicted, efforts are obstructed, etc. Challenges arouse anger. The subjective feeling aroused by such situations as well as the behaviour shown are referred to as anger. Perception of such situations sets a series of glandular and nervous (automic) changes in the body which result both in the subjective feelings and the explicit behaviour (i.e., fighting, arguing, etc.).

Normally, individuals respond to thwarting situations with anger reactions. If the response (anger) is commensurate with the provocation, it is said to be normal. Some individuals respond in an aggressive and violent manner for no sufficient provocation. This is abnormal and it needs psychological treatment. Anger generally lowers the efficiency of the individual, while mild anger in some situation is found to boost the efforts.

See: Agression. Emotions

ANIMATION: In visual display (as teaching devices) the creation of an illusion of movement by special effects. Animation arouses interest in children and it enhances the effectiveness of the lesson.

ANTERIOGRADE AMNESIA: Loss of memory of events and experience from a particular point of time occurring as a result of an emotional shock. After a severe traumatic experience (emotional shock) some individuals forget what has happened at the time of the painful experience or after that. The disorder is functional.

See: Trauma Retrograde Amnesia

ANTHROPOMORPHISM: The practice of attributing human qualities to animals, physical events, etc.

ANXIETY: A state of suspended unconscious (or sometimes conscious too) fear. In anxiety, the person is often not aware of the cause, but the mental and physiological symptoms of fright continues to exist. Increased heart beat, heightened blood-pressure, bowel upsets, feelings of frustration and helplessness, depression and sadness are the general symptoms of anxiety. Anxiety pulls down the efficiency of the person. If a person continues to be in an extreme anxiety state, he is likely to develop serious neurotic disorders and psychosomatic diseases like hypertension and gastric ulcers.

Eventhough anxiety is indicative of a morbid state, mild anxiety when one faces a difficult situation works as a spur for enhanced energetic action.

See: Fear Neurosis

APHASIA: Loss of speech. It is evidenced by the inability to understand written or spoken word. This psychological disorder usually occurs after severe emotional shocks. In motor aphasia the individual will not be able to speak (articulate) but will be able to understand written and spoken language. Psychotherapy and other clinical methods are used for treating this disorder.

See: Hysteria. Trauma

APPLICATION: Level 3 in Bloom's Taxonomy of educational objectives in the Cognitive domain. The making use of facts, principles, theories, etc. to tackle a problem. Application involves the use of known facts (or principles) to understand or solve an unfamiliar problem.

See: Taxonomy

APPRAISAL: A term often used interchangeably with measurement and evaluation. It means the process of determining present status of achievement, ability, etc. Though appraisal indicates more than simple measurement, it is not comprehensive enough to include all aspects of achievement in terms of objectives, for which the term evaluation is preferred. Appraisal is also used inter changeable with assessment.

See: Evaluation

APPERCEPTION: The mental process by which new experiences are absorbed in and assimilated by the mass of past mental associations, according to the Associationists. Similar ideas coalesce and form bunches–'the apperception mass'. New ideas related to the 'apperception mass' have the tendency to coalesce readily with it. This process is 'apperception'. This is how new ideas are received in the mind. Those ideas that are totally unrelated to past experiences, (i.e., ideas for which there is no proper apperception masses) tended to be rejected. So, in teaching, it is necessary to relate new ideas with related ideas, previously learned. According to the Herbartian plan, the preparation and testing of previous knowledge are intended to prepare the 'apperception masses' ready to absorb the new ideas.

See: Herbart, J.F.

APREXIA: A neurological disorder characterized by the inability to carry out motor responses to verbal instructions.

APTITUDE TEST: Tests for measuring the psychological characteristics that are predictive of success in some specific activity. Mechanical, spatial, musical, artistic, numerical, clerical, etc. are the aptitudes for which tests are available. High scores in the test predicts a higher degree of proficiency, if the person is given proper training. High score on a test of mechanical aptitude is predictive of success in mechanical, engineering and allied courses of studies. The well known Differential Aptitude Test (DAT) has sub-tests for measuring the aptitudes: Verbal reasoning, Number, Abstract reasoning, Space relations, Clerical spelling and language usage. Likewise, there are tests for measuring Musical aptitude (Seashore), Art judgement (Meier), Finger dexterity (O'Connor), etc.

See: Test

APTITUDES: The potential for learning specific tasks, like signing, painting, sculpturing, etc. Aptitude is a set of characteristics which is indicative of the capacity to develop proficiency in some skill or subject, after adequate training. The term 'aptitude' is usually reserved for denoting potential for specific and restricted proficiencies, unlike intelligence, which is prognostic of overall general proficiency. Aptitude is only a set of psychological characteristics that is indicative of future accomplishment, possible only with appropriate training. The present level of attainment in a specific task, therefore, is not an index of the aptitude. Musical aptitude of a person, for example cannot be judged reliably from his present level of accomplishment in singing. It is better judged by the person's 'unlearned' capacity to discriminate close differences in tonal memory, timbre, intensity, time, pitch and rhythm, etc. Performance scores of the individual on tests of these dimensions (i.e. Seashore's test of musical aptitude) are indicative of the level of success in musical proficiency in future. Musical aptitude, mechanical aptitude, neuromuscular co-ordination, scientific aptitude, etc. are some of the aptitudes for which standardized tests are available.

See: Ability

AQUINAS, ST. THOMAS: The European clergy man, theologician and educational thinker, the author of 'Summa Theologica'. He was born around 1225 and lived upto 1274 AD. The book 'Summa Theologica' is primarily addressed to students of theology, but it also contains his educational ideas. In the book is explained the methods of teaching that had developed in the higher institutions of learning in Paris–the 'lectio' and the 'disputation' (lecture, the discussion/debate). The link between the two was provided by the 'qustio'. St. Aquinas defined disputation as a syllogistic activity carried on between one person and another about a proposition which has been enunciated.

AREA TRAINING ORGANIZATION: Area Training Organization (Britain) is the regional organization responsible for the supervision of the preservice training of teachers in a geographically limited area around a university. It is often called an Institute of Education or sometimes as a School of Education. There are 18 such A.T.Os in England and Wales. The A.T.O. has a governing body consisting of representatives of Universities, training colleges, local education authorities and the Ministry of Education. The A.T.O's responsibility includes conducting examinations for the initial qualification for teaching and the award of diplomas with the formal approval of the Ministry of Education, further education of practising teachers and educational research.

ARISTOTLE: Aristotle lived between BC 386 and 322. Young Alexander was placed under his care for education and Alexander the Great, in return, later arranged to provide his great master with all facilities for his intellectual pursuits. Aristotle was strongly influenced by Plato and most of his views on education resemble that of Plato.

Aristotle considered education as part of politics and his educational ideas are dealt with in 'Ethics' and 'Politics'. Education is to produce men or women of right character with high mental and moral qualities. Individual is a member of society and inculcation of right habits is essential for a good citizen. As happiness is dependent on leisure, there should be also education for leisure. Education should result in rational living, that is, it should enable to guide the conduct of the individual by reason. The content of education at the first level should be for promoting physical health (through exercise) and for refining the mind (through literature.

art and music). Upto five years there should be no regular lessons, the children should learn through play. From 5 to 7 they have to observe older children learn. The children should not be allowed to mix with slaves and people of low culture. Elementary education should start at 7 years. Only useful subjects need be taught. According to Aristotle music, literature and art have powerful influence in building character. In the curriculum for the young boy, the stress should be on reading and writing, gymnastics, music and drawing. At the higher stages–subjects like biology, physics, ethics, medicine and logic were to be taught. He also stressed the need for inductive approach in teaching.

See: Plato. Socrates

ARITHMETIC MEAN (MEAN): The measure of central tendency most widely used in educational and psychological measurement. It is the sum of the scores divided by total number of scores. It corresponds to the 'average' in general use.

$$M = \frac{\sum x}{N} \;;$$

M : Mean
x : individual score
$\sum x$: Sum of all scores
N: Number of scores (Number of cases).

Mean is the most sensitive measure of central tendency (when the distribution is fairly normal) because all the scores are given equal weight in determining this index. So this single value is representative of the entire array of measures. It may be considered as the centre of gravity of the set of measures. The other measures of central tendency are, the median and the mode.

See: Averages

ARRANGEMENT ITEMS: Test items with jumbled arrangement of elements. The elements of the items have proper sequence, but in the test they are put out of order (jumbled). The testee has to put the elements in the proper order. Such test items are used in intelligence, aptitude, achievement and other ability tests. Verbal and nonverbal, including graphic, pictorial and diagrammatic types are extensively used in constructing arrangement items. A simple example is a sentence in which the words are jumbled like: Wild is animal a tiger.

ART: Those branches of knowledge that are primarily concerned with aesthetics. It is a collective term used to include subjects like music, painting, sculpture, dancing, etc. Sometimes subjects like pottery, weaving, basketry and other handicrafts are also included under (practical) arts. For e'xcellent performance in art, abilities like creativity, aesthetic perception and psychomotor coordination are necessary.

See: Humanities

ARTICULATION: Production of speech sounds. To articulate is to make the appropriate coordinated motor movements of the speech organs (like lips and vocal cords) in order to produce phonemes. Articulation ability is the capacity of the individual to produce well coordinated speech sounds speedily.

ARTIFICIAL INTELLIGENCE: Computer programs that simulate human problem solving. Robots have been designed in such complexity, that they can select components of equipment and assemble into structures. Some robots can even modify their operations according to the situation, generalize and even predict. But these operations are possible only within specified limits, limits set by the human brains that designed them.

ARTS: The wide subject area including language, literature, history, philosophy, economics, etc. The term is loosely used to include subjects considered other than 'science'. In many universities social science subjects, like anthropology, sociology, psychology, etc. are also included under the Art faculties.

See: Science

ASPIRATION: Intense desire to attain particular levels in social status, jobs, etc. Goals set by individuals are based on their aspirations. The level of aspiration should be related to the individual's capabilities and environment.

See: Level of aspiration

ASSEMBLY: The meeting of all the pupils and staff of the school everyday before the actual commencement of lessons. School assembly generally begins with prayer. An inspiring short speech touching some important subject or on a current topic by the head teacher or some other person is a common feature of school assemblies. General announcements are also given in the assemblies.

ASSERTIVENESS: Tendency to dominate over people and people's views. Assertive individuals, in a group, tend to "push" them in and at times appear even aggressive. It is also called self-assertiveness.

ASSIGNMENT: Any special duty given to the pupils. It may be a simple project or a problem to be undertaken by the pupils or a lesson to be mastered on the basis of independent study at home or in the school.

The term is also used to specify the contract of work to be completed by the pupil within a given time (Dalton Plan). Helen Parkhurst who initiated the Dalton Plan used the term in this sense.

See: Activity cards

ASSIMILATION: A process in Piaget's theory of concept formation. It is the process of reception and integration (accomodation) of a new experience into the schema (idea complex in the mind). When the child encounters a new experience which has some conflicting characteristics with previous similar experiences the schema then makes suitable modification to accomodate the new experience. This process is assimilation.

See: Piaget. J.

ASSOCIATION: The mental process of connecting ideas. Associationism, which was popular during the early decades of the last century, stressed the importance of association in learning. Smaller elements (simple ideas) combined together to form complex ideas. An idea to coalesce with the existing group of ideas (apperception mass) it should be related to them in some way. Similarity, contrast, proximity, etc. facilitated association of ideas. New ideas will be assimilated only if they are related to existing ideas. The methodology of teaching based on Herbart's works depended largely on the principle of association. Association is related to later developments like connectionism (S-R) and Behaviourism.

See: Connectionism

ATAXIA: A nervous disorder characterized by the lack of coordination of muscles. Lack of coordination may affect a particular part of the body (like the hand, in that case writing will be difficult) or the whole body (when keeping the body erect will be difficult). Ataxia may be due to organic or functional causes.

See: Functional disorder

ATHENIAN EDUCATION ANCIENT: The education prevalent in ancient Athens (in Greece) around 1000 BC. Education in Athens was very different from that of contemporary Sparta. In Athens, the ideal was individual excellence, and public usefulness. The Athenians emphasized the allround development of both body and mind and sought beauty and grace while the Spartans aimed at strength and hardihood. A well balanced personality was the aim of Athenian education. In Athens, during those times education began early in childhood with nursery rhymes and folklores and stories about animals and men. When the child was seven years old he was sent to the schools under the care of a slave. Schools were privately managed. Reading, writing, music, dancing and physical education formed the essential curriculum. During adolescence the boy went to gymnasia maintained by the state where swimming, boxing, etc. were also taught. Women were trained only for household affairs.

See: Spartan Education

ATTENDANCE OFFICER: An officer entrusted with the work of supervising the attendance of children in schools, in areas where compulsory education is in force. Their work is mainly concerned with the enrollment of all children of the eligible age group in the compulsory education area and the prevention of droppage of children from schools. When children are absent from school for an unduly long period or for reason unknown to the school, the Attendance Officer investigates the cases by involving the parents. In U.K., they are known also as School Welfare Officer or Enquiry Officer.

ATTENDENCE: Presence in school. Attendence is an essential pre-requisite for academic success. Regular attendance of students indicates proper motivation and congenial environmental conditions. Irregular attendance is often due to low motivational level in school work, parental neglect, ill-health, poverty, gangism, etc.

ATTENDING: Directing and focussing the senses to receive some stimulti. Attending is the set of the mind to perceive certain stimulations from the environment. An activity or thing that leads to pleasurable experiences is likely to receive better attention than others. Attending leads to observation which is the prerequisite for learning. Relating the thing to be perceived to one's needs is an effective way of ensuring attention.

Attention is selective and certain characteristics of the stimuli, like intensity, contrast, change, repetition and movement are found to facilitate better attention.

See: Perception

ATTENTION-SEEKING: An abnormal behaviour tendency, unconsciously motivated. A child to whom love or recognition has been denied by parents or teachers, often develops deviant behaviours, socially undesirable, like bullying, abusing, destroying, stealing, fire-setting, disobeying and playing baffoonery. These behaviours should be understood as an attempt to seize the recognition from others which they have been denied at home or school. Such children need counselling and not punishment to remedy the malbehaviour. When the home condition become too intolerable the children may resort to truancy and may even become delinquents. Recognition denied children can be also misled by ill-meaning people for their own purposes, by pretending to give them love and recognition in abundant measures.

See: Broken Home

ATTITUDE: An acquired pronness of a person to respond in a consistent and characteristic way when stimulated by a specific situation. It implies a readiness of the person to react in a manner typical of him to particular stimuli (usually social) and that this tendency is a learned one and not an innate trait. Attitudes have both a cognitive and an emotional content and this complex organization is a predisposition for a specific response when confronting the specific situation. A person's attitude towards 'Sex education' for example, consists of the cognitive element– his knowledge of sex and sexual behaviour of the society, etc. and the emotional component–his strong emotional feelings against discussing the matter with his children. His response to the question 'Would you like to have sex education in schools?', will largely depend on the predisposition he has acquired (attitude).

In short, attitude has the following constituents (1) an enduring predisposition to react in a characteristic manner when confronted with specific stimuli particularly social. (2) a cognitive element (i.e., ideas, opinions, etc.), and (3) an emotional component. Attitudes are usually described by words, 'favourable' or 'unfavourable, or 'like' or 'dislike'. Attitudes are relatively stable. As attitudes are strong determinants of behaviour (i.e., as people are strongly influenced by their attitudes towards reacting to particular situations), it is very useful to know about the attitudes of people to predict their behaviour in particular situations. Every person will have his own set of attitudes–attitudes towards groups of people, social practices, politics, wars and peace, etc.

See: Belief

ATTITUDE SCALE: A standardized attitude test which helps to classify people into broad categories with regard to specific attitudes. An attitude scale usually contains a number of statements (like, 'All schools should be co-educational institutions') usually between 12 to 24, which the person has to respond with 'agree' or 'disagree'. In another type a point-scale is given for responding 'strongly agree, 'agree', 'unconcerned', 'disagree' and 'strongly disagree'. Each item of the scale refers to a particular aspect of the attitude towards a social situation, an ideology, etc. For example, in attitude scales there may be items on co-education, vegetarianism, divorce, etc. These items are selected from a wide range of statements which have been subjected to try-outs and analysis. Those items which have high discriminative value (i.e., items that can discriminate clearly people who agree and disagree) only are selected for the 'scale'. So the final scale will contain only a smaller number of statements (upto 30 usually) which are found qualitatively and statistically sound.

Total responses of the person to the statements help to form broad conclusions about the person's attitude towards the object, person, situation, etc. An attitude scale often measures only one attitude (say attitude towards nuclear war).

Well known scales of attitudes are those developed by Thurstone and Likert. The techniques used in these scales are applicable for the construction of scales for any type of attitude. Bogardus' Social-Distance scale is meant to assess people's attitude towards racial and religious groups.

ATTRIBUTE: The discriminable quality of a thing or event that is subject to variation. The attributes of a piece of stone are its shape, colour, size, weight, etc. These attributes vary from one piece to another. The attributes of a person are all the discriminable features of his physical appearance, mental qualities, etc.

ATTRIBUTE DATA: The data represented in a nominal scale. They are mainly classification in categories i.e., as number of cases in different categories, like 'male', 'female', 'literate', 'illiterate' 'right handed', 'left handed', etc. It is also called categorical data and enumeration data. Census data is attribute data; it gives the numbers of people, households, etc. under different heads (categories).

ATTRITION: In language learning, it means language loss, which occurs when learner's competence in a language (mothertongue or other language) undergoes change which results in a reduction of knowledge or skills. This occurs when the learner no longer uses the language receptively or productively.

AUDIO-MATERIALS: Instructional materials that depend on auditory medium (hearing) for display. It is one of the most potent and versatile materials for learning, as practically any idea can be converted into verbal symbols which have auditory equivalents. The auditory signals can be received by the learner (i.e., listened to) remaining in any position (unlike in the case of visual materials in which the learner has to keep a particular posture and look intently towards the object). The audiomaterials can be used individually or in groups. Audio-tapes, gramaphone records, radio broadcasts, etc. are the most popular audio-instructional materials. In audio-visual aids like television and sound-films, the audio signals are transmitted in synchronization with visual signals.

See: Educational Technology

AUDIO CARD/AUDIO PAGE: An audio component used for individualized instruction. It can be carried on a separate audio tape or a special strip, etc.

AUDIO-INSTRUCTION: Learning with the aid of equipment that provide auditory (hearing) experience. Audio-instruction, when used as an exclusive method of learning uses no living voice of the teacher, it uses only the lecturer's talks and lessons presented by radio and cassette tapes, etc. or programmed lessons of a language laboratory. The student listens to the recorded lessons; there are facilities for recording his responses, which he can compare with the recording of the lessons. The method is widely used in the learning of foreign languages.

AUDIO-TAPES: Audio material recorded in open reel tape cassettes. It can be used in a variety of instructional situations either alone or along with other visual displays.

AUDIO-DISCS: Vinyl or compact discs on which audio signals (music, plays, etc.) are recorded. It is a relatively inexpensive device and is a readily available instructional resource.

AUDIO-ACTIVE COMPARATIVE (AAC) LABORATORIES: A type of language laboratory. It is a full scale system and may contain upto thirty carrels. The carrels are linked to the master console which is controlled by the teacher. Each carrel has a tape recorder as that of the master console. The master console monitors and controls all individual carrels either singly or in groups. The individual learner can work at his own speed. They can rewind their own tape, record on it and listen to their own responses.

The audio-active language laboratory (AAL), is not provided with tape-records as in the AAC and so recording and replay of individual responses is not possible in it. This is the difference between AAL and AAC.

See: Language Laboratory

AUDIO-ACTIVE LANGUAGE (AAL) LABORATORY: Full class system language laboratory. It may contain upto thirty carrels. The individual carrels are not equipped with their own tape recorders. The students receive learning materials from the master console. Students can hear via the microphones and headphones, but they cannot record their responses and replay. It works in lock-steps, at the pace controlled by the operator of the master console.

See: Language Laboratory

AUDIO-TUTORIAL (A.T.): The learning system using audio-tapes, usually along with other types of learning materials.

The learner is directed by recorded commentary. It is an individualized learning procedure.

AUGUSTINE, ST. (AD 354-430): Philosopher and theologician. His educational theory is described in his treatise on 'The teacher'. The book also deals with the origins of ideas. The pupil is taught to receive ideas from the teacher and the pupil's role is that of a passive recipient. Basic ideas of the 'direct method' of teaching languages can be traced back to this book. Teaching should be considered as an activity causing the pupils to learn. The liberal arts are the subjects to be taught–(grammar, dialectics, rhetoric, music, geometry, arithmetic and astronomy).

AUROBINDO GHOSE, SRI (1872-1950): The Indian Philosopher who propounded Integral Yoga, a philosophic system based on Indian Vedanta. His educational principles bear parallelism to his philosophic ideas. The first task of man is the discovery and knowledge of the powers, principles and processes of self-realization, and the second is a persistent personal effort for growth and changes. The example and influence of the teacher provides a further force. The main aim of education is to enable one to know oneself–the self-development. To achieve this, it is necessary to concentrate on physical, vital, psychic and mental powers of man. The student should observe himself directly all that happens to himself. Exercise controls direction and finally leads to mastery. The senses should be trained in accuracy, sensitivity, width and breadth. Training in aesthetics is part of vital education. It develops emotions and human habits. With observation and self-knowledge comes the need for concentration of vital energies. The students should choose their subjects of study, cultivate areas of interest, take examinations when they want. They should work regularly. The teacher should guide and the class size should be restricted to 4 or 5. The environment should be well organized. The unity of all knowledge should be emphasized and humanities and sciences should be brought together. A sense of oneness of mankind should be developed.

AUTHORING LANGUAGES (A.L.): Means for converting instructional sequences into computer software. There are different authoring languages.

Professional firms, can be requested for the production of computer-assisted learning packages, or skilled personnel can be requested for the selection of suitable authoring languages.

AUTHORITARIAN LEADERSHIP: Domineering leadership that keeps all functions of leadership to the leader himself (like the setting up of goals, planning activities, allocation of work, direction and supervision of functions). He will demand conformity and obedience and will not encourage free communication. There will be discipline in the group as long as the leader is powerful enough to exert his influence, but in his absence the group discipline tends to deteriorate, as the group member's identification with the group cause (group morale) is weak.

See: Leader, Democratic leader

AUTISM: Thinking centred on self. Autism is the tendency to indulge in thinking in terms of personal needs, emotions and desires without regard to reality. In Freudian psychology it is the thinking resulting from motivations of the id. When an individual is thwarted in his effort to satisfy a strong need, he is likely to resort to autistic thinking. Children's thinking to a large extent is autistic.

AUTOBIOGRAPHY: True sketch of a person's life history written by himself. Auto-biographies are very important records for guidance and counselling. The client is required to write his autobiographical sketch which should include information on his early childhood experiences, school career, relationship with parents and others, health problems, traumatic episodes in the family, etc. apart from basic biodata. The interpretation of biographical data is susceptible to subjectivity, nevertheless, it provides revealing data otherwise unobtainable. The counsellor uses autobiographical data to supplement test data and interview data.

See: Guidance

AUTOMACITY: Ability to speak a foreign language effortlessly, and spontaneously. In learning a foreign language and in achieving proficiency in it, the main handicap is the inability to produce speech, in the habitual manner of the native speaker, who need not attend to any aspect of the process involved in speaking. Articulation is habituated and automatic in his case.

This is automacity in speech. What one has to aim in the mastery of a foreign language is automacity in speech.

In other words, in language learning, it means 'fluent use'. It refers to the spontanity in the use of given linguistic structures.

AUTONOMIC NERVOUS SYSTEM: The sensory motor nervous system that is relatively independent of the central nervous system. It consists of the sympathetic and parasympathetic systems. This system activates and regulates the various internal organs like the heart, stomach, lungs, endocrine glands, etc. It plays a very important role, in collaboration with the endocrine system, in the arousal of emotional behaviour. Involuntary physiological processes like heart-beat, stomach contractions, secretion of ductless glands, etc. are stimulated and regulated by this nervous system. The sympathetic and para-sympathetic division of the autonomic nervous system have nerves connecting to the endocrine glands and the vital organs. Usually they have opposing effects on these organs. Heart rate increases with sympathetic stimulation, while it decreases by the action of the para-sympathetic system.

See: Central nervous system. Emotion

AVERAGE DEVIATION: A rough measure of variability or dispersion. It gives the extent of the average (mean) deviation of a set of scores from the arithmetic mean. It is obtained by finding the average of the deviation of each score from the mean, disregarding the algebraic sign.

e.g. Scores: 7, 4, 6, 5, 8....: Mean 6

Total deviations:

8	–	6	=	2
7	–	6	=	1
6	–	6	=	0
5	–	6	=	–1
4	–	6	=	–2

Total deviations of the scores from the mean, disregarding the algebraic sign = 6. So average deviation : is 1. (i.e. 6/6). It is also called the mean deviation or mean variation.

See: Dispersion

AVERAGES: The different measures of central tendency. When there are a set of observations, a middle value of the scores is worked out, which can represent the scores in the distribution by a single value. The average, therefore, can be considered to be descriptive of the group from which the measures are drawn. For example, if we know that the average marks obtained by a class in mathematics is 50 and another class is 60, we can draw inferences about the achievement level of the two classes and their relative standing. It is not necessary to know the entire distribution of scores to know about some of the important characteristics. In fact, it is not practical too, to consider the whole array of measures. The average helps in reducing the mass of data into a meaningful single value which is representative of the whole data.

There are three 'averages' used to measure central values in educational and psychological measurement viz., the arithmetic mean, the median and the mode.

In a normal distribution, arithmetic mean, median and mode coincide. In other cases they differ.

See: Central tendency

AVERSION THERAPY: A technique of behaviour therapy using a negative reinforcement (aversive) for eliminating the undesirable symptoms. It is often used for effecting behaviour modification in the case of persons with socially undesirable characteristics–like drug addiction, alcoholism, sexual deviations etc. The method involves the evocation of the undesirable response (for eg., drug injection) which will be immediately followed by an aversive stimulus, such as chemicals which produce unpleasant effects like nausea or vomiting, electric shocks, etc. If alcohol is taken immediately after injection of antabuse, the patient develops feelings of nausea which leads to vomiting. This course is repeated a few times.

See: Behaviour therapy

AYERE'S HANDWRITING SCALE: A standard for scoring pupils' handwriting, developed by Ayeres in 1912. This scale gives samples of handwriting in English, against which the given handwriting is compared. The teacher finds out the one most similar to standard samples and assign the grade accordingly. The judgement, to a large extent, is subjective.

B

BACKWARD CHILD: Usually the term is used to describe a child whose scholastic performance is markedly below the average performance of children of his grade or age, in most of the school subjects.

A child whose IQ is between 70 and 85 is also said to be a backward child.

Backwardness in most of the school subjects is designated as 'general backwardness' and backwardness in a subject or subject area (e.g., Mathematics or language) is called specific backwardness.

See: Retardation

BACKWARD BRANCHING: In programmed instruction and CAL, the program which requires the learners to repeat items (by sending them back to repeat). This is also known as wash back.

See: Programmed Instruction

BACKWARDNESS: Any form of retardation, mental or scholastic. 'Backwardness' is a general term used to denote mental or scholastic retardation. A mentally backward child is one whose mental age is below his chronological age (i.e. a child with a low I.Q.). Educational backwardness is characterized by consistent low performance in school. The term 'under-achievement' is used to signify that kind of backwardness in which the pupils work is much below his capacity as revealed by intelligence and other tests. 'General backwardness' means consistent low performance in most of the school subjects (like language, mathematics, etc.). General backwardness is generally due to low I.Q. low motivation, ill-health, emotional disturbance, poor learning habits, etc. Reasons for specific backwardness may be absenteeism, aversion for particular subjects or fear of the teacher handling a subject, etc. A 'slow learner' is a backward or retarded child who needs more time to learn and so is a backward child in the normal class.

BARBITURATES: Drugs producing lowered moods. Barbiturates (like phenobarbitone) are used as hypnotics (sleep inducers) and tranquilizers (for reducing tension and stress).

See: Amphetamine

BAR DIAGRAM: Graphical representation of the relative position of a variable in a distribution represented by bars. Bar Diagram or Bar Graph is used as a good visual representation of some attribute distributed differently in different populations. The proportional number of individual in the categories can be easily seen.

BARD-CANNON THEORY: The theory of emotion that states that the emotional behaviour is controlled by the hypothalamus. According to the Cannon-Bard theory, the autonomic changes (like increased heart and breathing rates, increased flow of blood to gross muscles, etc.) and the feeling of emotion (subjective experience of feeling) from the receptors (e.g., perception of a frightening situation) first go to the hypothalamus and then simultaneously to the higher centres of the brain (Cortex) and to the effectors (leading to attack or flight).

See: Emotions

BARRIERS: The obstruction one confronts in the efforts to reach a goal. A goal-directed activity is often beset with problems. The barriers obstruct the individual's progress towards the achievement of the goal. The barrier may be sometimes the individual's own inhibition apart from external obstructions. For reaching the goal the barrier has to be overcome. This can be done by either removing the barrier or by taking a detour (circuitous route) and if the goal is insurmountable, by abandoning it and substituting it with another goal in order to fulfill the same need. If the barrier confrontation leaves the individual in a state of indecision, frustration results. When one meets with difficulties (barrier) in achieving a goal, what is to be done is to study the situation, closely and formulate plausible methods for resolving the difficulty and then try them out.

See: Conflict

BASAL AGE: the term used in the Standford-Binet Test of Intelligence to denote the highest age level at which the individual is able to do all items assigned to that age level. The Binet scale consists of groups of items for each age level. If a seven year old child is able to do all the items beginning from the lowest to that assigned for age 8 years, his basal age is 8. (even though his chronological age is only 7). Even if the child is able to do a few items for the age-group 9 or 10, his basal age is only 8. Basal age roughly corresponds to mental age.

BASE-LINE DATA: Data obtained before starting a particular programme. Base-line data shows the original position, and any change that occurs afterwards can be compared with it in order to decide the effect of the new programme.

BASIC EDUCATION: The Educational theory formulated by Mahatma Gandhi in India around 1938, later developed into 'the Wardha scheme of Basic education' by Dr. Zakir Hussain and his associates. The main features of Basic education are—

1. Universal free and compulsory education for all boys and girls between the ages 7-14
2. Education should be imparted in the mother tongue
3. The educational processes should centre round some basic craft, like spinning, weaving, wood-work, etc.
4. The selected craft should make children into good craftsmen, and
5. In the craft-centered education all subjects to be taught should be integrated (correlated) to the central craft.

Education of character was stressed and the educated child was expected to be a worthy citizen of the country. Basic education, according to Mahatma Gandhi was 'education for life, through life and throughout life'.

Mahatma Gandhi's educational ideas were, in fact, an integral part of his philosophy of life. He envisaged a non-violent revolution resulting in political and economic freedom of the country. When he developed the ideology, India was a nation of 440 million people, economically very backward, struggling under the yoke of foreign administration well over a hundred years. Liberating the vast majority of the illiterate, poverty striken people was as important to him as the political liberation of the country. So from the very beginning, since his return from South Africa, his strategy had been multipronged, to attack inequalities, oppression and slavery from all quarters. He began his non-cooperation movement in 1920, and he inaugurated his Khadi (i.e., handspun cloth) movement also in the same year. In 1934 he started the Civil disobedience movement and following it, the campaign against untouchability. Then he started the All-India Village Industries movement intended for the economic regeneration of the villages. Basic education was, sequentially the last; the plan was prepared in 1937.

The background of his thinking is best revealed in the following words of his: "whatever may be true of other countries, in India at any rate, where more than 80% of the population is agricultural and another 10% industrial, it is a crime to make education merely literary, and make boys and girls unfit for manual work in life. Indeed, I hold that as the larger part of our time is devoted to labour for earning one's bread, our children must, from their infancy, be taught the dignity of labour. It is sad that our school boys look upon manual work with disfavour, if not contempt". And again: "The ultimate objective of this new education is not only a balanced and harmonious society, but a just social order in which there is no unnatural dividing line between haves and have-nots, and everybody is assured of a living wage and the right to freedom... literacy is not the end of education, not even the beginning... Literacy in itself is no education. I, therefore, begin the child's education by the teaching of a useful handicraft. My plan to impart education through the medium of village handicrafts, like spinning, carding, etc. is thus conceived as a spearhead of the salient social revolution fraught with the most far-reaching consequences. It will provide a healthy and moral basis of relationship between the city and the village and thus go a long way in eradicating some of the worst evils of the present". This gives in nutshell, his basic philosophy of education.

Mahatma Gandhi formally presented his ideas in a national conference of educationists, summoned in Wardha in 1937. He also made another revolutionary proposal: to provide the new type of education universally to all boys and girls of school going age. This requires huge financial resources which could not be mobilized through conventional governmental sources, so the work which is central to basic education (i.e. the handicraft) be made capable of creating wealth. The committee of educationists subsequently formulated the resolutions which are considered as the basic tenets of the scheme:

1. Free and compulsory education should be provided for seven years on a nation-wide scale.
2. The medium of instruction should be the mother tongue.
3. The process of education throughout the period should centre round some forms of manual and productive work and all other abilities to be developed or training to be given should, as far as possible, be integrally related to the central handicraft chosen with due regard to the environment of the child, and
4. It is expected that this system of education will be gradually able to cover the remuneration of teachers.

A committee under the chairmanship of Dr. Zakir Hussain, who later became the President of the Republic of India, subsequently drew up a detailed syllabus on the basis of the resolution, which became famous as the 'Wardha Scheme of Education'.

In the scheme of Basic Education, work is central, and instruction revolves around it. Work includes all activities which have personal, social and community significance. Work experience is also a medium for citizenship training. It is essentially an education for life and through life. The teaching of a basic craft (usually cotton craft: spinning, carding, weaving, etc.) is the essential part of education at the primary stage. Productive work makes the acquisition of related knowledge more concrete and realistic, but it also is a powerful means of developing the personality and character and to instil the dignity of labour. The basic craft selected for an institution, therefore, should fit into the natural and social environment of the school and should have the maximum educational possibilities. The study of the curricular content, so, should be connected to the three main centres of correlation: Craft work, natural environment and the social environment. Basic education, though emphasizes the role of productive work as the centre of activities, does not underrate the study of books.

The basic scheme aims to break the isolation between the school and the community. To enable this, school life itself should be organized as a living, functioning, community and the students should be encouraged to participate in the life around the school.

Student self-government is another important feature of Basic education, which affords continuous opportunity for development of qualities of democratic ways of living.

A large number of schools all over the country developed on the lines of Basic education ideology functioned very well for sometime. But now, only few institutions can stand up to the claims. Reasons for the relapse are varied and controversial.

See: Gandhi, M.K.

BASIC ANXIETY: Feeling of helplessness felt by the child if it perceives the environment as hostile. Basic anxiety in children originates from lack of affection and warmth in the family. It is accompanied by repressed hostility against the parents. The child tries to cope with the situation by usually resorting to neurotic strategies like showing strong tendencies of craving for affection, overambition and power, withdrawal from competition, etc. Basic anxiety directs the development of personality of the individual. This is the central concept of the theory of personality according to Karen Horney.

BASIC ENGLISH: A vocabulary comprising 850 words developed between 1926 and 1930 by G.K. Ogdon. He claimed that these words were sufficient to communicate all ideas and any kind of message. This vocabulary was used mainly for teaching those who wanted to learn English as a second language.

BASIC SKILLS: The three R's–Reading, writing and Arithmetic.

BATTERY: A collection of tests, usually used for measuring complex abilities. Eg. intellegence test batteries, scholastic test batteries, differential aptitude test batteries.

A test battery contains a group of related tests; independent and separate treated as a composite test. It also means different tests standardized on the same population or a group of tests administered to the same group of testees.

Achievement test batteries are used for collecting comprehensive data on pupil achievement. Such batteries may contain separate sub-tests within the battery, to assess learning outcomes in different content areas (like language, mathematics, science, etc.)

BEHAVIOUR THERAPY: The process of treating abnormal behaviour by the application of the principles of learning.

Abnormal behaviour symptoms are acquired by learning–as in the case of any other behaviour. Abnormal symptoms incapacitate the individual and so, to get the individual back to normal life, these symptoms are to be eliminated. Learning techniques can be used effectively for unlearning the unsuitable behaviour (symptoms) and for substituting them with suitable ones. Learning procedures based on classical conditioning and operant conditioning are used to evolve the various techniques in behaviour–therapeutical practice. The technique is found to be useful in the treatment of behavioural disorders involving psycho-neurotic problems, character aberrations, etc. Wolpe and Lazarus were the foremost in developing behaviour therapeutic methods.

See: Operant conditioning

BEHAVIOUR TESTS: Controlled situations that elicit responses typical of the individual. A behaviour test is intended to put the individual in a known psychological situation in order to observe and measure his reaction in that situation. Personality tests, attitude inventories, etc. are behaviour tests. These tests elicit the typical responses of the individuals which will help the psychologist to draw conclusions about their personality (or behaviour tendencies). Behaviour tests are also used to compare the behaviour or personality of individuals.

BEHAVIOUR: Anything that the organism does. According to the behaviourists 'behaviour' is the reactions of the individual which are observable. So behaviour has to be necessarily objective. As 'consciousness' and its effects as such are not observable, behaviourists have kept out these terms in dealing with mental phenomena. But the term behaviour, as now used, includes 'implicit behaviour' also which, though are not directly observable, can be reliably inferred from their effects (also called covert behaviour). Withdrawing of the hand when pricked with a needle is an explicit behaviour. The response to a question (problem) given by the person in written, spoken or any other way is an evidence of his implicit behaviour i.e. thinking. (How did you feel when I pricked you with the pin? The answer provides observable evidence of his thinking process).

BEHAVIOUR COUNSELLING: Counselling procedure undertaken on behaviouristic model i.e., on the basis of behaviour modification. It is based on the learning theory–operant conditioning. The counsellor's role is in the management of the learning situation; the maladaptive behaviour has to be substituted with adaptive responses. This is achieved by reinforcing the behaviour by positive or negative reinforcements. The techniques of behaviour therapy, like reciprocal inhibition, aversion techniques, successive desensitization are adapted and applied to suit the counselling situation.

See: Counselling

BEHAVIOURAL OBJECTIVES: The objectives of Education in terms of observable (and measurable) changes in behaviour. Knowledge of behavioural objectives enables the teacher to plan and implement learning activities and also to evaluate the outcomes of learning. The basic abilities in 'knowledge', in behavioural terms, for example, can be given as,

'The ability to recognise facts, names, dates, events, etc.'

See: Aim

BEHAVIOURISM: The school of psychology founded by J.B. Watson by 1913. He said that psychology being a science, should employ only scientific methods for studying mental phenomena. So psychology should adopt the objective, natural science approach. Psychology, upto that time, used mentalistic terms like 'consciousness', 'will', etc. for explaining behaviour, and used 'introspection' as a method of studying psychological phenomena. He said that the subject of psychology should be 'behaviour' because it alone was observable and measurable. Psychology, according to him, is therefore the study of behaviour. Hence he used the term behaviourism to emphasize his stand point. His book 'Psychology, from the stand point of a behaviourist' clearly explains his view. It is a land mark in the history of psychology.

He extensively made use of Pavlov's theory of conditioning, as it was based on objective experimentation. 'Behaviourism' as propounded by Watson had a great influence in the development of psychology since then. (His experiments on conditioned fear in children is well known). Phenomena considered to be unobservable like thinking, problem-solving, etc. are being studied experimentally under controlled conditions by the behaviourists.

See: Watson J.B.

BELIEF: An opinion or statement accepted and retained, critically or uncritically. The individual who holds the belief considers

it as a fact of truth and often his actions are guided by it. He is prone to overlook instances in which his belief does not agree with reality. One's religious views and political opinions are part of one's belief system. An attitude is a belief with an emotional core.
See: Attitude

BENEFIT-COST ANALYSIS: Process of working out the present value of benefits and costs of education. Benefits and cost analysis in education involves the identification of all benefits, direct and indirect resulting from education and the total cost involved in the process and their measurement. Benefits can be in the following areas:

1. Monetary returns (higher income one gets because of education)
2. opportunity the student gets for further education and the additional income possible thereby;
3. providing a wider choice of employment for the individual;
4. shielding the individual from unhealthy influences of technological and cultural changes; and
5. providing skills for meeting the new needs of a complex society like maintenance of records, preparation of statements, etc.

These benefits are called the internal benefits (benefits direct to the individual) of the system. The external benefits can be listed as

1. when the student becomes adult his children get informal education at home;
2. neighbours of educated people are benefitted because educated people have better social values;
3. educated people when interact in the job situation result in improvement of their work procedures;
4. national incomes increase;
5. administration of law and justice becomes less costly, etc.

Under the costs are included: Institutional costs, student cost, cost of administration and supervision and opportunity cost.
See: Cost of Education

BENZODIAZEPINES: The class of widely used tranquilizers. The common forms are chlordiazepoxide (librium) and diazepam (valium). These drugs produce depression of neural activity in the thalamus and hypothalamus and in the neurons of the spinal cord. The result is a tranquilized and sedated condition. They are used effectively for the treatment of neurotic anxiety. These drugs are less toxic than barbiturates.

BIAS: The attitude adopted by the experimenters that vitiates their findings. The word 'biased' is used in different senses. A 'biased observer' is one who has predetermined notions about the results of observation, or who shows favour or disfavour towards particular candidates.

In an experimental situation the experimenter may be enthusiastic about the work so that he will unwittingly encourage the individuals in the experimental group to achieve better. He can be biased even otherwise. He may collect only data that will substantiate his hypothesis, overlooking or ignoring others.

In selecting a random sample also 'bias' is possible. If the selection procedure is such that certain cases are more likely to be represented in the sample, it is called a 'biased sample'. 'Bias' introduces an error that is not due to chance. If some elements of the population are over-represented and others inadequately represented, the sample cannot be called random or representative. A sample selected from a telephone directory to represent the population of a city is a biased sample (In this sample, telephone users get over-representation and other go unrepresented).

See: Statistics

BILATERAL TRANSFER: A positive transfer of learning from one side of the body to the other. In this kind of transfer, the skill acquired by involving only hand or leg on one side of the body, resulting from training confined exclusively to that side, is seen transferred to the other side. For example, normally only right hand receives training in writing. But, even though no practice is given for the left hand, it is possible to write with the left hand.

See: Transfer

BILATERAL SCHOOL: A school which provides two types of education in the same institution–like academic education and technical education. Before the establishment of comprehensive schools, such schools were in existence in United Kingdom under the tripartite system.

BIMODAL DISTRIBUTION: A distribution which has two modes or peaks. When there are two modes in a distribution, it is suggestive of two distributions being combined and grouped as one. If the frequency distribution of the height of a sample of college students is composed of data for both male and female students, the distribution is likely to be bimodal. The distribution necessarily will have two peaks, as the mean heights for men and women are clearly different.

BINARY DIGIT: A digit system which employs only 0 and 1. (The decimal system employs numerals 0 to 9). Binary numbers are used in information theory and in computers. According to the binary system zero is denoted by 0, 1 by 1, two by 10, three by 11 etc. The place value of the digits, when shifted to the left is in multiples of 2, where as it is in multiples of 10 in decimal rotation.

Binary system	Decimal system
0	0
1	1
10	2
11	3
100	4
101	5
110	6, etc.

Computers use this system of notation because the two operations of switch-on (for number 1) and switch-off (for 0) of the electronic devices can be made use of in representing any number.

BINET, ALFRED: The French psychologist generally considered as the 'father of mental testing'. Binet (1857-1911) was born in France. Though his specialization was law, he later became immensely interested in medicine and science. He studied under Charcot and took a doctorate in natural science for his thesis on 'The nervous system of insects'. He wrote a book on 'Hypnosis' and another on 'Reasoning'. In 1905 he stressed the need for establishing an accurate diagnosis of intelligence, if the placement of feeble-minded children in special schools were to be carried out effectively. Between 1897 and 1905, Binet and his collaborators (particularly Theodore Simon) were involved in developing new tests for measuring higher mental processes. The first intelligence test appeared in 1905 as the joint work of Binet and Simon. It was a long test with sub-tests, which was based on the developmental norms worked out from data collected from a large sample of children. The items were of increasing difficulty extending from those for the infants upwards to that of average adult. The tests were arranged not according to difficulty, but according to age, which normal children could pass successfully. By means of this scale one could find the mental age of the child. The items for age three, for example, are: (1) Points to nose; (2) Repeats sentences of six syllables; (3) repeats two digits; (4) Enumerates objects in a picture; (5) Gives family name.

The Binet test was the forerunner of not only intelligence tests, but also of all kinds of mental tests.

See: Intelligence test

BINET-SIMON SCALE: The first intelligence test ever constructed. It was developed by Binet and Simon in France during the first decade of this century. A variety of items were used which involved a number of perceptual and reasoning processes. The concepts of mental age and Intelligence quotient (I.Q.) were developed on the basis of these tests. It was an individual test and included test items for children from early childhood to maturity. Various adaptations of this test have been made, in different countries, the most well known being Stanford-Binet Intelligence Scale.

BINOMIAL DISTRIBUTION: An algebraic expression of the general form $(p+q)^n$. Binomial expansion is a mathematical model, based on the principles of probability, used to explain the normal distribution. If two coins are tossed, the probable frequencies of the combinations (of Head and Tail) are given by the binomial $(H+T)^2$, which on expansion equals $(1)H^2+(2)\ HT + (1)\ T^2$. These values indicate that the relative frequency of 2 heads in 4 tosses is 1, of one head and one tail is 2 and two tails is 1. If there are 3 independent factors operating (i.e., for 3 coins), the binomial will be $(H+T)^3$ which is equal to $(1)\ H^3+3H^2T+3HT^2+(1)\ T^3$, for which the probability ratios will be:

All H (H^3) 1/8
(2) H (1) T = $H^2T)$ 3/8
(1) H (2) T = (HT^2) 3/8
All T (T^3) 1/8

If there are 10 coins, the binomial will be $(H+T)^{10}$. In that case the probability ratio will be: for All Head or All Tails (T^{10} or H^{10}): 1/1024, 5 heads and 5 tails, 252/1024, etc. It is assumed that all the coins are identical with regard to weight size, shape, etc. The coins in the example stands for factors which are independent and the occurrence of a Head (H) represents the presence of a factor and the occurrence of a Tail (T) to the absence of a factor.

If it can be assumed that an event or characteristic encountered in an educational or psychological measurement is influenced by innumerable independent factors in a random manner the relative frequencies of the events, also can be assumed to conform more or less, to the normal probability pattern, which is based on binominal expansion.

See: Statistics

BITS: Numbers according to binary notation. In computers the binary code is composed of 0's and 1's. All messages (information) are converted into bits. It is called binary because it uses only the two symbols that can be set by the electronic state 'off' and 'on' (i.e. switching on and off). '0' for off and '1' for on. All manipulations of the computers are based on these two operations. Switching on and off. Any information can be converted into this code because of its immense possibility. A four bit word for example–containing not more than four 0's and 1's (eg. 1010, 1100, 1111, etc.) can represent 16 symbols while words of eight bits can have 256 combinations, etc.

The word bit is coined from the two words BINARY and DIGITS.

See: Binary digit

BIO-FEED BACK: A new therapeutic method developed for normalizing the internal physiological conditions by voluntary control. The patients' internal physiological events like heart-beat, blood pressure, temperature, breathing and muscle relaxation are monitored directly to him as feed back. He will be able then to control voluntarily by practice the events to become normal. This method is used for treating certain types of anxieties and phobias, and particularly, psychosomatic diseases.

BIOGRAPHICAL METHOD: A method of child study which relies on biographical data. The individual has to record biographical data relating to : relevant incidents, his behaviour in retrospect, the developmental trends at various stages, etc. (Autobiography). The investigator also may collect data necessary for the preparation of the biography of the individuals. The data will include information on family background, early childhood, physical, social and emotional development, school career, etc. The biographical method is used for studying developmental trends in normal and exceptional children. This method of investigation is also called the life history method.

See: Guidance

BIOLOGICAL NEEDS: Basic needs that are directly related to the maintenance of life. Biological needs are: the need for air (breathing), water, food, elimination, sleep and maintenance of body temperature. Deprivation of these needs will upset the homeostasis (chemical bodily equilibrium) of the body which can be restored only on satiation of the respective needs. Bodily needs are operative from the time of birth and the satiation of these needs is essential for maintenance of life and well-being. These needs are also called physiological needs or primary needs. Other needs which appear later in life (after early childhood) are derived from the biological needs and so are called derived needs or secondary needs.

See: Needs

BIRTH TRAUMA: Emotional shock the newborn experiences during delivery. Freud asserts that the first severe shock that one receives during life is the birth shock. Trauma is a severe emotional experience, which is very often repressed and so forgotten. Birth trauma is universal, and the repression results in the formation of the first contents of the unconscious. When delivery is difficult and delayed the trauma will be abnormally severe and it will have its adverse effects in later life. Freud points out that there is no other change in the life of an individual as violent as that of his birth (delivery). The child in the uterus is in a shock protected, temperature controlled chamber and is suspended upside down, weightless. Nourishment, oxygenation and elimination are effected spontaneously for which it does not have to do anything. The moment it is ejected out, all the comforts disappear instantaneously. This is the rudest shock one experiences in life and if delivery is abnormal the distress will be aggrevated and the trauma will lead to the formation of the nucleus for serious unconscious complaints later in life.

See: Trauma

BISERIAL COEFFICIENT OF CORRELATION: The correlation coefficient used to show the relationship between two variables of which one is given as a continuous distribution and the other in two categories (dichotomy) and when both the variables can be assumed to be continuous and normally distributed.

The formula for computing Biserial coefficient of correlation is:

$$r_{bis} = \frac{X_p - X_q}{\sigma x}\left(\frac{pq}{r}\right)$$

Where, r_{bis} is the biserial correlation.

X_p is mean of scores on continuous variable of individuals in the higher group ('pass' group in the example).

X_q is mean of the continuous variable in the lower group ('failure' group in the example)

σx is the standard deviation of the total sample in the continuous variable.

Y height of ordinate of unit normal curve at point of division between p and q proportion.

p : proportion of cases in the higher group

q : proportion of cases in the lower group

In an examination, out of the 100 students, 70 pass and 30 fail, the mean on an intelligence test for the 'failure' group is 95 and for the 'pass' group is 105. Biserial correlation can be used to find out the degree of relationship between 'success' and 'intelligence'. (Both the variables, viz., intelligence and the marks for deciding pass-fail are continuous and normal). The intelligence test scores are given as a frequency distribution while pass-fail variable is dichotomized (given in two categories).

See: Point bi-serial coefficient of correlation.

BIVARIATE DISTRIBUTION: A frequency distribution involving two variables. Usually a frequency distribution involves only one variable (Univariate distribution). In certain situation two variables will have to be considered simultaneously, for example, to find out the relationship between height and weight, the relationship between scores on two different tests, etc.

Example: Bivariate distribution

Individual	Score in Test A	Score in Test B
A	25	6
B	32	8
C	17	9
D	40	13
E	50	15
F	24	6
G	29	5
H	37	12

BIVARIATE ANALYSIS: Experiments in which only two variables are involved one independent variable and one dependent variable, at a particular time. A variety of statistical procedures are available to analyse the data obtained from such experimentation.

BLOCK DESIGN TEST: A type of test in a nonverbal intelligence test battery. The subject has to arrange the blocks provided in a given pattern, to solve the problem.

BLOOM, B.S.: The well known American psychologist whose works on educational evaluation has received world-wide recognition. His books on 'Taxonomy of Educational Objectives' (of which he is the chief contributor) and his 'Handbook on Formative and Summative Evaluation' of student learning are masterly works. Bloom's influence in reforming school and college examinations all over the world was very great.

See: Taxonomy

BLUE PRINT: Specification chart for achievement tests prepared in advance, incorporating 'content' and 'objectives'. For achievement test it is usually a two dimensional grid–in one dimension is given the topics and in the other the type of operation to apply to the topic (objectives). The relative weightage to be given to the objectives and contents also are to be indicated.

The content has to be broken down into topics and sub-topics before preparing the grid.

Example: Test blue print of a test on 'construction of a test'.

Sl. No.	Objectives: Specific-ations	Content (Topics)
1	Recognises: terms, facts: 20%	Test, measure-ment, objectives, objectivity, validity, Reliability, Multiple - choice items (5 to 7 times)
2	Identifies specific facts 20%	Essay type examination Objective type examination (10 items)
3	Identifies concepts, principles 40 %	Character-istics of a good test, Conditions that pulls down reliability, validity, objectivity (12 items)
4	Evaluates information and data 10 %	Suitability of test items for different purposes (4 items)
5	Applies generali-zations and principles 10 %	Construct different types of items: essay, short answer, Multiple choice etc.

The blue print specimen shown above indicates only objectives in the cognitive domain. Objectives from the Affective and

Psychomotor domains also will have to be assessed along with the objectives in the cognitive domain, according to the nature of the topic.

See: Achievement Test

BOARD OF EDUCATION: Corporate, statutory body established for the management of policy implementation with regard to school education of a state. Usually the Minister for Education is the president or chairman of the Board. The members of the Board are generally educational experts, high officials, etc. The main function of the Board at the state level is concerned with the direction of educational programmes and the review of progress. Apart from such state boards, boards may be formed at regional levels also–like District Board of Education, County Board of Education, etc. In some countries like Sweden and UK, the term is used to denote the department of the Central Government responsible for education.

BORDERLINE INTELLIGENCE: Intelligence quotient roughly between 95-85. It is the intelligence of the dull average, i.e., of those between the 'average' and the 'morons'.

See: Intelligence

BORSTAL INSTITUTION: A residential institution for young convicted offenders below the age of 16. The purpose of such institutions includes both education and correction. The attempt in these institutions is to rehabilitate the children in society after release.

BRAHMANIC EDUCATION: The education in India that existed between 800 BC to early Christian Centuries. Chathurvarnya (caste system) began to develop during this period. Education was restricted only to young brahmins. The vedas and sacrificial scriptures formed the curriculum and the education was meant for the preparation for priestly life. At a later stage Kshatriyas and Vysias were also initiated to education. The pupils were trained for simple life and training continued for 6 to 8 years. At the second stage the curriculum included along with the Vedas, study of Sanskrit literature, dharmasastras (regulations regarding social life), arithmetic, medicine, grammar, astronomy, the works of Panini (400BC), Pathanjali (200BC) and Manu (Manusmrithi). The method of learning was mainly imitation and memorization.

As the art of writing was fully developed by that time, the student used to copy the texts on palm leaves. The gurus were forbidden from receiving any fees from pupils. Teachers were highly respected.

The brahmanic system of education resulted in strengthening the social discriminations that began to develop along with Chathurvarnya.

BRAILLE: The reading aids invented by Louis Braille, to help the blind to read by the sense of touch. Different patterns of embossed dots on a frame represent the letters of the alphabet. The blind reads by moving the fingers over these dots.

BRAIN-WASHING: Conditioning a person in a way against his own views. The attitudes, values and interests of people can be modified by subjecting them to severe stress and physical and psychological torture. The persons thus brain-washed are conditioned to modify their behaviour in a predetermined manner.

BRAIN-STORMING: The problem solving method, applicable in group situations, in which the individual is challenged and stimulated by interaction to produce ideas. In the group, the problem is posed and the individual members of the group are encouraged to speak out any idea that occurs to their mind without any restriction. The responses are received in a free and friendly way. The method is useful in obtaining effective and creative solutions to problems, by generating every plausible idea.

BRAINSTEM: The part of the brain minus the cerebrum and the cerebellum. It is the lower part of the brain which is linked to the spinal cord. The brain stem is involved in the control of various involuntary functions like breathing, heart-beat, digestion, sleep, etc.

See: Hypothalamus

BRANCHING PROGRAM: In programmed learning and in CAL, the method of presenting the frames which allows different responses. If the student gives the correct response, he is asked to proceed to the next frame. If the answer is a wrong one he is guided to the appropriate 'branch', depending on the answer. After completing the 'branch' frames, the student is steered back

to the main path. It is also called Intrinsic Program.
See: Programmed Instruction Linear Program

BRIGHT: A term loosely used to denote intelligent children. In terms of I.Q. scale a child whose I.Q is above 115 is considered bright, above 130 is termed very bright or brilliant.
See: Gifted

BROKEN HOME: Home in which the parents are separated (due to death, divorce, etc.) and the children suffer neglect. When death is the cause of separation the children may not necessarily feel neglected until an unkind step parent arrives. Discord between the husband and wife, which is serious and continued, leads to separation. In such families, the children may feel neglected. In a typical broken home there will be no mutual trust between the husband and wife, there will be frequent quarrels and fights and one or both parents may behave cruelly towards the children. The children are illtreated and they feel unwanted and neglected and will have no sense of security in the home. The proverbial step-mother aggravates the broken home conditions. But the presence of a step-parent necessarily does not create such a psychological environment for the child. Loving step-parents do not create broken home conditions. It has been found that various behaviour problems, including juvenile delinquency, are closely associated with broken home conditions.
See: Problem Children

BRUNER, JEROME S.: American psychologist and educationist, born in 1915. He strongly advocated the creative approach in education. The goal of education is not to prepare men for repeating what others have done but to equip people for doing new things–to prepare men to become creative and inventive. Education should transform people in such a way that they will not accept anything they are offered, without critical examination and verification. Education should endeavour to produce people capable of converting troubles into manageable problems, and for performing creative tasks, not capable of being computerized. Arts of all kinds should be cultivated leading to the maximum development of human excellence.

His contributions to developmental psychology, particularly cognitive development is well known. Generally, he is in agreement with the views of Piaget in child development. His works include: 'A Study of Thinking' (1956), 'The Process of Education' (1960); 'Toward a Theory of Education' (1966), 'Studies in Cognitive Growth' (1966), and 'The Relevance of Education' (1971).

See: Concept

BRYCE REPORT: The commitee constituted in 1894 under the chairmanship of James Bryce for recommending the best method of establishing a well organized system of secondary education in England. The main recommendations were–a central authority of secondary education under a minister for education, shifting of responsibility of secondary and primary education to local authorities, and the provision of scholarships to provide a ladder of opportunity for elementary pupils.

BUDDHIST EDUCATION: As Buddhism rejected the chathurvarnya (the four-caste hierarchy) of the Brahmanic cult, Budhist education was basically secular. Vedic study was not essential and the teachers were non-brahmins. All pupils belonging to all castes were admitted in monastic Viharas. Buddha was a great teacher, his sermon in the Deer Park attracted a large number of disciples. Buddha's main teaching of Astangamarga (Eight Fold Path)–right views, right intentions, right speech, right action, right occupation, right effort, right mindfulness and right concentration dominated the educational activities of the Viharas. Ancient centres of learning like Nalanda attracted students from far and wide.

See: Nalanda

BULLYING: Harassing a child by an older or a stronger one usually by the use of physical force. This form of aggressive behaviour, if found consistently in a child, should be considered as a serious behaviour problem needing specialized treatment, i.e., counselling.

See: Problem children

BUREAU OF EDUCATION: The Federal department of education of U.S.A. The functions of the Bureau are generally the collection and dissemination of educational information regarding organization, administration, policies and practices. The head of the Bureau is the Commissioner of Education and he is appointed by the President. Since 1953 the Bureau has been functioning under the Department of Health Education and Welfare. The original Federal department of education from which the present Bureau evolved was created in 1867.

BURT, CYRIL: Noted British psychologist. He had worked extensively on mental testing, scholastic backwardness, the nature of intelligence, and mental retardation. His famous books include 'Mental and Scholastic Testing', 'The Subnormal Mind', 'The Backward Child' and 'The Factors of the Mind'. His last work 'The Gifted Child' was published posthumously, in 1979.

See: Backward child

BUZZ SESSION: A short, small group discussion session. Buzz session is used as an effective means of achieving student participation. In buzz session, a problem is actively discussed upon by a small group of students for a short interval of time. The size of the group is between 3-6 and the duration between 5-8 minutes. The buzz groups are formed usually during the lecture when the class confronts a problem. As the groups are composed of a small number of members, all individuals will participate. There will be active communication and group interaction and this naturally stimulate thinking which leads to the generation of new ideas.

BUTLER ACT, EDUCATION ACT, 1944: The 1944 Education act of England which made the famous recommendation that education should be provided to every child according to age, ability and aptitude (3A's) (Education for all). Apart from other important recommendations it also recommended the raising of school leaving age from 14 to 15 and subsequently to 16. The bill was piloted in the British Parliament by R.A. Butler, the then President of the Board of Education.

BYTE: A group of adjacent bits, usually eight in number like the code for a letter, number, etc. used in computing and data processing.

C

C-SCORE: A normalized standard score with 11 units and a mean of 5 and standard deviation of 3.

See: Standard scores

CAMCORDER: A self-contained recording system which consist of a video camera, a recorder, batteries and other necessary accessories. Though it has more than 30 controls, it can be used very easily by opening the on/off control and the zoom. Focussing and exposure are automatic.

CAPACITY: A term generally used to indicate the ability to learn. It is the potential for accomplishment or ability to master some skill. Sometimes, it is also used to denote ability to perform some task, in which case it implies both potential and learning.

See: Ability

CAREER MASTER: A secondary school teacher in charge of the vocational guidance programme of the school. His work is chiefly concerned with the dissemination of occupational information. He collects details of the pupils, on their family back-grounds, health, developmental problems, intelligence, aptitudes, interests, personality traits, vocational aspiration, values, socio economic conditions, etc. He uses both test and non-test methods, for collecting data. He also collects and compiles information on different occupations, courses of studies, etc. Various methods like career talks, career conferences, career exhibitions and some vocational counselling are used for dissemination of occupational information. Both individual and group methods of guidance are employed.

The career master is often a regular teacher of the school, who has received in-service training in vocational guidance.

See: Guidance

CARREL: A small cubicle in a library, language laboratory etc. designed for individualized study.

CASE HISTORY: Collecting and assembling of data on the development of the individual in chronological order. Case history is a reliable narrative record of the development of the individual which helps the teacher, counsellor, psychotherapist, etc. to understand his problems and to formulate measures for remedial steps. A complete case history provides data on family and environmental background, antenatal and post-natal life, physical health, scholastic work, social, emotional and other personality characteristics, adjustment problems, etc. The case history aids in reconstructing a truthful record of the developmental trends and physical, psychological and social characteristics of the individual. It is a very useful record for the teacher, counsellor, sociologist and the psychotherapist.

CASE STUDY: Detailed study of the trends in development of the status of an individual or institution on a particular characteristic, undertaken with a definite purpose. The subject of study in this type of research is usually the individual. Case studies of a number of delinquents can be used to draw general conclusions of the causation, incidence, development, etc. of delinquency. In a case study, complete data on factors likely to be associated with the development of the problem: viz., physical and social environmental, family, school work, etc. are collected. Usually a case study is undertaken for studying in depth the dynamics of abnormal trends. But case studies are also conducted with a sample of normal children with a view to studying the normal trends in development. The case study employs observation to collect data on present status, apart from data collected from other sources, like school records, health records, interview reports obtained from parents, teachers, etc. The case study record in the final form is a narrative report which gives a full report of the 'case' and is a reliable segment of the life history of the individual.

A detailed case history will contain data on family background, social environment, pre-natal and post-natal development, childhood problems, health, physical, social and emotional development, intellectual and personality traits, scholastic progress, peer group relations, present problem (if any), etc.

For educational purposes a case study will include data on family, nature of birth, siblings, early childhood characteristics and problems, health, educational history and psychological characteristics. All items of information considered relevant to the focus of study (purpose) are collected. The methods used for collection of data are interview with parents and teachers, friends, scrutiny of school records, observation of behaviour, and testing.

On the basis of the data collected, a precise report is prepared which is called 'case history'. It will contain conclusions and recommendations (drawn on the basis of the generalization from data) which can be used for correctional, remedial or any special treatment suitable for the child. Since a case-study is comprehensive, it will reveal a lot of information about the child. When a complete understanding of the child is required a case study is undertaken.

Case studies can be either cross-sectional or longitudinal. When complete data on a particular stage of development of the child (e.g., a 6 year old child) are required 'crosssectional study' is attempted and when data on complete development since birth (or for a fairly long period) are required a 'longitudinal study' is undertaken. Longitudinal studies stretch over many years, while cross sectional studies are completed within a short period of time.

Case studies also can be undertaken for an institution, like a school, college, etc.

CASSETTE: Film or magnetic tape enclosed in a container that can be fed into suitable projectors, video or audio-player.

CATCHMENT AREA: The geographical area served by a school. It is the area from which the children are enrolled in a school. In urban localities it comprises only a few square kilometers while in rural regions it may extend to several square kilometers. Usually it is an area within a radius of 3-4 kms. for a primary school in fairly populated rural villages (as the assumption is that there should be a primary school within easy walking distance from the home of every child).

CATEGORY SYSTEM: One of the methods adopted for constructing 'Observation Schedules' for recording class room behaviour. Each schedule limits observation to only one aspect of class room behaviour or conduct at a time (e.g. questioning). For the specific behaviour, a set of fixed categories is constructed. A unit of behaviour observed can be recorded in one or other of the categories. The record would show the total number of units of behaviour that occurred in a period, classified in each category.

CARTRIDGE: A closed loop of audio-tape, video-tape or film enclosed in a container (cassette) that does not require rewinding.

CEILING AND FLOOR EFFECTS: The reduced efficiency of a test to discriminate at the lower and upper limits of performance. If a large number of testies obtain the lowest score possible (eg. '0') or scores close to it, there is no discrimination among them, likewise if a large number obtain the highest score possible (eg. 100) or scores close to it then the difference in their abilities also cannot be known.

CENTILE (PERCENTILE): A scale which divides the distribution into hundred parts. The centile scale is also called percentile scale. In this scale, there are hundred units or centiles. If a person gets a centile value of 50 (i.e., score equivalent to the centile 50) it means that half the number of individuals (i.e., 50% of the sample to which he belongs, is below him and 50% excels him. Likewise, a centile of 90 means that only 10% are above him). So centiles indicate the position (rank) of the person in the distribution.

Centiles are useful 'derived scores' and they are prepared as norms for tests.

The method of preparing centiles from a frequency distribution.

Centiles are obtained by preparing a cumulative percentage curve. From the curve a centile equivalent of the raw score can be easily read.

Cumulative Percentage Curve

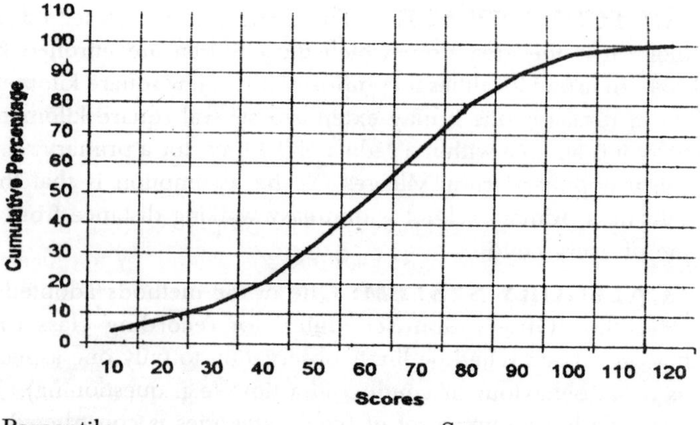

Percentile	Score
25 – Score 38	20 – Percentile 10
50 – Score 58	50 – Percentile 40
75 – Score 72	100 – Percentile 97

Example:

Class interval	Frequ-ency	Cumulative frequency	Cumulative percentage
110 _ 119	2	154	100.00
100 _ 109	3	152	98.70
90 _ 99	10	149	96.75
80 _ 89	16	139	90.26
70 _ 79	24	123	79.87
60 _ 69	25	99	64.28
50 _ 59	23	74	48.01
40 _ 49	20	51	33.12
30 _ 39	12	31.00	20_13
20 _ 29	7	19	12.34
10 _ 19	6	12	7.79
0 9	6	6	3.89
N : 154			

CENTRAL NERVOUS SYSTEM (CNS): The brain and spinal cord. It co-ordinates and integrates the different kinds of incoming sensory impulses. It is also the seat of thoughts, memory and emotions (brain). Muscles and glands are also stimulated by CNS to react.

See: Autonomic Nervous System.

CENTRAL TENDENCY: The property shown by sets of measures of variables to cluster around the centre. When measures on different variables relating to human qualities (like height, intelligence, etc.) are obtained, a large number of cases are seen centering round the average value of the score. If we take measures on the heights of 10 year old boys we find that the majority of children have height very close to the average. When we move up or down from the average the number of cases decreases.

This property of the measures of variables to gravitate towards the centre is called central tendency. The 'average' is the measure of the central tendency of a distribution.

See: Dispersion

CEPHALO-CAUDAL MATURATION: Physical development taking place in the infant from the head towards the limbs. In the new born infant the earliest coordinated movement is seen in the organs of the head and the head itself. This is because the development of the nerve fibres going to the muscles of the head takes place earlier than those situated more remote from the brain. The maturation of neural tissues proceeds in the order–from the head towards the limbs (cephalo-caudal means: from head to tail). The child will be able to lift its head in a coordinated manner far earlier than it can display coordinated movements of the legs. This sequence of maturation is also referred to as proximo-distal maturation, which means from near to distant.

CEREBELLUM: The large lobe, a part of the hind brain. It has close interrelations with the cerebral cortex and is directly involved in the proper performance of bodily movements (motor control).

CEREBRAL CORTEX: The outer layer of the cerebrum, about an inch thick. It almost corresponds to the convoluted (wrinkled) grey matter of the brain. It is the last part of the brain to appear in the animals, according to the data available on Evolution. Functionally it is the most significant organ; structurally also it is the most complicated organ with millions of neural connections. It is the cortex that initiates, coordinates and controls all complicated mental processes like thinking, problem solving, speaking, remembering, etc. Intelligence and creativity are functionally related to the potential of the cerebral cortex. Various areas located in particular parts of the cortex are found to control specific functions.

CEREBROTONIA: Personality type characterized by general restraint in behaviour. Cerebrotonia is a cluster of traits, the important characteristics of which are: tense posture and movement, general restraint, emotional control, poor sleep habits and preferences for seclusion when in trouble.

The classification is according to Sheldon's personality typing. Cerebrotonia is the temperament in which the predominant characteristics are inhibition, love of privacy, love of solitude, etc.

CHARACTER: Moral and ethical qualities of the individual. Honesty, dependability, consideration for others, cooperativeness, sociability, punctuality, kindness and the like are the components that go to form one's character.

CHECK-LISTS: A schedule for recording observation data. In investigations, the behaviour under study has to be observed and marked appropriately in the category for classifying the behaviour. Check-list is a crude form of a rating scale. Check-lists, are not very useful for the quantification of data, but are useful as tools for collection of pertinent data for a variety of other purposes. An item from a behaviour check-list of a student for example–When prevented from playing with his friends, in the play field–

- (He goes away)
- (He cries bitterly)
- (He protests and argues)
- (He withdraws and appears depressed)
- (Any other) ...

The observer has to put a tick mark in the appropriate place. When the child's behaviour is different from what are given in the alternatives, the observer can specify it as the last alternative and put the mark.

Check-lists are used for educational and vocational guidance, research, etc. It is one of the most widely used non-test techniques of behaviour study. It can be also used for preparing evaluation instruments for the collection of non-behavioural data–like school facilities.

CHI-SQUARE (χ^2) TEST: A statistical test used to determine whether the frequencies of distributions obtained in an experimental situation are different from those that can be expected theoretically. The chi-square test is used to compare 'observed' and theoretically 'expected' frequencies. The theoretical frequencies are worked out on the basis of some hypothesis. The χ^2 test is a test of independence in the sense that it is used to test the null hypothesis : that the observed frequencies do not differ from the expected frequencies. For example, if we toss a coin 200 times we expect to get the head 100 times and tail, 100 times. This is the theoretical frequency (expected) according to probability theory. But in an experiment of 200 tosses we may get 90 heads and 110 tails. The problem now is to find out whether the difference in frequencies is larger than that can be expected to occur by chance alone. If the differences are definitely larger, then one of the possibilities is that the coin might have asymetrical weight.

The formula used to obtain the value of χ^2, is

χ^2 : $(O\text{-}E)^2/E$, where

O : Observed frequency

E : expected frequency.

To find whether the value is statistically significant, the Table of critical values of chi-square should be consulted.

So we find that χ^2 is applicable to determine whether the frequencies of a distribution are different from those that can be expected to occur by chance.

When the frequencies are given in contingency tables (four-fold table) the formula used is–

$$\chi^2 = \frac{N(AD - BC)^2}{(A + B)(C + D)(A + C)(B + D)}$$

Illustration: In an experiment it was found that in a primary school 111 backward children, and 126 normal children regularly attended the school and among the 25 children whose attendance was low, 23 were backward and 2 were normal.

The problem was to find out whether the frequencies differ from what can be expected theoretically, i.e., whether normal achievement is independent of regular school attendance.

The contingency table showing the frequencies.

Attendance (%)	Normal	Backward	Both
At and above 85%	126 A	111 B	237
Below 85%	2 C	23 D	25
Both	128	134	262

χ^2, when worked out came to 20.56 which from the table of critical values for χ^2, is significant at .001 level of significance. This means that irregular attendance and low achievement are not independent, i.e., irregular attendance is also a factor associated with low achievements.

It should be noted that χ^2 is applicable for data obtained on nominal (categorical) data.

See: Hypothesis

CHINESE EDUCATION ANCIENT: The education that prevailed in China during the pre-Christian Centuries. The ancient Chinese were overconcerned about the preservation of their civilization. The aim of education therefore was dominated by social ideals. Education was universal and so schools existed in all parts of the country but practically all schools were conducted by private agencies. Elementary schools were held in the master's houses. Children began with the learning of the characters in the Chinese language (reading & writing) and memorization of sacred texts. Arithmetic was also essential. Elementary education lasted for five or six years. At the second stage the sacred books had to be translated and commentaries learnt and at the third stage the students were required to write essays and compose poems. The methods of teaching were primarily imitation and memorization. School examinations were common. Confucius emphazised 'noble living' and Lao Tze stressed the spirit that made the good man. Teachers were highly respected.

CHILD-CENTERED EDUCATION: Educational activities designed and implemented on the basis of the capacities, needs and interests of children. In child-centred education, the child is the centre of activity, that is, all programmes are geared to his requirements. Curricula, teaching methods, evaluation, cocurricular activities, etc. are planned accordingly. Such programmes make learning more interesting and meaningful to the children and so they become active participants in the teaching–learning process. The children receive ample opportunities for active learning, social interaction, problem-solving and creative works in the classroom. This will lead to the balanced development of the child's potentialities and personality.

This approach emerged as a revolt against teacher-centred and book-centred approaches in teaching.

CHOMSKY, NOAM A.: Formerly, Professor of Linguistics, Massachussets Institute of Technology U.S.A. He has done notable work in General linguistics and Psycholinguistics. His theory of Transformational–generative grammar–(of which the concepts of 'deep and surface structure', 'competence and performance', 'acceptability and grammaticalness')–are well known. His important publications are: 'Syntactic structure', and 'Aspects of the theory of Syntax'.

See: Language acquisition device

CIRCULAR BEHAVIOUR: Teachers' behaviour which induces the development of the same behaviour in children. The development of circular behaviour is particularly significant in the case of young children in nursery schools. Dominant and oppressive behaviour of teachers induces the children to develop resistance which is a manifestation of domination. Likewise, a balanced behaviour on the part of the teachers promotes the development of qualities of cooperativeness in children.

CLASS: A relatively stable group of children who receives the same educational treatment during a course term (usually a year). The class may be formed on various principles: by age, by sex, by ability (intelligence) or by achievement. Grouping of children in classes aims at achieving some sort of homogeneity in factors that are believed to be directly involved in learning.

The real difficulty lies in the fact that heterogeneity will always prevail, whatever principle is adopted for forming classes. It may help only in reducing heterogeneity of a particular variable. So some educators recommend flexible groups, classes regrouping as and when necessary.

A class is also called a standard. In some countries promotions of pupils to higher standards are based on the results of examinations conducted during the year. Those who fail are retained in the class to repeat the course for an additional year. This is called repetition of class.

Size of class or class size refers to the number of pupils in the class.

CLASS INTERVAL: Grouping of observation into equal and smaller units (for constructing a frequency distribution). When a big mass of data is obtained, it has to be condensed into a convenient size for handling, without damaging its original qualities. This is achieved by rearranging the data according to their magnitude and then dividing it into smaller equal units. A large array of scores obtained on a test can thus be converted into a frequency distribution. The size of steps in a frequency distribution is denoted by 'class interval'. Whatever is the number of observations (frequencies) the steps in a frequency distribution usually ranges between 8 and 16. The size of the class interval is dependent on the range of the scores and the number of steps in the frequency distribution. In short, the class interval is the range of the scores in each step.

Illustration: Distribution of scores obtained by 50 pupils in a test.

(Scores arranged in order of size)

7	25	38	49	63
12	27	39	52	63
12	27	40	52	64
12	29	41	59	66
16	33	43	59	67
17	33	45	59	68
18	36	46	60	70
18	37	46	61	71
19	37	46	61	71
24	37	47	62	72

Range of Scores: (72 – 7) : 65

Steps : 14

Class interval : 5

Class intervals	Frequencies
70 71	4
65-69	3
60-64	7
55-59	3
50-54	2
45-49	6
40-44	3
35-39	6
30-34	2
25-29	4
20-24	1
15-19	5
10-14	3
5-9	1

N = 50

CLASSICAL CONDITIONING: The type of conditioning established by Pavlov in which the sound of the bell elicited salivation in a dog when it was presented in paired sequence with the natural stimulus that would elicit the salivation (meat-powder). Pavlov confined the dog (which was hungry) in a sound proof cabin and first sounded a bell, and immediately after 5 seconds ingested meat powder into its mouth. This procedure was repeated a number of times and the saliva secreted in the mouth each time was collected and measured. After some trials, Pavlov withdrew food and repeated the experiment exactly as he did otherwise i.e., presentation of bell only, with no injestion of food. This time also there was salivation, the quantity collected being a little less. Once established, the salivation response tended to persist, even though food was not paired with the bell. Thus for the first time in 1911, Pavlov established the first conditioned reflex in the laboratory.

The meat powder in the experiment is the unconditioned stimulus (UCS) because it is the natural stimulus that elicit salivation. The salivary reflex which appeared when food was ingested in the mouth is called the unconditioned reflex (UR). The bell sound in the experiment is the conditioned stimulus (CS) and the salivation then occurred (which is the same reflex though less strong) is the Conditioned Reflex (CR).

This experiment proved crucial in psychology as it provided the technique for studying learning in its various aspects, not only in humans, but also in all organisms at the sub-human level.

See: Pavlov I.P.

CLASSIFICATION VARIABLE: The characteristics on which the experimental subjects are classified and the effects of which are intended to be studied in the experiment. The classification variables are not planned or created by the experiments (like the treatment variable over which the experimenter has manipulatory control) but are selected by him to find their correlates by means of the experiment. Age, sex, socio-economic status, religion, nationality, etc. are examples of classification variables, when they are selected for an experiment. Illustration: To study the effects of sex, socio-economic status and intelligence on scholastic achievement, the experimenter administers the achievement test under standardized conditions on a sufficiently large unselected sample of children. Then he finds the achievement level of each sub-sample classified according to the variables, sex, IQ, etc. The data on analysis show whether there is significant difference in the achievement levels of boys and girls, of pupils from different socio-economic levels, different IQ levels, etc.

The classification variables were present prior to the experiment and the experimenter does not manipulate them.

CLIENT-CENTRED THERAPY: Therapautie method which stresses the client's place in solving his own problems. The method was developed by Carl Rogers and is also known as Non-Directive psychotherapy. In this method, the client is encouraged in a very permissive situation to talk out his problems, which procedure is expected to lead to diagnosis and resolution. The therapist's role is mainly to help the patient to discover his own abilities for self-help. The therapist gives no directions or prescriptions. Roger believes that the client has the ability to rebuild his distorted self-concept if he is helped to develop proper insight in a free and uninhibited situation. Guidance as such, from the therapist, is minimal.

Rogerian approach is adopted in psychotherapy and counselling.

See: Rogers C.

CLINICAL PSYCHOLOGY: That branch of applied psychology that deals with the theory and treatment of abnormal behaviour. Clinical psychology is concerned with the theoretical foundation of abnormal and morbid behaviour which are functional in origin (i.e., without organic causes). It deals with the aetiology (causation), symptomatology, therapy (treatment), etc. of mental disorders which are of minor type, viz., neurotic problems and which are not characterized by any break with reality. The client affected with such disorders can carry on in his social set up, but have problems of adjustment and often has inward suffering (like anxiety). Psychotherapy, in its various forms (like psychoanalysis, non-directive therapy, behaviour therapy) is adopted to restore normal adjustment capabilities of the client. Sometimes drugs (like tranquilizers and antidepressants) are also given supportively. A Certificate in clinical psychology (theory and practice) is essential for practising psychotherapy.

CLIP: A short segment of a motion-picture film, or video-tape, used during the course of a lesson.

CLOZE PROCEDURE: A language development technique in which the learners are required to understand passages in which words are omitted at regular intervals (like 5th, 6th or 7th words) or from which certain parts of speech (like verbs, adjectives) are removed. It can be also used as a test in language comprehension.

CLOSURE: The tendency to perceive broken (unfinished) figures as closed ones. Three dots in space is seen as a triangle. It is the gestalt tendency to perceive things as wholes, closing the gaps.

See: Perception Gestalt

CO-EDUCATION: Teaching boys and girls in the same institution. In co-educational institutions boys and girls are not discriminated or segregated on the basis of sex. Even in many schools where both boys and girls are admitted, they are segregated in separate classes. They are not allowed free communication or social grouping. But in co-educational institutions free inter-communication and social groupings are allowed.

CO-OPERATIVE LEARNING: Learning that occurs in group situations by pupil interactions. If properly organised and guided by the teacher, learning will be very effective–it will have the advantages of both individualistic and competitive situations without the disadvantages of any. There will be collective reinforcement. The secondary benefits that accrue from co-operative learning are the development of better understanding among various social groups and the fostering of reciprocal friendships and cooperativeness.

CO-TWIN CONTROL: A method of studying the effect of environments on development (psychological) of the individual, keeping the effect of heredity constant. For co-twin studies, identical twins (monozygotic) are selected. As the identical twins possess almost identical gene composition they can be considered identical in heredity. So such individuals can form suitable subjects for studying the effect of any particular environment variable, on them. In co-twin control studies one individual from each pair is subjected to a particular treatment and their identical counterparts kept without the treatment, as controls. The difference after the treatment period can be reasonably concluded as being the effect of environment, since heredity and other factors were almost similar. Gessel's experiments on twins to study the effect of maturation is a good example. He selected a few pairs of 8 month old identical twins and one child from each pair was given systematic training in staircase climbing. The other children (controls) received no training. Results showed that there was an initial improvement in the staircase-climbing proficiency of the children who received training, but after the lapse of a few months there was no significant difference in the proficiency of two groups of children. From this he concluded that training given to children before they attain the appropriate neuro-muscular development (maturation) produced little effect on their performance. Co-twin studies have been extensively used to explore the effects of environmental variables on intelligence, mental diseases, delinquency criminal tendencies, etc.

COGNITION: Knowing: the mental process of acquiring and preserving knowledge. It is the complex process involving perceptual, conceptual and reasoning processes. In other words it is mainly the process of acquiring, preserving, applying, reproducing and generating ideas.

COGNITIVE DISSONANCE: Mental imbalance felt when two inconsistent cognitions about an object or event are experienced at the same time. Festinger developed this concept. When a new experience is felt which is in harmony with the existing cognitive systems, there is congruence or consonance of the system and the new component is absorbed into the existing system. But when the individual has to hold a new experience which is logically inconsistent with the existing cognitive system, he experiences discomfort. This is cognitive dissonance. To reduce this dissonance he is motivated to change his cognitions and attitudes. Cognitive dissonance, thus leads to attitude changes also.

COHORT: A group of individuals selected on the basis of a criterion (e.g. all children admitted in Std. I during an year) followed up over a period of time. In ordinary sense, it means a troop, a well defined section of an army. Longitudinal studies are usually based on collecting data from a cohort at various intervals of time. In child development studies, the method is to observe child behaviour and record them continuously or at fixed intervals of time (1, 2, 6 months intervals, etc.) from a sample of children born on a particular month of the year (e.g., in June 1980). This cohort of children admitted in Class I is followed up through their educational career till they reach the specified stage (say Standard VII). Such an investigation is called a 'Cohort Study'.

COHORT METHOD: Longitudinal study with a homogeneous group, in order to find out trends over a period.

In child study it is widely used. Samples of children from the same age groups are followed-up over a number of years. For example: for studying the development of social characteristics of young children, cohort (homogeneous groups), like the following may be taken:

3 year old at the beginning in 1980 →	4 year old in 1981 →	5 year old in 1981 →

The cohort method is often used in the investigation of assessing the extent of wastage and stagnation in education.

COMINIUS, JOHN AMOS (1592-1670): The great seventeenth century educationalist. Cominius was a Moravian priest, who was also a teacher. In 1638 the Government of Sweden invited him to work out a scheme for organization of the school system. He was migrating from country to country most of the time. His masterpiece 'Great Dictactic' was written in 1632, in Czech language but, later it was published in Latin. At the outset, he points out that the methods of teaching and learning should follow scientific principles. He postulates that education will be easy if it begins early, before the mind is corrupted; if the mind is duly prepared to receive it; if it proceeds from the general to particular; from what is easy to what is difficult; if the pupil is not overburdened by too many subjects; if progress be slow in every case; if the intellect is forced to nothing to which it is not naturally inclined; if everything be taught through the medium of the senses; if the use of everything taught be continually kept in view and if everything is taught by one and the same method.

Cominius produced text-books for children, which were revolutionary at the time. The books were appropriately illustrated. Goethe in his autobiography remarks that the only book for children in his youth was Amos Cominius' "Orbes Sensualium Dictus".

Cominius' fourfold division of schools are remarkably parallel to the modern structure.

1. Infancy–the school be the mother's knee (0-6 years)
2. In Childhood–should be the vernacular school (7-12 years)

3. In Boyhood–should be The Latin School or gymnasium (13 to 18 years)
4. Youth–should be University and Travel (18-24 years)

Cominius wanted education to be made universal.

COMMERCIAL SUBJECTS: School subjects aimed to prepare students for commercial jobs. Commercial subjects are offered in schools where diversified courses of curriculum are implemented. Commercial subjects usually include specialized training in type-writing, shorthand, book-keeping, etc. in addition to the general subjects like arithmetic, history and geography.

COMMON CORE: The compulsory subjects in the curriculum. It is also called the core curriculum when a curriculum consists of two parts, one compulsory for all students and another part optional. The compulsory part is called the core. Proficiency in the core subjects is essential in their own rights in addition to being necessary or instrumental in acquiring proficiency in the optional subjects. So they are provided compulsory for all. Mother tongue, Mathematics, Science, History and Earth Science usually form part of the subjects in the core curriculum.

COMMON SCHOOL: A school serving a particular region which does not impose any restriction on admitting children. All the children of the locality are entitled for enrolment in the school. In a common school, admission cannot be denied to any child on the basis of religion, sex, entrance examination result etc. (synonymous with neighborhood school).

COMMUNITY CENTRE: A centre for social, educational and cultural activities for adults and adolescents of a locality. The community centre is a meeting place and forum for the members of the community where different kinds of activities like, continuing education, recreational, cultural and social functions, etc. are organized.

COMPACT DISC READ-ONLY MEMORY (CD-ROM): Compact discs containing electronic information or data bases, often in the form of text files, graphic images, or motion sequences. Eg. dictionaries, electronic books, etc.

COMPACT DISC INTERACTIVE (CD-I): Computer system with compact discs containing audio, video and graphic information combined with interactive programs. The user can interact with the software using infra-red remote controls, joysticks or lightpen. The software often includes, apart from other programs, games and simulations.

COMPARATIVE EDUCATION: A study of the educational system of various countries of the world in terms of well defined parameters. In Comparative education, the emphasis is on the development of the educational systems in the various countries with regard to the emergence of philosophies of education, evolution of educational structures and their metamorphoses, control and finance of education, etc. Comparative education makes it possible to compare the trends in education in various countries. It also enables to draw meaningful conclusions on the influence of social and cultural factors, political ideology, etc. on the development of education and educational ideas, school practices, and financing of education. This is revealed by analysing the similarities and differences in the educational system in the various countries. Comparative education, to be useful, should employ only objective methods for analysis and interpretation.

COMPENSATION: The psychological defence mechanism against feeling of inferiority. The inadequacy felt by the individual may be real or imaginary. The individual may exert extraordinary effort, consciously (or unconsciously) to make up for the inferiority. The compensation usually results in an overcompensation; a short statured person may try to dress like a tall person and try to mix with such people. The compensation may also emerge in some undesirable manner, the man becoming a bully (to attract attention).

See: Ego degence mechanism

COMPENSATORY EDUCATION: Education provided for the children of the disadvantaged groups in order to make them cope with the regular programmes of the common school. Social deficit, because of the deprivation, has to be compensated to enable those children to profit from the school procedures.

See: Disadvantaged

COMPLETION ITEMS: A test item which requires the candidate to answer by filling up the blanks left in it. In the completion test-forms, one or more parts of a sentence, word, diagram, graph, etc. may be left blank. The candidate is to supply the missing parts. This is often included as a guided (objective) response test. The test content is fully structured and so far the item is objective. But, as the answers are not given as in multiple choice items, any type of free responses are possible, and in many situations the responses will have to be interpreted. This reduces the objectivity of the item. Even when correct responses are provided (in scoring keys) factors like illegibility, slip-shod drawing, etc. may necessitate subjective decision.

Completion tests are, however, useful in eliciting original and creative responses.

See: Objective test

COMPLEX: A term widely used by the Depth Psychologists to mean a constellation of repressed unconscious experiences around a central theme. 'Complex' means a bunch of ideas kicked down to the unconscious (repressed)–the ideas centering round a core and with a heavy emotional charge. The Oedipus complex, the well known complex according to Freud, is universal. The boy in early childhood develops a strong love towards the mother, which according to Freud is erotic and so unapprovable. So he is bound to repress the desires (unconscious) and at the same time becomes envious and aggressive towards the father (i.e., develops jealousy). Around this central theme more and more painful experiences are repressed which coalesce to form the Oedipus Complex. Even though the complex is unconscious, the behaviour motivated by it must be acceptable at the conscious level. The boy in adulthood may become extremely worried about the mother's health and welfare, when there is no reason to be so. He may even prefer a girl, elder than him or in some way similar to his mother, for marriage. This is due to the unconscious motivation springing from the complex. Jung used the term to signify another common complex–the inferiority complex. A man with some organ defect e.g. very short stature) may unconsciously build up a complex around this inferiority. As inferiority complex is unconscious, the person is not aware of the fact that his motivations arise from it. His behaviour at conscious level will appears to negate the idea of being short–he will dress up like taller men, will prefer friends who are taller, etc. The behaviour motivated by a complex will never be a direct expression of it, but a compensation in a disguised form. A person with an inferiority complex seldom appear inferior in the particular respect. Now people often use the term wrongly to mean feeling of inferiority and inadequacy (which is conscious).

See: Adler A.

COMPREHENSIVE SCHOOL: A secondary school with a variety of courses of study. A comprehensive school is a secondary school meant to cater for all students in a compact locality who are at the appropriate age limits. It offers a wide choice of subjects (electives) in both academic and vocational fields. The prime consideration is that the school should provide a variety of opportunity to accommodate all type of abilities, interests, needs, etc. of the pupils.

In some countries Middle schools (upper stage of primary) also adopt the comprehensive pattern.

In the U.K., a secondary school meant for all pupils of the district or area who are of the appropriate age (11 to 18 years) is called a comprehensive school. It provides courses of studies taught in all types of secondary schools.

COMPREHENSIVE TESTS: A test which has a wide coverage of subject matter. Comprehensive tests are usually used at higher levels of academic courses. There are comprehensive achievement tests covering wide areas of subject matter like Physics, Chemistry, Biology, History, Economics, etc.

COMPULSION: An unconscious urge to perform some action repeatedly. The unconscious urge in a compulsion is so strong that the individual will perform the same action over and over again in a ritualistic manner. If the individual is restricted from performing the compulsive acts, anxiety may develop. The individual does not know why he performs the act which does not help in achieving any purpose. It is irresistible. It may be sometimes a harmless action like the ritualistic touching of every lamp post on the way or verifying whether the door has been locked, repeatedly for a number of times. Sometimes the compulsive act may lead to problems, problems for the individual and for others: e.g., compulsive stealing (kleptomania–the stolen property is obviously not taken away for using) and compulsive fire setting (pyromania).

Compulsions are symptoms of deep-seated psychological problems.

See: Ego defence mechanism

COMPULSORY SCHOOL AGE: The age group for which school attendance is compulsory. In all countries where education is compulsory, there are appropriate statutory provisions for enforcing it. According to the law, it is the duty of the parent to enrol the child in the school, at the appropriate age and retain him there till he completes the upper age limit laid down. There will be penal provisions to deal with failure or neglect on the part of the parent. The Educational Act of 1944 (Butler Act) in Britain made education compulsory upto the age of 14 (which was subsequently revised to 16) according to the age, ability and aptitude of the children.

Regional administration or local education authorities are responsible for the enforcement of the provisions of the Act. Attendance officers are usually attached to the Regional offices to supervise the enrollment and attendance of the pupils. Generally the compulsory school age is between 5 years and 15 years (or 6 years to 14 years), etc.

COMPUTER MEMORY: The storing and retention of information in the computer. This is achieved by altering the states of a large number of mechanical and electrical devices of the computer by on-off switching. The meaning of the information at the address of each point in the memory units depends on the program supplied by the operator.

COMPUTER-MEDIATED MATERIALS: Learning materials that need a computer for display. Such materials can be classified under

1. Number crunching and data processing materials (i.e., as a complex calculator or data processor);
2. learning packages for individualized learning, permitting interaction and feedback;
3. substitute laboratory packages–simulations of complex experiments, training situations, etc.
4. data base system–storing and retrieval;
5. computer managed learning system–in managerial work, budgetary control, management of actual teaching-learning process, etc.;

6. interactive video-systems–to gain access to videomaterials stored on a random access video recorder.

COMPUTER: The computer machine and accessories: The computer machine and accessories constitute the hardware in computer technology and the rules and commands, transformed into programming language form the software.

Computers are used for processing information. There are mainly two types of computers: analogue computers and digital computers. Analogue computers work by rearranging the information into representative mechanical or electrical systems. In digital computers, usually, the binary code is used to represent the information. In this case, the machine can perform operations using the binary code program (algorithm) at rates like one billion per second. It is an electronic instrument that can store, select, create and transform immense quantities of information at a very fast rate. The computer has no moving parts (except the switches), so wear and tear is minimal. The set of commands for the computer is called the 'program'. For information processing, first make sure that the program (commands) is in the computer, then feed the information to be processed. This is the 'input' part of the machine. Processing takes place fastly. The processed information can be either stored or displayed visually or otherwise, or both stored and displayed at the same time. This is the 'output' part. The modern computer (ordinary micro-computer or personal computer) has a micro-processor (central processing unit – CPU) and an input unit and output unit. These are linked to keyboards and (monitor) display screen, (or other devices). The storage unit can perform two functions: first, keeping the information in a manner that cannot be changed (which is called read-only memory or ROM) and in a form that can be altered (or called random access memory i.e., RAM).

COMPUTER LITERACY: Knowledge of terminology related to computer system and ability to do computing. It includes the study of the history of computers, the working of the computer, their uses, their importance in progress, etc. and also the ability to do computing. To acquire computer literacy, first-hand experience and practice at computing are essential.

COMPUTER PROGRAM: The 'bit' of signs in some

language (FORTRAN, COBOL, etc.) which activates the computer to carry out a logical sequence of operations (calculations) to find out answers to the questions that it has been required to answer. The program is represented by means of an algorithm.

COMPUTER-MANAGED LEARNING SYSTEM (CML): Applications of computer, practically in all aspects of educational management like teaching, training, administration, managerial role, etc. For Time-table planning, budgetting, management of teaching-learning process, etc. also computers can be used. Software packages available for such areas of education are being widely used and becoming increasingly popular.

COMPUTER-ASSISTED LEARNING (CAL): Computer-Assisted (Aided) learning. The acronyms CAI, (Computer-assisted Instructions) CBL (Computer-based Learning) and CBE (Computer-based education) practically mean the same thing. The main feature of the CAL is that it enables the presentation of instructional materials to the students on a television screen or visual display unit (VDU). The student communicates to the computer usually by means of a normal type-writer key board or by using a mouse. Interaction between the learner and the computer is possible in a CAL program. The program is usually in the form of an audio-tape, floppy disc, video tape or their combinations. The machine facing the learner can be the terminal of a main-frame computer, or a mini-computer or a micro computer (personal computer).

CAL is not a teaching aid, because, teaching aids do not permit interaction with the learner. CAL is a total teaching system, which allows for mutual interaction, between the learner and computer. (It should be noted that in pupil–teacher situation the possibilities of interaction are unlimited while with the computer the range of interaction possible is limited). The CAL program in the micro-computer is intended to lead the student from one skill level to a higher one without any help or intervention from a teacher. The program will provide all the guidance to the student about what he is expected to do. It presents the stimuli (learning experience) in a structured manner. The student should respond individually, at his own pace. The program is structured in such a way that accurate and immediate feed-back can be given.

Educational programs, like drills and tests, multiple-choice tests, experimental aids, educational games, manipulative tests, simulations, etc. are some of the possible variety of CAL program.

The CAL is not suitable for very young children. The adequacy of CAL programs increases with age. Its appropriateness also depends on the subject matter. It is not suitable for teaching subjects with a high attitudinal content (like religion, literature, sociology, etc.) It is most suitable when the subject matter can be clearly analysed into statements which gives unambigous Yes/ No responses.

CONANT, JAMES BRYANT: Brilliant American Chemist who made remarkable contributions for the education of his country. Conant was the Advisor to the project which produced the first atom bomb. In 1943, his views in education were published in the 'Harvard Report'. He pointed out that there should be general education instead of liberal education. He wanted three levels of instruction based on scholastic ability. Admissions are to be selective, and foreign languages need be taught only to able students. He insisted that a language should be studied at least for 4 years. His famous works include: 'Education in a Divided World', 'Education and Liberty' and 'American High Schools today'. He wanted science to be taught to every child and that 'the gifted child should never be lost to the nation'.

CONCENTRIC METHOD: The method of arranging curricular experiences in a subject in expanding rings, as the course progresses. In this type of curriculum organization each topic or important unit is arranged in such a way to spread over a number of years. The simplest concepts of the subject are introduced first, depth, extent and complexity gradually increasing from year to year. This is in contrast to the Topical method in which case each topic is introduced and completed at that stage itself.

See: Curriculam

CONCEPT ANALYSIS: Breaking down of the various elements of a concept. Analysis of the concept is done as a preparation for teaching a concept – i.e., – concept attainment. The analysis scheme incorporates (1) the concept name; (2) the definition; (3) characteristics; (4) superordinate concepts; (5) subordinate concepts; (6) coordinate concepts and (7) examples. An analysis of the concept vitamin, for example: *Definition*–Organic substance present in some food stuffs essential for maintaining metabolic processes, etc.; *Characteristics*–Organic compounds, some water soluble and some fat soluble, some destroyed on heating etc.; *Subordinate concept*–Vitamin B has different members: B_1, B_2 etc.; *Superordinate concept*–Food materials; *Coordinate concept*–Proteins, fats, carbohydrates, etc; Examples–Vitamin A, B, etc. This type of analysis is suitable for planning lessons on concept teaching.

J.S. Bruner developed the principle of analysis of the concepts into conjuctive, disjunctive and relational concepts.

CONCEPT: An abstraction drawn from particular experience. The experiences of seeing, touching, etc. of different types of trees goes to build up the concept 'tree'. The concept 'tree' is abstract and has no particular shape size, etc. The common features present in all trees are abstracted, ignoring individual qualities. Likewise, the concept of 'man' includes all human beings irrespective of race, nationality or period of existence. The abstraction is done mentally after a series of perceptual experiences. Generally, a class name is a concept (like table, flower, star). The concept is abstract and can accommodate all the members of the class (e.g., table can be round table, metal table, dining table, etc.) because the concept includes only the common qualities present in all the members of the class. Words are used to denote concepts in symbolic form.

See: Generalization

CONCEPT ATTAINMENT MODEL: Class room teaching model useful for teaching concepts. The approach is inductive. The model was designed by Joyce and Weil based on the works of Bruner on concept attainment. The basic steps, as in any lesson, are planning activities, implementation of activities and evaluation. In planning the following steps are involved: Identification of goals, selection of examples, sequencing of examples and selecting the appropriate medium for presenting the examples (i.e., pictures, models, specimens, etc.). The implementation activities involve presentation of examples (in the proper sequence) and the analysis of characteristics. The final step in implementation stage is 'closure' that results in the definition of the concept and the giving of additional examples, etc. At the evaluation stage, the attainment is tested.

This model follows the naturally occurring process of concept formation–finding similarities, forming categories and abstraction.

CONCRETE OPERATIONS STAGE: The third stage in cognitive development in children according to Piaget. This period extends approximately from 7 years to 11 years. At this stage, the child has the ideas of 'conservation' of qualities, like volume, length, weight and he can apply the principle of 'reversibility'. The child is less ego-centric than he was at the pre-operational stage. He is able to classify objects on the basis of particular characteristics and can build up complex network of such categories. Logical transformation of ideas is possible and he applies transformations suggested by the symbols +, -, x, :, =, >, < and so on. Still he is dependent on concrete objects as a means of thinking. He may not need concrete objects to manipulate for solving problems but he has to use them as images in his mind. At this stage he will not be able to work with pure abstractions (as in the case of algebraic problems) or to formulate hypotheses and test them.

See: Piaget, J.

CONDITIONED STIMULUS: A stimulus producing a conditioned response.

See: Classical Conditioning

CONDITIONED RESPONSE: Response elicited by a conditioned stimulus.

See: Classical Conditioning

CONE OF EXPERIENCE: The experience resulting from the arrangement of educational programmes in order of abstraction, beginning from the concrete at the bottom to the verbal, symbolic at the top. This is the model developed by Edgar Dale in U.S.A. to explain the progression of learning experiences from the direct first hand participation to purely abstract representation. At the bottom of the cone is the direct experience, i.e., the experience resulting from direct participation in the concrete situation and at the top the experience is mostly verbal, i.e., based on text books, lectures, etc. This model effectively explains the importance of audiovisual materials as instructional aids. The order of progression from the bottom is: Direct, purposeful experience → Contrived experience → Dramatized experience → Demonstrations → Exhibits

→ Television → Motion pictures → Recordings, radio, pictures → Visual symbols → Verbal symbols.

CONFLATION: Combining two or more scores (or sets of scores) in different tests to give a compositive index.

CONFLICT: A situation in which the individual has to deal with two opposing forces in order to reach his goal. It often occurs in a goal directed activity. Sometimes the opposing situations may be posed by two positive goals (choose a course in medicine or accept a job offered), sometimes between two negative goals (a child may want to avoid doing homework and at the same time faced with parental threats) and in some cases between positive and negative goals (a child wanting to go for a cinema show which his parents would not allow). Conflicts have to be resolved satisfactorily. Continued exposure to conflicting situations may lead to neurosis and other mental disturbances.

See: Stress

CONFORMITY: Tendency of the individuals to adopt behaviour patterns of the group. Ordinarily, individuals tend to yield to group pressure when faced with situations in which their own opinions are in conflict with those maintained by the group. People easily adopt the 'normal' behaviour styles to avoid conflict with the group's mode of behaviour.

CONFUCIUS (551-478 BC): The aim of education according to Confucius, the Chinese Scholar, is to prepare the individuals for noble living. He stressed morality and the importance of relationships in society; relation between father and son, brother and brother, teacher and pupils and so on. Likewise, universal charity, justice, prudence and fidelity were cherished virtues. Family was considered important. Every village should have a village teacher. Classes were to be conducted in the teacher's houses. (As the boys had to pay fees to the teachers, only children of upper class parents could receive education). Confucius emphasized practical application of knowledge in daily life. The teaching started with reading, writing, memorization and imitation.

CONNECTIONISM: Learning considered as establishing S-R bonds. In 'connectionism' mentalistic terms like consciousness, thought, etc. are not used to explain the phenomena of learning. All learning is considered as resulting from linking a stimulus with an appropriate response. Learning is the process of effecting bonds between specific stimulus and (desired) response. Stimuli that present themselves in close temporal or spatial contiguity under various conditions tend to associate themselves.

Thorndike preferred the term 'connection' to describe the learning that resulted from his classical experiments on trial and error learning. Conditioning is also considered as a method of establishing connections i.e., S-R bonds. The term is behaviouristic and it uses only observable variables in explaining human and animal learning.

See: Association

CONSCIOUSNESS: Awareness of external and internal experiences. An individual who is awake is aware of the happenings outside as well as the mental processes taking place within him. Consciousness is often compared to a stream because the subjective contents of awareness change from moment to moment. For a long time, psychology was considered as the study of 'consciousness' and 'conscious processes'. As 'consciousness' is not observable and cannot be subjected to experimental manipulation, later psychologists avoided the term in explaining mental phenomena.

See: Behaviourism

CONSERVATION: The Piagetian concept of invariance in mass, weight or volume of a substance when subjected to transformation in appearance. The concept of conservation begins to develop, according to Piaget, towards the end of the pre-operational stage (2-7 years). A simple experiment will explain the meaning of 'conservation'. The child is shown two plasticine balls which he agrees are the same in size. One of the balls is pressed into the shape of a disc in full view of the child, and if he is asked whether the size has changed, the child upto the age of about four years, would say that the disc contain more plasticine. The child develops the concept of conservation gradually later, so that he would say that both contain the same amount of plasticine in spite of the transformation in shape.

See: Piaget, J

CONSISTENT BIAS: Bias of judgement working consistently in one direction. This occurs when people evaluate the characteristics of others, as when foremen rate workers, teachers rate pupils, etc. Recorded data on 'observation schedules' 'check-lists', 'rating scales', etc. are liable to this defect. A rater may be consistently severe, overstrict, etc. or consistently generous and lenient. In this situation, there will be no bias against any particular individual, but ratings will be biassed in one particular direction.

See: Bias

CONSOLE: The equipment incorporating the central panels and monitoring devices, etc. needed to control a computer. It is like a desk and often, non-movable.

CONSTRUCT VALIDITY: Evidence of validity of a test obtained by comparing the content of the test with the construct of the dimension intended by the test.

It is obtained by a scrutiny of the content of the test and finding out how far it justifies the construct of the dimension. A measure of construct validity is also obtained by finding the correlation of the scores on the test with ratings and other observational data on the same population with reference to the construct. For example, if intelligence is operationally defined as 'the ability to solve new problems', the content of intelligence test in question can be scrutinised on this basis and evidence can be obtained from expert opinion about its agreement with the construct (i.e., how far the content contains new problems). Ratings and other observation data can be obtained for the same sample for 'intelligence' and these can be correlated with the test scores. A high correlation indicates a fair degree of construct validity.

See: Construct, Dimension, Validity

CONSTRUCT: A precise explanation for a phenomenon that is not directly observable or measurable. A construct is a definition, explanation or theory in verbal, graphical or mathematical form of a phenomenon that can be inferred from its effects or from evidences. Many concepts in psychology like 'intelligence', 'interest', 'aptitudes', 'attitudes', etc. are constructs. These entities are not directly observable; they are inferred from behaviour 'caused' by them. Measurement of these qualities are also based on these overt behaviours. 'Intelligence', for example, is described to include a large number of characteristics–like, innate ability, allround mental ability, (unobservable); ability to deduce relationships, ability to make adjustment, ability to solve new problems (observable), etc. The construct of intelligence is built up from these elements.

In other words, a construct is a concept or inference based on processes and effects which are observable. 'Intelligence' is not directly observable, but the concept 'intelligence' can be developed from an analysis of various types of behaviour of people in situations which demand them to solve problems successfully. To cite another example: Freud concluded from the study of clinical records of a large number of cases that many actions performed by his clients were not motivated consciously. They did not know why they did it or for what purpose they did it. Closer study convinced him that many types of behaviour of people, both normal and abnormal, were motivated unconsciously and that the unconscious part of the self was the repository of all the forbidden, repressed desires. Dreams, psychoneurotic symptoms, etc. were symbolic reappearances of the repressed contents of the unconscious. From these observations he postulated that apart from conscious and pre-conscious there is another part of the mind 'the unconscious'. 'Unconscious' though not directly observable can be inferred from various actions of men. 'Unconscious' is a construct. So also are 'Id', 'Inferiority complex', 'Insight', 'Intelligence', 'Aptitudes', 'Attitude', etc.

CONTENT ANALYSIS: Research technique used to describe the manifest content of a communication (like a book, periodical, etc.) in quantitative and systematic terms. Books, articles, movies, etc. are subjected to content analysis to study the actual content and its nature. For example, ideas of citizenship, democracy and internationalism, etc. dealt with in a school text book can be objectively studied by content analysis. Each pertinent item is listed and the times they occur (frequencies) are tabulated.

CONTINGENCIES OF REINFORCEMENT: Specific periodicity relationship of reinforcers to the responses and stimuli that precede them. When a reinforcer is introduced after a fixed interval of time it is 'fixed interval schedule', when given after emitting a fixed number of responses, it is 'fixed number reinforcement schedule'. When reinforcement follows a given number of responses since the previous reinforcement it is 'fixed ratio schedule', and so on.

See: Reinforcement, Operant Conditioning

CONTIGUITY: Closeness of two occurrences in space (spatial contiguity) or time (temporal contiguity). One of the postulates of Hull on learning is that a stimulus and a reinforced response occurring in close temporal contiguity tend to be connected with the stimulus (after sufficient trials) so as to evoke the response later. Guthrie's view on learning, on the otherhand, is that any stimulus and response occurring in close temporal contiguity (irrespective of a reinforcement sequence) tend to be connected. Stimuli occurring in spatial contiguity also tend to become connected.

See: Classical Conditioning

CONTINGENCY COEFFICIENT: An index of the degree of association between variables of which at least one is in the ordinal scale and the two variables are expressed as classes or categories. Contingency coefficient (C) is directly derived from Chi-square. Contingency coefficient closely approximates Product Moment Correlation when the number of categories are large (5x5 table and larger), the sample is large and the variables are normally distributed. For computation of C, the measures are first converted into cell frequencies. The relationship is given by the formula.

$$C = \sqrt{\frac{\chi^2}{N + \chi^2}}$$

Illustration: Degree of association (correlation) between Literacy status of parents and Educational backwardness (in a sample of primary school pupils):

Scholastic status	Both parents illiterate	One parent illiterate	Both parents literate	Total
Normal children	21	7	100	128
Backward children	55	25	54	134
Total	76	32	154	262

The X^2 value for these cell frequencies worked out to 38.83; and the contingency coefficient for this value works out to 0.85. This means that the two variables are highly correlated–illiteracy of parents has a strong adverse influence on the educational achievement of their children.

CONTINUOUS VARIABLE: A variable capable of sub-division (i.e., in which values in fractions are possible). Length is a continuous variable, because the quantity can exist in both integral or fractional values; like, 2 cm or 2.17 cm. There are no gaps in the continum in the case of such a variable. Most of the psychological qualities like intelligence, aptitudes, mathematical ability, linguistic ability, etc. form continuous series when measures on them are obtained.

See: Variable

CONTRASTIVE ANALYSIS: Making comparison of structures of the second language with structures of the native language as a means of better learning. The learner compares the structures of both the languages. Analysis of the features of the structures will help the learner to tackle problems to be faced in learning. Contrastive analysis is also used for formulating the principles for constructing teaching aids for the second language.

CONTROL: In experimentation, identifying the variables likely to affect a phenomenon and keeping them constant or varying them according to the plan of the experimenter. Experimental control is exercised in order to enable the experimenter to vary only one variable (independent variable), the effect of which on the dependent variable he wants to find out. This he achieves by keeping all other variable, likely to affect the experiment constant, or by blocking them.

See: Experiment

CENTRAL PROCESSOR (PROCESSING UNIT, CPU): The main part of a computer system containing the main storage, the arithmetic unit and control unit.

CONTROLLED OBSERVATION: Observation made on the basis of predetermined objectives. In controlled observation, the focus of the object or situation under investigation, the timing of observation, the behaviour to be recorded and the method of recording are previously determined. Controlled observation as a method of research, is used particularly in child study. For example, to study the spontaneous play of young children, situations are contrived with toys (and companions) in play chambers where children engage in play activities of their own. They are observed without being seen by them and the behaviour is recorded in preplanned record sheets. In controlled observation the experimenter limits his range of observation by specifically defining the things to be observed and how to observe and record them, on the basis of the purpose of the study.

CONVERGENT THINKING: The thinking process involved in solving problems which have only one solution. Most of the conventional problems are of that type, i.e. which permits only one solution. Strictly following the principles of reasoning, whoever attempts the problem, can arrive at only the same answer. What the thinker does is only that he analyses the problem and discovers the answer for which all cues were already there. Convergent thinking only finds out the unique solution to the problem, it cannot produce anything new or original for which Divergent Thinking is the mental process involved. This classification of thinking is based on Guilford's work.

See: Divergent thinking. Creativity

COURSE-WARE: In computer terminology, 'instructional software'. It may also mean the actual instructional materials comprising the content and the instructional techniques incorporated in the CAL.

See: Computer Assisted Learning

CORE SUBJECTS: The 'compulsory' subjects in a course. It is that part of the course that all students undergoing the course have to take. Along with the core subjects 'electives', 'optionals', etc. are also offered from which the students are free to choose any subject. Mother-tongue, mathematics, science, social studies etc. usually form the core subjects, in most of the secondary schools.

CORPUS CALLOSUM: The band of nerve fibres that connect the two cerebral hemispheres. It is believed to have no function other than serving as a communicating system between the two hemispheres.

CORRECTION FOR GUESSING: A method sometimes adopted for reducing the effects of guessing in the scores obtained by an individual in a test. It is often used in the scoring of objective tests containing multiple choice and true-false items.

When confronting a multiple choice situation the candidates are tempted to guess the answers when they do not know the correct ones, unless they are forewarned that they will be penalized for guessing, by reducing their marks. The total correct scores obtained from candidates for whom no such warning have been given, will generally be spurious, as they contain the scores which they have hit by guessing. So, in such cases, to get a better measurement of the scores, proper corrections will have to be applied. The extent of operation of chance for guessing depends on the number of options for the items. Larger the number of options, lesser is the chance factor. In a true-false test (two option items), the chance factor is 50%.

The corrected score is obtained by applying the formula:

$$S = R - \frac{W}{(n-1)}$$

where

S: the corrected score

R: the number of correct responses

W: the number of wrong responses

n: the number of options (alternatives)

For a two option test and true-false test, therefore, the correction formula is:

$$S = R - W$$

The correction formulas have to be applied with caution when a number of items are seen left unanswered.

See: Power Test, Speed Test

CORRECTION: The process of making a measured quantity more accurate by minimizing the effect of the inaccuracy component. Usually all measurement in education and psychology are based on estimates of parameters (real values). The real values are not at all possible to find out by known methods. But the probable effects and extent of the vitiating factors can be identified and estimated within limits. This is also an estimation. When this value is known, with its help, a correction can be made to the original estimate (usually by adding or subtracting the error estimate) in order to get an estimate closer to the real value.

Appropriate statistical techniques are available to meet specific situations needing correction.

CORRECTION FOR ATTENUATION: The correction

applied to correlation coefficients to reduce the effects of unreliability of the scores in the two measurements. A correlation coefficient corrected for attenuation will give more accurate value, by reducing the effects of the errors of measurement.

The correlation between two measurements will be lower than the true value, as one or both sets of scores incorporate errors of measurement (like low reliability). So to estimate a value nearer to the true coefficient of correlation a correction is applied to the obtained value by using the formula

$$r_{tt} = \frac{r_{xy}}{\sqrt{r_x \, x \, r_y}}$$

in which

r_{tt} : correlation between the true scores in variable 1 and variable 2.

r_{xy} : correlation between obtained scores in variable 1 and variable 2 (x and y).

r_x : reliability coefficient of variable 1, (x).

r : reliability coefficient of variable 2, (y).

CORRELATION: In statistics–The degree of correspondence or relationship between two variables. Suppose two variables A and B tend to vary together, i.e. when A increases B also tends to increase or when A increases B tends to decrease, they are said to be correlated. If, when B increases A also increases then correlation is positive and when B decreases A increases the correlation is negative and if an increase or decrease in A does not increase or decrease the value of B, they are not correlated. Maximum possible positive correlation is 1 (i.e. complete correspondence) and maximum negative correlation is –1 (complete disagreement) and when change in one variable does not in anyway affect the other variable the correlation is 0. So the coefficient of correlation can vary from +1 to –1, through 0.

Height and weight of boys is positively correlated, accident proneness and mental alertness is negatively correlated and height and artistic aptitude has no correlation.

The index of correlation according to Pearson's Product moment method is the mean of the z–score products of the two paired variables.

i.e. $$r = \frac{\Sigma Z_x Z_y}{N}$$

When the position of the two variables are given in ranks, Spearman's rank order formula is used to obtain the correlation:

$$\rho = 1 - \frac{6\Sigma D^2}{N(N^2-1)}$$

where ρ is the rank order correlation, åD^2 is the sum of the differences of each rank squared, and N= the total number of cases.

Other coefficients of correlation are the phi-coefficient, Biserial coefficient, Point biserial coefficient, etc.

See: Biserial coefficient of correlation

CORRELATION MATRIX: A table showing the correlations between each sub-test to each other sub-test. The correlation matrix provides complete data on intercorrelations of all the sub-tests. Preparation of a correlation matrix is the first step in Factor Analysis.

CORRELATION RATIO: The index of association of two variables, when they are continuous but the relationship is not linear. It is denoted by (h). An example of a situation in which nonlinear relationship in two continuous variables is encountered is when the correlation between psychological performance and chronological age are to be obtained. In this case there is rapid increase in performance in the earlier years which slows down after reaching a peak.

CORTICAL LOCALIZATION: Locating areas in the brain that are involved in specific functions. Particular areas in the cerebral cortex have been found to be in control of certain functions. Extensive research has established that 'learning' is localized in the temporal lobes, sight is localized in the occipital region of the brain, the left hemisphere controls language in the majority of individuals, etc.

See: Cerebral Cortex

COST OF EDUCATION: The total expenditure of a government on education. The most important items under which funds have to be spent are: Teacher's salaries; salaries of non-teaching staff, equipment and furniture, books, maintenance of properties, rents, taxes, light, fuel, water, noon-feeding, student health service activities, training of teachers: inservice and preservice, administration and supervision (inspection), printing text-books etc.

COUNSELLING: The psychological assistance provided by an expert to an individual facing adjustment problems, in a permissive interview siluation. The counsellor's aim is not to tell the client what he should do (prescriptive advice) but to help him to resolve his problems by himself. The counsellor helps by questions and hints to guide the client see the nature of his problem realistically and explore solutions to overcome it. So in a sense it is a therapeutic session. Counselling is a process in guidance.

There are three well-known approaches in guidance–Directive, Non-directive and Eclectic. In Directive counselling the counsellor directs the process by suitable questions and suggestions to guide the client to the goal while in Non-directive the counsellor, in a permissive attitude, encourages the client to talk out whatever he feels important and thereby resolve his tension and find out the solution by himself. Eclectic counselling uses all methods (including directive and non-directive) to help the client resolve his problems. Carl Rogers developed the techniques of Non-directive methods in counselling and psychotherapy.

See: Guidance

COUNSELLOR: The specialist who discharges guidance functions. The Counsellor's work in a school is to organise vocational guidance activities and help children with problems of personal and scholastic adjustment. So he has to organise vocational information service, vocational and personal counselling and help children in career planning. Usually he is a trained teacher with a master's degree in psychology (with specialization in Guidance and Counselling) or with a diploma in guidance.

See: Career master

COUNTER BALANCING: In experimentation, one of the techniques adopted for equalizing the effects of extraneous variables on the dependent variable. This is often done by arranging the order in which various levels or values of the independent variables are presented to the subjects.

See: Design of Experiment

COUNTY SCHOOL: A school maintained by the Local Education Authority (LEA) in the U.K. The entire cost of the school is met from public funds.

COURSE WARE: Educational programmes prepared for computers. It is part of the 'software'. Courseware can be divided into three types based on the teaching approach: drill and practice lessons, tutorials and simulations. In the drill and practice type the principle involved is mostly that of programmed learning–employing operant conditioning principle. The tutorial type aims at guiding the students for discovery learning. The computerized teacher intervenes when necessary. Simulations are used for experiments. The students can simulate experiments on their own.

COVERT DIMENSION: Aspects of behaviour that are not observable. Behaviour is either observable or unobservable. Speech is observable but thinking is unobservable. Unobservable behaviours are called covert behaviour. Many of the internal stimuli like, hunger contraction of the stomach, headache, etc. are covert stimuli. Likewise 'attitudes', 'interests', etc. are covert dimensions, which cannot be observed and measured directly. Their manifestations appear in observable behaviour when expressing verbally or choosing an activity, etc. Covert behaviour is also referred to as 'Implicit behaviour'.

See: Overt behaviour

CRAIG METHOD: A method of teaching to read letters and words making use of muscle sense (kinesthesis). The letters or words are cut out from sand paper and over the rough surface the children have to trace the letters with their finger tip and simultaneously read aloud the letters or word–forms. This is meant for the age group 3-5 years.

CREATIVITY: The thinking that produces an idea that was nonexistent up to that time. Creative thinking produces ideas that are original and unique. An example will illustrate the point. A music composer invents new melodies, tunes and rhythm in combinations for a film song; the talented singer reproduces it for the audience. The tune will be original to extent the music composer is creative, the song will be exquisite to the extent the trained musician is endowed with musical aptitude. Creative productions appear in all areas of human accomplishment, scientific inventions, artistic and literary works and so on.

Experiments have shown that 'creativity' is a unique trait and it is not identical with intelligence. Those who score high in creativity tests often do not get scores to that degree in Intelligence tests and (vice versa), though creative individuals are found generally only among those who score above average in intelligence tests.

Paul Torrence and his associates have produced a number of tests of creativity.

Guilford's 'Divergent Thinking' and de Bono's, 'Lateral Thinking' are approximate synonyms of creativity.

See: Divergent thinking. Lateral thinking

CRETINISM: Stunted growth resulting from thyroid dysfunction. This disorder occurs in a small percentage of children. Subnormal functioning of the thyroid gland from early childhood results in cretinism. In this condition physical growth of the bones and hair is retarded. There is marked mental retardation also. Thyroid extract administered during the early stages produces remarkable improvement.

CRITERION: A standard against which an observation, object, etc. is evaluated. For example, validity and reliability are the most important criteria for judging the quality of a test. An external criterion is a standard which is predetermined, usually arbitrarily, for making judgement on observations, e.g., criteria for selecting candidates for a job may be based on marks obtained in examinations, aptitude test results and performance at the interview, etc.

In testing, criterion is the standard which is accepted as a clear representation of the dimension, against which a test is validated. The criterion is claimed to be a valid representation of the dimension, therefore, a test which claims to measure the dimension should have high positive correlation with the criterion. Scholastic achievement scores are sometimes taken as criterion for validating intelligence tests. The rating of the foreman of an industrial unit is a criterion for validating a mechanical aptitude test.

CRITERION FRAME: In programmed instruction it is equivalent to a Test Frame.

See: Programmed Instruction

CRITERION-REFERENCED TEST: Tests prepared on the basis of pre-fixed external criterion–like the attainment of definite learning objectives, standards or levels of achievement. Almost all teacher-made tests (unit tests, termly tests, etc.) are criterion-referenced, since they attempt to evaluate the desirable outcomes of the carricular unit. Criterion-referenced tests are not primarily meant for comparison of pupil performance; they are used for assessing the strengths and weakness of the pupils in each unit of the curriculum.

For comparison of pupil performance, Norm-referenced tests are used.

See: Norm-referenced testing

CRITICAL RATIO (CR): The statistical index which shows how far a difference between two groups (in scores, values etc.) is statistically significant. The difference between the mean marks of two classes of pupils in a test may be large; but it cannot be said that the difference is actually due to difference in achievement (i.e., ability) because the difference may occur also due to various other chance factors. If the obtained difference is larger than that can be expected to occur by chance factors, then we can say that there is difference in achievement and that it is a real difference. If the differences is within the range that can occur by chance, it is rejected as being nonsignificant. The critical ratio method is used to find out the significance of differences between means and other measures. Critical ratio is obtained by dividing the obtained difference in the measures by the standard error of the difference between the measures.

$CR = \frac{D}{\rho_D}$, in which CR is the critical ratio, D the obtained difference and sD is the standard error of the difference between the measures.

In the case of differences between means sD is obtained by the formula

$$\sigma_D = \sqrt{\sigma^2_{M1} + \sigma^2_{M2}}$$

in which sM_1 is the standard error (SE) of the mean of the first measure and sM_2 is the SE of the mean of the second measure.

See: t-test

CRITICAL CUT-OFF SCORE: The lowest score adopted for selection of candidates for a course of study or for a job. Individuals who get scores below the cut-off score will not qualify for the selection. The 40% mark required for passing many examinations is a cut-off score.

CRITICAL PERIOD: In imprinting, the decisive stage at which maximum imprintability is possible. Imprintability is impossible or difficult before or after.

See: Imprinting

CRITICAL LEARNING PERIODS: Specific periods in childhood when individuals can acquire specific skills. At the critical periods, least effort is needed to acquire the skill. Opportunity missed at the period will require greater effort later to attain proficiency (and probably lowered proficiency).

See: Maturation. Readiness

CRITICAL PERIOD HYPOTHESIS (CPH): The time limit set for the acquisition of mother-tongue. Lenneberg fixes this limit around puberty, the time which coincides with the completion of the differentiation and specialization of brain functions. He also suggests that the learning of a second language would be more difficult after this period, since the mother tongue learning capacity would have atrophied by then.

CROSS CULTURAL STUDIES: Research on trends, phenomena, etc. in different cultural groups. Cross cultural studies are useful in understanding various human problems as they occur in different societies. Investigation data of mental ability (intelligence) of different cultural and ethnic groups are available. Such studies have shown that the belief that certain races as a group are more intelligent than others is a myth. When culture-fair tests are administered the differences are found to be negligible. Various social problems like delinquency, religious and communal tensions etc. have been subjected to cross-cultural studies. The UN study on 'social tensions and attitude towards war' is a well known report of a cross-cultural investigation. The results of achievement surveys (on mathematics, science, etc.) conducted in various countries (using the same achievement tests), enable us to compare the performance of students all over the world.

See: Longitudinal Studies

CRITICAL SUCCESS FACTORS (CSFs): Also called 'moments of truth' (in Total Quality Management). CSFs are indicators of the success of the institution that will satisfy its beneficieries. They are the pivotal activities of the school-like the teaching-learning process. Some of the important CSFs are (1)

High pass rates (2) Improvement of teaching stategies (both internal indicators) and (3) greater sensitivity to community needs and (4) greater satisfaction of parents; (both external indicators).

CROSS SECTIONAL METHOD: A method used to find out developmental trends by studying groups of individuals at a particular point in time. Such studies are usually conducted as surveys and data on particular variables (like sociability, aggressiveness, etc.) are collected at particular points in time (may be at intervals of 6 months, 1 year, or at age 5, 6, 7, 8 ....). In this method it is not necessary to take repeated measures from the same individuals. Usually data on various groups (like 5 year old, 6 year old, etc.) are collected on the same traits, if groups, representative in each age range, are obtainable. Longitudinal studies require more time for completion, while cross sectional studies can be completed within short periods. The method is widely used in psychological and sociological research.

CROWD: A group of people gathered at a place usually by chance but having a common centre of attention. The members of a crowd do not possess a comon purpose for assembling there, but something that happens draws the attention of all of them, e.g., accident at a road junction, a quarrel in a market place etc. The members of a crowd interact, the topic of interest being the current incident. Usually the members remain passive, but sometimes emotion gets flared up and the members become aggressive. When the reactions of the members become violent and unmanageable the crowd is called a mob.

CROWTHER REPORT: Report of the Central Advisory Council (England, 1958) on the Education of young people of the age group 15 to 18. The report highlighted the waste of ability due to early leaving and so recommended raising of the school leaving age and provision of access to further education for all young people. Appointment of the 'Beloe Committee' was on the basis of this report and that committee recommended that 'Certificate of Secondary Education' should be made obtainable through examination for any secondary school pupil.

CUE: A subtle signal or a subdued suggestion. It is also used to denote a command signal for a specific event to occur. In programmed learning it means a 'hint'.

See: Prompt

CUEING: In CAL, the hint or cue supplied to elicit a response for a frame. This becomes necessary when the learner has to make a difficult response. In such cases a hint, like the first letter of the word, is given as a cue. When a cued response is provided, it is necessary to follow it with an uncued frame for the item, using a slightly different phraseology.

See: Computer-Assisted-Learning

CUISENAIRE RODS: Also called Cuisenaire–Gettengo rods. A teaching aid devised by George Cuisenaire for teaching basic number concepts. It consists of a set of wooden rods (or wooden blocks). The smallest is an one centimetre cube which represents the number 1. The rods are of different lengths from 1 cm to 10 cm. They are also coloured. Each rod corresponds to a number.

CULTURAL DEPRIVATION: Absence of stimulation from a cultural environment. This happens in the case of social groups living in isolation, cut off from the main stream of culture as in the case of tribal people inhabiting jungles, the slum dwellers, gypsies, etc. Such groups will have their own culture, but it will be generally static and with little relevance to the social and cultural environment of a fast developing world. Education of the children in such societies poses a variety of problems, particularly if the aim is to bring them closer to the main stream of culture. The stunting affect of cultural deprivation is to a large extent irreversible. Compensatory education programmes are planned for such children, which essentially function as a preparatory part of their regular education. Culturally deprived children are also known as culturally disadvantaged children.

See: Disadvantaged

CULTURE EPOCH THEORY: The theory that stresses that the educational process should follow the stages of the evolution of culture in human society. This theory was based on the teachings of the French philosopher Condillac. The theory had some influence on the educational practice of the European countries during the nineteenth century. According to this theory, the child should pass through all the stages of the development of mankind before attaining maturity. A particular stage of development of the individual should corresponds to a specific stage in the development of the human race. Acquiring linguistic skills, number concept etc. should be gained by the child in the same way as the pre-historic man acquired them, but within a short telescoped period. Education is the systematized process of enabling the child to undergo the experience of all the important stages of the development of the race within a period of few years. The theory stresses that there is a parallel between the march of human race from savagehood to culture and the development of the young child from birth to maturity. So, in educational practice, products of instruction should be drawn from the culture of the race, from the epochs or periods that are appropriate to the particular stage of development of the child.

CUMULATIVE SCALING METHOD: The method developed by Guttman for attitude scale construction, in which the items are ordered in such a way that a person who responds positively to an item will respond so to all items of lower rank in the scale. An example of Guttman scale method applied to measurement of height: A person who positively responds to the item: "My height is more than 5'6"." Will respond positively to the items "My height is more than 5'4" and 'my height is more than 5'2", etc.

Guttman's method helps to know whether the scale measures only one dimension or not. So it ensures the selection of statements that measure only one attitude.

See: Attitude scale

CUMULATIVE RECORD: The longitudinal, comprehensive record of pupil growth maintained for a specific period of schooling. The cumulative records are maintained for specific stages–like primary stage and, secondary stage. It will contain identification data, essential family details, physical data including health apart from scholastic data. Personality traits, interests, aptitudes etc. also will have to be recorded from time to time. The teachers will have to tap all relevant sources to gather pertinent data. The methods used for collection of data are observation, interview, socio-metric tests, etc. (in addition to those collected from school records). As the data collection process is continuous and comprehensive, cumulative records give a reliable and complete picture of the personal growth and development of the child.

CURRICULUM: All pedogogic experiences offered by an educational institution. 'Curriculum' denotes the totality of educational experience in terms of aims and objectives, contents of learning, methods of instruction and evaluation of outcomes of learning— all in relation to the harmonious development of the personality of the child. Curriculum should be guided by (1) a sound philosophy that determines the aims and objectives in terms of values, (2) sociology to determine its direction in terms of socialization and acculturization, citizenship and economic productivity and (3) psychology to determine the ordering and organizing of experiences in terms of the needs, capacity and age of the child.

'Curriculum' is also used to refer to a course of study for a particular stage; like age, standard, age group etc. It essentially contains the objectives, contents or units of learning, hints on appropriate learning experiences and evaluation of learning outcomes. Often it is supplemented with a curriculum guide which will provide detailed instructions on teaching techniques, instructional aids, process of assessment, etc.

See: Syllabus

CURSIVE SCRIPT: Script used in writing by joining letters. Cursive script used in writing English aids in increasing speed in writing. Writing in print script in which letters are unconnected takes more time.

CURVILINEAR RELATIONSHIP: The relationship shown in a situation in which the points plotted for two variables takes the form of a curve rather than a straight line. The relationship of variables expressed for correlation coefficient is usually linear, that is, the plotted points of the two variables approximate a straight line. Suppose that a variable (x) first increases as another variable (y) increases and at a certain point even though x continues to increase y begins to decrease (or remains steady), then the relationship between x and y is said to be curvilinear, because the graph representing their relationship will be a curve. Speed in many psychomotor activities are seen to decrease when fatigue sets in. So when the graph is plotted for this relationship (speed at different time intervals) a curve results. The relationship is curvilinear.

D

DALTON PLAN: The method of organizing class activities by providing monthly assignments to pupils. The Dalton plan was developed by Helen Parkhurst around 1920 at the Dalton High School, Massachussets, USA. According to this scheme, the pupil is given monthly assignments in each subject to be completed within the period. The student is free to organise his work (i.e., choosing the assignments, the mode of approach to be adopted, etc.); but he has to complete the work by his own efforts and record the results of assignments. Individual work, group activities and conferences, etc. are also used as means of learning. The progress of the students are recorded in 'job cards'.

DAME SCHOOL: The early elementary schools in Britain, the forerunner of modern schools. In Britain and in some European Countries, usually in the country parts, schools for children of tender ages were conducted by elderly women. The school was normally conducted in a part of the house of the teacher. The rudiments of reading and number were the subjects taught to the children. The 'Dame School' is considered to be one of the earliest type of formal educational institutions.

DATA-BASE SYSTEM: The processed information stored in the computer which can be retrieved as required.

Apart from processing of information, the computer can also be used to store it. The stored information can also be retrieved when required. The teachers can now use computers to create data-bases, that can be used in a whole range of institutional situations.

DATA TABLET: A device for inputting graphic materials into a computer by writing on its (electromagnetically sensitive) surface using a tight pen or other forms of suitable styluses.

DAY-SCHOOL: The school for pupils living at home. 'Day-School' pupils live at their own homes, because the school is meant to serve only (usually) the pupils of a particular locality.

Children go to the schools every day from their homes. Such schools do not have boarding or hostel facilities for outstation students. The students in Day Schools are referred to as 'Day Scholars'.

DE-SCHOOLING: According to Ivan Illich, the author of 'De Schooling Society' (1971) schools are expensive bureaucratic establishments which are inefficient to educate the young. For developing countries, particularly, deschooling would be a better alternative.

See: Illich, I.D.

DECILE: The points that divide a distribution of scores into 10 equal parts. So there are nine decile points in the distribution, corresponding to the percentiles, 10, 20, 30, 40, 60, 70, 80, 90 i.e., the 10th percentile being the first decile.

Decile rank, like percentile ranks is a derived score.

See: Percentile

DECOMPENSATION: Lowering of personality integration occuring as a result of extreme stress. When stress becomes overpowering, common defences to restore normalcy fail and the individual resorts to inappropriate and exaggerated defence patterns, which may lead to disintegration of personality at physiological (shattered health) psychological (emotional instability) or social (inadequate social behaviour) levels.

See: Ego defence mechanism

DECOY: Another name for a distractor in a multiple choice test.

See: Multiple choice item

DEDUCTIVE METHOD: Teaching which proceeds from the general to the particular. In deductive teaching the students are guided to apply principles, rules of operation, etc. to acquire understanding about new phenomena. The process is parallel to deductive reasoning. By deductive learning the students gain not only the ability to apply the knowledge in the new situation but also acquire deeper knowledge and implications of the principle. Teacher's guidance should be minimal, in deductive teaching, the teacher leaves the students to discover the relationship between the principle and the situation in which it is supposed to operate.

See: Inductive method

DEDUCTIVE-DISCOVERY METHOD: Organisation of learning experience in such a way that pupils make inferences about particular situations which imply the application of principles already learnt. Suppose that the teacher wants to teach primary class pupils that air is matter. He devises situation in which the pupils experiment with empty bottles being dipped down in water with mouth open. They think about the problem and infer that water does not enter the bottle because there is air inside. When the bottle is reversed, bubble comes out and water gets in and this makes them think that water and air cannot exist inside at the same time. Air requires space. So air is matter. They deductively apply the knowledge and make the discovery.

DEFECTIVES: Persons with some defect. Physically defective persons have some organ or sensory handicap or impairment, as in the case of the blind, the deaf, the crippled, etc. Mentally defectives are persons with very low intelligence who usually need institutional care (like the idiot and the imbecile). Morally defectives are those who are anti-social and immoral, i.e., delinquents. Minor aberrations i.e. defects in physical, mental or moral characteristics do not require any specialized type of institution or schooling. They can be educated in ordinary schools by using special methods of teaching. Also called the Handicapped.

DEGREES OF FREEDOM: In statistics, the number of values in a set that are free to vary. Example: there are five scores: 3, 4, 5, 6, 7. The mean of the set of scores is, 5. The deviation of this scores from the mean are 2, 1, 0 -1 and -2. The sum of these deviations is zero. In a set of 5 scores like this, there are five deviations, only 4 of which are free to be altered, since the sum of the total set of deviations should be 0. When the 4 are fixed, the fifth is automatically determined. Degrees of freedom in this case is 4, meaning that only 4 scores can vary. In this case the degrees of freedom can be represented by (N-1), i.e. the total number of cases minus one. The concept of degrees of freedom has wide applications in statistical analysis, particularly when dealing with small samples.

DELINQUENT: A young offender. A delinquent child is usually in his adolescence. The term is legally applied to a young offender convicted by a juvenile court. Various environmental conditions and early childhood experiences have been found to be associated with the incidence of delinquency. These are: parental rejection and neglect, cruelty suffered in early life, severe mental shocks, gang and slum influence, etc. The prime cause is that these children did not have opportunities to internalize moral and ethical values. Psychologically unfavourable environment in their cases have worked to produce a psychopathic and antisocial personality. The offence committed by delinquents are usually theft, house breaking, minor sex crimes, etc.

Juvenile courts direct the authorities to provide these children with institutionalized care in reformatories and correctional schools (Borstal Schools) rather than sentencing them to prison terms. Remedial education facilities are provided in these institutions with the intention of rehabilitating them in society to lead a normal and productive life.

See: Sociopathic disorders

DELTA WAVES: Low frequency waves present in the brain (1 to 3Hz) generally during deep dreamless sleep.

See: Alphawaves

DELUSION: A persistent false notion held by an individual. Delusion is a wrong judgement arrived at by the individual about particular things and situations. A person who believes that others are watching him with a suspicious eye while walking along the road is suffering from delusion. His judgement is wrong because the people on the road do not show any special interest in a particular person all the time he moves along the road. Delusion may sometimes assume morbid dimensions. A man may claim that he has discovered a wonderful remedy for cancer but nobody is intelligent enough to understand his discovery. This type of delusion is called 'Delusion of grandeur'. Another man may complain that people are trying to poison him (This is 'delusion of suffering a persecution'). The most significant symptoms of the mental disorder 'paranoia' are systematic delusions.

See: Hallucination. Illusion

DEMOCRATIC LEADERSHIP: Leadership that shares responsibilities with members of the group. In democratic leadership, the leader encourages participatory role of the members in setting up the goals, planning activities and supervising the functions. There will be sharing of responsibilities; inter-communication at all levels will be uninhibited. Under democratic leadership, group morale will be high.

See: Leader

DEMOGRAPHIC VARIABLES: Population variables. The important demographic variables concerned with education are: number of members in the family, occupation of parents, educational status of parents, annual income and socio-economic status of family and housing conditions.

DENIAL: The psychological defence mechanism characterized by one's unconscious refusal to accept responsibility or involvement. Also called Escapism. Disagreeable realities are ignored and the individual refuses to face situations that lead to unpleasant experiences.

See: Ego defence mechanism

DEPENDENT VARIABLE: The effect of a cause, or the consequence of an antecedent. In a typical experiment we have to deal with two variables–the independent variable and the dependant variable. If a teacher is interested in finding out whether a new method of teaching a topic is better that the one he uses, he plans an experiment to try out the new method. In that case the new method is the independent variable (antecedent, cause) and the improved result he obtains is the dependent variable (effect, consequence).

See: Independent variable experiment

DEPRESSION: A feeling of hopelessness marked by lack of interest in anything. A person in depression is withdrawn and shows practically no interest in anything surrounding him. He may feel forsaken, shameful, weak, etc. Eventhough he feels terribly unhappy he is not often aware of the cause of his unhappiness. Depression is a common symptom of psychoneurosis and also depressive and manic-depressive psychoses. Morbid depression is treated with antidepressant drugs like Imipramine and Amphetamine. Psychosurgery (prefrontal lobotomy) gives relief in many cases of depressive psychosis. All individuals are liable to experience short spells of depression in life as a result of disappointments, frustrations, etc. But this will be only a passing phase and happy mood will be regained in due course. But if a person is found continuously in a state of depression he is likely to develop serious mental disorders.

See: Anxiety

DEPRIVATION: Withholding something of importance needed by the organism. If the opportunity for getting the objects for satisfying a need is not available, the individual feels deprived. In animal experimentation, rats deprived of food or water are often used. When a strongly felt need is denied, the organism strives for satisfying it (i.e. strongly motivated). This produces the behaviour in which the experimenter is interested. A food-deprived rat quickly learns to jump upon to a platform and press a lever in a problem box in order to get food pellets. A satiated rat will not be active and so cannot be trained to press the lever.

A group of people cut off from the main stream of civilization and remaining in exclusion is said to be a culturally deprived group. Tribals living in seclusion in the interior of the jungles, the nomads, etc. are considered culturally deprived as they get no opportunities for sharing the fruits of civilization with others.

Denial of a need either due to inaccessibility to achieve satisfaction or by wilful obstruction set by others also results in deprivation. Educational deprivation may be for example, the result inadequate schooling facilities in the area, or due to denial of admission to certain categories of children in the schools. Criminals undergoing solitary confinement suffer social deprivation.

DEPTH PSYCHOLOGY: Psychology which deals with the dynamics of deep seated motivations and behaviour considered to be related to such motivation. Depth psychologists are interested in behaviour motivated by the unconscious. Psychoanalysis of Freud, Individual Psychology of Adler, Analytical Psychology of Jung and the psychological systems of later Neo-Freudians, (like Horney, Fromm, etc.) are collectively referred to as depth psychology.

DERIVED SCORE: A score obtained from a raw score by some processing method in order to make it more meaningful. A score obtained in an Intelligence test, by itself does not convey much meaning. But when the mental age equivalent or the I.Q. equivalent is derived from it, it becomes meaningful. Percentiles, Standard Scores, like Z-score, T-score, etc. are derived scores.

See: Raw Scores

DESCRIPTIVE STATISTICS: Statistics that is used to describe populations and samples. Statistics is widely used to describe the properties of samples or of populations. The arithmetic mean, the median, the mode, percentages, etc. are commonly used for describing the characteristics of populations. It has wide application in the social sciences including Demography.

See: Statistics

DESENSITIZATION (SUCCESSIVE): A technique of behaviour therapy, used in the treatment of phobias and neurotic anxiety. The method involves the gradual exposure of the person to the object of his fear and simultaneously providing a state that is incompatible with the anxiety. The therapist prepares a list of situations (which is called a 'hierarchy'), graded accordingly to the degree of fear, which the respective situation would arouse, starting with almost a neutral stimulus to those which evoke fear, gradually in an increasing order. The least evocative situation is presented to the individual when he is in a state of relaxation. Each situation is presented repeatedly until the person seems to tolerate it, without experiencing anxiety. Relaxed state is incompatible with anxiety and fear (when a person is in fear he is in a state of muscular tension). So if the situation can be faced in a relaxed state it can be assumed that the anxiety has been eliminated or reduced. A person suffering from phobic fear of spiders may be presented with the hierarchy (1) A picture of a spider, held at a distance (2) The picture brought closer (3) a small dead spider placed at a distance (4) the spider brought closer (5) a small live spider held at a distance (6) the live spider brought closer (7) A large spider held at a distance (8) a large live spider brought closer.

The method is also used by encouraging the person to imagine (visualize) the scene in the hierarchy.

See: Behaviour therapy

DESIGN OF EXPERIMENT: The plan for carrying out the processes required for testing a hypothesis. In designing an experiment the factors to be considered are:

1. the variables (independent and dependent) and their nature;
2. the method of controlling the intervening variables (i.e., the extraneous variables that are likely to affect the dependent variable);

3. the treatment procedures (i.e., the activities adopted for testing the hypothesis) and
4. the method of measurement.

An experiment requires

1. at least two groups, one being the control group;
2. the random arrangement of subjects to the groups; and
3. the manipulation of at least one independent variable.

See: Experiment

DETENTION: Retaining a pupil in the same class consequent on failure in examination. The practice of making children repeat classes when they fail in examination is followed in many countries. This is detention. Low performance (i.e., failure to come up to the standard prescribed by the school authorities) results in detention and, as a consequence, the child has to repeat the same class till he qualifies himself for promotion. Eventhough the validity of this practice is highly questionable it still persists. Detention is also known as 'repetition of classes'.

Retaining children in school after regular school hours with some assignment to complete within a specified time, is adopted by some teachers as a punishment. This is also called detention.

DETERMINISM: The assumption that every occurrence has a cause (or causes). It asserts that nothing just happens, by accident or without a reason. Freud stressed the importance of 'psychic determinism' in explaining the origin and development of mental diseases. He said that every symptom has a cause. Likewise, it is assumed that beliefs, interests, values, etc. one possesses are necessarily the products of past experiences the individual had undergone.

DETOUR PROBLEM: A problem in which the solution depends on going around a barrier. Detour problems are usually designed for studying problem-solving behaviour in young children and animals. In a problem-solving situation for young children a child was made to stand on one side of a wire fence and on the other side was placed a toy. As the fence obstructed the child from reaching the toy, to take it, he had to go along the side of the fence and walk up to the other side (i.e. detour or go in a roundabout way). How fast the children solved the problem (and also their behaviour in the situation) provided the index of their problem solving ability. Such detour problems are devised also for studying the problem-solving behaviour of chimpanzees and other apes.

DEVELOPMENT: The term used to denote functional maturity. Development signifies the level of maturity attained in a particular function. In 'development' the stress is on function and not on size. Physical development means the level of capabilities achieved as a result of passage of time, while physical growth means, the increase gained in the size and weight of the tissues of the body. Development occurs both as a result of 'maturation' and 'learning'. Maturation is dependent on growth.

See: Growth. Maturation

DEVELOPMENTAL PSYCHOLOGY: Study of the behaviour of individuals at various stages of development; prenatal to adulthood and old age. Developmental psychology is concerned with the study of the growth and development of the individuals with special emphasis on the trends in functional maturity. The various psychological characteristics during pre-natal and neonatal life, infancy, childhood and adolescence in the development of the areas like physical, emotional, social, sexualm, etc. form the subject of developmental psychology. It may be also treated as Child Psychology, Child Development, Adolescent Development, etc.

DEVIATION I.Q.: A kind of standard score in intelligence test in which the arithmetic mean is equal to 100 and the standard deviation is approximately 15. It is an intelligence quotient obtained by converting the raw score into the normalized standard score on the scale in which the mean is 100 and the SD is 15 or 16. (The traditional IQ is the ratio between the mental age and the chronological age, but the Deviation IQ is obtained by converting the distribution of scores for each age group, to a normalized one with a mean of 100 and SD of 15). The score obtained by an individual is measured by the extent to which it deviates from the mean in terms of the SD unit.

The norms of Weschler's Intelligence Scale are given in Deviation IQ.

DEWEY, JOHN (1859-1952): The great American educationalist. He was a philosopher, psychologist and teacher.

Like Pestalozzi and Herbart he had his own experimental school, "the Laboratory School", which he founded in 1896 at the University of Chicago. All the theories he proposed were based on his practical experience. His important works: 'The School and Society', 'Child and the Curriculum', 'How we think', 'School of Tomorrow', and 'Democracy and Education' appeared between 1902 and 1916.

He was a pragmatist, like his senior contemporary William James. According to him process is more important than product, in thinking. Education should prepare individuals for social life that exists at the time and also prepare them to accept tradition, at the same time train them to anticipate new needs and accept vision of a new social order. The emphasis should be on the emergence of thinking individuals. Inquiry method and inductive reasoning are to be stressed in learning. The curriculum should be child-centred and there should be ample opportunities for working together to solve common problems. Dewey said that education is not simply a preparation for life, but life itself.

In his 'Democracy and Education' he states .... "the educational process has no end beyond itself, it is it's own end... the educational process is one of continual re-organizing, reconstructing transforming..." Teaching method is to be understood as a way of ordering of the total development of the child's powers and interests. The child has to be helped to express himself constructively in relation to the tasks generated from his sharing in the life of the school and the human community at large.... The departmentalization of curriculum and the systematic succession of studies have to give way to an elastic programme of activities.

DEXTERITY: Proficiency in using hands and fingers resulting from neuromuscular coordination. Dexterity is characterized by quickness and precision. The speed and accuracy with which a person is able to use his fingers in manipulating objects (like picking up small nails from a tray) is the index of his finger dexterity. When organs on both sides of the body (e.g., both right and left hands) can be used with comparable dexterity the person is said to be ambidextrous.

DIAGNOSIS: Identification of pupil's disabilities. This is done by the analysis of pupil's responses in scholastic work, both oral and written. By systematically observing the pupil for a period of time, behaviour problems can be diagnosed.

DIAGNOSTIC TESTS: Educational tests designed to find out specific weakness (and also strength). All school tests are in a way diagnostic tests, as they can also indicate weakness of the students along with their strength. But they cannot show clearly weakness in specific areas. Diagnostic tests are constructed and administered to meet this need. To find out whether primary class children have mastered the proficiency in various aspects of addition (like zero difficulty, carrying, etc.) tests designed to test these areas are constructed and administered on the student. Analysis of their responses will reveal specific difficulties (diagnose). Appropriate remedial teaching can then be given to the child.

See: Remedial Education

DIALECTICS: The method of explaining phenomena in terms of the interaction of opposing forces. Hegel formulated the dialectical principle. Every dialectical process (logical process) starts with a 'thesis'–a system of factors in a particular relationship. The relationship also incorporates contradictions. As the system develops, the contradictions become explicit and operative. This stage is called 'antithesis'. The interaction of the opposing forces affects one another and leads to the emergence of a modified system in a new 'synthesis'.

DIASCOPE: An optical projector which throws the magnified image from a transparent slide or film on to a screen. Diascope is used as a visual aid in teaching. The image can be projected on to a wall of a darkened classroom.

DICTIONARY OF OCCUPATIONAL TITLES (D.O.T.): Classified list of occupations with definitions of occupations, published by the Ministry of Labour, U.S.A. The D.O.T. as it is popularly known, has more than 40,000 titles of occupations. When it was first published in 1939, it had only definitions of 18,000 jobs.

See: National Classification of Occupations

DIDACTIC METHOD: The method of teaching exclusively based on information transfer from teacher to pupil. Didactic methods expect only active listening on the part of pupils. No active participation in teaching-learning activity is expected. Heuristic method which is diametrically opposed to this method, originated as reaction against this method.

DIFFERENTIAL FORGETTING: Difference in the rate of forgetting two events. Incorrect responses (responses that were not reinforced) are forgotten at a faster rate than the correct ones (responses that have been reinforced).

DIFFERENTIAL THRESHOLD: The smallest difference in the intensity of two stimuli of the same kind that becomes perceptible. The differential threshold (DL) of a sense modality (say sight, hearing) differs from one individual to another. Suppose a blind folded individual has in his hand a kilogram weight, and small weights are added to it one by one, 5 gms, 10 gms, 20 gms and so on until the subject reports that he feels a difference. The amount of weight added to the original weight in order to make the subject feel the difference, gives the measure of the differential threshold for that stimulus (weight). Likewise, differential thresholds for other sense impressions like sound, light intensity, temperature, pressure, etc. also can be found out. Differential threshold is also called 'Just noticeable Difference' or JND.

See: Just Noticeable Difference

DIFFICULTY INDEX: The difficulty level of a test item determined experimentally. The test is administered on a representative sample of pupils and the number of pupils doing an item correctly and wrongly are computed. From this data Difficulty index is worked out. If the number of pupils doing the item wrongly (and omitting) = w, Total number attempting the test: N, then Difficulty index of the item is

$$\frac{W \times 100}{N}$$

See: Facility index

DIGIT SPAN: A short term memory (STM) task, which requires the subject to recall the number of items in the correct order immediately after a presentation. Digits like, 7, 2, 3, 9, 6, 0, 8, 1, 5, etc., are presented tachistoscopically and the subject has to recall the digits in the correct order. Letters also are used in the place of number. The average number that persons could recall is about 7. The digit span is found to vary with intelligence, the nature of the material presented, its meaningfulness, etc.

The digits may be also presented auditorily (i.e. in the spoken form) and the children required to repeat them after an interval of 2 seconds.

DIGITAL CODING: Conversion of messages in the binary code. The message in this system is transformed into binary code signals of 0's and 1's. Digital coding is compatible with computers. The quality and efficiency of the transmission will also be superior in the digital code. This conversion also makes it easy to transmit signals through glass optical fibre cables which can carry signals as pulses of light.

See: Analogue coding

DIGITAL AUDIO-TAPE: A recent innovation of audio-recording. Vinyl discs are being displaced by digital compact discs since 1992. Digital Cassette Tape Recorders are also now available. In digital audio-tape recording, the original sound vibrations are analysed for frequency and intensity and the analysed information is recorded in digital form on audio-tapes. When decoded for playback, the fidelity of reproduction is very high. It has no losses in sound quality since there is no distortion like that when converting sound into magnetic intensity and in reconverting it into sound on play back, like that occurs in vinyl disc.

DIGITIZER: A device for converting graphical images into digital signals so that they can be handled by a digital computer.

DIMENSIONS: A particular, measurable aspect of an entity or phenomenon. Properties or attributes of a phenomenon that can be subjected to measurement is a dimension, e.g., intelligence, introversion, language proficiency, extraversion, neuroticism, etc. are dimensions of personality.

DIORAMA: A type of model usually improvised by the pupils themselves for the learning of history, geography and social sciences. The models are based on curricular items and often they depict some scene or incident in history. Diorama helps children in visualizing historic events.

It is a still visual display system. The diorama combines three-dimensional models, figures, etc. in the fore-ground with a two dimensional painted background. It creates a naturalistic effect of the scene. Useful for teaching topics in history, drama, geography, natural science, etc.

DIRECT METHOD: Learning a foreign language more or less in the same manner as one acquires mastery over the mother tongue. The child taught by this method gets ample linguistic experience by first hearing the spoken form in a natural situation in a graded order. Order of teaching is just as in the case of language development in the child; hearing, speaking, reading and writing. The use of mother tongue is almost prohibited. Direct method implies the learning of language by associating linguistic elements directly with experience and not through mother tongue.

DISADVANTAGED: Group of people (or individuals) for whom opportunities have been denied for social and cultural development. For those people who are cut-off from the main stream of culture, like tribals, gypsies, etc. chances for development are limited. So they suffer from various handicaps–physical, social cultural, economic, etc. Specific compensatory programmes of varied types will be needed to draw them to the main stream of society. The term 'Deprived' also is used to denote disadvantaged groups.

See: Deprivation

DISCIPLINE: Orderly behaviour, keeping of order in the class room and school. Once it implied the implicit obedience to rules of conduct laid down by the authorities. Now it is preferred to signify orderly behaviour, punctuality and exercise of self-control without any external pressure, compulsion, or threat of punishment. It is voluntary obeservance of rules of conduct which has bases on moral obligation and ethical principles.

DISCOVERY METHOD: Learning experiences that lead the students to draw inferences, solve problems, etc. by themselves. The teacher employing this method will give only the minimum guidance for the students to learn the new topic–the students begin to work in a situation which is only minimally structured. Manipulation of data, reasoning, finding relationships, etc. are left to the learner. In its extreme form it is called the 'heuristic method', in which case the student, who is given practically no guidance, has to solve the problem as the scientist solved it originally. In the class room situation, using lecture-demonstration, this method can be applied in a less rigorous form. By proper questioning, timely explanations, etc. students' thinking may be directed to arriving at the conclusions, themselves.

Discovery method can be used in the case of lessons developed inductively or deductively.

This method is applicable to individual and group work and also for project type activities.

See: Heuristic method

DISCRETE VARIABLES: Discontinuous variables. In discrete variables, values are obtained as whole numbers. The values cannot exist as fractions. In other words, in their case, there are gaps between the measures. Sex is such a variable. The sex of an individual may be either male or female (the freaks exempted). Salary scales are usually given as multiples of 10. The number of books in libraries, the number of children in families, etc. fall under this category of variables. It is also called discontinuous variables.

See: Continuous Variable

DISCRIMINATING POWER: The effectiveness of a test item in discriminating different levels of ability tested by it. Determination of the discriminating power (index) of each item of the test is an important step in item-analysis. Correlation of the item with the whole test gives the index of discrimination of the item. As the test as a whole is intended to measure a particular dimension (say intelligence), the correlation of individual items with the whole test will necessarily be an index of its validity also. To find the discriminating power of a test item, the scored test sheets are first piled up in ascending order of the total score. The pile is divided into two halves: the top 50% (or 30%) of papers and bottom 50% (or 33%) of papers. Then the number of testees doing each item correctly in the top group and those in the bottom group are counted. Larger the differences between the two (H-L) higher the discriminating power or discrimination index. The differences between the responses in the High and the Low groups are subjected to statistical procedures to work out the discrimination index. Biserial correlations and other short-cut methods are used to find out the discrimination index.

See: Item analysis

DISORIENTATION: An abnormal state of mind characterized by the person's inability to identify time, place, persons, etc. accurately. The disoriented person may feel perplexed and confused. This is an unmistakable symptom of mental disorder, the severity of the disease depending on the degree of disorientation.

DISPERSION: The property shown by a set of scores (or values) to deviate from the centre (means) or spread around the mean.

See: Central Tendency

DISPLACEMENT: Shifting of emotion from one person or object to another. The psychological mechanism (usually unconscious) which helps to avoid conflicts and ambivalent feelings. Hostile feeling towards a person may be shifted to a neutral object or person. Scape-goating of minority groups is a case in point.

See: Ego defence mechanism

DISSOCIATION (BY VARYING CONCOMITANTS): In concept formation, the differences in the individuals of a class tends to be overlooked (dissociated) and the qualities they have in common are abstracted. This process is basic for concept formation.

DISSOCIATION: Breaking away of ideas associated in memory. It results in the inability to recall some incident or ideas connected with an incident. Strong unhappy emotional experiences often lead to dissociation of ideas.

A part of the personality of the individual breaks away and sometimes functions exclusively as a separate one. This leads to the development of multiple-personality. Emotional shock (traumatic experiences) and continued stressful existence leads some individuals to the development of multiple personality. There are clinical records of such persons who occasionally behaved as two or three mutually exclusive independent personalities.

See: Multiple personality

DISTANCE EDUCATION: Educating students staying in their own places of residence situated away from the central institution. In distance education, the students are not required to be present in the school or college or to remain in full time engagement in the institution. They can carry on education without upsetting their work. They are, of course, enrolled in the central institution, which is often called an Open University, from which they receive regular lessons, assignments, etc. Their work sheets and answer papers will be sent to the institution. There will be regular communication between the student and the teacher. Radio and television, audio-tapes, videotapes, computer lessons, etc. are also used for instruction. To make up for the deficiencies resulting from lack of face to face contact between the students and teachers, periodical 'contact programmes' are organized when the students and teachers meet at a place and spend a fortnight or so in discussions, project work, practicals, etc. This is also called Distance teaching.

Distance education is considered by some people as a step towards de-schooling society.

See: Open University

DISTANCE LEARNING: Almost synonymous with 'correspondence course'. Recently, apart from printed notes, lessons are provided through television, radio, video, etc. for students taking correspondence courses. The main defect in such programmes is lack of interaction between the tutors and learners even though there is limited feed back. Periodical short term contact courses are held in Distance learning programmes in order to make up for this deficiency.

DISTRACTOR: The alternative incorrect answers given along with the correct answer in a multiple-choice test. It is also called, decoy or option or alternative.

In a multiple choice test, there will be usually 3 incorrect answers given along with the correct one. The number of distractors among the alternatives should be at least 3, in order to reduce the effect of guessing. Even in a multiple choice item with 4 alternatives, there is 25% chance to hit the correct answer by guessing. Increasing the number reduces this effect. For practical convenience the alternatives are limited to 4 or 5.

The distractor should appear as a correct answer. A distractor which is totally unrelated to the situation will not be functional, i.e., even those who guess widely will not choose it. In that case the actual number of alternatives for the item is got reduced by one. As its function is to distract the individual who does not know the correct answer, it is called a 'distractor'.

Example:

Which place lies closest to the equator ?

A. New Delhi
B. North pole
C. Singapore
D. Sydney

Alternative C, Singapore is the answer, A, B and D are distractors. Distractor 'B' 'North Pole' least likely to be chosen by anyone, because those with elementary knowledge of geography know that the poles are farthest away from the equator. So, it is not a functioning distractor; it is unfit to be included as one. Colombo or some other place not very far away from the equator would be a proper choice.

In the standardized tests, usually, distractors are selected from the mistakes committed by the candidates. For this, the test is first administered in the open-ended form (free-response) without alternatives. The candidates are free to write their answers. The three wrong answers which receive the maximum frequencies are selected for the distractors.

See: Multiple choice item

DISTRIBUTED PRACTICE: The method of learning a new task which depends on the spreading of the practice sessions over period of time. The new task is broken down into small units. The task units are practised with rest intervals, i.e., distributed over a time with rest periods. This method is recommended for learning new materials (like poems) and for the mastery of complex skills.

Maximum efficiency is found to be achieved by using distributed practice and massed learning in combination–distributed practice followed by massed practice.

See: Massed Learning

DIVERGENT THINKING: The thinking that produces new and creative solutions. Conventional problems, however complex (like mathematical problems) have only one solution which is unique. By scientific reasoning the same solution can be found out by any one who is competent. This is convergent thinking. But in certain situations many answers may be possible for the same question, but still there may be some which are productive and original. The thinking involved in such situation is creative and it is called Divergent Thinking. Guilford proposed these two types of thinking in his 'Structure of the mind' in 1967.

The mental process that leads to inventions and production of high artistic works is divergent thinking.

DOMESTIC SCIENCE: The group of school subjects which imparts knowledge and skills in home-making and management.

The subject includes cookery, home-economics and budgeting, needle work, child care, housecraft, etc.

DOMINANCE: According to the Mendelian theory of heredity some genes in the male chromosomes (or female chromosomes) suppress the effects of their matched genes in the female (or male) chromosomes of the zygote. The genes that suppress the effects of their pair is the 'dominant genes' and the gene that is suppressed is the recessive gene.

One of the cerebral hemispheres in each individual will be functionally more powerful than the other. If the left hemisphere is dominant the individual will be right sided i.e., his right hand, right leg, etc. will be functionally superior to their respective left counterparts. In a vast majority of individuals the left hemisphere is dominant (Left cerebral dominance).

Some individuals possess personality traits that enable them to control the members of the group in which they are also one. The traits that usually go with dominance are assertiveness, aggressiveness, etc. Dominance is contrasted with submissiveness.

DOUBLE SHIFT: Two batches of pupils attending the same school in two sessions, usually in morning and evening.

When there is a sudden increase in enrollment (due to statutory compulsion or otherwise) or when funds are inadequate for building construction, as an expedient measure, double shifts are adopted in existing schools to serve the needs of the pupils of the locality. In schools working on double shift, one batch of pupils attend the classes in the morning session and other batch in the afternoon session. There will not be much difference in the instructional hours of the two sessions. Shortage in instructional hours of such schools (when compared with the normal schools) is usually compensated by increasing the number of working days.

A school working on double shift accommodates double its capacity of students, so there is saving of money that would have to be spent on building construction. If the same set of teachers are to handle both the sessions of the shift, there is saving on teacher cost also. As the practice is likely to affect the efficiency of the school adversely, double shift is adopted only as a temporary stop-gap arrangement.

DOUBLE BLIND DESIGN: An experimental research design in which both the subjects and the experimenter involved in the experiment do not know whether they are assigned to the experimental group or the control group. This condition is difficult to achieve in practice, when large sample experiments are conducted, but it ensures better control of variables.

See: Design of Experiment

DOWN'S SYNDROME: Mongolism. The genetic defect (chromosome abnormality) characterised by flattened facial features, stubby fingers, and low I.Q.

DOWNWARD FILTRATION THEORY: The theory that education given to one class of people (in a undeveloped country) will trickle down to people of lower strata. the educational endeavours of the East India Company in India (around 1830) were based on this theory. The assumption was that if the Company undertook the responsibility of educating the influential upper class of society, as time went on, the new culture would descend to the lower classes. The Company did not accept any responsibility for the education of the masses till 1854.

DRIVE REDUCTION: The release of tension caused by a drive. In other words it is the restoring of physiological balance of the body (homeostasis). Example: Denial of water for a long time causes thirst (drive) and this drive forces the organism to activities that leads to drive reduction (restoring of physiological balance). The activity related to the drive i.e. water seeking slows down (after satiation) and subsequently ceases. Likewise, mating reduces sex drive.

DRIVE: Drive is an internal state of the organism which induces it to react to the environment. This psychological state is characterized by the upsetting of the chemical balance of the body (homeostasis) by depletion of water (thirst), nourishment (hunger), oxygen (suffocation) or by the accretion of hormones (eg. sex) or waste products (urine, excreta, etc.). When the body balance is upset, the individual is forced to action that seeks to restore the balance. When the need is met, there will be drive reduction and the organism's activity ceases. Physiological drives are closely related to the survival of the organism. Deprivation of the need drives the organism to activity (motivates) that leads to the satiation of the need.

See: Homeostasis

DROPPAGE: Premature leaving from school. For example, a child enrolled in a school is expected to complete the years, necessary for attaining permanent literacy. Leaving the school before that, results in wastage both for the pupil and for the state. Adverse conditions that are found associated with droppage are, parental neglect, poverty of parents, low motivation, unsuitable curriculum, ununderstanding teachers, gang influence, etc. The rate of droppage in primary schools is very high in developing countries.

See: Wastage School refusal.

DYNAMOMETER: An instrument used for measuring the force applied by the organism in a particular activity, e.g., A hand dynamometer is used to measure the strength of hand grip.

E

E-MAIL: Electronic Mail. In E-mail, messages are transmitted by one user to another through computer terminals. Messages can be sent to distant sites down telephone lines and other telecommunication channels.

EARTH SCIENCES: The branch of study dealing with the interior and crust of the earth including oceans and atmosphere; it comprises the study of geology, geography, oceanography and meteorology.

EDUCATIONAL LADDER: The vertical structure of the educational system (school system). The educational system is considered as a ladder, each rung being a standard or class. Substages in the structure may have definite units which signify particular curricular stages. The structure 4+3+3, may denote 4 years of lower primary, 3 years of upper primary and 3 years of secondary education. The structure 5+4+3+2, may mean 5 years lower primary, 4 years upper primary, 3 years secondary and 2 years higher secondary education.

EDUCATIONAL PLANNING: Drawing up programmes of educational action for future periods on the basis of predicted needs and resources. Educational planning has two facets: planning for quantity and planning for quality. Expansion of educational facilities will be needed consequent on the increase of population. So, formulation of plan schemes for expansion will include: the processes of estimating additional enrolment during the period (1 year, 5 years, 10 years, etc.) and from that, the additional number of class rooms (with furniture and equipment) to be constructed, the additional number of teachers to be prepared and appointed, etc. The cost of these additional requirements along with the cost of auxillary services like noon-feeding, health services, etc. will have to be worked out. It will be also necessary to estimate the expenditure needed for expansion of administrative and supervisory machinery consequent on the additional increase in enrolment.

In developing countries, quantitative expansion is occurring at a fast rate and so educational planning has become an imperative need to cope up with the situation.

In planning for quality, the main emphasis is on implementing programmes that will improve the professional competence of teachers (by updating preservice training and by providing inservice education, etc.), revamping of curricula and preparing text books and teaching-learning materials based on it, effecting improvement in evaluation procedures, etc. on the basis of up-to-date knowledge in those areas. Research and experimentation on all aspects of education will have to be undertaken in order to ensure progress.

Another important factor in educational planning is the realistic estimation of resources that can be mobilized from various agencies, governmental and non-governmental. As resources are scarce, all possibilities of resources mobilization have to be explored. At the next stage, estimates of funds that are to be allocated for the various programmes are to be made. In planning, the order of priority of the programmes also will have to be indicated. Each plan scheme should indicate the objectives against which its progress can be assessed. It should also indicate the arrangements for implementation, follow-up and evaluation.

An educational plan, to succeed, should be drawn up after considering all relevant factors: the background, lacuna and shortfalls in previous plans, future needs, objectives to be achieved, resources that can be moblized, the personnel concerned in implementation, the optimum time frame for completion of various activities, etc., i.e., it should be realistic. There are plans for various periods of time: like 1 year plan, 5 year plan, etc. A long-range plan for periods covering over 10 years is usually called a Perspective Plan.

EDUCATIONAL ADMINISTRATION: The organization and management of the educational system. It includes the organization and its operations that are intended to carry out the policy of education laid down by a state. Its ultimate purpose is to provide adequate facilities for the personnel to carry out the pedagogic functions in the schools. To achieve this, there is the vast system comprising the schools, the teachers, etc. Educational administration involves the assignment of duties to different categories of staff and an effective follow-up and supervision. The general set up of educational administration in a country more or less conform to the following pattern:

1. Education minister:
   Policy formulation; Budgeting of educational funds; Review of progress; Educational Planning.
2. Advisory Boards:
   To advise the minister on policy matters and other technical matters.
3. Director of Education:
   Overall control and supervision of all programmes, allocation of funds to different agencies. assisting the government in planning; review of progress.
4. Local authorities:
   (may be regionwise, or districtwise, etc.)
   Control and supervision of schools, salary disbursement to staff, collection, computation and transmission of information and statistics. Financial control of expenditure, institutional planning and areawise planning, etc.
5. The Schools:
   Various educational activities.

EDUCATIONAL AGE: A derived score, like mental age, which tells the performance of the students in the school subjects, in terms of the average performance of the specific age-group. An educational age of 8 means that the performance of the individual in all the school subjects considered, is equal to that of the average performance of eight year old children in those subjects. The chronological age may be equal to, less than or greater than, the educational age. A child whose chronological age is 10 and educational age is 11, is accelerated by one year. If the educational age of a child is 8 and his chronological age is 10, he is said to be retarded (backward) by two years.

See: Age equivalent

EBBINGHAUS, H.B.: Famous German experimental psychologist (1850-1909). His studies on memory, remembering and forgetting are well known. In an experiment in which he himself was the subject, he took 33 trials to learn a list of 15 nonsense syllables, so that he could repeat them once without error. After 6 days it took him only 11 trials to relearn them to the same standard, thus he had made a savings of 22 trials. From repeated experiments of this kind he constructed 'the curve of retention'.

See: Saving method

EDUCATION: The process of developing the potentials of man to the optimum level in order to enable him to lead a productive and happy life in society. Learning is the psychological process that enables man to acquire the competencies required to develop his potentials. Learning, in other words, is the process that produces permanent behaviour changes in man when he undergoes experience. The permanent behaviour changes that occur when an individual is exposed to an experience, can be either desirable or undesirable, socially and for the individual. Education is concerned with the production of behaviour changes that are only desirable. Teaching is the process of providing proper learning experiences to the children, so that they acquire desirable competencies in cognitive, psychomotor and affective domains– i.e. knowledge, skills, values, attitudes and appreciations.

Education ensures the preservation and continuity of everything good in the culture of the people and simultaneously prepares them for progress and prosperity. Education is, thus, the most powerful instrument of social change and national integration. It is in due recognition of this fact the Kothari Education Commission assigned the subtitle 'Educational and National Development' to their Report. The report begins with the aphoristic statement that "the destiny of India is being shaped in her class room",–a statement which sounds platitudinous, but nevertheless, totally true and reminds everyone that a country cannot progress beyond its schools.

EDUCATIONAL SOCIOLOGY: The branch of study that deals with the role of education in the development of knowledge, skills, values and attitudes that help to transform society towards a better social, economic and political order. It is also concerned with the analysis of the social factors that affect the development of education. So problems like social mobility, social status, women's status, school droppage, etc. are also topics generally dealt within educational sociology. The school-community relations, likewise, is also of interest to the educational sociologist. 'Sociology of Education' is often used to denote theoretical exposition of the social problems related to education while Educational Sociology is preferred when the stress is on practical applications.

EDUCATIONAL TECHNOLOGY: The application of scientific discoveries and technological innovations for the improvement of efficiency of the schools programmes. It is mainly concerned with the harnessing of non-human resources to supplement human skill in implementing the curriculum. Teaching machines, programmed instruction materials, audio-video materials, and computers have thus found their place in schools. Information technology and communication theory have contributed a lot in this revolution.

See: Information Technology

EDUCATIONALLY SUB-NORMAL (ESN): Children with moderate or severe handicap (mentally, physically or emotionally). Such children can profit very little from normal school programmes. So in many countries they are given education in special institutions-schools for the E.S.N.

EFFECTORS: The tissues which respond to the stimulations starting from the sense organs (receptors): It is the responses of the effectors which result in behaviour (reflexes or complex neuro-muscular activity), overt or covert. The effector tissues are either muscles or glands and are activated by nerve impulses starting from the central nervous system or peripheral nervous system. The smell of desirable foods (stimulus) will stimulate the salivary glands to secrete saliva. An unexpected sudden explosion produces startle reaction in which case a large number (effectors) are involved. Perception of a dangerous situation causes the adrenal glands (effectors) to release appropriate doses of the hormones from them which reinforce the autonomic nervous activity which prepares the organism for flight or fight.

See: Receptors

EFFERENT: The neurons which carry messages from the brain and spinal cord to the muscles and glands. Efferent neurons are also called motor neurons.

See: Afferent

EFFICIENCY OF EDUCATION: In economic terms, it means the ratio between the total national effort on education to the total 'returns to Education'. Efficiency has two aspects: internal efficiency and external efficiency of the educational system. Internal efficiency means the qualitative and quantitative changes occurring in the total intake of students (i.e., without wastage and stagnation and total utilization of amenities like buildings, equipments, etc.

provided). By external efficiency is meant the success achieved by the system in meeting the needs of the state in relation to manpower: both in quantity and in quality.

EG RULE: A method of teaching by induction which uses a series of selected appropriate examples (egs.) for formulating rules. From scrutiny of the particular examples, the learners elicit the common features, which lead to the formulation of the rules. Examples (eg)–Rule.

See: Ruleg

EGO: Approximately, the 'self'. Freud divided human mind into three strata, viz., the super ego, ego and the id. Id is that part of the mind from which all desires spring. Actions guided by the forces of the id are concerned only with the fulfillment of wishes and do not care for ethics, morals or reality. This part is almost unconscious. Ego corresponds roughly with the 'self'. It is directly concerned with reality. Ego tests the desires against reality and only those that agree with reality are pursued. Other desires are either abandoned or repressed. Super ego roughly corresponds with 'conscience'. Actions at this level are tested against morals ethics, etc. Parts of ego and super ego are unconscious.

EGO DEFENSIVE: Mental mechanism adopted to protect security of the ego. Defensive mechanisms of behaviour develop when situations threaten the 'self'. The mechanisms are usually compensatory, e.g., when a person feels inadequacy to cope with a situation, he projects his 'weakness' to some external elements of the situation (Projection). The classical example is the bad workmen's complaint about the tools.

EGO-DEFENCE MECHANISM: The unconscious (and conscious) psychological devices adopted to protect self when there is threat–either perceived or imaginary. The defences are raised in order to reduce anxiety, cognitive dissonance, trauma, etc. and to restore a feeling of well-being. The reactions may be in the form of attack, withdrawal or compromise. The common defence mechanisms are Fantasy, Reaction-formation, Repression, Projection, Regression, Displacement, Denial, Compensation, Introjection, Insulation, Isolation and Sublimation.

See: Cognitive dissonance

EGO-INVOLVEMENT: Involvement of self or identification:

'Ego involvement' implies that the person has identified himself with the cause or situation which is in agreement with his interest, abilities, values and aspirations. As ego involvement leads to direct self participation, the performance of an individual in such situations will be at a higher level than on which ego-involvement is less. People derive satisfaction from a task in which they have ego involvement. To boost production, the techniques adopted by managements are contrived to ensure better ego-involvement of the workers.

See: Identification

EGYPTIAN EDUCATION (ANCIENT): Education in Egypt that prevailed during the pre-Christian centuries. Education that flourished in this ancient centre of civilization was representative of one that suited an autocratic state. The aim of education was therefore practical and moral. Elementary education was provided for all children, which commenced at the age of 5 years. Even though the state did not provide for the education the organization was directly or indirectly controlled by priests. At the elementary stage the 3 R's dominated the curriculum. Advanced education was organized at the temples. Ethics, philosophy, law, administration, architecture and mathematics were taught at this level. One main aim was the preparation of scribes (for copying, writing and account keeping). Memorization and imitation were the methods used. Transcription was compulsory. Discipline was severe and corporal punishment common. Teaching went hand-in-hand with priesthood.

EIDETIC IMAGERY: Images reproduced from memory with exceptional clarity. Certain individuals could reproduce all the details of a situation or incident very vividly. This is sometimes referred to as photographic memory. Some children could often tell from memory almost all the objects in a picture, even when there are a large number of unrelated objects. Eidetic imagery is operative only during a short period after the removal of the objects.

ELECTRA COMPLEX: The feminine counterpart of Oedipus Complex. It is the complex that develops in girls like Oedipus complex in boys. According to Freud, girls in their infancy pass through this stage. The girls develop strong erotic feelings towards the father which leads to concomitant jealousy towards the mother. The feelings associated with this experience are repressed and the individual is not aware of this 'complex' as it is an unconscious phenomenon. An individual who has not resolved this complex may develop adjustment problems later in life, particularly in marital life.

See: Oedipus Complex

ELECTRO-CARDIOGRAM (ECG): Record of heart activity. The record of the phases of heart activity are obtained by connecting electrodes from the electro-cardiograph to various points on the chest of the person. On a ribbon like paper heart activity is recorded.

See: Lie-detector

ELECTRO-ENCEPHALOGRAM (EEG): Record of the electrical activity of the brain. Electro-encephalogram (EEG) is obtained by applying the electrodes of the Encephalograph to the scalp. The potential changes in the brain are amplified and recorded on a moving strip of paper. Activities from different areas of the brain can be simultaneously recorded. Normal activity of the brain is represented by a wave with a frequency between 8-13 Hz. This is the alpha rhythm. When the person is awake (with eyes open) the alpha waves are replaced by waves of frequency between 14-22 Hz. This is the beta rhythm. This rhythm becomes more pronounced when the person is in an anxiety state. When the person is drowsy or asleep EEG records waves of frequencies between 4-7 Hz (the theta rhythm) and waves of frequency upto 3-5 Hz (delta rhythm).

EEG is used for diagnosing disorders of the brain. It is also used for studying the brain activity in different types of mental processes. The EEG is a component of the Lie-Detector.

See: Lie-detector

ELECTRODERMAL CHANGES: Changes in the electrical conductivity of the skin. Electrical conductivity of the skin varies under different conditions. Dry skin is more resistant to an electrical flow. Sweatliness increases the conductivity of the skin. Electrical resistance of the skin decreases when emotions are aroused. The electro-dermal changes are measured by the instrument 'Psycho-galvanograph'.

ELECTRONIC BRAIN: The master computer. A modern electronic machine (computer) which can store, manipulate and reproduce a large amount of information, which in some way resembles the functioning of the human brain. The electronic brain could handle an immense quantity of data in a very short time and can do tasks it has been instructed to do according to the programs keyed into it. It works only within these limitations. The potential of the human brain to produce new creations (originals) remains unchallenged.

See: Computer

ELECTRONIC BOOKS: The simplest tape comprising a computer and controlled data source and a sophisticated data retrieval system. A variety of a vast information (like texts, graphics, diagrams, sound, animated pictures, video sequences, etc.) can be stored in different media (like video discs, compact discs, etc.)

ELECTROSTATIC COPYING: A reprographic process for producing a large number of copies from an original. It first produces electrostatically charged images of the original on a plate or drum and then uses this to transfer pigment particles to the copy paper. (Also called xerography).

ELEVEN PLUS EXAMINATION: Testing programmes conducted in U.K. by the Local Education Authorities for admission into selective Secondary Schools, before the introduction of Comprehensive School System.

This system was in vogue in United Kingdom for allocation of children to different types of secondary schools such as Grammar schools or Secondary modern schools. The examination was held for the children of primary schools at about the age of 11. The children were required to take an intelligence test, a test of English composition and a test in arithmetic. Teachers' ratings were also taken into consideration. An interview was also held if necessary. Eleven plus examination was used to stream children to the different types of schools.

EMILE: The educational classic written by Rousseau (1762). Emile is a fictitious boy whose educuation is described in the book. As a young child he learns from his own experiences– sensory and motor activities, motivated by his own curiosity. He is encouraged to run, swim, jump, climb, etc. Counting and weighing, measuring distances, copying figures, etc. done on his own accord improved his sense of discrimination. Speech and music also formed part of the work. As the child grows agriculture or carpenting form part of his activities. Even arithmetic and geometry were taught not in their formal manner, but as experiential activities. As he grew up, astronomy, geography, etc. enter his study, not through books, but directly from nature. He makes field trips and visits from which he learns how to live with people. When he reaches maturity he takes up physical sciences, ancient languages, etc. and finally philosophy, and religion. 'Habits' Rousseau said, resist proper learning and so he claimed that the only habit he would like to teach Emile was the habit of forming no habits. The treatise is considered as the manifesto of 'Natuaralism' in education.

Rousseau's ideas on women's education, however, were regressive. In this context he discusses the education of a model girl 'Sophie' who has no individuality and her only duty is to please man and bear and bring up strong children. Her duty is to provide a good home for her family.

See: Naturalism, Rousseau, J.J.

EMITTED RESPONSE: A response produced spontaneously i.e. without an external stimuli (like the random exploratory activity of the rat in a cage). It is a term widely used in Skinner's theory of operant or instrumental conditioning. A rat which had been deprived of food for the past one day, when placed inside the Skinner box, engaged in a variety of activities, like running around, jumping, scratching the box, pressing the lever, etc. These specific activities were aroused just randomly without any specific stimulus that could be connected to them. Such a random behaviour is called an emitted response. An emitted response may result in drive reduction (i.e. pressing the lever with the paw which will release food pellet). The right response will be one of the emitted responses. In Skinnerian conditioning this response is said to be reinforced and so it tends to persist.

See: Operant Conditioning

EMOTION: The complex mental state subsequent to the perception of a situation involving or leading to pleasure or pain. The dominant feature of this mental state is 'feeling'. When an individual, for example, faces a threatening situation he has to act immediately and vigorously either by fighting or fleeing. The body prepares for this emergency, by increasing heart beats and breathing, by directing more blood supply to the gross muscles, by throwing more glycogen into the blood stream and so on. All these go to energize the body, and the changes effected by the physiological reactions are felt as 'emotion'. Emotion is the state of preparedness and the feeling accompanying it. Feeling can be either pleasant or unpleasant. At birth the child is seen to possess only one emotion-startling reaction. Later this emotion develops into three main emotions–fear, rage and love. From these three basic emotions, a large number of emotions proliferate as the child grows.

Emotion is the basis of all 'interests' and 'motivations' and so is directly related to all human performance; so also it is the basis for all happiness and misery.

See: Emotional maturity
Bard-Cannon Theory
Autonomic nervous system
Endocrine glands.

EMOTIONAL MATURITY: Attainment of appropriate level in the control of emotional behaviour: Emotional behaviour develops from just an 'excitement' pattern at the time of birth to a number of complex set of behaviour by early adult period. An emotionally mature individual will display emotional behaviour appropriate to the situation and his age. An adult reacting to a situation like a child (i.e. by overreacting to the provocation) is emotionally not mature. In an emotionally mature individual the overt emotional behaviour is commensurate with the degree of arousal (i.e. strength of the emotion arousing stimuli).

Emotional instability is an indication of emotional immaturity. An emotionally unstable response is characterized by the lack of agreement between the emotional response and the provoking stimuli.

See: Emotions

ENACTIVE-ICONIC AND SYMBOLIC: The three sequential models of children's development as postulated by Jerome S. Bruner. The three stages are characteristically represented by the behaviour

1. Enactive i.e. purely motor responses;
2. Iconic i.e. responding to pictorial images or models; and
3. Symbolic i.e. languages and abstract ideas. This sequence

is in agreement with Piaget's stages of development: sensori-motor, pre-operations, concrete operations and formal operations.

See: Bruner, J.S.

ENACTIVE LEARNING: A term used by Doslon and Bruner to denote learning through direct experience as opposed to learning through indirect experience (i.e. through media).

ENCODING: Transferring an information into a code i.e. signal. The code can be converted to get back the information. The light energy impinging on the retina is encoded as electrical impulses and are conveyed to the brain along the optic nerve. In the brain these impulses are converted (decoded) to visual experience.

ENDOCRINE GLANDS: The ductless glands. The endocrine glands throw their secretions–the hormones–directly into the blood stream. The hormones have an important role in the growth and development of the individual and also in influencing and controlling a variety of physiological and psychological functions. The important endocrine glands are: the adrenals, thyroid, parathyroid, the pancreas, the gonads (sex) and the pituitary.

ENRICHMENT PROGRAMME: Additional learning experiences provided for the gifted children. The progress of intellectually gifted children in school work is faster than the normal pupils. Some may have giftedness in other areas like music, art, etc. If these children are not given challenging tasks to cope with their abilities, not only that their full development is endangered, but also it is likely that they develop behaviour problems. So schools will have to organise enrichment programmes either along with daily work or as co-curricular or extra-curricular activities.

ENURESIS: Bed-wetting. Habitual involuntary (often in sleep) discharge of urine after the age of 3 years. It may be due to psysiological causes. It occurs also in the case of emotionally disturbed children and children who feel parental neglect. In chronic cases suitable medical or psychological treatment will have to be provided.

ENVIRONMENT: Physical and social surroundings of the individual. The environment includes all the elements of the surroundings, inanimate, animate, human, and also the social institutions man has built up that come into direct or indirect contact with the individual. So it includes the physical environment, social environment, cultural environment, etc. The environment has decisive role in guiding the growth and development of the individual and in directing his behaviour from time to time.

The term 'environment' used in the context of nurture-nature controversy means all the elements that influence the individual, other than hereditary factors. In that sense 'environment' may includes intracellular (inside the cells) intercellular (between cells) and intra uterine environment, in addition to the external environment.

Heredity (genes) sets limits to the growth and development, proper environment ensures growth and development possible within these limits.

See: Heredity

EPIDIASCOPE: An optical projector with combined functions of an episcope and a diascope. Enlarged images from opaque objects like diagrams, graphs, etc. from a printed page (episcope function) and images from transparent slides or films (diascope function) can be projected on to a screen or wall. It is an easily portable optical instrument and is widely used as a visual aid in class room teaching.

EPISCOPE: A projector which throws magnified images from opaque matter on to a screen. Pictures, charts, graphs, diagrams, etc. from a printed page, or a photograph on a non-transparent paper can be projected on to a screen in a darkened room. Used frequently as a visual aid in class room teaching.

EQUAL APPEARING INTERVAL SCALE METHOD: The method developed by Thurstone in scaling attitude test items. The steps involved in the construction of a scale on equal appearing interval scale are:

1. collection of a large number of statements, which relate to the expression of attitude (e.g., attitude towards nuclear war);
2. A panel of judges scrutinising and assigning each selected item a position on an attitude continuum between one extreme to the other (ranging from 0.0 for the most extreme

statement in unfavourable direction, 5.5 for neutral statements and 11.0 for most extreme favourable statement);

3. Median value for each items (from the pooled values of the judges) is computed and the scale positions is assigned to all the items; and
4. The items are finally selected from among those statements for the test so that they spread as far as possible evenly along the scale from one extreme to the other.

See: Attitude scale

EQUALIZATION OF EDUCATIONAL OPPORTUNITY: The situation that ensures equal opportunity for all citizens for pursuing education. This is a precondition for universal education. To ensure equalization of opportunity, there should be a school within reasonable distance from the home of every child, where all the children of the locality are admitted without any discrimination. It is the responsibility of every welfare state to ensure equalization of educational opportunity for all its citizens, i.e., by providing schools, noon meals, and financial and other assistance to poor students.

EQUIVALENT GROUPS: Two matched groups selected for an experiment. The control group and the experimental group are made equivalent generally, either by matching by pairs or matching by frequency distributions. In matched pair groups, the procedure is to assign one of the pairs to the experimental group and the other to the control group, the individuals in a pair being almost similar. In an experiment on trying out a new method of teaching a topic in mathematics, an intelligence test and an initial mathematics achievement tests were given to a sample of 220 children. Among them 30 pairs had almost equal scores in the two tests. From each pair one individual is assigned to the control group and the other to the experimental group.

The two groups will be equivalent in this type of matching. The mean, the standard deviation, etc. of the two groups will be almost identical. The difficulty in this method is that to get a sample of appropriate size, selection will have to be made from a much bigger sample.

In matching by frequency distribution, equivalence is achieved by equalizing the frequencies in each class interval for the two groups with regard to the variables to be controlled. For example, as in the case of the example under matched pair group, the tests (for intelligence and mathematical ability) are administered to a fairly large sample: say 150. Individuals are selected to match the frequency distributions in the two groups. In this case the mean, the standard deviation, etc. of the two groups in the two tests will be approximately equal. It is easier to match by frequency distribution than by pairing individuals.

Matching is the process which results in the control of the intervening variables.

See: Control

ERASMUS, DE SIDERIUS (1466-1536): European thinker. The aim of education according to Erasmus was to prepare men to enjoy life to the full. Mass methods could not be expected to prove successful in education, as both nature and capacity of individuals vary. In his 'Liberal Education of Children' he gives the following simple rules: "Do not hurry, wait till the proper stage is reached..." Avoid a difficulty which may be either ignored or postponed. When the child has to encounter a difficulty, make him approach it gradually and make the task as interesting as possible". He stressed the maxim 'understand, arrange, repeat'. Corporal punishment should be resorted to only in extreme cases. There should be no rote learning. Education should be a public endeavour.

ERGONOMICS: The study of the relationship between man and his working environment–which includes the work, the equipment (machines and tools) and the surroundings. The study helps to find out the problems arising from physiological and psychological characteristics of the individual in relation to his work situation. This is also called 'human engineering'.

EROTICISM: Pleasure derived from sexual stimulation. Psychoanalytical view of eroticism is that all pleasure derived from tactile stimulation (i.e., stimulation of sense organs of touch) is sexual in nature.

In early infancy, tactile stimulation anywhere in the body, gives pleasure. The erotic zones of the body begin to differentiate only at later stages. From the whole body, at first, it shifts to the mouth (sucking infants derives erotic pleasure) then to the anal region (both defecation and retention are pleasurable) and by adolescence, to the genitals.

See: Freud, S.
Psycho-sexual development

ESSAY: A short narrative treatise on a given topic; a prose composition on a particular topic; free response test requiring extended written answer.

The essay has been the main mode of response obtained from students as evidence of learning till recently. Even now, to a large extent, it is. But when the objectivity of essay type examination was shown to be questionable in various investigations, attempts were made to improve them and to find alternative methods of evaluation. The attempt at improving essay type examination resulted in designing better questions.

As we require evidence of attainment with regard to the higher and composite objectives of learning (like analytical and critical thinking reasoning, etc.) the use of essay as a means of testing will always find a place among the evaluation techniques. For the assessment of the ability in organizing ideas in sequential thinking and in creative thinking in different subjects, essay type answers will be needed.

See: Objective tests

ESSENTIALISM: The educational philosophy that emphasizes the primacy of the conservation of the best of the traditions of a society and the promotion of intellectual growth of the individuals. William C. Bagley (1874-1946), a well-known essentiatist in education, wrote: "...if democratic society is to meet the conflict with totalitarian states, there must be discipline that gives strength to the democratic purpose and ideal. The electorate should be literate". Education should deal with the transmission of cultural heritage and intellectual training, but it should also consider secondary goals of physical health, emotional health and vocational competency. The core of the curriculum, according to the essentialists, contains the essentials. At the elementary stage it should be reading, speaking, writing, spelling and arithmetic and at a later stage, history, geography and sciences. Art, music and physical education are of secondary importance. In the secondary schools the essentials at the primary stages are improved in breadth and depth. Subjects like algebra, geometry, trigonometry, calculus are to be introduced. Vocational subjects are also added, but they are less essential.

ESTIMATES: Income and expenditure forecasts for a future period worked out with the help of trends in income and expenditure for the previous years. In preparing estimates for educational planning, factors relating to quantitative expansion (additional school building, salary for additional staff, etc.) as well as qualitative improvement (like curriculum planning, in-service education, provision of better teaching-learning materials, etc.) are taken into account. Budgets are prepared on the basis of estimates.

Similarly, population estimates are worked out for future years from trends in population growth. If the annual increase in population of a country for the past few decades was 1.5%, forecast of population, say 5 years hence, will be approximately 7.5% of the total population (1.5 x 5).

Any measure, predicted likewise from past trends is an estimate.

ESTROGEN: The female sex hormone, which is directly related to the development of secondary sex characteristics and libido.

See: Testosterone

ETHOLOGY: Study of animal behaviour. It deals with the investigation into the nature and functions of animal behaviour, and how and why some kind of behaviour was helpful in the survival of the species. This branch of study was developed by Konrad Lorenz and Niko Tinbergen.

EURHYTHMICS: A system of physical training which uses music to facilitate co-ordination of movements. The method was developed by E.J. Dalcroze in the fifteenth century. Music is used as an aid to stimulate rhythmic impulses in the body which helps in coordinating body movements.

EVALUATION: Assessment vis-a-vis values. In educational context, it means the appraisal of expected outcomes of teaching. The expected outcomes are listed in specific terms (as behavioural objectives) like 'ability to recall facts' and 'ability to apply knowledge in new situations to solve problems'. Evaluation aims to collect data on the growth of pupils in terms of the competencies they have attained as a result of schooling. It enables the pupil to understand his strength and weakness and the teacher to assess the efficiency of his teaching. A variety of measurement techniques are used for evaluation, viz. unit tests, interviews, practical tests, etc. while examinations are used for screening purposes (i.e. for deciding promotion). Evaluation is used as an inbuilt procedure and an integral part of the curriculum, a continuous process, which is intended to aid pupil growth and improvement of curriculum implementation.

See: Examination

EVENT SAMPLING: The method of child study that uses the recording of particular behaviours (e.g., aggression). In event sampling technique, the experimenter looks for particular behaviour (like shyness, cooperative play, etc.) and record it. The event occurring any time during the day will have to be recorded. To formulate useful conclusions, the child will have to be observed for a period of time extending to months.

See: Longitudinal study

EX-POST-FACTO RESEARCH: The research design that seeks to unravel a problem retrospectively. The phrase means 'after the fact'. The investigation starts with the dependent variable (which can be observed and measured at present) and works backwards to find out the independent variables (antecedents or causes 'occured in the past'). The investigator starts by observing the conditions and situations existing at the present time and search back in time to find out the causal factors. Eg: an investigator is interested in isolating the factors associated with droppage. He takes a representative sample of drop-outs and collects data on all variables connected with their school lives: like, family conditions such as socio-economic status, educational status of parents, number of members in the family, birth order, parental attitudes, and conditions in school such as scholastic status, interest in school work, sociability, emotional stability, behaviour problems, peer group relations, hobbies, attitude towards teachers, teacher's attitude towards the drop-outs, etc.

After collection of data on all pertinent variables, the plausible causal factors of droppage can be ascertained by appropriate statistical procedures.

See: Design of Experiment

EXAMINATION: The traditional testing procedure used for assessing student progress. Examinations have been and are an integral part of the educational system. Examinations used to be the terminal stage of a particular course of instruction and promotion to the next course was based on the results of the examinations. Till recently, examinations depended largely on essay type questions. When various research studies have proved that the reliability and validity of essay type tests were highly questionable, attempts have been made to improve examinations by using objective type questions.

Examinations are now used to:

decide promotion of students, award certificates, degrees, etc. and select (screen) candidates for awards, scholarship, jobs, etc.

Instead of depending on a single examination or a few examinations to decide the progress of pupils, a process of continuous pupil evaluation is now preferred. Pupil growth in every aspect is continuously assessed and all major decisions are made on the basis of evidence of growth, from the practical, written and oral work of the pupils collected throughout the year.

See: Internal Examination

EXCEPTIONAL CHILDREN: Children who deviate from the normal in any trait of human quality, physical, mental or emotional. There are two categories of exceptionality: supernormal (above normal) or sub-normal (below normal). Take for example eye-sight. There are some who have excellent visual acuity, colour discrimination, etc. while some are visually handicapped and partially or totally colour blind. Likewise, there are children with excellent hearing ability while some who are hard of hearing or even deaf. As these children, whether super-normal or sub normal, are very different from normals and they need special treatment and care according to the degree of deviation.

The following are some of the characteristic types of exceptional children: Academically or artistically gifted, athletically talented, partially sighted, blind, deaf, physically deformed, mentally retarted, etc.

EXERCISE: Practicing of learning tasks. Learning becomes more effective by repeating the learning tasks. This is implied in 'the law of exercise' (Thorndike). Children in schools will require adequate practice for developing their proficiency to the maximum. As the time available in school is hardly sufficient for learning new tasks, teachers give daily assignments to be done at home. Home exercises are beneficial not only for raising the academic skills, but also in developing in children the habits punctuality and hardwork.

EXISTENTIALISM: The philosophy that stresses the significance of subjective factors like intuition, introspection, emotional commitment and feeling of aloneness. According to this approach a person is free to choose what he decides to become. He is free to act and is responsible for his acts. The person is always alone, separate from the physical universe and other human beings. Living is a confrontation with the dangers and threats of existence, particularly freedom and death. The existentialist teacher has the utmost respect for freedom and he expects the students to accept the consequence and outcome of all their actions. The aim of education should be to teach people to live together in peace. Education should develop understanding and cofeeling with people of other nations. Existentialism can be traced back to Kierkergaard, Nietzche, Satre, Camus, etc.

EXPERIENCE: The subjective concomitant of a stimulation. The 'conscious' condition accompanying a stimulation is experience. The stimulation can arise from the internal (i.e. from within the body) or external environment. All past learning is also referred to as experience. Sometimes the term is used to signify all the stimulation an individual receives at a time.

Experience, being subjective, is unobservable and cannot be measured. But in many situations we receive verbal reports of experience as reasonably reliable evidence–as when an individual reports that he 'feels cold', 'it is causing pain', etc.

See: Behaviour, Consciousness

EXPERIMENT: A procedure undertaken for finding out the relationships between variables. An experiment is designed and carried out to establish the effects of one variable (independent variable) on another (dependent variable) or to trace the antecedents of a consequence. In the simplest form, it involves only one independent variable (antecedent, cause, etc.). The investigator exercises every control over all conditions (intervening variables) that are likely to affect the dependent variable (consequence) and then introduces the variable, the effect of which he wants to study. As the control results in keeping the effects of the intervening variables under check, the effects of the new variables under study can be identified clearly. For example: a teacher thinks that a new method he has improvised (Method A) in teaching a topic in science may be more effective than the traditional method (Method B). To test this hypothesis he plans to design an experiment. He selects two classes of students which are equivalent. This is for controlling the intervening variables (see equivalent groups). Then he uses method A in one class (independent variable) and method B in the other class (the second independent variable) in teaching the same topic. After the period of instruction he gives an achievement test on the topic to both groups. The results of the test by Method A is the dependent variable in experimental group: (say D_A) and by method B is dependent variable in the control group (say D_B). If the difference between D_A and D_B is large enough to be statistically significant he can conclude that method A is more effective than method B.

See: Design of Experimen, Statistical Significance

EXPERIMENTAL PSYCHOLOGY: Study of psychological phenomena experimentally. This branch of psychology deals with the study of behaviour in the completely controlled situations of the laboratory. Scientific instruments are often used for control and measurement. In experimental psychology the experimenter and the subjects are both human beings. Phenomena like reaction time, conditioning, perception, attention, concept formation, etc. are experimentally studied under laboratory conditions. Non-human organisms like animals, birds, insects, etc. are also used as subjects for the experimental study of sub-human behaviour.

EXPERIMENTAL EXTINCTION: Elimination of a learned response (conditioned) experimentally. It was first demonstrated by Pavlov. Extinction of the conditioned response is achieved by eliciting the response (CR) a number of times without reinforcing it. In the classical conditioning experiment: first the dog was conditioned to salivate at the sound of the bell and then in a number of subsequent trials the bell was sounded but the food was not given immediately on salivating. This resulted in the gradual extinction of the conditioned reflex.

But it was seen that a conditioned reflex which was thus become extinct, reappeared spontaneously after some time.

See: Classical Conditioning

EXPERIMENTAL NEUROSIS: Experimentally induced neurosis: Pavlov first demonstrated the phenomenon with dogs as subjects. The dog was first conditioned to salivate to a sound of a particular wave-length. Then, in the place of the CS, sound with wave-lengths close to it were presented in a random order alternatively with the CS and the animal was forced to discriminate between them. As the two stimuli resembled very much, discrimination was extremely difficult. Repeated exposure to this treatment made the animal tense, excitable and emotionally maladjusted. Neurotic symptoms (like irritability, increased blood pressure, etc.) were developed experimentally. This experiment helped to understand the causation of neurosis and the adverse effects of continued exposure to situations in which the individual has to make difficult choices i.e. exposure to a state of conflict for a long time.

See: Classical conditioning

EXPLICIT: An action that can be observed by other persons. This is also referred to as an overt activity. Explicit actions are objective. 'Speaking' is explicit but 'thinking' is not (implicit).

See: Implicit response

EXPLORATORY DRIVE: An animal's spontaneous urge to wander about or examine unfamiliar environment. A rat, when put inside a problem box will immediately start running, jumping, scratching, etc. and will explore almost every nook and corner of the box. Exploratory drive is almost identical with curiosity.

See: Drive

EXPOSITORY MATERIALS: The introductory materials presented in audio-instruction sessions. An expository material is meant as an overview of the lesson. It may be a complete lesson or instructional sequences without reference to other materials. It prepares the learner for the new lessons. It is useful for self-instructional programmes also.

EXTRAPOLATION: Inferring (projecting) values outside the range of obtained values on the assumption that the same trend or pattern observed within the observed range will continue outside it. A graph can be extended beyond the points for which values of the variables are obtained, if there is strong evidence that the trend will follow beyond the level of obtained measurement.

If the population of a country is found to increase at regular rate (say 2% annually) a projection for a future year can be worked out from known data of the previous year.

See: Interpolation

EXTROVERSION: One of the bipolar type of personality traits (according to the Analytical psychology of Jung) used to describe and explain behaviour. Jung said any individual can be placed somewhere in a continuum with the two poles: Introversion–Extroversion. Extroversion is characterized by high sociability, preference for outdoor life, active participation in social situations, talkativeness, expressiveness and showmanship qualities. Extroversion-Introversion is one of the major three dimensions of personality, proposed by Eysenck, the other two being Neuroticism-Stability, and Psychotism-Normality.

Extrovert is a person with dominant characteristics of extraversion.

See: Introversion, Jung.

F

F-RATIO: The ratio of variance. If the variance of one sample is V_b and the other V_w, the F-ratio is given by the relation,

$$F = \frac{V_b}{V_w}$$

If the value is 1, it means the variances of both samples are the same and so the distributions are similar in respect of the variable in question. The departure of values from 1, is indicative of difference in variance. Larger the difference, grater the difference in the variables, i.e. the two samples are dissimilar. In analysis of variance, F-ratio is used to test the independence of two or more groups. F in that case is,

$$\frac{\text{Variance between groups}}{\text{Variance within groups}} \; i.e. \frac{V}{V}$$

Values of F-statistics for different degrees of freedom for different levels of significance can be obtained from the Table of F-ratios.

See: Analysis of variance

F-TEST: The statistical test for determining the significance of the difference between two variances. F-test yields the F-ratio which shows the extent of the difference between the two variances. This is used to find out whether two groups differ or are similar, F-ratio is obtained from the formula,

$$F = \frac{V_1}{V_2}$$

where V_1 is the variance of scores in group-1 and V_2 variance of scores in group-2. If the value of F-ratio is close together (depending on the total number of cases in the sample) it can be assumed that there is no significant difference between the two distributions.

In analysis of variance (ANOVA) involving a number of groups, F-test is applied to find out whether each group is different from the other. For example, if teaching methods T_1, T_2, T_3 are tried out in groups g_1, g_2, g_3 (which have been equated), the F-tests will determine whether the differences in the variance of the distribution of scores between the groups (g_1, g_2, g_3) are larger than, same, smaller than the variances of the scores within the groups. The variances within each group occur due to chance, while variance between groups is due to the difference in treatment. So the ratio between the variance between groups and the variance within groups will indicate whether the differences (if any) are larger than that can occur by chance and whether the distributions are different or the same. In other words it shows whether the three methods yield different results. The F method was developed by Ronald E. Fisher.

See: Analysis of variance

FACE VALIDITY: A test is valid if it tests the quality it claims to test. A valid test of intelligence measures intelligence and only intelligence. Precisely, the validity of a test is determined statistically by its degree of agreement with the criterion it purports to test.

Face validity is a non-empirical, non statistical type of validity. It is the validity that is apparent from an examination of the test. If the items of an intelligence test, on scrutiny, appear appropriate for testing intelligence, it has face validity.

If the test lacks face validity the items have to be refined till it gets face validity before empirical validation is attempted.

See: Validity

FACILITATOR: A leader in a group who helps in the learning of the participants. He may act as a leader of a group discussion to stimulate the thinking of the group members, as a catalyst. He may give suggestions, but not teach. His approach should be permissible and democratic.

FACILITY INDEX: The degree of 'easiness' of a test item. It is the percentage of students who answer the item correctly out of the total number of students who take the test. A facility index of 10 means that 10% of the students who take the test are able to do the item correctly. This also means that 90% of the students fail in the item, i.e. for the 90% the item is difficult. So the difficulty index of the item is 90.

See: Difficulty index

FACTOR ANALYSIS: The complex statistical procedure used for isolating irreducible factors of a complex ability. By administering a test (e.g., intelligence test) containing a large number of subtests on a sample of population, data can be obtained on intercorrelation of each sub-test with the other. By subjecting these correlation to factor analysis, factors of the particular ability emerge. Thus factors of 'intelligence' 'personality', etc. have been evolved. This is a highly sophisticated technique intended for studying the characteristics of complex abilities or qualities by isolating the factors constituting them. There are various methods of factor analysis, like 'centroid method', 'principal axis method', etc.

It was Charles Spearman, who evolved Factor Analysis in order to isolate the factors of intelligence. In 1904 he established the 'two factor' theory of intelligence. Subsequently much was done in the field and more and more refined methods were developed. L.L. Thurstone developed the 'Multiple Factor Analysis' on the basis of which, he extracted primary mental abilities (factors) from a series of intelligence test data.

The aim of all methods of factor analysis, is then the resolution of a set of variables into a smaller number of 'factors'. The resolution is done by analyzing the intercorrelations of variables. The analysis will yield 'factors' which bear all characteristics of the original measures.

See: Primary mental abilities

FACTOR: The unique quality common in a number of tests. The 'factor' is isolated or extracted by factor analysis.

FANTASY: Vivid imagery of scenes, persons, activities, etc. experienced by individuals. The imagery may be coherent as in dreams and day-dreams, but usually has no relevance to reality. Often, fantasies are imaginary fulfilment of desires and urges that are hard to achieve in reality. Occasional indulgence in fantasy is not harmful, but excessive indulgence is a symptom of psychotic tendencies.

FEAR: Fear is an emotional reaction originating from the perception of danger or threat. The perception of danger triggers a series of bodily changes mediated by the autonomic nervous system and reinforced by the endocrine secretions, particularly of the adrenals. It is characterized by tension and on arousal of fear, heart beat increases, the flow of blood to the visceral organs slackens but to the gross muscles (like thigh and calf muscles) increases, coordinated activity becomes difficult, breathing rate speeds up, red cells and glycogen are thrown into the blood stream in large quantities, sweating is accelerated and cerebral activity (higher mental activity) inhibited to some extent. Apart from the cerebral cortex, the hypothalamus is also involved as it is the control centre of fear reaction. The adrenalin thrown into the blood stream also facilitate the neural activity connected with the fear reactions. Fear prepares the organism for fight or flight, i.e., escape from danger. The body is energized and prepared for escape from the threatening situation.

See: Emotions

FEEBLEMINDEDNESS: Very low level intelligence. Individuals whose IQ is lower than 60 is considered as feebleminded. This includes the moron, imbeciles and the idiots. Feebleminded children cannot be taught in normal schools. They have to be provided with special schooling programmes.

See: Intelligence

FEED BACK: Return of output information to the control centre, when they are used for evaluation of the processes and for improvement of inputs. If the impact of the teaching of a topic is fed back to the teacher he can make an assessment of his activities and effect improvement in his future teaching activities. Knowledge of the results of what one does is feed back. Feed back aids in regulating the working of a system for better efficiency, as the incoming output information makes it possible to readjust the working.

Feed back is a reinforcer in learning situations. 'Concurrent feed back' results when the information is received as and when the process is ongoing. Concurrent feedback is automatically operative in many learning situations particularly in motor learning (like drawing, cycling). 'Terminal feed back' is the feed back that is obtained at the end of the operation. Feed back can be either intrinsic (as in motor learning) or extrinsic (as marks or scores supplied to the student).

FEEDER SCHOOL: A lower level school from which children on promotion are generally admitted to a higher level school. Around a secondary school, for example, there may be two or more middle schools from which students pass on to the secondary school. These are the feeder schools of the secondary school.

FEELING: It is the subjective concomitant of emotions. Feelings are either pleasant or unpleasant. Excitement, tension, happiness, joy, love, sadness, disgust, etc. have their feeling tones.
See: Emotions

FELT BOARD DISPLAY: An adhesive display board. The board surface is covered with flannel, felt, etc. Display materials cut out and backed with the same material (Flannel, felt, etc.) adhere to the board. It aids in easy movement and rearrangement of the display materials. So it can be used with advantage where rearrangement of pieces can be used to demonstrate some fact: like the Pythagoras theorem.

FICTIVE GOAL: Unrealistic goal. Term used by Adler to denote the unrealistic goal set by the individual to compensate his inferiority.
See: Goal

FIELD THEORY: The theory that attempts to explain human behaviour as a resultant of the interaction between the forces within the individual and forces outside, in the environment. Kurt Lewin (1890-1947) who propounded this theory adopted an analogy from physics to explain his stand. Like a magnetic substance in a magnetic field is influenced both by the forces in the field and the force in the substance, behaviour of man in his environment is dependent on the interaction between the person and the environment and is expressed by the relation B=f (P,E) i.e. Behaviour (B) is a function of the interaction between the person (P) and the environment (E). Gestaltists' influence on Lewin is clear in this exposition.

The individual person is to be considered as a field system consisting of various psychological forces (originating from needs, knowledge, etc.). In the case of the child his personality system is mostly undifferentiated and as it grows the personality system expands and differentiation takes place and many subsystems develop. It is the nature of the balance of the subsystems, that is the strong determinant of his behaviour in a given environment. The psychological environment also expands, in space and time as the child grows. The psychological environment is not exactly the geographical environment, according to Lewin. It includes some aspects of the geophysical environment but it really is the psychological field (which may contain also elements in his imagination and fantasy), with which he is concerned. The person and his psychological environment constitute his 'life space', which is analogous to a magnetic field within which is placed a magnetic substance, free to interact. The psychological field is that part of the environment as perceived and understood by the person and it is related to his needs. Objects in the field may have forces with different magnitudes which he calls 'valences'. Valences may be positive, negative or neutral, i.e. attracting, repulsing or static. Attraction is a vector directed towards the object and repulsion is a vector directed away from the object. (That is, the forces have not only magnitude but also direction). If two or more vectors, act at the same time, displacement of some kind is the resultant. When there is an imbalance in the equilibrium, the vectors act in such a way that the resultant restores the equilibrium. What happens when a person's attempt to strive towards a goal is thwarted? Then one of his subsystems is in a state of tension, and when the interruption is removed, it restores its original activity. If the particular activity is not possible a substitute activity that will reduce the tension will be adopted. So barriers produce frustration, but the attempt of the individual then will be to overcome the barrier and if it is found insurmountable, either to abandon it or provide another substitute goal. As Field theory makes use of vector analysis and Topology, it is also called Topological Psychology.

See: Gestalt, Life space

FIVE STEPS: The five-steps in a lesson plan according to Herbart. Planning a lesson according to the Herbartian method, was very popular with teachers in primary and secondary schools in various countries of the world till recently. The steps are: (1) preparation; (2) statement of aim; (3) presentation; (4) consolidation (generalization); and (5) application. Class room lessons, whatever the method used, often conform broadly to this pattern.

See: Herbart

FIXATION: Any particular characteristic of an earlier stage of development remaining persistent without being substituted with the appropriate one for the late stage of development. The concept is largely used by psychoanalysts. Thumb-sucking in an adult is a fixation. Excessive dependence of a married son on his mother is usually a symptom of 'mother fixation'.

Any behaviour or habit becoming persistent and inflexible may also be said to have fixated.

See: Psychoanalysis

FIXED RATIO REINFORCEMENT: Reinforcement given for every correct response emitted only after a fixed number of correct responses. In the fixed ratio reinforcement schedule, reinforcement is given only for the correct responses emitted only after emitting a fixed number of correct responses, say, 3rd or 6th or 9th, etc.

See: Operant Conditioning, Reinforcement

FIXED INTERVAL REINFORCEMENT: Reinforcement given for every correct response emitted only after a fixed interval of time. In fixed interval schedule, reinforcement is given only for the correct response coming after a fixed interval of time after the preceding correct response (Say 30 seconds).

See: Operant Conditioning, Reinforcement

FLESCH FORMULA: A standard formula designed to obtain a quantitative measure of 'readability' of textual material. The formula is based on the number of syllables in a sample of 100 words of the textual matter and the number of sentences in the sample.

See: Fog index, Readability

FLIP CHART: A device for displaying information. The Flip Chart consists of a number of sheets of paper (with the information recorded) fixed to a rod or display board by clamping along the top edges. Each sheet can be flipped forwards or backwards.

FLOODING: A technique in behaviour therapy which employs exposure of the patient to massive doses of the feared stimuli. In flooding, the patient is exposed to continuous presentation of the obnoxious stimuli which evokes severe anxiety in him. The patient is prevented from taking recourse to escape reactions.

He is encouraged to discover that the traumatic experience he anticipates, do not occur and that the anxiety disappears. The procedure will be repeated till the anxiety disappears. This may be done either in real life situations or in imagination. This is also called implosive therapy. The method has been found to be particularly effective in treating neurotic obsessions.

See: Behaviour therapy, Implosion

FLOOR: The lowest degree of the dimension measured by a test. 'Floor' indicates the lowest score possible to obtain in a test. If in a test of 100 items, nobody gets below the score '5', score 5 is the floor. All good and valid tests will have a few items below the 'floor level' to accommodate 'foot room'. This is meant to accommodate a lower level of ability, in case it occurs.

FLOPPY DISK: Magnetically coated disc of standard radius used as a medium for storing data in digital form, for use in computers.

FLUCTUATION OF ATTENTION: Periodical shifting of attention: Attention is the focussing of the scenes towards objects, situations, etc. in order to effect better perception. Shifting of this focus i.e. what was central once later becomes peripheral, is what is referred to as fluctuation.

See: Attending

FOCUSSED INTERVIEW: Interview which stresses on a particular event or experience. This technique is made use of by the interviewer in exploring a particular problem. It is used in counselling or psychotherapy. The interviewer, instead of adopting a general line of enquiry, helps with cues to focus attention of the client on a particular relationship, work situation, etc. which are closely related to the problem.

See: Counselling

FOG INDEX: Numerical value of 'readability' of a text.

See: Readability. Modified fog index.

FOLK WAYS: Minor norms of social behaviour. For example: in modes of dressing, people in a society have to conform to the norms prevailing in the society. Nonconformity with regard to a folk-way does not affect the welfare of the society and there is no punishment inflicted for nonconformity. Even if a man dresses himself ludicrously people tend to ignore it.

FOLK SCHOOL: Schools for continuing education (Denmark). Originally they were Evening Schools meant for vocational education of adults. Later they were also used to provide general education to employed adults. Cultural programmes also form part of the school work.

FORGETTING CURVE: The rate at which the ability to recall decreases until totally forgotten. The important results of experiments on retention and forgetting can be summarised as follows: Meaningful materials are better retained than meaningless materials; materials which have pleasant emotional tones tend to be better retained than unpleasant materials. Retention is greater when the material is learned with an intention to recall.
See: Memory

FORM BOARD: A kind of performance type intelligence test. It is a plane board (usually wooden) from which different shapes like circle, triangle, star, square, etc. have been cut out. The testee is blindfolded and is required to insert the cut out figures in the correct holes. The testee has to feel the shape of the cut out piece and the holes and make the correct judgement for solving each problem. The form board was first devised by Seguin (known as Seguin's Form Board) and is widely used for testing children and mentally defectives.
See: Performance test

FORMAL OPERATIONS STAGE: The final stage of cognitive development in children, according to Piaget. The child enters this stage around 11 years and it extends upto 16 and beyond. At this stage the child needs no concrete associations to solve problems. He is capable of considering all possible ways of tackling a problem. Thinking becomes more flexible and he can make use of information from a number of different sources for meeting the present situation. He is capable of hypothetical or deductive reasoning.
See: Piaget. J.

FORMAL DISCIPLINE: The doctrine that states that 'faculties' of the mind can be strengthened by training. This is also known by the name 'faculty psychology' and John Locke (1632-1704) was to some extent resposible for initiating this doctrine. The Aristotlean faculty psychology was the basis for this theory. According to their view, education consisted in habituating the faculties of the mind by disciplining them by exercises. Mental power or faculty can be increased by such training. Powerful intellectual capacities result from rigorous training of the mind. Mental power is more important than the knowledge acquired, because a person who has such perfected faculties could learn or do anything difficult. The mind is a blank slate (tabula rasa) at birth. Education provides the exercises which results in the formation of intellectual capacities. Education should begin with bodily exercises because a sound mind can exist only in a sound body. Classical languages (like Latin and Greek) and mathematics were considered most suitable for the training of the faculties. The study of these subjects was thought to be powerful enough to strengthen and sharpen the various faculties of the mind. In the elementary schools the stress was on subjects that had scope for drill work like spelling, arithmetic and grammar. Control in the schools was very severe and corporal punishment was common.

FORMAL LANGUAGE: The typical language of the middle class people according to Bernstein. In a middle class family the child is exposed to a linguistic environment which places great value on verbalization and conceptualization. So the child develops proficiency in the use of a language, which uses complex structures, with appropriate adjectives, adverbs and conjunctions. The stress is on abstract symbolism. This language is suitable for logical arguments, discussion of relationships, etc. This language–formal language is also called the 'Elaborate Code'.

FORMATIVE ASSESSMENT: The assessment, the purpose of which is primarily to aid the development of the student. The assessment is continuous and there will be regular feed back to enable the pupils to remedy their defects. Formative evaluation, which is continuous and comprehensive will also provide evidence of strength and weakness of the curriculum and the school procedures.

Summative assessment, on the other hand, is provided at the end of the course and is mainly intended for assessment of pupil performance.

See: Summative assessment

FORWARD BRANCHING: The type of Programmed Instruction method by which the learner is required to move forward by several frames if he makes a correct response. It is also called wash-head. He can skip a few frames as he already possesses the knowledge presented in those frames.

See: Wash back.

FRACTAL COMPRESSION: Image compression technique based on fractal theory. It enables very high compression ratios to be achieved for use in electronic books.

FRAME OF REFERENCE: Internal standards against which properties of objects, events, etc. are judged. It is usually the broad contextual system in terms of which object, situation, etc. is judged. The person whose height is just below normal will not be judged as short statured when he is in the midst of a set of very short people. Events, objects, etc. are thus judged in terms of frames of reference which are drawn largely from the contextual-setting.

FRAME: The subject matter or instructions which appears on the monitor or television screen at a time in a CAL program. It is a short piece of the text (i.e. subject content) or text and diagram or diagrams alone. The 'frames' are prepared by the CAL writer after careful analysis of the subject matter. The content is then structured and frames are prepared and arranged in proper sequence. The materials are tried out on selected samples of students before they are finalized.

See: Programmed Instruction, Computer-Assisted-Learning

FRATERNAL TWINS: Twins developed from two separate ova fertilized by two separate spermatozoa. Even though the two individuals are conceived more or less at the same time, as the ova and sperm cells are different, the gene make up of the two zygotes are very likely to be dissimilar. They may be of the same sex or of different sexes. Their "inheritance" may not be identical, but as they are usually brought up together in the same environment by the same parents, a higher degree of correlation is often obtained in their intellectual performance and personality traits, than that between ordinary siblings.

See: Identical twins

FREE FLOATING ANXIETY: General state of anxiety. The individual is constantly under tension but does not know what causes him to be apprehensive. The main symptoms are: irritability, hyper-sensitiveness, irregular breathing, loss of sleep, fatigue, etc.

It is a state of high emotional excitement characterized by heightened blood pressure, sweating, shortness of breath, etc. with a feeling that something terrible is going to happen. The individual remains in a state of intense fear, but he cannot trace the cause of his fear to any object or situation. This is a common symptom of serious neurotic disorders.

See: Anxiety

FREE ASSOCIATION (OF IDEAS): A method of probing the contents of the unconscious, developed by Freud. The psychologist uses this method for diagnosis and for planning psychotherapeutic procedures.

The therapist encourages the client to talk about the dream that he had the previous day (or on any other day). This may be used as a starting point for further talk in an uninhibited manner. Whenever the client hesitates, the therapist encourages him to continue. The underlying principle is that when ideas are allowed to come as freely as they occur in the mind without any conscious inhibitions, the ideas, desires, etc. repressed and remaining in the unconscious may express themselves in the conversation of the client, more often in a disguised form. The free association session will help the psychoanalyst to make a preliminary diagnosis. Free association session has also therapeutic effects.

In the laboratory, the free association test is used for purposes other than clinical. It is used for studying the nature of association of ideas and for assessing the wealth of ideas and creativity possessed by an individual. For this purpose the individual is presented with a set of stimulus words (like Flower, Sky, Blood, etc.) for which he has to speak out all words that comes to his mind for each stimulus word (with or without time limit), and from the quality of the responses conclusions can be drawn about some traits, like creativity, imagination, etc. of the individual.

FREE-RESPONSE TESTS: A test in which the items require the individuals to respond in his own words. In a free-response test, predetermined responses are not provided from which the candidate has to make a selection. Since there is no pre-fixed responses (as in the case of multiple choice items) the possibilities of the way in which responses can be given are many and diverse. The response can be a word, a phrase, a sentence or even a lengthy essay. Free response tests are useful in assessing the ability to give original responses–productive, creative, new, etc. The great disadvantage of these type of items is that interpretation of responses and their scoring becomes very difficult, and so reliability tend to be low. Essay type questions, open end questions i.e. those without given options) tests of creativity, projective tests, etc. are examples of free response tests.

See: Objective test

FREE-RESPONSE QUESTION: Open-ended question. No alternatives are given, from among which the testee has to choose the correct one. The answer has to be supplied (written down) by the pupil. Free-response questions are used to obtain productive and original responses.

FREQUENCY MODULATION: A system of radio communication in which sound signals are transmitted as electromagnetic waves by varying the frequency of a carrier wave.

FREQUENCY: In statistics, the number of times a value or score occurs. It is used in classifying data. When data are arranged in a Frequency distribution, it is the number of cases occurring in a class interval.

Example: The score obtained in a test by 20 students were:

15 17 18 20 12
13 14 14 19 11
15 13 12 10 16
11 17 18 12 14

The scores in frequencies:

Score	Frequency	Score	Frequency
10	1	15	2
11	2	16	1
12	3	17	2
13	2	18	2
14	3	19	1
		20	1

When grouped into a frequency distribution we get:

19 - 21 2
16 - 18 5
13 - 15 7
10 - 12 6

FREQUENCY DISTRIBUTION: Condensed data with the number of times each measurement (frequency) occurs between equal small steps of the scale. When the mass of data (measurements, observations) collected is very large, it has to be first reduced to a convenient size, without jeopardizing the basic characteristics. This is done by constructing a frequency distribution from the data. The steps involved in constructing a frequency distribution are:

1. Finding the largest and smallest measurements in the array. This gives the range.
2. Deciding the number of steps in the distribution. The number of steps depends on the nature and range of scores. Usually the steps range between 8-15.
3. Deciding the class interval of the steps.
4. Writing down the steps in ascending order, usually beginning from the bottom
5. Recording the frequencies with tally mark in each class interval.

Illustration:

Scores obtained by 50 pupils in a test:
36, 70, 61, 46, 41, 17, 39, 7, 40, 67, 71, 63, 33, 19, 72, 69, 45, 27, 18, 59, 43, 17, 68, 44, 54, 35, 25, 63, 46, 64, 60, 49, 33, 59, 12, 29, 18, 47, 24, 38, 60, 52, 71, 66, 37, 12, 16, 62, 59, 37: Total 50

Highest score 72
Lowest score 7
Steps 14
Class Interval 5

Class interval	*Tallies*	*Frequency*
70-74	||||	4
65-69	||||	4
60-64	~~||||~~ ||	7
55-59	|||	4
50-54	|	1

(Contd.)

Class interval	*Tallies*	*Frequency*
45-49	~~||||~~ |	5
40-44	||||	4
35-39	~~||||~~	5
30-34	|||	3
25-29	|||	3
20-24	|	1
15-19	~~||||~~ |	6
10-14	||	2
5-9	|	1

N : 50

The range of the class interval 5-9 is actually from 4.5 to 9.5, size of the class interval (9.5–4.5) : 5; class interval 70-74 ranges from 69.5 to 74.5 and so on.

FREQUENCY LIST (WORD): Word counts: word counts or frequency lists give the number of times each word is used among all those that are used in writing or speaking, (usually in common popular use). The best known pioneering work in the field was that of E.L. Thorndike and Lorge (1944) and that of Michael West (1953). Thorndike's data was based on two word counts and a semantic count from four different samples of various kinds of printed matter in English from among about 4.5 million running words. Part I of the list, 'The Teacher Word Book' (TWB) gives a list of 20,000 words. Michael West's 'A General Service List' (GSL) contains 2000 words which was prepared as a basis for English language teaching. The Dolch 'Basic Sight Vocabulary' is a very popular word list used in the teaching of reading at elementary level in the U.S. (BSV). Sight words are those words whose meaning the reader grasps almost at sight. They are basic because they are essential among the service words that are used in all writing. These 220 words are particularly important in the case of those who learn English as a second language. Another well known word list is that of L.A. Hill.

FREQUENCY, LAW OF: One of the laws of learning: Law of frequency is the same as the law of exercise (Thorndike).

It states that "other things being equal, the more often a response is made to a stimulus, the greater the probability that this response is aroused by the stimulus in future".

See: Thorndike, E.L.

FREUD, SIGMUND: The founder of psychoanalysis and the theory of unconscious. Sigmund Freud was born in 1856 in a town in Czechoslovakia. His parents were Jews. The family moved to Vienna where Freud lived and worked for about eighty years. After early education Freud took up medicine. He was particularly interested in neurology and speech pathology. He discovered the anaesthetic properties of cocaine, for which he was awarded the Nobel Prize. He became a competent neurologist and practitioner. It was then that he came into contact with Joseph Bruer, a well known practitioner, who was using talking cure for treating mental disorders. In 1885 Freud met Charcot who was using hypnosis for studying hysteria. Freud used hypnosis for release of emotions (catharsis) which led to the elimination of symptoms. Later, he developed his classical method of treating functional mental disorders-psychoanalysis. The patient was to lie on a sofa in a relaxed position and touching the forehead he prompted the patient to start talking. Such psychotherapeutic sessions were effective both for diagnosis and therapy. The speaking out sessions helped in the resolution of the unconscious conflicts which resulted in the elimination of the symptoms. It was from the clinical data that accumulated from this therapeutic practice that he formulated his theories of the unconscious, dreams, personality, psychosexual development and the role of unconscious motivation in the normal life of the individual. Free association and dream analysis were mainly used for diagnosis and treatment of functional disorders like phobias, anxieties, conversion symptoms and other neurotic conditions.

The impact of Freud's work on practically every aspect of modern life during the early part of the last century was immense. His works stimulated further research in the working of the abnormal mind–which led to the proliferation of different systems of psychotherapeutic practices. He died in 1939.

See: Psychoanalysis

FROEBEL FRIEDRICH (1782-1852): The German educationist; one of the protagonists of childhood education and originator of 'kindergartens'. Froebel exercised a great influence on progressive education throughout the world. According to him, childhood is not merely a preparation for life; it has its worth by itself and possibilities of creativeness. At this stage the duty of the educator is to lead the child through situations that will help him to relate his experiences, one with the other. The child can realize his own personal unity only in that manner, i.e., by creative self-expressions. His book 'Education by development' emphasises the importance of child-centered education. Play and art are most essential elements in the education of man. Play is an important phase in the spontaneous development of the child. Play combines attention and relaxation, purpose and independence, rule and freedom. Froebel's efforts were particularly concentrated on the education of pre-school children. His name is synonymous with the kindergarten.

See: Pre-school education

FRONTAL CORTEX: The front (anterior) part of the cerebral cortex. It has no sensory or motor functions. It is mainly involved in inhibitory functions. When it becomes overactive, the individual may suffer from depression. In case of severe depression, it is sometimes surgically separated from the brain (frontal leucotomy).

FRONTAL LOBES: Lobes of the cerebral cortex, in the front of the brain. Important association areas of the brain are located in the frontal lobes. Lowered functioning of the frontal association areas often results in the failure in coordinating and synthesizing actions into a pattern and to plan and manage routine activities.

In certain types of chronic anxiety and depression, partial removal of the areas of the frontal lobes (prefrontal lobotomy) or severing of the nerve fibres to and from the frontal lobes (pre-frontal leucotomy) is found to do some good.

See: Cerebral Cortex

FRUSTRATION: It is the mental distress resulting from obstructions and thwarting of activities directed towards the fulfillment of needs considered important. Frustration, when very intense and continued, can lead to neurotic conditions and mental break-down.

When a goal-directed activity, motivated by a strong need, meets with an insurmountable barrier or obstruction, the situation created is said to be frustrating. Individuals are likely to encounter a number of frustrating situations in life. The frustration is resolved by abandoning the goal or by striving for a substitute goal. Setting unrealistic goals (goals beyond one's reach), wrong perception of the situation (i.e., imagining that other people are hostile), etc. make some people feel frustrated frequently.

See: Conflict

FRUSTRATION TOLERANCE: Ability of an individual to stand a frustrating situation without developing neurotic symptoms, like regressive reactions (eg. temper tantrums), depression, etc. Some individuals are able to resist frustration and carry on efficiently and happily without developing maladjusted behavior. Some people, on the other hand, develop symptoms of tension, anxiety and depression, which pulls down their efficiency in mental and physical tasks. People who are more tolerant to frustration are generally less prone to mental break-downs.

FT-FRAME: In CAL, the frame that appears at the end of a program. They contain actual evaluation items. No cues will be supplied in the FT frames and responses to FT frames are not reinforced.

See: Computer-Assisted-Learning

FUGUE: It is a neurotic behaviour characterized by almost complete disorientation of the personality. The individual in fugue is unable even to recall his identify. He may be found aimlessly roaming in places far from his home. He is often unable to remember his name, age, relatives, etc. and of happenings during the period before the fugue state. On recovery he is completely unable to recall all what has happened during the fugue. It is believed that fugue is caused by serious neurotic disorders resulting in a dissociation of the personality.

See: Dissociation Multiple personality

FUNCTIONAL AUTONOMY (IN HABIT): The characteristics of habits to persist even after the motivation for the development of the habit has ceased. Habits are developed as action sequences to satisfy some need that has been aroused (i.e., motivated) and satisfied. But once the habit has been formed, it persists, even though the motivation that led to its development is absent. An example in point is the case of a hunter who continues to hunt even when he has plenty of meat on hand as he needs. The habit of hunting developed because the hunter had to satiate hunger. The habit persists even when the need is absent. A multi-millionaire's greed for further amassing of wealth is also related to this phenomenon.

FUNCTIONAL LITERACY: The literacy that will enable the individual to cope with the literacy requirements of adult life. It is not simply the ability to read and write, but also the ability to protect oneself from exploitation. A functionally literate person knows his rights and responsibilities as a citizen of the country.

FUNCTIONAL DISORDER: A disorder that affects only the functioning, while the organ concerned remaining structurally normal. Functional disorders are not due to pathological conditions of the tissues of the organ. Stammering for example, can be either organic (i.e. originating from organ defects) or functional in origin. Stammering caused by organic reasons can be corrected only by restoring the normal structure of the organs (by medicines or surgery) while stammering due to functional disorder can be eliminated by psychotherapy and speech therapy. Functional stammering is often caused by early painful (emotional shock) experiences related to speech. Many mental symptoms like loss of memory (amnesia) loss of speech (aphasia) loss of feeling of touch in certain parts of the body (anesthesia) loss of motor control of limbs (paralysis), etc. are functional in origin. These symptoms can also occur due to organic causes. Only differential diagnostic procedures can find out whether a symptom is organic or functional in origin. Functional disorders can be successfully treated by psychotherapy.

See: Organic

FUNCTIONALISM: The school of psychology which stressed the importance of processes of mental life as the main concern of psychology. Conscious experience was interpreted in terms of abilities and their uses. It is one of the oldest schools

See: Structural psychology

FURTHER EDUCATION: Education available after regular school life, apart from that provided by Universities.

G

GAGNE'S MODEL OF LEARNING: The six categories of learning postulated by Gagne. In addition to classical conditioning (Signal learnig) and operant conditioning, Gagne lists the following types of learning:

1. Chaining of behaviour learning
2. Verbal association learning
3. Multiple discrimination learning
4. Concept learning
5. Principle or Rule learning and
6. Problem solving

See: Learning

GALTON, SIR FRANCIS: British doctor, Charles Darwin's cousin. Worked extensive on 'heredity' and showed that 'genius' was inherited in his published study of British geniuses in 1869. He introduced statistical methods in psychology and is considered as one of the pioneers of psychometrics. He also developed correlation techniques to explain his findings.

Even though he was not directly involved in any educational work, it was his pioneering work (and also that of Karl Pearson, both English men) that helped to introduce statistical methodology for educational and psychological measurement, testing and research.

GAME: An activity which involves competition and is pleasurable. There are arbitrary rules and constraints for each game and the participants have to play their roles within that framework.

GANDHI, MOHANDAS KARAMCHAND, MAHATMA: Nationalist leader of the Indian independence struggle, the apostle of non-violence. He was born in 1869. Gandhi's activities were not restricted to freedom struggle alone, he was a visionary whose concern was a total revolution, resurgence. So concurrently with his nationalist independence movement he had plans of social, economic and industrial revolutions. The educational reformation had been the last compaign in the series, nevertheless, he considered it pivotal for progress in all other fields.

His view on education was that the British system of education created a new class of people drawn away from the tradition and culture of the country. Education is not the mere training in literacy and literature. Good education should help to draw out and stimulate the spiritual, intellectual and physical faculties. Education should stress creative activity. Teaching and learning should be more concrete and so manual work should have an important place in school's work. The school should be conceived as a minature society and all educational programmes should have social orientation. In a country where the vast majority of people are poor, illiterate and exploited, education should be instrumental in the transformation of the lives of people. His educational ideas were proposed as a challenge to meet this situation. It was in a National Conference of the political leaders, in 1937, at Wardha, that he formally declared his ideas of education. He said that India needed a new type of education and it should be universal. "The ultimate aim of the New Education is not only a balanced and harmonious society" by also a social order in which there are no dividing lines, everybody is assured of a living wage and right to freedom... Literacy is not enough... a useful handicraft also should be taught... it should help to generate progressive self-reliance in all aspects of balanced life, physical, social, moral and cultural. The children while learning, should learn through their work, a part of which should go to maintain the school... learning of a craft is therefore central.

The conference subsequently appointed a committee under the chairmanship of Dr. Zakir Husain to prepare a plan for the implementation of the scheme. (The plan became famous, as the Wardha Scheme of Basic Education) Mahatma Gandhi was assassinated in 1948.

See: Basic Education

GATE FRAME: In programmed instruction, a branching programme that presents a key question, the answer determining route to the next frame.

See: Programmed Instruction

GCE-O AND A LEVEL EXAMINATION: The GCE (General Certificate Examination–U.K). The 'O' level (ordinary) examination which remained as the school leaving examination till 1988 was replaced by GCSE (General Certificate of Secondary Examination). GCE A (Advanced) level is now the school leaving examination for 18 year old students. A pass in 'A' level is the normal entrance qualification to higher education.

GEARY'S TEST: A simple test used to find out whether a given distribution differs from a normal distribution. it is based on the comparison of the average deviation (AD) of the distribution with its standard deviation (SD). It is computed by using the formula :

$$Z = \frac{a - 0.7979}{0.2123} \text{ in which}$$

$$a = \frac{AD}{SD};\ 0.7979 \text{ and } 02123 \text{ are constants}$$

The z is then compared with the standard z values (for two tailed tests) for significance.

This test should be applied only to cases in which the number of cases is larger than 40. If in an obtained distribution, the SD is 12.7 and AD is 10, the value of z will be -0.1258 (Negative sign has no significance and so may be dropped). The value 0.1258 does not reach the level of significance (5% level) and so the distribution does not diverge significantly from normality.

GENERAL DEDUCTIVE MODEL: The class room model used for teaching concepts and generalisations. With regard to the aims it does not differ from general inductive model, the differences are in the process adopted for achieving the goal. In general, there are three basic steps as in every lesson : Planning deductive activities Implementation of general deductive activities and evaluation of the outcomes. Planning is concerned with the identification of goals and preparation of examples. Implementation has four steps : presentation of abstractions (i.e., the generalisation to be learned), clarification of terms (clarification necessary for understanding the characteristics of the concepts), presentation of illustrations (i.e., for illustrating the concept of generalisation. At the fourth stage in implementation the pupils generate their own examples. The outcomes of the learning are tested at the Evaluation stage.

GENERAL INDUCTIVE MODEL: A model of classroom teaching very suited for teaching concepts and generalizations. It uses the inductive approach. General inductive model teaching keeps motivation at a high level and ensures thinking and active pupil involvement. It helps the development of a number of processes and skills, viz., perceptual and observational skills, the ability to form interferences and conclusions etc. These steps involve the three essential ones : Planning, implementation and evaluation. Planning involves the identification of the goals of the lesson and preparing examples (i.e., particular examples from which generalizations are to be drawn). Implementation stage activities includes : Presentation of the example and closure (i.e., drawing the generalization) and providng more examples. At the evaluation stage, outcomes of learning with particular regard to the process and skills are tested.

GENERAL INTELLIGENCE: The 'G' factor of intelligence according to Spearman. It is the all-round intellectual efficiency of the individual. it is judged by the capacity of the person to make successful adjustments in different situations. It is also defined as the ability to draw relationships, solve new problems and to abstract generalizations. General flexibility in coping with different situations in order to make effective adjustments is also an attribute of general intelligence.

Common intelligence tests are usually tests of General intelligence.

As General intelligence is a very strong index of educability, it is often used as a predictor of academic success.

See: Intelligence. Factor Analysis

GENERAL MATHEMATICS: Essentials of mathematics included in the core curriculum of schools. This term is used to include the fundamental operations in mathematics, elements of algebra, geometry and trigonometry and arithmetic. Particular emphasis is on practical applications.

GENERALIZATION: Generalization: Abstracting common elements from particulars and drawing conclusions on that basis.

The particulars (objects, situations, events, etc.) may appear very dissimilar but there may be common elements in all the individual entities. The abstraction of the common characteristics and its definition is what is implied in generlization. Formulation of concepts, hypotheses, theories, etc. uses generalizations of varying degrees of complexity. The word 'cat' is a generalization, a concept derived from observing cats of various breeds. Forming of the concept 'cat' involves only a few steps of observations and abstractions. But the generalization used in 'the theory of evolution' involves innumerable observations and abstractions at complex levels.

Generalization includes the process of observation of particulars for abstracting common elements and the clear formulation of the generalized concept.

GENERALIZATION-STIMULUS: Responding to a stimulus closer in magnitude to the one for which conditioning has been effected. A dog conditioned to salivate at the sound of a tuning fork of a specified frequency may salivate to frequencies closer to the original one. The strength of the response in this case is often found to decrease when the difference is large. A child who has developed a conditioned fear for white rabbits, may show fear reaction at the sight of a cotton roll resembling a rabbit placed at a distance.

See: Concept. Classical Conditioning

GENERATIVE GRAMMAR: According to Noam Chomsky, 'A system of rules that in some explicit and well-defined way assigns structural descriptions of sentences'. It is also explained as the brain programmes that are followed in generating the sentences in a language.

See: Chomsky. Noam

GENETIC METHOD: A method of child study based on observation of the development of children from birth (even from intra-uterine period) to maturity. The same set of children are observed during the period of their development i.e. longitudinally, and developmental data are collected for the entire period. Conclusions are drawn on the basis of the longitudinal data.

GENETIC EPISTEMOLOGY: The principle of development of knowledge according to Piaget. Epistemology is the study of the structure of knowledge. So genetic epistemology means the study of the origin and ways in which knowledge develeps. Piaget postulates that the basic mechanisms which determine the individuals encounters with the environment are 'organisation' and 'adaptation' which he calls 'functional invariants'. The child's intellect is already organised in a primitive way. Organisation and adaptation, though are not varibale, the child's actions are variable. The child will be adopting a number of mental structures according to his level of development. This will lead to the introduction of new material into the existing strucures which consequently are restructured. The development of the system takes place in a heirarchical order. All children are likely (within broad ranges) to pass through similar experience at comparable stages in their lives; so the children at a particular stage are likely to have similar structures than children of different ages.

According to the conclusions based on the investigation conducted on his own children, Piaget postulated that there are four stages in development, viz:

1. Sensory motor stage (0-2 years)
2. Pre-operation stage (2-8 years)
3. Concrete operation stage (7-11 year)
4. Formal operation stage (from 11 year)

See: Piaget, Jean

GENIUS: An individual whose intelligence quotient (I.Q.) is 140 and above. The outstanding qualities of the genius are: high level of adaptability in complex and varying situations, quickness in solving complex and difficult problems and a high level proficiencies in abstracting generalization and drawing conclusions. He has a very high capacity for academic work (academically gifted).

The genius comprises far less than 1% of the total population.
See: Intelligence. Mental Test

GENOTYPE: Genetic characteristics passed on to individuals through genes, such as physical qualities like height, colour of skin and texture of hair and mental qualities like intelligence, aptittudes and psychomotor abilities.

See: Phenotype

GERIATRICS: Study of the diagnosis and treatment of problems and diseases of old people. Like children, old people also have peculiar problems. The process of ageing necessitates the application of special methods of diagnosis, treatment and nursing. So a special branch of medicine has come up recently which deals with this area.

GESSEL'S TEST OF CHILD DEVELOPMENT: The norms of child development established by Gessel and his colleagues. It is one of the early studies on child development. Norms of developmental behaviour of children from birth to 3 years were prepared by examining hundreds of children periodically. The children were observed under controlled conditions. Normal behaviours at particular stages of development according to Gessel's scale (American 1934) are–

Age	Normal behaviour
At 2 weeks	Lying down, lateral head movement
6 weeks	Vertical eye coordination
3 months	Reaching for objects
5 months	Say da—da
9 months	Finger grasp
13 months	Build with 2 blocks
16 months	Turn book pages
21 months	Name 3 objects
25 months	Understand 2 propositions
28 months	Points out missing parts of pictures
35 months	Remember one of 4 pictures

GESELL ARNOLD: Founder of the famous child study centre, 'Gesell's Institute of Child Development' in New Haven, USA. The team under him produced developmental norms for children from birth to age 16. His influence on child rearing practices were remarkable.

GESTALT: A configuration or pattern. The Gestalt psychologists proved that sensory experiences are organized into meaningful 'wholes' and not experienced simply as disparate isolated bits. A song is heard as music and not as bits of notes distributed in time. Three dots put on a paper is perceived as a triangle. The tendency of the brain process in perception is to close the gaps (spatial and temporal) in order to get a balanced meaningful pattern. The sensory input is reorganised by the perceptual processes in order to produce this effect. 'Parts' are not perceived as parts but as components of a 'whole pattern'. The Gestalt theory was, to a large extent, responsible for exploring the perceptual process and in establishing the importance of the perceptual field in problem solving activities.

See: Wertheimer Max

GESTALT PSYCHOLOGY: The school of psychology, the founders of which were Wertheimer, Kohler and Koffka. They demonstrated the inadequacy of analytical approach in the study of behaviour. It was Wetheimer's work on the phi-phenomenon (i.e. apparent motion seen as in the case of still pictures of the motion picture frames projected on the screen) that led to the formulation of the Gestalt theory. With a series of ingeniously conducted experiments, the Gestal tists showed that in perception, bits of sensory experiences are organised into meaningful patterns- 'wholes'. In organizing a perceptual experience, gaps in an organisation are either overlooked or closed so that the situation is perceived as a 'whole'. A rhythm struck is not experienced as bits of unconnected sounds, the constellation Pegasus is not perceived as separate stars but as a pattern. The Gestaltists have shown that problem-solving is not jsut a trial and error process. It is a result of insight. A problem is a situation in which either the component parts are not in the proper order or that there are gaps in it. When the parts can be manipulated and arranged (mentally) in their real realtionship to the whole situation, the gap automatically closes. Solution emerges automatically when the perceptual field is thus restructured in order to get the correct configuration. The contribution of the Gstalt psychologists is largely in the fields of perceptual process and in thinking and problem solivng. The Gestalt School was found around 1912.

See: Wertheimer Max. Insight

GIFTED: Very highly talented in any area of human activity. An individual whose I.Q. is 130 or above is intellectually gifted, one whose performance is very outstanding in school work is academically gifted. Those who can produce original ideas are gifted in creativity. Likewise, there is the musically gifted, artistically gifted, etc. There are also persons gifted in athletics, games and so on. The number of gifted people in any area of performance is usually far less than 1% of the population.

GIFTEDNESS: The term is often used loosely to denote exceptionally high capacity. Potential for excellence in different areas of human endeavour is present in many individuals (like athletics, art histronics, etc.), but usually the term is applied restrictively to 'academic giftedness'. 'Giftedness' in fact, should include capability to develop excellence in any area of human endeavour that society values.

GLUMATIC ACID: A drug believed to have effects on improving intelligence. Its effect on average or above average intelligence is practically insignificant but it is found effective in raising the performance level of dull children by about 10 I.Q. points. It is one of the important amino acids that constitute animal protein.

GOAL: The destination or end result expected. The goal is set depending on the 'level of aspiration' of the individual. One will reach the goal only if his 'level of ability' and effort are commensurate with his level of aspiration.

GRACIA EFFECT: Sometimes, conditioning between Stimulus and response occur even when they are not contiguous (i.e. occuring at the same time or close to in time). Gracia showed that animals learn S_1–0–R_1 (predictive associations) even though S_1–0–R_1 occur hours apart.

See: Conditioned response

GRADE EQUIVALENT: Scores of a standardized achievement test converted into their equivalents in 'grades'. The average performance of children on a standardized achievement test for specific grades are found and from that, grade equivalents are worked out. Suppose on a standardized test in Mathematics score 30 is the mean for standard 5 and 40 for standard 6, 5 is the grade equivalent of score 30 and 6 is the grade equivalent of score 40. The individual's score obtained on a test is thus converted into the equivalent grade. For example, suppose a boy in grade 6, obtains a score of 30 in the test, his grade equivalent is 5. That shows he is retarded by one year. The grade equivalents make raw scores more meaningful.

See: Age equivalent

GRADE REPETITION: The practice of requiring the pupil

who fails in the examinations to repeat the class for an additional year. The practice is based on the assumption that the examination is a valid and sensitive procedure for deciding promotions and that the promoted pupils have attained the necessary proficiency for pursuing study in the higher class and the failed pupils have not attained that proficiency level to benefit from instruction in the higher grade. All those assumptions are questionable and many studies have shown that the failed pupils' real progress during the repeating year is negligible, when the effect of increase in mental age is partialled out. Detention is more an administrative expedient than an educational (remedy). Even though everybody is skeptical about the soundness of the procedure, it still remains to stay, because in a crude way, it reduces the heterogeniety of the class, which is inconvenient for the teachers who mostly depend on using 'mass methods' of teaching. Mass teaching is not suitable for slow-learners and backward children. During the repeating year also the failed children receive only the type of treatment they received the previous year which did only very little good for them.

It is because of these problems that various educational commissions and educationists have recommended the abolition of 'failure' and the introduction of alternative methods for it, particularly at the primary stage. One such alternative is the 'ungraded unit' which permits all pupils to move forward according to the pace of progress of each pupil. Individualistic methods of instruction are used and the children need not be held back for lack of progress. Deficiences will be diagnosed and remedial measure adopted during the regular work. A child may take five years for covering a normal curriculam of four years, but the delay is not due to failure. It is to provide additional time for making up his deficiencies. So there is no waste of time or frustration and shame consequent on failure.

See: Non graded Elementary School

GRADED READERS: Readers prepared in a serial order based on reading difficulty, for the learning of languages. Grading will be on the basis of word difficulty, linguistic content, etc.

GRADES: In organization of schools, the hierarchy of classes grouped for instruction. In evaluation, symbols used to signify pupils performance in schools work.

In evaluation procedures 'grades' are often used to signify

pupil performance. As raw scores as such has only limited meaning, various measures are adopted to derive other more meaningful scores from raw scores. One such derived measurement is the 'grade'. Usually, letters are used to represent grades, like A, B, C, D, E and so on. 'A' refers to a high grade of performance, B average and C low. Assigning class, like class I, class II, class III, etc. in University examinations is also based on this principle.

In schools, children are grouped for instructional purposes, according to age, scholastic performance, etc. Each group of children pursue studies during the year in one class. The children pass on to the next higher unit, on promotion. Each, such relatively permanent organization, is called a grade, class, or standard (and sometimes, a 'Form'). The progress is from class 1 to 2, from 2 to 3, and so on.

GRAMMAR SCHOOL: Now a misnomer. Some schools founded for providing free education for boys in a neighbourhood locality during the fourteenth century in England, was first called Grammar Schools. The stress in those schools, was the learning of Latin grammar. The name was retained even though the schools have changed totally. Even now a small percentage of schools under the local Education Authorities in U.K retain the name.

GRAPHIC RATING SCALE: A measuring technique for the appraisal of behaviour qualities, by observation. It is a refined form of a rating scale.

Graphic rating scale consists of a line on which points are marked with numbers assigned to denote the degree of trait concentration at the points, with short description of the trait level at the points. The trait (quality) is supposed to be spread on a continuum and the markings on the line show the degree of concentration of the trait at the points. The experimenter (rater) observes the particular individual and assign a position for him in the scale, considering the degree of the particular quality possessed by him. Graphic rating scales are used for collecting data on behaviour traits like, emotionality, sociability, self confidence, etc. To render the data more reliable, two or three experimenters observe the individual and make the ratings. Mean value obtained from the pooled ratings will be more dependable. Graphic rating scales are used for guidance, counselling, research, etc.

See: Rating. Rating Scale

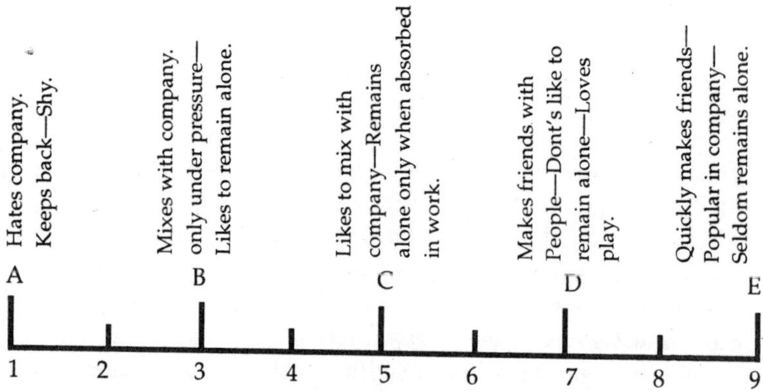

SOCIABILITY

GRAPHIC RATING SCALE

GRAPHIC PLOTTER: The electro-mechanical device which can be used to draw graphs, diagrams, etc. according to the signals supplied by a computer.

GRAPHIC TABLET: A device for interaction with the micro-computer. It is a kind of electronic notepad. The user can draw diagrams and write words on it, which the micro-computer will understand.

GRAPHICACY: It is the ability to think in terms of shapes, colours, etc. visually and spatially and the mastery of certain skills based on it like drawing, writing, etc. The term is parallel to literacy, numeracy and oracy.

GREGARIOUSNESS: The tendency of man and some other organisms to form groups. Gregariousness is one of the instincts of man, according to McDoungall, i.e. man has a basic urge to associate himself with others in social groups and that this tendency is inborn and is not a result of learning.

GRID METHOD: Simplest method of producing an enlarged version of graphic material, whether on chalk-board, marker-board or any other medium. It involves covering the material to be copied with a pattern of square grid lines (or preferably covering it with a transperent sheet on which the grid has been drawn). The grid lines will enable the student to prepare an enlarged copy of the original material. It is a teaching aid (T.A.).

GROUP THERAPY: Psychotherapy (or counselling) undertaken in a group situation. In this method the clients or patients with similar problems, symptoms or needs are brought together in the therapist's room and encouraged to discuss their problems. The therapist often assumes a non-directive role. The group situation facilitates free discussion, which leads to the reduction of anxiety which helps the individuals in resolving their problems. This method is not suitable for severe and chronic problems.

See: Psychotherapy

GROUP TESTS: A test that can be administered to a group of persons at a time. The testees assemble at a place and the administration is done under standardized conditions. General instructions are given orally by the Test Administrator. Specific instructions will be normally provided in the test sheets themselves. All the candidates begin to answer the tests simultaneously. Individual instructions are not given. The great advantage of group tests is that it can be administered to a large group of individuals within a short time. Verbal and nonverbal, paper-pencil tests are most suitable for group testing.

Most of the achievement tests, some of the intelligence, aptitude and personality tests are prepared in the form of group tests. (eg. Otis Alpha Nonverbal Intelligence Test, Eysenck's personality inventory, etc.)

A 'group test' can be administered as an individual test, but an individual test cannot be administered to a group.

See: Test. Individual test

GROUP BEHAVIOUR: Behaviour of man in groups. The group exerts influence (or pressure) on people so that they behave strangely when they are in different types of groups–social organizations, religious organizations, crowds, mobs, etc. Individual needs, attitudes, values, etc. submerge to a great extent in the general pressure exerted by the group and the individual's behaviour in groups often tends to conform with the general trend of the group in the situation.

See: Crowd Mob

GROUPING: Classroom organisation of pupils for instructional purposes. Depending upon the nature of activities children are grouped on the basis of different criteria like age, achievement, interest and friendship. A child can move from one group to another for a second activity.

GROWTH: Increase in size of body tissues, with coordination and integration occurring naturally, which result in better functioning of the organs. Maturation is a result of growth.

See: Development

GROWTH CYCLE: The rate at which growth takes place in different body tissues. Growth does not occur at a regular rate in the different tissues, but it has cycles or periods of different rates. At some stages, the rate will be slower and at other fast, but it takes place in an orderly manner, so that growth at a particular stage can be predicted with reasonable accuracy in the case of any child. In other words, even though each child has its own tempo of progress in growth (slower or faster than normal), the general order of progress is almost the same in all the children. The cyclic characteristics is observable in all aspects of growth of children, viz., body size, height, weight ossification, muscle size, etc.

See: Development

GUIDANCE: The psychological assistance given to an individual facing adjustment problems, by a competent person. Guidance is not simply giving advice to individuals. The purpose of guidance is to help the individual to solve his problem by himself. The guidance expert assists him by non-directive suggestions to explore the problem and find out the realities and devise solutions appropriate to overcome the difficulties. When the person develops the proper self-concept and is able to face realities of the environment his adjustment difficulties will disappear. The duty of the guidance personnel is to enable the individual to achieve it.

The individuals may encounter adjustment problems, practically in every field of his activity. Accordingly, there are different specialized guidance services like vocational guidance, educational guidance–personal guidance, etc.

Guidance services available for resolving adjustment problems is called adjustmental guidance, and guidance services provided along with school career to aid smooth progress of the pupils is called 'developmental guidance'.

See: Counselling. Vocational guidance

H

HABIT: A learned behaviour which become persistent and remain as a characteristic mode of behaviour of the person. Habits, being learned behaviour are formed according to the principles of learning. Habits may be motor or verbal skills, general behaviour in confronting social situations, a way of thinking, etc. In practical life, as the individual is likely to face identical situations in a large number of times (in which the same type of responses are required) the acquisition of habits to tackle such situations is convenient and less effortful. But when new elements are also present in the situation, habitual mode of approach will often prove unsuccessful; but people who show too much rigidity in their habits tend to cling on to habits that do not work, instead of modifying their approach to suit the situation. It is to highlight this defect of habits that Rousseau said that, "the only habit I will teach Emile is the habit of forming no habits".

See: Learning

HABIT HIERARCHY: Complex habit built up by simple habits in graded order. A complex skill (learned response or habit) like swimming involves the integration of simpler elements like hand movements, leg kicking, chest positioning, etc. The complex habit is integrated from simpler habits in a hierarchical order: Complex skills like typing, writing, speaking, etc. are learned in this manner.

HABIT INTERFERENCE: An already acquired habit (learned response) adversely affecting the learning of a new task. When a new response is required for an old stimulus, habit interference occurs. Habit interference is also called Negative transfer.

See: Negative transfer

HALLUCINATIONS: A disordered perception characterized by experiencing (i.e. seeing vision, hearing speech, music, etc.)

without any external stimulation. This is an abnormal symptom seen in psychotic patients. The patients will describe vividly that they see angels, ghosts, etc. or hear songs of people who were dead years ago. The difference between an illusion and a hallucination is that illusion is only a distorted perception, for in the case the illusion stimulus situation is present and it can be identified, whereas in hallucination there is no stimulation that can be identified. Certain drugs like L.S.D., hashish, marijuana also produce hallucinations. Such drugs are called hallucinogens.

See: Psychosis Paranoia

HALLUCINOGEN: Substances or drugs that produce hallucinations (false perceptions like flying through the clouds, hearing people talking who were dead long ago, etc.). The common drugs producing hallucinations are: mescaline, marijuana, Lysergic acid diethelmide (L.S.D).

HALO EFFECT: Favourable or unfavourable impression biasing a judgement. If a judge (rater) has a favourable impression about a person, his rating on him in the traits he has to assess is also likely to be influenced by the impression. So all his ratings will be biased towards one side (favourable). So, to neutralise this bias it is desirable that when rating scales are used, at least two judges make the ratings on the basis of independent observation and then take the pooled judgements. Another method employed to reduce halo-effect is to rate the individuals trait by trait and not all the traits person by person (i.e., if there are ten traits to be assessed for 20 individuals, and the first trait is 'cheerfulness' rate all the candidates for the trait 'cheerfulness' and then proceed to the second trait for all and so on.

The effect of bias in assessment is due to the personal impression created by the student in the mind of the rater in some other aspect. The influence of the bias may be favourable or unfavourable. A well-behaved boy may be given an unduly higher rating by a teacher when he has to rate him for the trait 'leadership'.

See: Rating Rating Scale

HANDOUTS: Notes, sketches, etc. on a specified area designed for lectures. It may be complete sets of notes, or a single sheet containing a sketch or diagram. Any write-up or leaflet on a subject is also called a hand-out.

HARD COPY: Information, typed or printed or reproduced in any other form on paper. Information temporarily displayed on screen or held in store coded on tape is called soft copy. See: Soft copy.

HARD-WARED: The term used to signify the program already incorporated into the structure of a computer. The hard-wared program cannot be varied by the software programs.

HARTOG COMMITTEE REPORT: The Report of the Committee presided over by Sir Philip Hartog in 1929. The Committee studied all aspects of education in British India. The Committee reported that the universities failed to produce the right type of leaders needed for the country... the social atmosphere only partially developed ... there was definite lowering of standards due to indiscriminate admissions... there was competition between universities... that the work in secondary schools was of poor quality... The Committee recommended that teaching and unitary universities were ideal for the country but affiliating universities were a necessity... University degrees should be made a requirement for employment... Universities should do extension work. Regarding secondary education, the Commission, observed that it was dominated by the matriculation examination and the failure rate at the matriculation stage was very high. The important recommendations regarding secondary education were:- ... pupils to be diverted to non-literary pursuits with retention of middle vernacular schools with diversified curriculum and diversion of boys to industrial and commercial careers at the end of the middle stage, the improvement of teacher training and improvement of service conditions of teachers. With regards to Elementary education, the Committee pointed out that wastage and stagnation occurring at the primary stage was of collossal propotions. In British India, for example, out of 100 children enrolled in class I, only 18 reached class V in 5 years. This occurred due to wastage (premature withdrawal of children) and stagnation (retention of children in a class for a period of more than one year). This resulted in relapse into illiteracy of the drop-outs. There was no systematic effort for adult education... poverty, illiteracy and conservatism compelled the parents unwilling to admit children in schools... Social differences also created difficulties in rapid infusion of primary education... The committee further recommended: that there should be better distribution of primary schools according to the needs of the localities. The curriculum should be revised, education in rural areas should be related to the lives of the people; teacher training programme should be expanded (as only 44% of the teachers were trained). Teacher's salary scales should be upgraded. The inspection process should be improved. The government should undertake the responsibility of mass education... the minimum duration of primary education should be 4 years, and there should be a common school system.

See: Sargent Report. Kothari Education Commission Report

HAWTHORNE EFFECT: The improvement found in the performance of people when they feel they are observed. When people form subjects in an experimentation, the change in situation (novelty) and their awareness of the experimental procedures help to improve results. The observed performance therefore will not be completely due to the experimental treatment. To minimise this effect in experiments, often two groups are taken; in the control group a placebo treatment (a treatment which has no effect on the variable studied) will be provided. Hawthorne effect affects equally in both groups and so it will not vitiate the difference between the performance of the two groups.

HECTOGRAPHIC DUPLICATING (BANDA): A simple non-photographic method of producing copies of single sheet materials. It is also known as Spirit Duplicating or Banda. It can be used for producing multicolour copies. The process involves preparation of a master copy (hectograph master) by typing, writing, drawing, etc. on the special sheet of plain glossy paper which is in contact with the dye side of hectograph transfer sheet of required colour. The transfer sheet has a coating of a special aniline dye. Some of the dye is transferred to the underside of the hectographic master where a reversed image is produced. By using different colour master sheets, one after another, multicoloured masters can be produced.

HERBART, JOHN FRIEDRICH (1776-1834): One of the most influential of early educational psychologists. Very early in life he was attracted to teaching ... he even visited Pestalozzi's experimental school to see the practices there. He founded a pedagogic institute, a practising school for teacher training in East

Prussia, Germany. In 1835 he published the 'Outline of Educational Doctrine'.

Herbart held that, experimentation in psychology was impossible. His 'Science of Education' in 1806 and the 'Text Book of Psychology' in 1816–clearly explain his theory and practice of instruction. He postulated that the contents of the mind originated with bits of experience (sensations). These bits of experience combined to form 'ideas' in the mind. Ideas exhibits both attractive and repulsive forces. Ideas which are related do not resist one another; they tend to associate themselves (coalesce) and become 'apperception masses'. It is against the background of previous experience (apperception) that a new idea is assimilated. An idea which cannot be related to an apperception mass will be naturally rejected. So teaching should proceed from the known to the unknown and new ideas should be always related to previously known ideas. Thus he stressed the importance of 'interest' in learning. He formulated four broad stages in instruction.

1. 'Clearness': It means that the pupils should see the issue clearly, which is the pre-requisite for assimilation
2. 'Association', which means connecting the new ideas to the ideas contained in the apperceptive mass of the pupils
3. "System" which means, emphasizing the qualities of the different elements which the newly associated idea consists and relating them to the total context and purpose of the lesson.
4. 'Method' which implies the application of the new idea in new situations.

Herbart said that teaching should be

1. concrete or illustrative,
2. 'continuous',
3. 'elevating' and
4. 'applying the discovered truth to reality'.

His disciples later modified the 'stages' into the famous 'Five Steps' of lesson planning: 'Preparation', Presentation', 'Association' 'Systematization' and 'Application'.

His major contribution was in the field of psychology applied to education. Herbartian psychology, continued to influence schools all over the world during the latter half of the nineteenth century and first decades of the last century. His doctrines of 'apperception' and 'interest' were pivotal concepts in his theory. Ideas of similar kind (related ideas) coalesce in the mind and form 'apperception masses'. New ideas can be received and assimilated readily to the extent to which they have similarities with the apperception masses. Dissimilar ideas will be repelled. All teaching should begin by preparing the mind to arouse the right apperception, before the new experiences are presented. When this happens interest also is aroused.

Herbart postulated five steps (originally it was four) for a lesson:

1. Preparation
2. Presentation
3. Association
4. Systematisation and
5. Application.

For class-room teaching, some teachers even now follow these steps with modifications. One weakness advanced against the Herbartian procedure is that it gives only limited scope for pupil activity.

See: Five Steps

HEREDITY: The biologically transmitted qualities from the parents to the offsprings. The determinants of heredity are the 'genes' contained in the chromosomes of the germ cells from the parents from which the individual develops. The genetic materials that determine the qualities of the individual are contained in the DNA molecules of the genes. It is believed that the limits to one's physical and mental growth are set by the inbuilt 'codes' of the DNA molecules. So also are characteristics, like skin colour, hair distribution, body shape, etc. 'Heredity' sets limits to the maximum development possible for an individual, provided ideal condition for growth are provided. The congenial conditions for full growth will not be available for most individuals. So the growth attained will be less than what is possible under inheritance.

Apart from biological heredity, there is another legacy, which the individual inherits. This is social heredity. Social heredity is all that has been handed over to the individual 'as an inheritance' from the society to which he belongs. This includes, language, customs, manners, collective beliefs, arts and all other aspects of culture. In setting limits to the development of the individual these factors also have an important role. Social heredity can be better considered as a part of the 'environment' to which the individual belongs, possibly the most influential zone of the environment.

See: Environment

HEURISTIC METHOD: The method of teaching science in which the learner is placed in the learning situation that enables him to discover the principles himself. According to this principle the pupil has to explore and discover the scientific facts, principles and laws in the same way as the scientist do. The teachers' role is minimal. The learner has to pose the problems (for which the teacher can help) and then work forward on his own to obtain the solution. As the scientist, he has to design the experiment, conduct it, make observations and recordings and draw the inferences. Though it is not often possible to conduct science classes in this manner, it is important that for all science teaching, the spirit of heurism has to be maintained. 'Discovery methods' lean heavily on the principle of heurism.

See: Discovery method

HIDDEN CURRICULUM: The informal and unobstrusive curriculum, neither drawn-up by anybody nor consciously implemented by anybody, but present in the school system which reflects the values of the society of which it is a part and the interests of the management which runs the school. Social values, character traits (and also social discrimination, political or religious indoctrination), etc. are imparted to the students by the hidden curriculum. It essentially favours the dominant groups.

See: Curriculum

HIERARCHY: Organization characterized by the combination of simple elements built up in a pyramidal manner to form complex units in a graded order. Concepts and habits are built up in this manner. In concept formation, percepts of particulars are formed from simple sensory experiences. Some percepts combine to form more complex percepts. By abstracting the common elements in the precepts, generalizations are made and thus concepts are formed.

Likewise, habits (like cycling, typing) are built up by the combination of simpler skills in a hierarchical manner.

In the cognitive domain of educational objectives, the simplest and most elementary one is the objective 'knowledge' and the most complex is 'evaluation'. The hierarchy is: Knowledge–Comprehension–Application–Analysis, Synthesis–Evaluation.

Need hierarchy: Abraham Maslow held that man's need for need satisfaction never ends. When one need is satisfied, another claims the place at a higher level. This trend is in a hierarchical order. At the bottom there is the physiological needs (need for air, warmth, food, water, elimination, etc.) and at the top 'self actualization needs'. Maslow's hierarchy of needs is given below:

Self actualization (Top)
need (fulfillment of one's potential)
Aesthetic needs (order, symmetry, beauty)
Cognitive needs (to know, explore)
Esteem needs (to achieve, to gain approval and recognition)
Belonging and love needs (to be accepted and belong)
Safety needs (feel secure and safe)
Physiological needs (thirst, hunger, etc.) (Bottom)
See: Drive Need

HIEROGLYPHIC WRITING: The ancient method of writing used in some countries, like Egypt. In this form of writing, pictures were used to represent objects and ideas.

HIGHER ORDER CONDITIONING: Conditioning effected on a new stimulus with the help of a previously conditioned stimulus. In higher order conditioning, stimulus more and more remote to the original conditioned stimuli are conditioned to the original response. In Pavlov's experiment, the dogs used to salivate at the sound of the bell. It was found that the dogs began to sativate even before the sound of the bell, that is, on hearing the footsteps of the assistant who used to carry the food. This is higher order conditioning. More remote the new stimulus, more difficult it is to condition it. Many learnings that takes place by 'association' can be ascribed to higher order conditioning.

See: Classical Conditioning

HIPPOCAMPUS: The area of the brain that is involved in the processing of short-term memory (STM). It is situated in the temporal lobe of each hemisphere.

HISTOGRAM: Display of frequency distribution graphically by means of rectangular bars. It is one of the most useful methods of visual presentation of data grouped in the form of a frequency distribution. The histogram is also called a column diagram. It can quickly reveal the proportional status of the variable in each class interval, as well as the general shape of the distribution.

Example: Scores obtained in a test by a group of pupils, as shown below can be represented graphically in a bar diagram.

Class interval	*Frequencies*
80-84	1
75-79	2
70-74	2
65-69	5
60-64	8
55-59	12
50-54	9
45-49	6
40-44	3
35-39	1
30-34	1

N : 50

In the histogram the frequencies are represented by the area of the respective bars.

HOLDING POWER: The efficiency of a school in terms of the number of children remaining in the school (without droppage) till they complete the specific stage. In a school which has a high holding power, droppage rates, absenteeism, etc. will be low. The schooling programmes in such a school would be necessarily attractive.

Holding power is also used to mean the right of a school (statutory or otherwise) to retain the child there till he completes the specified stage.

HOLISTIC ASSESSMENT: Assessment in terms of 'wholes'. Usually for assessment, the complex human qualities to be measured are broken down into components, and the components are subjected to measurement. This analytical method is generally used in the measurement of human qualities (like intelligence, aptitudes, personality, etc.). Combined data obtained from fractional measurements often fail to give the correct picture of the person. So it is desirable that assessment of the person 'as whole' should be obtained in order to make correct predictions of behaviour. The proponents of this view point, therefore, holds that the personality can be best assessed by studying the person's behaviour as and when he functions in real life situations (in social relations).

See: Test

HOLOPHRASTIC SPEECH: Single-word speech of the child. This generally occurs between the age one and 12 (to 2) years. The child uses a single 'word' for the idea which the adult would express in a sentence. The word; 'doll' when uttered by the child may mean 'give me the doll', 'there is bread there', etc. according to the context.

HOMEOSTASIS: Maintaining equilibrium of the physiological and psychological balance. Body has the natural power to maintain balanced conditions, for its proper functioning, for example, when body temperature is upset, there is inbuilt mechanism in the brain (thermostatic control centre) to restore normalcy. When foreign bacteria invade the body, the body temperature spontaneously rises and this aids in the destruction of them, which results in the restoration of body balance. The urge for the elimination of waste products also leads to the maintenance of balance. When body chemistry is upset the physiological system automatically tries to maintain the balanced state.

When the psychological balance is upset, then also there are mechanisms to restore it. When thwarted from achieving a goal, the individual tries to find a substitute goal. If that is not possible, he will try to blame others for his failure or curse the times. This restores the psychological balance. The tilted balance will be restored somehow by successful or unsuccessful modes of behaviour.

HOOK-AND-LOOP BOARD DISPLAY: A kind of display board working on the principle of the felt board. The board surface, in this case is covered with a material with many tiny loops. The backside of the display materials are covered with special materials which has a large number of lining hooks. When placed against the surface of the board, the hooks engage with the loops and the display materials stick on to it. It can be used for the display of materials relatively heavier.

HORMIC PSYCHOLOGY: The psychological system that stresses the importance of 'purpose' in human behaviour. William McDougall was the proponent of Hormic Psychology or purposive psychology. All behaviour has a goal orientation. McDougall identifies the following characteristics for goal seeking behaviour: it persists, it varies, it terminates and it improves with repetition. How is the individual motivated? The fundamental motives are natural and hereditary, which he called 'instincts'. He listed such eighteen instincts for man. Other motives are derived from instincts and the individuals prompted by these motives, strive for the goal. Bernard, another hormic psychologist, was of the view that it is the social environment that determines the goal and provides the motive force, more than the instincts.

See: Schools of Psychology

HORMONE: The secretion of an endocrine (ductless) gland. Hormones are complex chemical substances and they react quickly with the target organs sensitive to them as the secretions are directly poured into the blood stream. Some of the hormones (like adrenalin) act very rapidly but for a short period only while others provide long lasting signals for controlling slow processes, like growth and reproduction (like sex hormones).

See: Endorcrine glands

HUE: Colour. The subjective visual experience of colour produced by light waves of different wavelengths on the retina.

HUMAN RESOURCE MANAGEMENT: Effective human resources management in education is based on the assumption that the school has a set of well planned and fully integrated strategies for action which lead to optimum performance from the people who are responsible for determining the quality of education offered by the institution. This implies that Human resource management–HRM of school service depends on the capabilities, motivation and accountability of the people who provide it (teachers and supporting staff).

See: Total Quality Management

HUMANITIES: Subjects which deal with man and his life, achievements, history, etc. Humanities are those subjects in which man is central. Subjects like literature, language, art, history, culture, religion, politics, civics, etc. are subjects grouped under humanities. It is one of the two broad areas of curriculum for schools and colleges, the other being science.

HUMANISTIC EDUCATION: The educational view point that developed in Western Europe during the 14-15 centuries, as a sequel of Renaissance. The scientific movement of the times began to influence the thinking of the people. It began to undermine the foundation of monastic and scholastic education that prevailed. Feudalism also started to disintegrate. The humanism that developed as a result of these had two distinct features–individual humanism and social humanism. Individual humanism emphasized freedom of thoughts, opinion and creative expression. So, according to it the aim of education was to provide a liberal education to develop all round personality–development of the body, mind and spirit leading to individual excellence. The aim according to social humanism was general social welfare. It emphasized a rich and full life, not simply of the individual but of the society. So religious instruction was to be integrated with scholastic training. Education should be democratic. They emphasized the study of history, geography and science. The curriculum should be drawn in agreement with the social needs of the people. Discipline was to be mild and teachers to be friendly with the pupils.

HUNTER COMMISSION (REPORT): The report of the commission set up in British India in 1882, to examine the practical implications of 'Woods Despatch'. The main recommendations were that: elementary education should be expanded; entrust all state schools to local boards; a proper system of grant-in-aid should be adopted for the maintenence of the schools. Primary education should be treated as a preparatory course for higher education. Religious instructions should not be carried out in government schools.

See: Wood's Education Despatch

HUSSAIN, DR. ZAKIR: Indian educationalist, known as the chief architect of the Wardha Scheme of Education (Basic

Education). In the first conference of National Education, which met in Wardha in October 1937, Mahatma Gandhi in his speech, broadly outlined his ideas on education–a national system of education suitable for India. The conference then appointed a committee under the chairmanship of Dr. Zakir Hussain the noted educational thinker, to prepare a detailed syllabus on the lines of the resolutions on Basic Education, within a period of two months. Dr. Hussain submitted the report which came to be known as 'Zakir Hussain Report'. The Report contained sections on the 'objectives' and 'principles of Basic Education', 'detailed syllabus', suggestions for 'the training of teachers', 'examination', 'supervision' and 'administration'. This document was also known as the 'Wardha Scheme'. Dr. Zakir Hussain, later became the President of the Republic of India.

See: Basic Education Gandhi Mahatma

HYDROCEPHALY: A condition resulting in mental deficiency characterized by an increased volume of cerebro-spinal fluid in the brain cavity: The head of the child suffering from hydrocephaly will be usually large and heavy.

HYPNOSIS: Induced sleep-like state. It is produced by suggestion. The individual is required to sit or lie in a reclining pose and made to relax and the hypnotist gives the suggestions to go into sleep, in a monotonous voice, repeatedly. Those who are highly suggestible easily go into the hypnotic state. The psychoanalysts, claim that in this semi-sleepy state, the patient finds it more easy to bring to the conscious level, repressed wishes and ideas in less disguised forms, as the 'censor' at this stage is weak. The client may respond to the therapist's questions and follow his directions. Suggestion is also given as a therapeutic process for the elimination of symptoms. The trance-like stage in hypnosis is often followed by sleep. On waking up, the individual scarcely remembers what has happened during the hypnotic session.

See: Psychoanalysis Suggestion

HYPOTHALAMUS: The part of the nervous system, situated below the cerebral hemispheres, close to the pituitary gland. It is the underside of the thalamus. It is about an inch in length. It has neural connections with the cortex, pituitary gland, reticular formation and the autonomic nervous system. Hypothalamus is the internal sense organ that controls homeostasis. It has a decisive role in the expression of emotions and is also connected with the functions involved in metabolism and sleep. This part of the brain is involved in motivation also.

See: Homeostasis Reticular formation

HYPOTHESIS: A tentative proposition formulated to explain a phenomenon, event, situation, etc. Hypothesis originate as a guess from a series of observations made about an event. The hypothesis so proposed, if found consistent in similar situations without exceptions, helps in explaining the phenomenon, but still it is questionable, as it has not been tested and proved valid. On experimental testing and try-out if the hypothesis is proved correct, it is accepted as a conclusion, generalization, principle, etc. To cite a simple common example: daily experience in handling balloons, air pumps, etc. may lead the children to form a general conclusion that volume of air gets reduced when pressed. This will further lead to broader generalizations: the volume of air decreases with pressure or volume of a gas is inversely proportional to the pressure. This is a hypothesis phrased in a testable form (i.e., operational hypothesis). If it is tested experimentally and proved valid the hypothesis assumes the status of a principle or law. In this case it is the well known 'Boyle's law'. A hypothesis that fails to hold its validity on testing, will be discarded.

In educational and psychological experimentation also hypothesis testing is of crucial importance. All valid generalizations have their origin as hypotheses. For example: Various observations led psychologist to hypothesize that practically any stimulus can be substituted in the place of a specific stimulus that produced a particular response. This hypothesis was experimentally verified and found valid, and became famous later as the 'principle of conditioning'. Creative and experienced teachers, likewise, pose many answers (hypothesis) to their difficulties (like 'x' method will help to improve hand-writing or creative expression, etc.) and then put them to trial and accept those that are found valid and defensible.

See: Experiments Null hypothesis

HYPOTHETICO-DEDUCTIVE REASONING: The reasoning that employs postulates or assumptions (unprovable or unproven) as starting points to arrive at useful conclusions. The hypothetico-deductive approach is widely used in geometry. Many theorems in Euclidian geometry are based on postulates and definitions which are accepted as facts that need no proof. By using this method logical deductions can be made from the postulates. Freud's 'Id', 'Ego' and 'Super-ego' are assumptions which cannot be tested or reproduced experimentally. He used these concepts to explain convincingly a variety of abnormal and normal behaviour. Likewise Hull's learning theory (which accepts assumptions like 'drive', 'habit' 'strength', etc.) and Eysenck's 'Introversion-Extroversion theory' are based on deduced propositions arrived at by hypothetico-deductive reasoning. The conclusions are useful, eventhough basic assumptions are not testable.

See: Deductive method

HYSTERIA: A neurotic condition characterized by dissociation and conversion reactions. As hysterical attacks were more common among young girls, it was believed that the disease was caused by the movement of the womb. Hence the name hysteria. Now it is used as a general term for the functional disorders characterized by anxiety, trance-like states, functional anaesthesia (loss of touch), amnesia (loss of memory), partial paralysis, etc. Freud and his associates have thrown much light on the mechanisms of hysteria. The cause is often traced to unconscious motivation (i.e., some repressed forbidden wish appearing in a disguised form). The patients often display a totally different personality during the hysterical state (multiple-personality caused by dissociation of personality). Conversion symptom like functional paralysis is also common. Hypnotic suggestion and other psychotherapeutic steps were employed to eliminate the symptoms. Other systems of treatment like behaviour therapy are also found effective in the treatment of hysteria.

See: Hypnosis Psychoanalysis

I

ICE BREAKER: Activity designed to establish proper rapport with participants, learners, clients, etc. so that they become receptive. Preliminary questions, brief talks, a short paper, etc. can be used for this purpose.

IDEAL: An acronym for a stralegy of problem solving. 'I'-Identification of problem, 'D'-Definition of problem, E-Exploration, A-Acting on strategy and L-Looking for effects.

IDEALISM: The philosophy that postulates that 'reality' is a world of minds, ideas and forms. The human mind creates ideas, mind only is capable of creation, cognition and volition. An Absolute mind creates reality and controls the world. The value of an idea can be determined by the degree to which it corresponds with the body of knowledge already in existence. Human behaviour is purposive and by an exercise of free will individuals strive for values. As idealism stresses the supremacy of mind and ideas, it follows that education should emphasis training of the mind and mastering ideas. Education should cater to the needs of the mind, body and spirit. The importance of freedom and rationality is also to be reckoned with. The students should have the freedom to exercise free-will and should have opportunities for evolving and discovering ideas. Sensory training must be subservient to learning by reason. The schools should strive to perpetuate and enrich the traditional values. Idealism can be traced back to Plato.

See: Philosophy of Education

IDENTICAL TWINS: Monozygotic twins (uniovular twins)—produced from one fertilized ovum. It occurs one in many thousands of conceptions. In this case each chromosome of the fertilized ovum splits into two laterally, and the two move away from each other to the two sides of the fertilized cell and then separate at the middle and develop into separate zygotes. The twins born from such conceptions will be of the same sex and will be almost identical in shape and other physical and mental characteristics as they share almost identical gene combinations. They are therefore supposed to share identical heredity.

As heredity is the same for identical twins, study of such twins reared together and reared apart is used to find out the effect of heredity and environment in the development of the individual.

See: Fraternal twins

ID: The deepest and inaccessible stratum of personality, according to Freud. The Id is almost totally unconscious. It is at this stratum that the primary and primitive urges originate. The strivings of the Id are only concerned with wish-fulfillment, regardless of reality, ethics and morals. As the urges are most basic and are more often related to crude animal drives like food and sex, often the fulfillment of them will be either impossible in reality or morally or ethically atrocious. So many of such wishes are to be repressed to the unconscious. It is these repressions that lead to the development of various neurotic and psychological symptoms, according to the psychoanalysts. In short, basic desires originate in the id and it is totally unconcerned with reality or morality.

See: Ego Super ego

IDENTIFICATION: Accepting persons, things, institutions, ideas, etc. as part of one's self. In 'identification' the individual becomes ego-involved with a person or a thing, so that its problems are felt as his own. Identification with a cause determines one's devotion to and involvement in it.

According to psychoanalytic theory, identification is a defense mechanisms of adjustment. It helps to resolve conflicts and tensions. The person (in threat of failure) identifies with someone powerful and restores security by sharing the success achieved by the person, of course, in fantasy.

See: Ego-involvement Ego defensive

IDEOGRAPHIC APPROACH: The method of studying one individual closely for personality assessment. In contrast to nomothetic approach, which leads to generalizations, this method is suitable only for understanding the qualities of an individual. Observation (and some testing) is the main method of data collection Case studies are prepared and conclusions are drawn.

See: Nomothetic approach

IDIOT: Among mentally defectives, the lowest grade. The individual whose IQ is below 25 is considered an idiot. The mental age of an idiot will be below 4 years, i.e. he will not even possess the mental capacities of a child of 4 years. He will not be able to attend to his own needs, without the help of others.

See: Intelligence

ILLICH, IVAN D.: The educational thinker who advocated the 'deschooling' movement. He was born in Vienna in 1926. In 1956 he was appointed as the Vice-Rector of the University of Puerto Rico (West Indies) where he met Reimer, author of the book, "The school is dead". Illich's views in education are revolutionary. He contends that in the present system of schooling individual freedom is lost, ...the school takes away a large part of the early life and it conditions individuals to predetermined patterns of behaviour. The curriculum is compulsory... the 'hidden curriculum' which is very powerful, helps only to develop devisive tendencies in people by sorting pupils into social groups. Cost of formal system of schooling is very high. So, he advocates 'deschooling'. Societies should provide institutions like libraries, cinemas, etc. for education. Supervision should be by a small band of experts. What is needed is complete access to all sources of learning, by what he calls the 'opportunity web'. There are three ways of encouraging learning;

1. by intellectual leadership of individual teachers working through personal relationship;
2. skill exchange operating through the willingness of craftsmen to share their experience with the learners, and
3. by grouping of young people. His book 'Deschooling Society' appeared in 1971.

See: De-schooling

ILLUSION: A distorted or mistaken perception. In an illusion the experience and the objective situation do not agree. The parallel sides of a straight road appear to converge at a distance. A 20 cm line drawn close to the sides of lines of length 100 cm and 200 cm appears shorter than it actually is. In dim light a thick string may be seen as a snake. The movement seen on a cinematographic screen is an illusion. Muller-Lyer illusion is a well known example of an illusion that can be demonstrated experimentally.

Things are not perceived in isolation. They are seen as a part of the whole field at the time and so distortions are apparent in many in such situations.

See: Perception Gestalt

IMBECILE: Mentally retarded individual whose IQ is between 25-50. The mental age of such individuals will be around that of children between 5-7 years. Special educational treatment is necessary for them in order to make them at least partially independent.

See: Intelligence

IMPLICIT RESPONSE: A response that is not directly observable. Thinking and problem-solving are implicit responses. The occurrence of such responses can be inferred only from evidence (i.e., responses connected with it: eg., answer given to a problem). Also called a 'covert' response.

See: Explicit Overt behaviour

IMPLOSION: The Behaviour therapy technique which requires the patient (client) face the situation he is most frightened of.

See: Flooding

IMPRINTING: A learning that occurs in birds (and possibly in animals and humans) at the earliest stage of development (on the day of hatching). If the mother hen is removed and the hatchlings are given a surrogate mother (a man or a model bird) the infant birds would follow the surrogate mother exactly as it would have followed the real mother. Imprintability of young monkeys has been demonstrated with model mothers made of wirenets. Imprinting will be most effective if the infant gets the surrogate mother immediately after birth, without much time lag, i.e., during the critical period. It was Lorenz who first studied systematically the process of imprinting.

See: Critical period

INCENTIVE: The reward one receives for motivated behaviour; the incentive satisfies a need, for the fulfillment of which the individual acts. In animal experiments the incentives usually provided are food, water, freedom, sex object, etc. Performance of an individual improves when there is a strong motivation, so incentives (as bonus, promotion, positions of honour, etc.) are offered by employers for accelerated production.

See: Reinforcement Rewards

INCIDENCE: Rate of occurrence of an event, situation, etc. within a specified period. Incidence rate of a disease, for example, tells how many persons out of a defined population contracted the disease during the period (may be a month, year, etc.). It may be expressed as a percentage. Incidence rate of droppage gives the percentage of pupils dropped out from a school, district, state, etc. or from a class, age group, etc. during a year, out of the total number of pupils enrolled.

INCIDENTAL LEARNING: Learning that occurs in situations which are not contrived for effecting learning. A child that goes with his parents on a train journey learns a lot about the locomotive, railway stations and other things he saw enroute. A large proportion of one's learning occurs incidentally.

INDEPENDENT VARIABLE: The variable, the effect of which on another variable (dependent variable) the experimenter wants to study. In an experiment to determine the factors that affect the volume of a gas, 'volume' is the dependent variable, because it is dependent on two conditions (variables) viz. 'pressure' and 'temperature'. 'Pressure' and 'temperature' are the independent variables, because these variables can vary independently while volume remains dependent on them. If a teacher wants to try out the effectiveness of a new method of teaching (say M) on the achievement of pupils (say A) then M is the independent variable and A is the dependent variable.

See: Design of Experient, Dependent variable

INDIVIDUAL TESTS: Tests that are administered to only one person at a time. In Individual Test administration, as instructions have to be given orally by the tester to the testee under standardized conditions, only one person can be attended to at a time. Scoring is also done, usually, as the test is in progress. The testing time in the case of individual tests is also much longer than in the case of group tests which are administered to groups of individuals at a time. For individual tests, the testee is not required to make his response on an answer sheet, he responds by manipulating things, speaking out, pointing out with his fingers, etc. The administrator will record the responses. Performance tests, projective tests, etc. are individual tests. When illiterates or handicapped individuals are to be tested, an individual test is the choice. The Binet Test, the first intelligence test developed, was an individual test.

See: Group tests

INDIVIDUAL PSYCHOLOGY: The system of psychology developed by Alfred Adler (1870-1937). Adler was a close disciple of Freud at the beginning. Later, he deviated from Freud and stressed that the prime factor that motivates all behaviour was the individual's striving for superiority and not sexuality as Freud claimed. Behaviour disorders originate from feelings of inferiority or insecurity. The method of encountering the psychological situations arising from a feeling of inferiority differ. Some people may repress the painful experience (unconscious) while others over-compensate. A very common inferiority situation is faced by individuals who have some organ defect (like shortness of stature, lameness, etc.). The threat of inferiority is met by compensation. The person who is hard of hearing will develop extraordinary skills in attention. Girls, from early childhood, experience feelings of inferiority associated with their sex. To compensate, they strive to outshine men in fields which are known to be man's prerogatives. When the feeling of inferiority is extremely painful, it may be repressed and there will be a displacement of the drive to another goal. 'Inferiority complex' is the result. A short statured person's inward aggression may be sublimated by a career in law, preaching, medicine, etc. He will never be aware of the fact that his 'inferiority complex' was the basis of his achievement. The personality of the individual develops as a result of the encounters of the individuals with the social environment. The child begins to develop a 'style of life' in this manner as early from his fifth year. The 'style of life' of the first child, 'the only child', 'the pampered child', 'the neglected child', etc. are liable to be distorted. Alderian treatment of psychotherapy stresses the need for exploring the goals of superiority in order to find the life style of the patients. Recovery is effected when the person is able to view the situation objectively and modify his style of life.

See: Adler Alfred, Depth Psychology

INDIVIDUAL DIFFERENCES: The differences in characteristics of individuals–mental and physical. Qualitatively all individuals of the human race are alike. In physical and mental makeup there is no qualitative difference. In biological functioning also there is no difference, e.g., the physiological processes of digestion is the same in all the members of the human race. All the known aptitudes (like musical, artistic, spatial, etc.) are possessed by all the individuals of the race. So also are the other intellectual and physical capacities. Eventhough all are similar with regard to qualities, every one is different from the other when we consider the degrees in which the qualities are possessed by each individual. Eventhough all people possess hair, its distribution over the body, colour, texture, etc. differ from individual to individual. In body-form, motor coordination, arm strength, visual acuity, colour discrimination, intelligence, aptitudes, etc. every one is quantitatively different from the other. In personality qualities, like sociability, emotionality, cheerfulness, etc. also each individual is different from the other. As the gene make up of each individual is different from all others, everyone has to be unique and without a prototype. (Monozygotic twins have very similar gene combinations and so are very similar). In each quality, the range of difference is wide (e.g., I.Q. may range from 20 points to 200) and it is these differences that make the teacher's task difficult in teaching. The teacher has to deal with a group of children, heterogeneous in every respect. Planning in education has to take cognizance of this problem, if it is to succeed.

INDIVIDUAL TESTS: A test of statements (or series of questions) on a range of behaviour traits, meant for testing personality, interests, attitudes, beliefs, etc. They are usually self-administering devices. The subject has to read through each item and check whether it is characteristic of him or not. Examples:

I do my home work promptly. Yes .... No.

I cannot start conversation with a stranger. Yes..... No.

See: Group tests

INDIVIDUALIZATION: Individual-centred teaching. Organizing teaching programmes to suit individual needs of children. In classroom situation the teacher has to devise learning activities by providing learning aids and materials and he has to give personal guidance in order to enable the pupil to move at his own pace. All good teaching necessarily incorporates the spirit of individualization.

INDUCTION SCHEME: Training courses organised for new recruits or new promotees. In the Education Department, such training programmes are periodically held for newly appointed inspectors, headmasters, etc.

INDUCTIVE METHOD: The method of teaching which rely on the process of thinking that leads to the learning of generalizations and principles (i.e., from particulars to general). The teacher's role in inductive methods of teaching is to help the students to organise the given information to form their own hypothesis. At the next stage, the students, with or without the help of the teacher, try to produce more evidences (instances) which may confirm or disprove the hypothesis. Then, those hypotheses that are proved, are accepted as conclusions. To cite a simple example–children can be led to discover the relationship between the circumference and the diameter of a circle (P) by their own activity, by drawing circles of different diameters, measuring the circumference and diameters, tabulating the results, etc. The children formulate the hypothesis usually in the following order : smaller diameter smaller the circle, increasing the diameter, causes increase in the circumference. The increase appears regular and so must have some constant relationship between the two. The circumference may be a regular multiple of the diameter. This leads them to make more observations and finally to arrive at the relation C/D is almost the same irrespective of the size of the circle.

Inductive methods are particularly applicable in the teaching of broad generalizations and principles. The teachers' interference in the students' thinking should be minimal.

See: Deductive method

INFANT SCHOOL: The term used to denote all types of pre-primary institutions meant for children of the age group 2-5 years.

INFORMAL EDUCATION: Education taking place outside the formal institutions of learning like schools and colleges. The term is often used to denote all types of incidental learning that take place through media whose professed aim is not teaching; like the newspapers, radio, television, cinema, etc. In informal education, there is no teacher-pupil relationship and no rules operate to control it. As the modern man is exposed to a variety of vast stimulations from the media around him, the quantum of knowledge he acquires through informal education may be much greater than that he receives through formal education. Formal education, however, prepares and helps him to capitalize most from the informal stimulations.

The term is also used to denote the parallel arrangement for education of children or adults who cannot attend regular schools. The term 'Non-formal education' is preferred by some to specify this type of educational programmes. Adults who have missed schools, drop-outs (i.e., those who have left schools prematurely), etc. are provided education in some countries in this manner. The programmes, timings, rigours of schedule, etc. of the formal school system are unsuitable for them. So adult schools, schools for drop-outs, etc. are conducted in the non-formal way. The programmes are planned according to the needs of the educands, so also are the scheduling of work hours, working days, etc. Everything is flexible in the nonformal school, of course except the objectives.

See: Non-Formal Education

INFORMATION TECHNOLOGY: "---the Scientific, technological and engineering disciplines and the management techniques used in information handling and processing, their applications, computers and their interaction with men and machines, and associated social, economic and cultural matters", (Unesco definition). Information technology is concerned with the creation, collection, storage, transformation and distribution of information.

In short, it is the revolutionary innovation that has been effected in the collection, preservation and dissemination of information as a result of the convergence of the complex technologies–computing, micro-electronics and telecommunication.

INSIGHT: A method of problem solving. According to the Gestaltists problem-solving results from perceptual reorganization of the field constituting the problem. This principle was demonstrated in the famous joint-stick problem Kohler designed, in which the subjects were chimpanzees. A banana was placed at a distance outside the cage that could not be reached with the hand or with the two given sticks, separately. The animal for some time tried with the hands and the sticks separately and then appeared to have abandoned the trial. [The components in the problem field were the banana, the bars of the cage and the two sticks that could be joined. The real difficulty was the distance.] Later the animal commenced to play with the sticks for some time and then suddenly it inserted one end of the stick to the hole at the end of the other stick. Then it used the combined long stick to move the banana towards the cage. The discovery was sudden. The Gestlatists argued that the mental process involved was really the reorganization of the perceptual field (i.e., reorganizing the components of the field in the proper relationship) which was not based on trial and error. It is a mental operation occurring suddenly, which they called 'insight'. Problem solving occurs by insight.

Good learning in many situations also occurs by insight– i.e., by reorganization of the perceptual field.

See: Gestalt. Learning

INSTINCT: An unlearned complex behaviour appearing at a specific period of development of the individual. Earlier psychologists, including McDougall, argued that a large part of human and animal behaviour was instinctual. Some important instincts are: gregariousness, curiosity, sex, acquisition, aggression, (nest-building and migration in animals, birds), etc.

The Instinct Psychologists argued that as in the case of reflexes, complex connections existed in the nervous system for the instincts. Instincts were necessary for the survival of the organisms. The connections for some of them, like aggression, were present from early stages of life, while 'sex' instinct became active only at a later stage. Motivated behaviour, they argued, has its origin in the instincts.

Evidences from later studies have proved that the instinctual behaviour was to a large extent 'learned'. Changes in body chemistry consequent upon hormonal changes, etc. necessitated the individuals to react in stereotyped ways to restore equilibrium with the environment, in instances like fish migration.

See: McDougall William

INSTITUTIONAL COST: The total cost of establishing and maintaining an educational institution. It has three main components: capital cost, equipment cost and operating cost. Capital Cost is non-recurring and it includes cost of land, buildings, laboratory, library, etc. Equipment cost includes cost of furniture, utensils, laboratory equipment books, etc. Operating costs can be considered under two heads– Non-divisible operating costs and Divisible operating costs. Items under non-divisible operating costs are: salaries of administrative and establishment staff, pension, gratuity, rent, interest, taxes, maintenance cost of buildings, repair cost of equipment, contingent expenditure, etc. Divisible operating cost includes: teacher salary, current expenditure on laboratory, books, periodicals, etc.

INSTITUTIONAL PLANING: In Educational planning, formulating of development plans in terms of resources and targets according to specified time-frame, for a school or an institution.

See: Educational Planning

INSTRUCTION: The procedure adopted for the modification of human behaviour. It is almost synonymous with 'teaching'. 'Instruction' refers to the specific tasks carried out in terms of some predetermined objective in order to effect some desirable changes in the behaviour of the individual. Instruction is concerned with the determination of objectives, the ordering, manipulating and controlling of a sequence of events (learning experiences) to produce the modification of behaviour in the learners. The outcome of the instructional process is measurable and it includes changes in 'knowledge', 'skills' 'interests', 'attitudes' 'values', etc. Such changes in behaviour are necessarily desirable in terms of the aims of education.

'Instruction' is sometimes used in a restrictive sense viz., the training of skills. 'Teaching', on the other hand, has broader meaning, it implies behaviour change at all 'domains' and at all levels of learning.

See: Education Teaching

INSTRUMENT: In evaluation and testing, an improvised aid that can be used to obtain measures of dimensions or an aid that collects evidences of particular behaviours. Tests, questionnaires, inventories, check-list, rating scales, etc. are called instruments.

They are called instruments because they facilitate measurement.
See: Test Tools

INSTRUMENTAL CONDITIONING: Operant conditioning (Skinner). Emitting a particular response is instrumental for producing the situation for satisfying the need. In Skinner-box, the food-deprived rat has to press a lever for releasing a food pellet. The food is the reinforcement for pressing the lever. The reinforced response (bar pressing) is the 'conditioned response'. For getting food, bar pressing is instrumental.
See: Skinner B.F. Operant Conditioning

INSTRUMENTAL ENRICHMENT: The method of training planned to improve children's thinking ability and problem solving skills in class room situation, based on the ideas of Feuerstein.

INTELLIGENCE: A very broad term in cognitive psychology used to signify the overall mental ability. It is described as the innate, alround mental potential. Spearman defined it as the ability to deduce relationships. A host of mental operations are involved in it, like clear perception of the situation, analysis of the situation, finding out the relationships of the elements in the situation, relating the present experience to experiences of similar kind in the past (remembering), closing gaps in the mental structure (problem solving) and verifying the validity of the conclusion. Test constructors prefer to define intelligence as the ability to solve new problems. Spearman on the basis of factor analysis claimed that intelligence has two factors–one general factor (G) and a few specific factors (S). The general factor pervades almost all mental activities, while each specific factor indicates a particular ability in a restricted field. Thurstone's analysis has shown a number of group factors.

Some psychologists are of the view that intelligence is genetically fixed and the influence of environment is only secondary. Others claim that both are equally significant. Hebb postulated that intelligence has two components A and B. 'A' indicates genetic potential and 'B' the actual mental capacities developed as the result of interaction between heredity and environment. A and B are not directly measurable and so, Vernon included intelligence 'C' also; C is what is obtained by a scientific testing procedure which is expected to be an approximate of A and B.

See: Factor, Binet, Alfred, Primary mental abilities, General Intelligence

INTELLIGENCE QUOTIENT (I.Q.): The widely accepted index of mental ability. The concept was developed by Lewis M. Terman and his associates at Stanford University during the revision of the Binet Scale intended for American population. I.Q. is ratio of the mental age to the chronological age, and to avoid the fraction in the result, the obtained value is multiplied by 100. Thus

$$\text{I.Q.} = \frac{\text{Mental age}}{\text{Chronological age}} \times 100$$

'Mental age', as the first index of intelligence, developed by Binet, denotes the mental level attained by the child on the basis of the performance of representative samples of children at different age levels. The tests were grouped for year levels, like that for 5 year olds, 6 year olds, etc. If a child is able to complete the test assigned for the age group 6, irrespective of his age, he has a mental age of 6. If his chronological age is 5, he is accelerated by one year and if 7, he is retarded by one year. So, when using the mental age concept, the chronological age also should have to be specified.

An I.Q. of 100 at any age, signifies the average intelligence for that particular age-group. Thus, if an eleven year old child is able to complete the test standardized for the 11 year old group, his mental age is 11 and his I.Q. is 100

$$(i.e. \frac{11}{11} x 100 = 100)$$

I.Q. above 100 indicates superior intelligence and I.Q. below 100 signifies sub-normal intelligence. The rough categorisation of individuals on the basis of I.Q. is–

I.Q.	*Class*
Above 150	Genius
140 - 150	Brilliance
120 - 140	Bright
110 - 120	Superior
90 - 110	Average (normal)
80 - 90	Dull
70 - 80	Borderline
50 - 70	Moron
20 - 50	Imbecile
Below 20	Idiot

Moron, imbecile and idiot come under the category, 'feeble minded' and special educational procedures have to be provided for them. Idiots are almost ineducable and they often need institutional care. The group comprising bright, brilliant and genius form the 'gifted' who also need special educational procedures (enrichment programmes) to develop their potential to the optimum.

The distribution of I.Q. among a population is supposed to conform roughly to the law of normal distribution. So 'geniuses' and 'idiots' are extremely rare in a population and a large proportion (roughly above 60%) of people have I.Q. between 90-110.

The I.Q. of a person remains almost constant throughout life until deterioration of the cells of cerebral cortex sets in as a result of ageing. But in the case of intellectually active individuals lowering of I.Q. occurs only slowly. At the early ages, as the rate of development of children differs, (although the pattern of development remains similar), there may be some inconsistency in I.Q. in particular cases. A child at age 4 may show a mental age of 5 which indicates an I.Q. of 125, he may at a later stage (say at 14 years) come down to I.Q. 110 or go upto 135. As cerebral development continues upto late adolescence almost around the age of 16 or 17, an individual attains his maximum mental age. So I.Q. for adults are obtained from the ordinary tests by using the formula $\frac{MA}{CA} \times 100$ taking the basal age, i.e., CA as 15 or 16, irrespective of their chronological age. But for special Adult Intelligence Scales developed exclusively for adults, Deviation I.Qs. are used. Interpretation of I.Q. should be done with care and caution as it is largely dependent on the type of test used, the mode of testing (i.e., individual, group, verbal, performance, etc.) testing environment and so on. So the results obtained from two or more tests is always desirable.

See: Intelligence, Binet Alfred, Abilities, Deviation I.Q.

INTEGRATION: The various educational activities organised in ordinary schools to integrate children with special needs i.e. disabled children. This practice is undertaken in response to the suggestion that it is beneficial to de-institutionalize handicapped children and place them in the mainstream.

INTELLIGENCE TEST: Test of mental ability–that is, primarily, the ability to solve new problems. Intelligence tests require the testees to solve a number of new problems for which earlier learning will not be of much help. The tests may use a variety of media like words (verbal tests), diagrams and sketches (non-verbal tests), manipulation of objects (performance tests), etc. The first test of intelligence was published in 1905–by Alfred Binet in France. Subsequently, Intelligence tests have been developed in various countries in the world, including India. Tests are now available for all age-groups and also for individuals with different kinds of disability.

See: Intelligence, Binet, Alfred

INTER-INDIVIDUAL: Differences in qualities existing among individuals. The term 'individual differences' generally means inter-individual difference. Each individual is unique. In any characteristic, like–skin colour, shape of nose, intelligence, individuals differ. This difference between individual and individual is 'inter-individual difference'.

See: Individual differences

INTERACTIVE VIDEO SYSTEM: A very efficient system of mediated instruction. It uses a computer to gain access to video materials stored in a video recorder. It is a fully interactive computer-mediated learning programme. It can be used over a wide variety of individualized and group learning programmes.

INTEREST: The mental condition of an individual to voluntarily seek an activity (or object, person, etc.) or continue in an activity. Activities that give satisfaction and pleasure to the individual are interesting. The degree of attention an individual bestows on an activity gives a rough indication of his interest. Interests are mostly learned response or tendencies. Frequent involvement in an activity (say chess playing) that leads to pleasurable experience, leads to the development of interest in that activity. Those activities that are related to need satisfaction (e.g., working for positions of honour, money, etc.) are also interesting. To motivate a pupil in an activity the teacher has to arouse interest in him for the activity.

Interest inventories are used to measure expressed interests. Vocational interest inventories are widely popular.

See: Attending

INTERNAL EXAMINATION: Examination conducted by the school or college for its own students. Internal examinations are used for the assessment of student's progress within the institution. Its purpose is mainly to decide promotions, find out areas of weakness in the teaching-learning process and for curriculum evaluation. Internal examination is also called 'internal assessment'. Though external examinations are helpful for inter-school comparisons or for selection and screening of candidates for jobs, internal examinations have great significance as a pedagogic process, since the teachers who have taught the students themselves are the examiners. So they are more useful for evaluation of personal growth and the evaluation of learning and teaching at the same time.

See: Examination

INTERPOLATION: Estimating a value between two given values or points (in a graph) when there is a demonstrable trend in the measures obtained in the dimension. Suppose there is an increase of 10% in the population of a country, every 10 year period. The population for the years within this ten year period for which census data were not collected, can be estimated from the available census figures. The average annual increase in population is roughly 1% (10/10), so estimates of population for any intervening year could be calculated. This is interpolation. Interpolation is also employed for preparing norms for tests. If the mean in a scholastic standardized achievement test for the age group 12 is 50, and for 13 is 60 and 14 is 70, by interpolation the mean (norm) for 12 year 6 months can be estimated as 55, norm for 13 years 6 months as 65 and so on.

When a graph is plotted with a known set of values, any other value read from the graph is an interpolated value.

Interpolation (like extrapolation) is useful in estimating measures for which data has not been collected.

See: Extrapolation

INTERVAL SCALE: In the scales of measurement 'interval scale' is the third one (Nominal, Ordinal, Interval and Ratio scales). In interval scales the intervals between two adjacent units are equal. There may be an arbitrary zero, but this zero does not signify a point at which the quality measured is non-existent (zero). Eg., in the measurement of temperature in centigrade scale, 0°C does not mean 'no heat state'. But as the distance in the thermometer from 0°C to 100°C is divided into 100 equal units, the interval, between each successive scale division i.e. 1°C, is equal.

In psychological and educational tests, for which measurement is based on the number of correct responses (like intelligence tests, tests of memory, school marks, etc.) it is assumed for practical convenience, that the intervals between two score points are equal. Zero Score in such tests does not signify absence of the trait/ quality. Such tests belong to the interval scale.

See: Nominal scale, Ordinal scale, Ratio scale

INTERVENING VARIABLE: Variables that interact between an independent variable and a dependent variable.

If a random variable, which can facilitate or inhibit the response in question, is present between a stimulus and the response, it will vitiate the response. Such a variable is an intervening variable. So in an experiment, the intervening variables will have to be identified and controlled in order to ascertain reliably the effect of the independent variable on the dependent variable.

Needs, incentives, attitudes, habits, etc. have been identified as intervening variables in psychological experimentation with human beings.

See: Variable, Design of Experiment

INTRODUCTION FRAME: In a CAL, 'Introduction Frame' or I-Frame is the first frame in a program. The introduction frame introduces a new fact or a piece of information for the first time. There will be several I-frames and they appear at the beginning of every new stage. I-frames thus introduces new materials in the early parts of every program.

See: Computer-Assisted-Learning

INTROJECTION: A psychological defence mechanism. It is a crude form of identification. When the subject cannot counter a threatening situation, he may internalize the aspects of the threatening situation and identify with the agressor. It is the opposite of Projection.

Unconscious interiorization of the qualities of a person held in high esteem, is also referred to as introjection.

See: Ego-defence mechanism Projection

INTROVERSION: Withdrawn, inward looking type of personality according to Jung.

See: Extroversion, Jung, Carl.

INVENTORIES: A device used for the appraisal of characteristics which are typical of the individual, like interests, personality, attitudes, etc. Inventories are usually a collection of statements or questions that are used for finding out the typical response tendencies of the individual, i.e., his characteristic ways of responding in social and personal situations. Therefore, there are no right and wrong responses for inventories. Usually an inventory is in the form of a questionnaire, wherein responses in the form of 'yes' or 'no' are given and the individual is required to check them and mark those that appropriately apply to him. Inventories contain statements relating to a number of situations to which the individual is required to respond.

There are standardized inventories for the appraisal of various aspects of personality, like introversion extroversion, neuroticism, emotional stability, social adjustment, interest, attitudes, values, etc.

Inventories contain a number of items, often above 20. If the inventory contains larger number of items, it is more reliable than one containing a fewer number of items. A few items from an adjustment inventory (A Questionnaire) are given below:

1. Do you find it difficult to start conversation with a stranger?
   Yes – No – Doubtful
2. Do you laugh easily?
   Yes – No – Doubtful
3. Do you daydream a lot? Yes – No – Doubtful
4. Can you stand the sight of blood?
   Yes – No – Doubtful

The items can be also given in the form of statements (e.g., I find it difficult to start conversation with a stranger.
Yes – No – Doubtful).

See: Test, Questionnaire

IPSATIVE ASSESSMENT: The present attainment of an individual compared with his earlier attainment in order to assess individual growth.

ISLAMIC EDUCATION (EARLY): The education that prevailed in Arabia and other Islamic countries around 700-1000 AD. Arabs' quest for knowledge enabled them to develop a culture rapidly and by 10 century AD there came up well-known centres of learning at Baghdad, Bassora, Bukhara and Cairo. In Islamic Spain, there was a widely organized system of schools during this period and the trend soon spread throughout the entire Muslim domains.

The aim of Islamic education was mainly search of knowledge and persuit of natural sciences. It was practical and scientific. Reading was considered a necessity. Education began with religious training, memorizing Koran. It was intended to develop leaders, improve conditions of life, etc. The impact of this education was immense. It led to the improvement of agriculture by irrigation, regulation of legal codes, production of paper, textiles and artillery. Vocational education was stressed and also commercial training. Training in architecture was provided but there was no provision for art education. Education was universal and free. Both boys and girls received elementary education and higher education was open for all. Curriculum in the elementary stages comprised: reading, writing, arithmetic, religion, grammar and science. At higher levels algebra, physics, chemistry, Arabic, medicine and jurisprudence were introduced. At the university level medicine, astronomy, mathematics, agriculture, music, navigation, physics, literature were included. At the elementary stages though repetition and drill formed the main method of learning, at higher stages, laboratory training, travel, etc. were included.

The universities of Cordova, Seville and Salamanca were world famous and the university of Cordova had a library with half a million books.

ISOLATE: A pupil (boy or girl) not chosen by any of the classmates (or group) for play, work or any other activity. Isolates are objectively found out by administering a sociometric test. This test requires each of the children in the group to write down the names (2 or 3 usually) of their classmates in the order of preference, with whom he would like to play, work, or near whom he wishes to sit, etc. If a pupil's name has not been chosen by any one, he is an 'isolate'. An Isolate rarely chooses others also as friends. He prefers to remain lonely. He may be having emotional problems. Prompt guidance (counselling) will often help to resolve his problems.

See: Sociogram, Rejectee, Neglectee

ITEM ANALYSIS: The process of determining the qualities like 'discrimination' and 'difficulty' of the individual items of a test. The primary function of item analysis is to find out: (1) How far an item can discriminate between different levels of ability (discrimination index) (2) What percentage of the testees fail to answer the item correctly (difficulty index of each item) and (3) the effectiveness of the distractors in multiple choice tests. Item analysis is thus the process which leads to the selection of items for the final test which are qualitatively and statistically good. 'Discrimination' means the power of an item to discriminate the differences in the quantity measured at different levels of ability (like low, average, high levels, and so, is an index of validity of the test).

For item analysis, the empirical version of the test is administered on a representative sample (around 500). The answers are scored and piled in ascending order of the total scores. From the pile, top 27½% and bottom 27½% of the papers are taken for item analysis, discarding the middle 45%. (Other fractions also can be taken, like top 1/3 and bottom 1/3 or top 25% and bottom 25%, etc.). The top 27½% is the high achieving group the bottom 27½% is the low achieving group. The following steps are undertaken at the next stage.

1. The number of individuals doing each item correctly in the top and bottom groups are counted and recorded.

2. Number of testees choosing each alternative answer is found out and recorded.

(i) Discrimination index of each item is worked out from the difference in number of correct responses for it from the upper and lower fractions. For example, if the upper and lower piles consisted of 300 papers each and for an item the total number getting correct response in the upper group is 250 and in the lower group 100, a rough value of discrimination will be provided by the equation $D = (U-L)/N$, where D is the discrimination value, U : number of correct responses in the upper fraction and L : number of correct responses in the lower fraction and N : the number of papers in each pile. The discrimination value in this case works out to 0.5. In actual practice more sophisticated formulas are used to compute the discrimination indices from the data. An item which has discriminative value around 0.5 or 50% is statistically the item with the highest discriminative power, but values above this are also chosen as they are useful in testing ability at levels higher than the average. Items with low index of discrimination are rejected as they cannot differentiate between high and low performance. A good discrimination value suggests that the item can identify the criterion and also that it can indicate differences in the ability (i.e., it is valid).

[Note: The upper pile indicates higher level performance and the Lower pile, the lower level. So, for a good item, more persons in the upper pile should choose the correct response than in the lower pile].

(ii) Difficulty level of an item is given by the total number of wrong responses in the upper and lower piles taken together.

It can be found out by using the formula.

$$\frac{(U + L) \times 100}{2N}$$

Difficulty indices help in choosing items at different difficulty levels.

(iii) To find out the quality of distractors (alternatives), the number of times each distractor was selected in the upper and lower piles are computed.

Suppose in a multiple choice item with 4 alternatives (of which one is the correct answer) 600 students choose the answer as follows:

A	B	C	D	E
80	10	350	70	90

Obviously C is the answer. The distractor A, D and E have been selected by a fairly good proportion of candidates missing the correct answer, but B is chosen only by an insignificantly low percentage. This means it cannot attract those who make guesses, and so, is non-functional. So this question item really has only 3 functioning distractors. Therefore distractor B will have to be discarded and a functioning one selected instead.

Item analysis is an essential procedure in standardizing a test.

See: Test, Standardized test

ITEM DIFFICULTY: The percentage of individuals who miss the item (i.e., who either choose the wrong answer or omit the question) in an achievement test (or test of ability). An item is 83% difficult if 83% of the individuals who take the test miss it, i.e., fail to do it correctly. An achievement test usually has items at all difficulty levels from 0 to 100, i.e., from items that all candidates can do correctly to items that nobody could do. In fact, theoretically, an item that nobody can do or that every body can do serves no purpose, and their inclusion in the test is a waste. Still they are included for providing 'floor' and 'headroom' for the test. For an achievement test, items with difficulty indices around 50 are often preferred. In that case the test is administered under strict time limits. A test with a large number of difficult items is usually given without time limit.

See: Test, Ceiling and Floor effects

ITEM BANK: A large stock pool of scientifically prepared test items preserved ready for bonafide users.

J

J-CURVE: A frequency curve plotted from data collected from situations in which all are expected to behave in a particular uniform manner. In such situations (eg. behaviour of drivers in overtaking vehicles) as most of the individuals attempt to observe closely the rules laid down or conform to the norms, the highest frequency will be for total agreement and the least will be for total neglect of the rules. So when the data is represented graphically, the curve will take the shape of J, reversed. Attitudes on social problems expressed publicly often takes a J distribution, while private recordings of the same attitude deviate from the J shape to resemble a bell shape (normal distribution).

JACQUES-DALCROSE, EMILE: The Swiss Professor of music (Harmony). He was born in 1865. He founded the 'Dalcrose method' for infant schools. He stressed the relationship between rhythmic movement and music. Appreciation of music is gained through rhythmic movement. So he recommended 'Eurhythmics'. Eurhythmics should not be regarded merely as dancing and physical exercise. By learning to appreciate rhythm, the children gain a sense of continuity and coordination which is essential for the total development of the human being. It helps to elevate altruistic qualities.

JAMES, WILLIAM: Famous American Psychologist (1842-1916). His classical work 'Principles of Psychology' was published in 1890. He taught at Harvard University for 35 years and his book 'Talks to Teachers and Students' which appeared in 1900 had remarkable influence on generations of teachers all over the world.

His theory of Emotion (James-Lange theory) is well-known.

JAMIA MILLIA ISLAMIA: Famous university established in Aligarh in 1921; later shifted to Delhi in 1925. Its objectives were 'to broaden education of the youth on their own cultural heritage, without rejecting what is true and useful in the culture of others and to build character by providing adequately for the intellectual and emotional needs of the growing mind by replacing the discipline of fear by the development of initiative and responsibility'. Jamia Millia Islamia has under it a residential university, a residential High School, a residential Primary School, The Jamia Education Centre, The Jamia Chemical Industries and Urdu academy. Students from various parts of India are enrolled in the Jamia.

JEFFERSON, THOMAS: The statesman considered as the chief architect of democratic education in the USA. He was not a professional educator. The bill which the introduced in the Virginia Legislature in 1779, outlined a state system of universal education. He proposed districts of 5 or 6 square miles each containing a school. The bill required the masters to be paid by local taxation. There should be a secondary school to serve a few elementary schools and every boy and girl should receive three years of free and compulsory education. Further education (public secondary and higher) should be selective. The bill urged also for the secularization of Schools and Universities.

JESUIT EDUCATION: Educational system developed by the Society of Jesus, founded by St. Ignatius Loyola in 1534. It was organized on a military basis. The most important feature of the system was its organization and methods. The administration of a Jesuit college was in the hands oı a Rector who was considered both as a prefect of studies and a prefect of discipline. The methods recommended for teaching are codified in the document, 'Ratio Studiorum' published in 1599. Both teachers and pupils were subjected to rigorous supervision under the system. Instruction was free. The courses lasting each one year were named, the lower, middle and upper grammar, followed by a course of humanities and a course in rhetoric of 2 years duration. History and geography were taught at this lower levels and mathematics at the advanced level. 'Lecture' and 'explanation' were the methods adopted for the instruction of literary courses. Constant repetition was emphasized at the younger stages. Examinations and tests were regular, corporal punishment was allowed and discipline was very severe. Though the Jesuits were interested in elementary education, the stress was on secondary and college education.

Even before the death of the founder, Jesuit Colleges were established in many Italian towns. Now Jesuit institutions are functioning all over the world.

Christian brothers were the first to grade elementary school pupils into 'classes'. They introduced the phonetic method of teaching. Memorization was encouraged only for things understood.

JESUS CHRIST: Jesus as a great teacher. Jesus Christ represents the personality of the ideal teacher. The methods he used to educate his illiterate, ignorant people were most appropriate; for the efficiency of which history is the proof. Both the 'content and method' were his own, like the didactic method of Socrates. He used parables to explain his points which provided to be most effective with the illiterate audience. Jesus wrote no books, the gospels were compiled from the reports of his disciples. It was love that attracted the people towards him. He was aware of their needs and problems, it was after perfect understanding of the people that he attempted to transmit the truth he believed. He used examples, simile, analogies and parables at the appropriate time to clarify his points. He used concrete examples and referred to familiar phenomena in nature. Occassionally he made references to incidents from the Old Testament, before presenting a new idea, which kept his audience motivated and receptive. In his parables and illustrations he brought in objects and situations that interested them, like sowing, shepherding, fishing, etc. He scolded his disciples for not asking questions and he always encouraged them to talk about their doubts. He used very simple language for explaining complex and abstract ideas. Though he often talked about the kingdom of God, he also taught them the right relationship between man and man and man and God. He taught them about civic responsibilities. He stressed that slavery in any form should not exist. He discouraged the urge for competition and acquisition. He preached only what he practised. There was not a single occasion in which his action diverged from his words. His love, integrity, tolerance, compassion, courage, humility, mercy, diligence and forgiveness were the personal qualities that made him the ideal teacher.

JEWISH EDUCATION (ANCIENT): The Hebrew education that prevailed in the Fertile Crescent extending from the Persian Gulf to the Mediterranean (Palestine) during the pre-

Christian centuries. The people believed in the omnipotent benevolent creator (Jehova) and that the Hebrews were his own chosen people. So moral discipline was very important to them. The family was in control of the early education of children. Father-mother-child relationship was considered very important. All children were given the same type of training and education was democratic. Vocational training was considered essential. The girls were trained by the mother. History of the Hebrew people, Torah and Talmud had to be studied. Education was compulsory for boys in the elementary schools. Domestic training was necessary for girls. The main agency of education was the family. Boys went to the elementary school or the synogue after completing their education at home. Methods used were mainly oral, memorization was emphasized. Discipline was rigorous. Some precepts in the Talmud indicate that they were aware of the principle of interest, individual differences, etc.

JOB SATISFACTION: The contentment the worker receives from the job and the job situation. Job satisfaction is not solely dependent on wages; other factors like work environment, job prospects, worker-management relationship, worker–co-worker relationship, opportunities for self-expression, etc. are also important for it. The worker will be unhappy if the job demands abilities and qualities that he does not possess for effective execution of his duties, even if other conditions are favourable. Vocational guidance before placement will help a long way in ensuring job satisfaction because it helps the individual to choose a career in which he is likely to succeed. Vocational counselling will be required for persons who are dissatisfied in their job. Job dissatisfaction will lead to the development of further complex problems for the worker as well as to the management.

See: Vocational guidance

JOB ANALYSIS: Analysing job activities by observing the worker at work and collecting data on work and work environment, management relations and job prospects in order to obtain the nature of all the component activities of the job. Job analysis includes details on all the requirements for the job, and it indicates what types of physical, psychological and social characteristics are needed for the workers in the job for succeeding in it.

Industrial and vocational psychologists conduct job analyses which are effectively used for selection, screening, guidance and also for modifying job activities for better production.

See: Ergonomics

JOY STICK: Lever used to control a cursor, write on a video display unit or in videogames, etc.

JUNG, CARL GUSTAV: The founder of the psychological school: Analytical Psychology. Jung (1875-1961) was born in Switzerland. His early interests were in philosophy and natural sciences. Later, he pursued medical studies and took a degree in medicine in 1900 and then went to Paris to study psychology. In Zurich, he first came into contact with Bluer who was interested in 'word association' as a method of clinical diagnosis. This acquaintance brought him closer to the significance of 'unconscious motivation' in mental disorders and thus he became interested in Freud's theories. In 1911, he met Freud and they became close friends. The friendship lasted only a short time as he differed with Freud in his views on the sexual nature of 'libido'. For Jung, it was 'psychic energy' that could manifest itself on different levels of intensity in any activity strongly related to power, hunger, sexuality, hatred, religion, etc. Sexuality was only one of its manifestations. So Jung severed his connections with Freud and developed his own theory of personality which he termed 'Analytical Psychology'.

A very prominent contribution of Jung was the theory of 'psychological types' – 'extroversion-introversion'. His concept of the 'unconscious' was also different from that of Freud. His 'unconscious' includes a 'personal unconscious' and a 'collective unconscious'. The unconscious includes the individual factors in the personal unconscious and the dispositions inherited from the person's ancestors in the 'collective-unconscious'. The collective-unconscious is more or less common to all the individuals sharing a culture. The collective unconscious contains both the instincts and their correlates which he calls the 'archetypes'. Archetypal images tend to emerge in dreams.

Jung's therapeutical practices are aimed to help the patient become a 'wholeman'. The hidden potentialities of the patient are to be integrated with the active and dominant aspects of the personality as a result of the treatment.

See: Extroversion, Introversion

JUNIOR SCHOOL: In U.K. School for children between the ages 7 and 11; corresponds to primary school, elementary school, etc. elsewhere.

JUST NOTICEABLE DIFFERENCE: The smallest change between two stimuli that can be identified. For example, in an experiment the subject is blind folded and required to identify the weight closest to 200 gm. from a set of 201, 202, 203, 204, 205, 206 gm., etc. The 200 gm. weight is first placed on the palm of the subject and subsequently other weights one by one in a random order with 200 gm. weight given before every new weight is placed on the palm. If the subject can discriminate only the 205 gm. weight as heavier (and others above it) the 5 gm. increase in 200 gm. is the just noticeable difference (j.n.d.). Just noticeable difference in the other sense modalities like visual, auditory, tactile (touch) also can be measured. This is also called the Differential Threshold.

JUVENILE: In legal sense, an individual who has not become adult. In most countries, a young person below the age of 18 is considered a juvenile. An adolescent is also referred to as a juvenile. As a juvenile is exempt from adult responsibility, there are separate courts and penal codes for young offenders. Most of the convicted juveniles are sent to reformatories or correctional institutions. There are also provisions for rehabilitation of juvenile convicts after the prison terms.

K

KANT, IMMANUEL (1724-1804): Great German Philosopher. He pointed out that man was the only creature that needed education. Education should include nurture, discipline, moral training and instruction. Education should start in infancy and children should be educated for the future and not for the present. During the first stage, discipline should dominate instruction but later the order should be reversed. Physical education should be emphasized. Moral education is necessary for all children. He was an adherent of the 'faculty psychology' school. His ideas are contained in his paper 'On Education'.

See: Formal discipline

KENDAL'S TAU: The coefficient of correlation obtained from data in the form of rank orders of each item (person or variable) in the two variables.

KERALA EDUCATION ACT 1958: One of the early legislations on education promulgated in India after independence. The aim of the Act as laid down in it, was to provide for the better organization and development of educational institutions, providing a varied and comprehensive educational service throughout the state of Kerala. The architect of the Act was Prof. Joseph Mundassery, the noted literary luminary in Malayalam, teacher and politician, who was the Minister of Education in the communist ministry. It was the first communist government in the world to be democratically elected to power.

The Act provided for a number of progressive changes in the education of the state. In summary they are

1. The government to pay the salary of all teachers and non-teaching staff in Aided Schools (i.e., Private Aided) direct through the Headmaster of the school
2. Teachers of aided schools to be appointed by the managers of those schools

3. The conditions of service relating to salary, pension, provident fund, insurance and age of retirement applicable to teachers of government schools to be applied to all teachers of aided schools
4. empowering the government to take over the administration of in aided school if the Manager neglects to perform any duty imposed on him by the Act
5. Local education Authorities to be constituted in a local area for the purpose of associating people with the administration of education
6. State Education Advisory Board to be constituted to advise the government on matters pertaining to educational policy and administration.
7. the government to provide free and compulsory education throughout the state within 10 years from the commencement of the Act and
8. no fee to be charged from pupils in primary schools.

Regarding the appointment of teachers in aided schools, section 11 of the Act laid down that the Public Service Commission should be empowered to select candidates for appointment of teachers in government and aided schools. The teachers in aided schools should be appointed by the Manager, only from among the candidates selected by the Public Service Commission for the district. This clause had to be deleted as there was stiff opposition from a section of people against it. The inclusion of Clause 11, in the Act was one of the main causes for the downfall of the Ministry in 1959.

The Act and the Kerala Education Rules framed under it have helped to streamline, systematize and consolidate all education activities in the state. Security of tenure was assured for all categories of teachers, so that teachers in private schools were to enjoy almost all the rights enjoyed by teachers of government schools.

KEY: The prepared answers for scoring a test. It contains the correct answers or a scheme for interpretation of the responses, prepared for scoring the test. A key is a necessary requirement for an objective test. It is usually in the form of a coded sheet or a stencil with window cut out at the positions of the correct answers. In the case of the coded sheet the key can be placed alongside the answers given in the answer sheet of the tests, for easy reference. The stencil key, is placed over the answer sheet, and as there are openings only at the positions of correct answers in the sheet, all the correct responses made by the candidate will be seen through the windows.

See: Scoring, Scoring Stencil

KEY BOARD TERMINAL: In computers, key board incorporated with the computer terminal, similar to a type-writer.

KILPATRICK, WILLIAM HEARD (1871-1965): American educationist (Teachers College, Columbia University) known as the exponent of the 'Project Method'. He wanted pragmatism to be applied to education. Kilpatrick considered learning essentially a creative and dynamic activity and the teacher's task was only to guide the pupils. For achieving this purpose he recommended the 'projects'. He advocated the importance of community service by children. 'Education for a changing civilization', 'Education and Social Crisis', 'Remaking the curriculum', 'Teacher and Society', 'The Project Method' and 'Foundations of Methods' are his well known works.

See: Project, Project Method

KINESTHESIS: The muscle sense of movement. Kinesthetic sensory receptors are present in the muscles, tendons and joints. We can touch any specified part of the body with the hand, blind-folded. This is possible because the sensations of the position of the arms are received through the kinesthetic receptors and these sensations reach the brain from where appropriate motor impulses go to the effector muscles of the arm. Walking, writing and other voluntary psychomotor skills depend largely on the kinesthetic sense. Impulses from the brain coordinates the action. Kinesthesis means feeling of motion. We can open the door of our room in the dark and move inside freely without bouncing on to any furniture. Kinesthetic memory guides us to do this.

KINESTHETIC PERCEPTION: The perception resulting from the movements of muscles. All muscles of the body contain receptor nerve cells and effector nerve cells which are stimulated when muscles move. So changes occurring in the positions of muscles become conscious experience. This is kinesthetic sensation. Co-ordinated movements of the body are possible because of the control and feed-back provided by these nerve cells.

The movements of the eye and vocal cords in reading produce kinesthetic perceptions associated with the stimuli and likewise movements of eye, hands and arm in writing and drawing produce co-ordinated kinesthetic perceptions. These perceptions lead to the learning of these skills. Our ability to move inside a familiar dark room is dependent on kinesthetic perception.

KNOWLEDGE: The complex abilities of the cognitive domain. The process and products of cognition. The two other domains of abilities relate to the psychomotor domain (physical skills) and affective domain (attitudes, appreciation, values, etc).

See: Taxonomy

KOHLBERG, LAWRENCE: The social psychologist whose theory of moral development is well-known. He was professor of social psychology at the University of Harvard. He was highly critical of the hidden curriculum which functions against the growth of individuality of the learner. The individual should develop to attain the final stage of moral development, the stage at which he is capable of recognizing and accepting abstract ethical values concerning justice, reciprocity and equality of human rights and respect for the dignity of human beings.

See: Moral development

KOTHARI EDUCATION COMMISSION: The Indian Education Commission, 1964-66. The unique feature of this commission was that it has brought within its ambit all aspects of Indian education at all levels, pre-primary, primary, secondary and university. As the commission felt that education is the most powerful instrument of national development, the report was given the sub-title: "Educational and National Development". The Chairman of the Commission was Dr. D.S. Kothari, Chairman of University Grants Commission and the Member Secretary J.P. Naik, the well-known educationist. The commission had eleven members from India, and one each from Japan, France, U.K., U.S.A. and U.S.S.R.

The commission indentified three levels at which it was necessary to bring about the desired educational revolution, viz.

1. Internal transformation of the educational system to relate

it to life, needs and aspirations of the people. To achieve this it was recommended that work-experience should form integral part of general education, vocationalization of secondary education, improvement of professional education and research.

2. Qualitative improvement. It can be ensured by adopting a common school system, making social and national service compulsory and by developing all modern Indian languages.
3. Expansion of educational facilities mainly on the basis of manpower needs and by recognising the importance of equalization of educational opportunities. To realize this goal science education should become an integral part of all school education and scientific research should be developed.

In all educational endeavours, the stress should be on the inculcation of high values – social, moral and spritual. These approaches are necessary to increase productivity, achieve national integration and accelerate modernization.

The main recommendations of the commision were:

Educational structure. 2 or 3 years of pre-school education, 7 or 8 years of primary education, 2 or 3 years of secondary education followed by 2 years of general higher secondary or 1 to 3 years of vocational education. Only 50% need take general stream.

Age of admission in school should be 6+.

There should be two types of schools, 10 years secondary and 12 year higher secondary. Working days should be 234 for schools and 216 for colleges for an year.

The first public examination should be at the end of standard 10.

The three language formula should be followed in all schools– in lower primary school only the mother tongue or regional language; in upper primary, mother tongue and national language; and in secondary school, mother tongue, Hindi and English or a modern foreign language.

Regional imbalance in schooling facilities should be removed and there should be adequate provision for free education and scholarships. Special programmes should be organised to promote the education of girls and weaker sections of society.

Common school system should be enforced. This will help in bringing the different social classes together.

School-complexes should be organized to upgrade the qualities of primary and secondary schools.

Guidance and counselling should become integral part of school education. National service and social service should be made compulsory for all students. This will also help in breaking the isolation existing between schools and society.

Curriculum should be upgraded.

Teacher education programme should be revitalized. For primary teachers with SSLC, it should be for 2 years and for secondary teachers after degree, 1 year.

Text-books and learning materials should be provided to deserving students free of cost and efforts should be made to abolish tuition fees at the school stage.

Quality schools, as pace-setters should be started in selected areas. To raise the economic, social and professional status of teachers, their salary scales should be raised appropriately. Evaluation procedures should be improved. There should be radical reform in the teaching of science and mathematics. State Institutes of Education should be established in all States, to carry on programmes of training, inservice education and research.

National and State Boards of Education should be established— their main duty will be concerned with prescribing and maintaining standards.

See: Sargent Report, Mudaliar Report

KUDER-RICHARDSON FORMULAS: The formulas used for determining the reliability-coefficient of a test. The formula derived by G.F. Kuder and M.W. Richardson is based on the method of rational equivalence. Rational equivalence implies that if a test is reliable (i.e., if the reliability coefficient is high), then the intercorrelations of the items of the test should be high and the correlations of the individual items with the whole test should also be high. Such a test when split into two halves in any manner should be approximately equivalent. The formula which is also known as KR-20 is:

$$r_{11} = \frac{n}{(n-1)} x \frac{\sigma t^2 - \in pq}{\sigma t^2}$$

Where

r_{11} : reliability coefficient of the whole test

n : number of items in the test.

p : proportion of the group answering the items correctly.

q : proportion of the group answering the item incorrectly (1-p).

st^2 : Standard deviation of the test scores.

Approximation formulas to KR-20 are also used.

KR-21 is:

$$r_{11} = \frac{n\sigma t^2 - M(n-M)}{\sigma t^2 (n-1)}$$

in which

r_{11} = reliability of the whole test

n = number of items in the test.

st = SD of the test scores

M = mean of the test scores

See: Reliability

KURTOSIS: 'Peakedness' or 'Flatness' of a frequency distribution as compared with normal distribution. A distribution which is more 'peaked' than the normal is said to be leptokurtic and one which is flatter than the normal is platykurtic. Thc normal curve is mesokurtic (i.e. between leptokurtic and platykurtic).

KYMOGRAPH: An apparatus used to record or measure activities and their variations occurring during known intervals of time (e.g., the number of times a rat runs around, jumps, etc. in a minute). It is usually a rotating drum on which is wrapped a smoked paper. A stylus attached to the activity box records the activities on the smoked paper.

L

LABELLING: The sociological tendency of people to dub an individual as a member of a category and then treat him as such. The boy labelled as a 'bully' rarely gets a fair deal from others. Likewise, a boy labelled 'dull' is often neglected.

Also known as 'Pygmalion effect' and 'self-fulfilling prophecy'.

See: Pygmalion effect

LABORATORY METHOD: The method of teaching that emphasizes direct experience and the use of materials for learning. This method is particularly applicable to the teaching of science and is closely related to the 'heuristic method'. It stipulates that problems should be studied in the laboratory. It includes field experience as well. The stress is on student activity, in posing problems, formulating hypothesis, collecting data, designing experiments, drawing conclusions, and preparing reports.

See: Heuristic method

LADDER OF OPPORTUNITY: In schooling, the selective process of admissions. Opportunities are not equal, but according to merit or other criteria.

LAISSEZ-FAIRE SITUATION: A situation in which the individual can do anything he pleases. Laissez-faire situation can be compared to a disorderly market place. A laissez-faire group is only an aggregate of people in which every one does what he likes, without consideration for discipline and order. Contrasted with the laissez-faire situation are the democratic situation and the authoritarian situation. A laissez-faire leader is one who is totally incapable of exercising any kind of discipline among his followers.

See: Leader.

LANGUAGE DEVELOPMENT: Trend in child's mastery of communication skills. The development of language skills depends on intelligence, health, and the verbal stimulation the child receives.

Girls as a group, learn to talk earlier and at a faster rate in the earlier stages. The general trend of language development are: (1) The first words used by children are monosyllables, and nouns. (2) In sequence, the next series of words they learn are those denoting actions like, give, go, come, etc. (3) From around the age of 1½ years they begin to use adjectives like 'good', 'bad', 'hot', etc. (4) Almost at the same period they begin to use adverbs like here, there, etc. (5) Prepositions and pronouns appear at a later stage. Children can name the colours: red, green and blue by around the age of 4 years. The average size of vocabulary of children who receive adequate linguistic stimulation:

Age	Size of vocabulary
1 year	25 words
2 years	250 words
3 years	850 words
4 years	1600 words
5 years	2100 words

The size of vocabulary differs from culture to culture.

LANGUAGE LABORATORY: Interactive self-learning arrangement for language learning consisting of cubicles, electronic equipments, and a console. There will be a large control table and microphone, for the instructor. Tape recorders are also used. The instructor communicates to the learner through the microphone. Each learner is provided with a cubicle containing all equipment.

LANGUAGE ACQUISITION DEVICE: The inherited capacity of children to extract the rules of language usage from the mass of spoken words the child hears, according to Chomsky. LAD operates when the child is exposed continuously to hear spoken language. It is an automatic system.

See: Chomsky, Noam.

LASER PRINTER: A printer used for preparing single master copies of high quality which can be then used for photocopying or offset lithography. Laser printers usually operate from electronic originals. The original documents are normally transferred to a laser printer directly from a word processor or desk-top publishing system. The advantage is the very high print resolution. Usually the whole page is printed at a time whether it contains texts, illustrations or tables.

LATENT LEARNING: The learning that occurs without external evidence. Much of such learning occurs when the individual is in a learning situation (like television viewing), but outwardly remaining passive. Evidence of the learning appears in late performance.

LATERAL THINKING: Creative thinking or problem solving. The term as used by de Bono is almost synonymous with divergent thinking. In 'lateral thinking' the strategy is not to direct thinking in a straight course, but to try out possibilities which are outside the normal track.

LAW OF PARSIMONY: The well known maxim applied in natural sciences, which states that one should always choose the simplest explanation possible for explaining observed phenomena. In other words it means that, if an event can be interpreted in terms of a lower physical faculty, in no case should one resort to do the same in terms of a higher faculty.

LAWS OF LEARNING: Though various schools of psychology, like Gestalt and Behaviourism have contributed richly to the development of the 'Theories of Learning', it is the name of Thorndike that is associated with 'the Laws of Learning'. Thorndike, on the basis of his extensive studies of 'trial-and-error' learning [with his famous problem box with cats as subjects] formulated five major laws of learning. They are:

Law of effect,
Law of exercise,
Law of readiness,
Law of repetition, and
Law of disuse.

Law of effect, states that, 'When a modifiable connection between a situation and response is made and is accompanied or followed by a satisfying state of affairs, the strength of that connection is increased.

Law of exercise: The chance of a particular response to be elicited by a particular stimulus, is dependent on the number of times both have occurred together. This is also called Law of frequency.

Law of readiness: When a person is ready to respond in a particular manner he derives satisfaction from doing it.

Law of repetition: The occurrence of a Stimulus–Response Connection, produces a tendency for it to occur again.

Law of disuse: The less frequent the occurrence of a Response–Stimulus Combination, the more difficult it will be for it to occur again.

See: Learning, Operant Conditioning, Gestalt, Motivation

LEADER: Member of group who directs its activities. The leader represents the entire group and he has influence over all the members of the group. His role is central with regard to goal setting, planning, formulating group ideologies and in directing and controlling all the activities. Maintenance of group cohesion, order and discipline are also his responsibility. Group morale and the efficiency of group functioning are also dependent on him. There are three styles in which leaders exercise their influence viz. democratic, authoritarian and laissez faire.

See: Democratic, Authoritarian leader, Laissez-faire situation

LEARNING PACKAGE: A unit of independent learning materials used in distance learning. It may be prepared as programmed learning materials, brochures, lesson notes, etc. In preparing a package for a particular target population, the objectives of the lesson, tests to assess student performance, the strategies to be adopted for completing the tasks, the validation of the materials and the method of implementation, etc. are to be considered.

See: Distance learning

LEARNING THEORIES: Learning is the change in behaviour of organisms when they undergo experience. Vast research has been done on the conditions and nature of learning and various theories have been advanced for explaining the phenomena. Among them of particular interest to educators are – Associationism (Herbart), Classical conditioning (Pavlov), Trial and error (Thorndike), Contiguous conditioning (Guthrie) and Operant conditioning (Skinner).

See: Association, Classical Conditioning, Trial and Error, Contiguity, Operant Conditioning

LEARNING: Sustaining changes occurring in behavior as a result of experience (i.e., exposure to stimulation). Behavior may be explicit (like speaking, writing, cycling, singing, etc.) or implicit (like thinking, problem solving, etc.). Learning, therefore, effects changes in both such activities, explicit or implicit. A behavior change that occurs due to other causes is not considered learning (e.g., that due to maturation). Learning in symbolic form, is, S-O-R (S-Stimulus; O-Organism; R-Response) which means connecting a particular stimulus with a specific response in the organism. Learning is, in other words, the process of acquiring responses. The process of learning is blind with regard to the desirability of the response. The same principles of learning apply to the acquisition of both undesirable and desirable responses. An individual can be taught to share anything which he has with others in need of it; to pick one's pocket or commit any atrocious deed to seize another's property.

The potential of the human nervous system, particularly the cerebral cortex is so immense, that any kind of exposure to experience is likely to result in some learning. This is known as the inevitability of learning. Of course, the degree of learning effected is dependent on a number of other factors, both intrinsic and extrinsic (like intelligence, interest, habits, mental stress, etc.).

Earlier psychologists stressed 'the association of ideas' as central to learning and the method they used for studying learning was mainly introspection. But the crucial experiment of Pavlov in 'conditioning' shifted the emphasis to the application of objective methods in studying the process of learning. The contributions of the psychologists like Watson, Hull, Tolman, Thorndike, Skinner, Guthrie, Wertheimer, Kohler Bruner and so on towards the development of the theories of learning have influenced greatly the practice of teaching in schools and colleges.

The desirability of the learning outcome is dependent on the nature of experience as pointed out earlier, that is why Watson declared that he could make an individual a criminal or a priest, out of the same child. It is education that decides the purpose of learning; education is concerned only with the production of desirable behaviour changes.

See: Education, Maturation

LEARNING PHASES: Gagne's division of learning phases. There are eight phases according to Gagne.

1. Motivation: The preparation by arousal of previous knowledge and interest.

2. Apprehending: the presentation of the lesson by the teacher
3. Acquisition: the new ideas first entering short-term memory and then passes on to long-term memory.
4. Retention: the encoded ideas get stored in long-term memory
5. Recall: the process of getting back the learned materials from memory
6. Generalisation: The recall and the application of recalled ideas to new situations involving generalizations – 'transfer of learning'
7. Performance: the learner proves what he has learned and
8. Feedback: enables the pupils to understand how well he has learned.

See: Five Steps

LEVEL OF ASPIRATION: The highest achievement one desires in a particular field. It may be in any field: academic, occupational, social, political, etc. The individual's effort towards achievement is always based on his level of aspiration. Faulty self-concept is often responsible for the fixing of unrealistic levels of aspiration which very often leads to failure and disappointment. One has to fix one's level of aspiration commensurate with abilities, opportunities, etc. in order to succeed.

See: Achievement motive

LIBERAL EDUCATION: Education that is intended to broaden the mind and rid it of narrow views and prejudices. Liberal education discourages early specialization and early vocationalization. The stress is on the study of a wide range of subjects including humanities.

LIBIDO: According to Freud, the 'life energy' which propels all human activities. It is closely associated with 'id' the unconscious stratum from which all desires and urges originate. It is the energy of the life's integrating forces. The energy of the libido is predominantly sexual in nature according to Freud. Sexuality to the Freudians implies any pleasure resulting from tactile stimulation (even the thumb sucking of the infant!) In short, Libido is the life energy that is available for all unconsciously (and consciously) motivated activities.

See: Freud, Sigmund

LIE DETECTOR: Device which helps in recording bodily changes associated with an arousal of emotion.

Emotions produce a large number of bodily reactions like the quickening of heart beat, release of more red blood cells and sugar into the blood stream, constriction or arteries taking blood to the internal organs (visceral) and dilation of arteries to the gross muscles (like the thigh or calf), sweating, reduction of skin conductivity, increase in breathing rate, discharge of more adrenalin into the blood stream, alterations in the electrical waves generated in the brain, etc.

Sometimes, for criminal investigation of the suspect, measurements of some of the above body effects are taken while interrogation. By attaching electrodes to his body, polygraph records which include recordings from electro-encephalogram for measuring brain waves, electrocardiograph for heart activity, manometer for blood pressure, psychogalvanogram for skin conductivity, etc. are taken after exposing him to some aspect of the crime situation. On perception of it, the criminal is likely to be emotionally aroused (in spite of voluntary effort to conceal the evidence). The physiological concomitants of the emotion will be recorded automatically by the polygraph. The data will be indicative but not decisive. So it is not accepted as legal evidence, but is used for criminal investigations.

See: Emotion

LIFE-SPACE: The environment, including the individual, at any moment within which his social and psychological interaction exists. According to the Field Theorists (Kurt Lewin) a person's behavior takes place in his life space. The life space of a researcher working inside the tent in the antarctic is so restrictive, that he is not congnizant of the vast expanse spreading before him. He is psychologically involved within a small 'capsule' of space.

According to the Field theorists the 'Field' is the life space consisting of the person and his psychological environment. (Psychological environment is the environment as perceived by the person at the time and it is related to his needs). The behavior of a person at a time is dependent on the 'forces', in the life space, interacting at that time.

See: Field theory

LIGHT PEN: Pen like device that is used to enter new data or alter existing data by moving across the face of the light sensitive monitor screen of computer.

LIMBIC SYSTEM: The part of the brain involved in the control of motivated behaviour. It is situated around the brain stem, and includes amygdala, hypocampus, part of hypothalamus and the septal area.

LIMEN: The sensory threshold. There are two types of limen– the Absolute limen (AL) and the Differential limen (DL). The absolute limen is signified by the minimum value of a physical stimulus (like light intensity) that will arouse a sensation (sensation of sight). The lowest intensity at which a tonal stimulus (Sound) can be identified as an auditory sensation (Hearing) is the absolute limen (threshold) for auditory stimulus. The minimum amount of stimulus change required to produce a sensation of difference is what is referred to as differential limen (Differential threshold).

See: Differential threshold, Just noticeable difference

LINEAR RELATIONSHIP: The relationship of two variables that can be represented graphically by points on a straight line. Linear relationship of two variables indicates that they are directly related, i.e., that one variable changes with the other in such a regular manner that when their values are plotted on a graph, they approximate a straight line. The relationship between height and weight of children upto a particular stage of development (say up to 12 years) is roughly linear.

See: Curvilinear relationship

LINEAR PROGRAM: In programmed learning and in CAL, the method of sequencing the frame which presents the contents in a straight path which does not deviate to any side. Each frame calls for only one response. The progress is from a lower level of skill to a higher one. Eventhough the progression is straight, without branching, it may contain examples, illustrations, analogies, etc. To prepare the frame, the complex subject matter is first analysed into very small components and then they are arranged in a linear sequence. Before final selection of the frames, they are subjected to actual try-out. It is also called Extrinsic program.

See: Branching program

LINK-FRAME: In CAL, a frame introduced to associate

two parts of understanding of a new item. It is usually in the form of a Test-Frame which can connect together at least two facts. As the lesson progresses and become increasingly complex more and more link-frames may become necessary to link difficult concepts, by association, comparison or contrast.

See: Computer-Assisted-Learning

LITERACY: Ability to read and write (in one's own mother tongue). UNESCO definition is: 'A person is functionally literate when he has acquired the knowledge and skills in reading and writing which enables him to engage effectively in all those activities in which literacy is normally assumed in his culture or group'. Literacy, as generally meant, is characterized by one's ability to use reading and writing effectively in one's day to day activities, like writing personal letters, filling up forms, reading news paper, etc. Five years of primary school education is believed necessary to effect permanent functional literacy.

LOCKE, JOHN: English philosopher (1632-1704). His important works were 'Some thoughts concerning education' and an essay, 'Governing Human Understanding'. According to him the mind of the new born infant is like a blank slate (tabula rasa). After birth, mind fills itself with contents through experience. Experiences are of two kinds; ideas received through sense organs which are representations of the external world and ideas which are formed by mind through reflection. Ideas have two types of qualities – primary qualities and secondary qualities. Primary qualities are objective, irrespective of human experience, like number, motion, space, etc. Secondary qualities are those which are produced in the minds, like colour, taste, smell, etc. In some aspects his views were anti-conservative – he rejected book learning. Reading and writing, he said, were necessary but not the main processes. Locke wanted a method of education capable of stimulating initiative, independent judgement, observation and rational thinking. Language should be taught through conversation and not by rules of grammar. He favoured the study of subjects like science, geography, astronomy, mathematics, history, the Bible, accounting and the vernacular. He recognized the importance of the manual arts and he also included travel as a part of education.

LOGOTHERAPY: The psychotherapeutic procedure developed by Victor Frankl which is based on rational thinking about values; unlike the probing of emotional depths – as in the case of psychoanalysis. It is effective in cases where the person is distressed with situational problems for which he has no easily available philosophical solutions.

See: Psychotherapy

LONG-TERM MEMORY: Information preserved in the mind which has high functional significance. The information stored in Long-term memory is highly organized. Simple facts and concepts are organized into more complex hierarchical models. The information will be available for retrieval (recall).

See: Short-term memory

LONGITUDINAL STUDY: Study of an individual or a group of individuals, continuously over a period of time, in order to discover trends in development. Most of the well-known studies on child development were longitudinal investigations. In child development studies, data on the sample of infants at birth (neonate) are collected on various physical and psychological characteristics and the process of data collection continues throughout the period of infancy, childhood, pre-adolescence, adolescence and early adulthood. The periods of development can be segmented, like, infancy, early childhood, late childhood, adolescence and then longitudinal studies can be also planned for such sub-periods. The method, though time consuming, gives the most useful data on development. In longitudinal studies, observations are made on the behavior of the same sample of individuals throughout the entire period of investigation.

The alternative method of child study often used is the 'cross sectional' method.

See: Cross-sectional method

LURIA, A.R.: Famous Soviet psychologist. He had been the Head of the Department of Neurophysiology and Psychophysiology of the University of Moscow. He has published large number of papers on various topics in psychobiology of which those on the brain processes, language acquisition and thinking are of particular interest to educators. His main works are 'Higher Cortical functions in Man and Traumatic Aphasia'. Many of his researches were based on the data obtained from brain-damaged patients.

M

Mc NAIR REPORT: Report of the Committee constituted for recommending measures of reforms in the methods of recruitment and training of teachers and youth leaders in U.K. The Committee was constituted under the chairmanship of Sir Arnold Mc Nair, in 1944. The main recommendations of the report were: conditions should be improved so that sufficient number of men and women of quality would be attracted to the teaching profession. The salaries of the teachers should be substantially increased. Administration of teacher training may be either through a 'school of education' under each University or by setting up a Central Training Council. The teacher training course should be of three year duration, from 18 years, with three years probation after qualification. There should be specialist teacher in Arts and Crafts, Music, Physical Education and Domestic subjects, etc. The report was welcomed as a 'teacher charter'. The Area Training organisations were formed on the basis of this Act, so also was the National Advisory Council for training and supply of teachers.

MACAULAY'S MINUTES: The document on Indian Educational Policy prepared by T.B. Macaulay and accepted by the Viceroy, William Bentinck. The minute was the basic document that guided the educational efforts in British India, almost till the attainment of freedom. The important recommendations in the minutes were:

1. The medium of instruction in Indian Schools should be English
2. Government should codify Hindu and Muslim laws in English
3. All funds appropriated for education should be best utilized for English education alone
4. The colleges or schools of native learning need not be abolished forthwith

5. No portion of the funds should be spent on printing of oriental works, and
6. Funds are to be utilized for imparting to the native populations a knowledge of English literature and science through the medium of English language. The minutes was dated 2.2.1835.

MACHINE SCORING: Scoring answer sheets by means of electronic test-scoring machines or by other mechanical means. The commonest type of scoring machines requires the individuals to mark the answers by darkening the space provided against each alternative, in the answer sheets, with a special pencil whose lead is an electric conductor. The marked answer sheets are fed into the machine which has been previously keyed (set) for scoring the test. The machine electronically scores the answer sheet and counts the number of conducting points at the position of correct answers and prints the total number on the test sheet. This gives the total score obtained by the individual.

Scoring will be perfectly objective if the machine has been properly set for the test and the machine works in good order. Hundreds of papers can be scored in an hour. Many types of electronic test-scoring machines are available, which functions on different principles.

MADRASSAH: Institution of higher learning prevalent in India during the Muslim period. Only selected children were admitted in the madrassahs. The candidates were prepared for the professions like teaching, judiciary, medicine, etc. Girls were not admitted in the madrassahs.

MAGNETIC BOARDS: Display (and writing) boards which make use of magnetic parts that enables the display items to be fixed to the surface of the board. There are two main types: Magnetic chalk boards and Magnetic marker boards. Magnetic chalk boards consist of sheets of ferromagnetic material with specially painted surface which can be used as an ordinary blackboard, for writing or drawing. Display items made (prepared) with a back layer of magnetic material can be moved about on its surface. Magnetic marker board is made of a thin sheet of ferromagnetic material like mild-steel mounted on thin wooden plank. The display materials can be made from special magnetic rubber, by cutting out the required shapes. Non magnetic materials can be also used in which case they should be backed with magnetic rubber backs.

MAKARENKO, ANTON SEMYONOVICH: Famous Soviet educator. He was born in a working class family in 1888. He started his career as a teacher in 1905 in Kryukova. From the very beginning he was keen on establishing close contact between the school and community. In 1911 he took up a Primary School in Dolinskoya station where he introduced various after-school activities. After the great October Revolution, he was put in charge of a school with 1000 pupils. To unite the pupils into a close-knit Collective, he organized their working by breaking them into teams. In 1920, the Department of Education authorised him to organize a colony for homeless children and Juvenile delinquents. He developed the colony–Gorky colony–into a remarkable educational establishment. His experience have taught him that the most powerful educative force was socially useful productive labour. In the beginning, productive labour of the students was limited to farming and manual training. General development and physical, political and aesthetic developments were also stressed. Work was the basis of the whole educative process and the centre of all activities. In 1927, he founded a commune on the outskirts of Kharkov and this commune soon developed into a model collective. Here also the emphasis was on socially useful productive labour. The commune gradually became self-supporting and by saving money it was able to build two factories of its own. Along with the development of industrial skills, general education was also provided, i.e. polytechnic education.

In the commune, the students had to work 5 hours a day and study 4 hours at school. The school work included physical and cultural education, drama, painting, dancing, gymnastics and literary classes. Annual field trips were also provided when the students met the best workers of the country. From 1937 Makarenko spent his time in Moscow, writing. He died in 1939.

MALADJUSTMENT: Behaviour of the individual that does not result in harmonizing the individual with the demands of the environment; or inappropriate or wrong behaviours displayed in a situation. The maladjusted behaviour often creates more problems for the individual. It is also likely to develop anxiety in the individuals. A well adjusted child mixes with his class-mates, converses with them, shares experiences with them, enjoys with them. If a child consistently keeps aloof from his group and sits all alone, moody, it can be assumed that he has developed withdrawal behaviour. This is a maladjusted behaviour. This behaviour leads to lowering of his efficiency and to the development of anxiety in him. Another boy, when confronting a situation attacks the adversary verbally or physically for no apparent reason. This is not the appropriate behaviour required of in such a situation. This actually leads to further complications. Such inappropriate behaviour tendencies, if become permanent, may lead to serious adjustment problems. Most of the maladjusted individuals have emotional problems. Maladjustments range from minor behaviour disorders like lying, bullying, stealing to criminal and antisocial tendencies (like house-breaking, killing, etc.)

See: Adjustment

MAN TO MAN RATING SCALE: Rating of a person made on a profile of a man with whose description of characteristics he resembles. The experimenter will be provided with a number of verbal descriptions of people, with different personality characteristics. The persons who are to be rated, will be compared with these descriptions of personality and the experimenter will then assign one which resembles him most.

See: Rating Scale

MAN-A COURSE OF STUDY (MACOS): The controversial curriculum project carried out in USA by Peter Dow based on the work of Jerome S. Bruner. It was developed as a social studies teaching kit. The kit comprises course materials, films, etc.

MANAGEMENT BY OBJECTIVES (MBO): A management approach that stresses (1) performance targets initiated periodically by the employee (2) mutual agreement on a set of goals by both employees and employers, and (3) periodic review of the achievements against the goals, by the employee and the management.

MANAGEMENT STRUCTURE: All the organizational arrangements. It comprises the roles, governance, finances, policies and the working conditions of the organization.

MARGINAL MAN: A person who is forced to live in two societies that have antagonistic cultures. Marginal man's position is ambiguous because he has to live in two cultural groups that have contrasting values. He has to identify with both the groups, but neither group fully accepts him. An example of marginal men is constituted by the immigrant population in a country.

MARKER BOARD: White board used in class room in the place of conventional blackboards. It is made of large sheets of white or light coloured plastic material. The surface texture of the board is made suitable for writing or drawing with felt pens, markers, crayons, etc. of any colour.

MASLOW, A.H.: Famous American psychologist, whose contribution towards motivation theory has received wide recognition. He postulated the heirarchical structure of human needs–physiological needs (air, food, warmth, safety) psychological and social needs of love, recognition, belonging, self-esteem and self-actualization. His published works are: 'Motivation and Personality', and 'Towards a Psychology of Being'.

See: Needs, Drive

MASS MEDIA: Modern media of communication–like newspapers, radio, television, etc.–which have an extensive coverage at a time. The application of mass-media on nonformal education, continuing education, distance education, complementary education, etc. has assumed gigantic proportions during the past few decades. The advantage of mass-media is that it can reach a large clientele at a time and can utilize multisensory materials (visual, auditory, etc.) as needed for making the message more realistic. Satellite transmission and computerization have made it possible to transmit incredibly large amounts of information across the globe in split seconds. All nations, both developed and developing, utilize mass media for a variety of educational purposes.

MASSED LEARNING: The method of learning units of study continuously without rest periods. Massed learning is contrasted with distributed practice in which meaningful subunits are learned with rest periods in between the learning sessions. A combination of distributed and massed learning is found to be more useful than either singly, particularly for learning things by heart.

See: Distributed practice

MASTERY LEARNING: Even though pupils differ in the rate at which they learn (speed) and in their style of learning, mastery of any kind of knowledge is possible for any learner, if he is given appropriate learning experience and adequate time. (according to Benjamin. S. Bloom).

See: Bloom B.S.

MATCHING ITEMS: A type of objective type test item which requires the candidate find out pairs that are related. Two columns of associated items in a jumbled order are given. The testee is required to pair the items on the basis of their relationships. One of the columns should contain 2 or 3 times in excess. This is necessary to reduce the effect of guessing.

Matching type questions are usually used to test knowledge of relationships like events and dates in history, countries and capitals, books and authors, etc.

See: Objective test

MATURATION: Muscular and neural development occurring at particular stages of growth of the organism which enables it to perform activities spontaneously (i.e., without learning). A particular level of tissue development is necessary for the organism to use those tissues effectively in a coordinated manner. The child at birth is not able to lift its head. Two months after birth it could do it because the muscular tissue around the neck has grown to sufficient size and strength by that time and the neural connections controlling the neck muscles have been established. The ability of the child to perform certain functions, likewise, appear sequentially at different times, like: ability to stand erect, walk, climb a staircase, take small objects with the fingers, articulate speech sounds, etc. Unless the child has reached the particular stage of maturation for a task, no amount of teaching will help in effecting appreciable learning of that task (eg., 5 month old baby cannot be taught to walk). Behaviour resulting from maturation is different from that is consequent on learning. The difference is that, in the former case, the behaviour appears spontaneously, whereas in the latter behaviour results from exposure to experience.

See: Growth Cycle, Development, Learning Readiness

MAZE: A device used for studying learning in which there are a number of path-ways with wrong turns and blind alleys but with an exit to the goal. Mazes are used to study animal behaviour. Very simple mazes like the T-maze are used for studying the behaviour of simple organisms like earthworms, but complex mazes are used for experimentation using higher level animals (rats, cats, etc.). Finger mazes are used as an item in the performance tests of intelligence.

See: Performance tests

MEASUREMENT ERROR: Error in observed values due to chance factors (not due to mistakes made in measuring). In educational and psychological measurements it is not possible to keep out the influence of chance factors on the values obtained by measurement. The score obtained on the same test by an individual varies from administration to administration. Various factors that occur by chance, other than his ability, influence his performance each time. Some factors like fatigue, disease, lack of motivation, poor ventilation, etc. have the tendency to pull down the score he would have obtained (true score) if all conditions were ideal. Guessing, on the other hand is likely to boost the results. Measurement error, theoretically, is the difference between the observed value and the true value. Though the true value cannot be obtained, it is possible to estimate it from an estimate of the measurement error. As the true value of measurement error also is not possible to get, only an estimate of it can be obtained. By statistical procedures an estimate of measurement error can be obtained. This error is called standard error of measurement: ST_x. It is obtained by using the formula

$$ST_x = S_t \sqrt{(1 - r_{tt})}$$

where, St_x is the standard error of measurement of obtained score

St = standard deviation of the scores

r_{tt} = reliability coefficient of the test

See: Standard error

McDOUGALL, WILLIAM: British psychologist (1871-1938). A versatile scholar whose contributions to various branches of psychology are notable, but his name is particularly associated with 'the theory of instincts', (which had been rejected by many scholars later), purposivism in psychology and group dynamics. His main works are: 'Text-Book of Social Psychology', 'The Group mind' and 'Outline of Abnormal Psychology'.

See: Instinct

MEASUREMENT: The process of quantification. Any quality of a thing, event, etc. exists in varying amounts and these amounts can be represented by number, symbols, etc. 'Measurement is defined as the assignment of numbers to objects and events according to logically acceptable rules.' The purpose of measurement is to find the exact position of a dimension in a scale. Measurement is basic to all scientific studies. Qualities, properties, etc. cannot be fully understood without an understanding of the relative position or status of that quality in a continuum that begins from a point of reference (usually zero) from which it increases. For a scientific study of various phenomena in education, psychology and other social sciences also exact measurement is necessary.

The term 'Measurement' in education is reserved to denote the quantification of a characteristic (i.e. assign position in a scale) or a set of characteristics. Evaluation, on the other hand, is collection of data by measurement (or otherwise) against the learning outcomes (objectives) expected by the curriculum.

See: Appraisal, Evaluation

MEDIAN: Measure of central tendency, above and below which 50% of the cases occur. The median is the score value that cuts the distribution into halves. In other words, it is the midpoint in a set of scores when they are arranged in ascending order.

When there are extreme cases in the distribution (when the distribution deviates too much from a normal distribution) median is more useful than mean to understand the central tendency of the distribution.

The formula for computing median (Mdn) from a frequency distribution is:

$$Mdn = l + \left(\frac{\frac{N}{2} - F}{fm} \right) i$$

When l = lower limit of class interval in which the median lies

N = Number of cases

F = Sum of scores in all intervals below l

fm = Number of cases within the interval in which the median lies.

i = Size of class interval

See: Arithmetic mean Mode

MEMORY SPAN: The range of items one can hold in memory at a particular time. The memory span of an individual is determined under laboratory conditions by exposing verbal or numerical items, one at a time for a short interval of time with the help of a tachistoscope (in the case of visual material). The maximum number of items recalled after a single presentation gives an index of the memory span. In the case of auditory memory span, the memory span is the maximum number of items recalled after a single presentation of items presented auditorily (i.e., spoken out) under controlled conditions. In visual presentation nonsense syllables, digits (for digit span), etc. are used.

MEMORY: Retention of experience as evidenced by recognition or recall. It involves the process of remembering. Remembering has two phases: recognition and recall. Recognition is the identification of a previous experience, when it occurs again, while recall is the retrieval of an experience (thing previously learned) to consciousness. Memory is sometimes treated as short-term memory (STM) or primary memory and long-term memory (LTM). We remember for a few seconds a complex telephone number but it cannot be recalled after dialling. This is short-term memory. Secondary memory or long-term memory, on the other hand, is characterized by unlimited capacity – it can store and retain complex materials during a considerable period of time. Scientific study on memory began with the classical experiment conducted by Ebbinghaus with nonsense syllables.

See: Ebbinghaus, H.B.

MEMORY DRUM: One of the first apparatuses used for studying the phenomenon of remembering. Units (e.g. printed words, nonsense syllables, etc.) to be memorized are fixed on a cylinder (drum). The drum is then encased in a cover. Through a slit on the cover, each unit to be memorized is exposed for controlled intervals of time by mechanically rotating the drum. The technique was first used by Wilhelm Wundt.

See: Wundt Wilhelm

MENOPAUSE: The stage at which menstruation ceases. This occurs around 40-45 years in the case of most women. During this period, as in adolescence, the body is subject to various hormonal changes which lead to a variety of physical and psychological problems for women. Hypertension, anxiety and emotional instability are some of the symptoms generally associated with menopause. Other symptoms generally seen are: feeling of insecurity and being rejected, varying moods and feelings and hot flushes. These changes are concurrent with the changes taking place in the ovarian glands, due to tissue changes and atrophy— which results in the sudden changes in the hormonal balance of the body. It does not mean that every woman at the menopausal stage is nervous, melancholic or quarrelsome. It means that as the changes occurring in the body chemistry, there is a condition which make women more prone to these symptoms.

The difficulty consequent on menopausal disturbance can be overcome by counselling and medication.

MENTAL HYGIENE (HEALTH): Applied psychology dealing with the methods of maintaining mental health. Mental hygiene deals with the dynamics of the social and environmental factors that produce emotional strains which lead to mental ill-health and the ways and means of maintaining a balanced and healthy personality. Mental hygiene practices ensure normal development of children, enabling them to make appropriate adjustment and lead a happy life. Mentally unhygienic environment (such as threats, neglect, etc.) produces anxiety and other incapacitating symptoms in children.

See: Emotions

MENTAL AGE: The level of intelligence of an individual in relation to the average intelligence of the individuals of his age group. A boy of 5 years of age is said to possess a mental age of 6 years when he is able to achieve the average score of the 6 year old children in a standardized intelligence test. If the boy is able to achieve the average score of five year old children, his mental age is 5 years, i.e., his intelligence is that of the average child of his age group. The mental age may be equal to, or above or below, the chronological age. Mental age is denoted by the abbreviation, M.A. It was Alfred Binet who developed the concept of Mental Age (M.A.).

See: Intelligence, Intelligence Quotient

MENTAL DEFICIENCY: Low mental capacity characterized by IQ less than 70. It is caused by genetic factors and so exist from birth and is irreversible. It is not due to any brain disease. About two percent of the population is usually found to be mentally defective. Special educational programmes are needed for such children.

MENTAL SET: Readiness for perceiving something. Mental set is a prerequisite for learning. Interest on the task on hand usually produces the proper mental set. A psychologist will readily notice the behaviour of people in an unruly mob, while an untrained man fails to notice many details, because the psychologist's mental set ensures better attention to all details of the specific situation.

MENTAL TEST: Tests that are designed to measure qualities or abilities that are characterized as mental–like intelligence, aptitudes, personality, etc.

Mental tests can be broadly classified into two types: Tests of maximum performance and tests of typical performance. A test of maximum performance, as the name implies, is a test intended to obtain the maximum level (highest level) of performance possible for the individual. So essentially they test abilities and capabilities. Tests of intelligence, aptitudes, scholastic achievement, etc. fall under this category. A test of typical performance on the other hand, is intended to obtain data on behaviour qualities typical of the individual and in this type of tests there is nothing that can be signified as high or low performance. These tests are aimed to measure those qualities that are basic to the person's adjustment in social and interpersonal relationships. So tests of personality, sociometry, interest, attitude, etc. are tests of typical performance, essentially because they are not abilities and so there is no question of maximum performance.

In tests of maximum performance the scores may be vitiated by 'guessing' and in the case of tests of typical performance, by 'cheating' or 'faking'.

See: Test

MESMERISM: The act of inducing hypnotic states. Anton Mesmer who used the method to cure some minor mental troubles, believed that it was 'the animal magnetism' that passed from the charmer to the client that put the client in the hypnotic state. It was Charcot and later Freud who developed the method as a technique of therapy. Freud believed that the contents of the unconscious could be brought up to the conscious by inducing a hypnotic state by using proper suggestions. He also succeeded in eliminating some symptoms in neurotic patients by giving suggestions at the hypnotic state.
See: Hypnosis

META COGNITION: Thinking about thinking.

METALANGUAGE: Implies the set of terms used to talk about the language, like grammatical terms.

METHOD OF PAIRED COMPARISON: A ranking method which requires the rater to compare and rate each individual or object with every other. Suppose it is required to find out the order of preference of 4 social organizations: 1, 2, 3, 4. The individual has to mark his preference, firstly between 1 and 2, then between 1 and 3 and then 1 and 4, 2 and 3, 2 and 4, and 3 and 4. From this, a final scaling is possible which can indicate how one social organization stands in relation to all others in the views of the testees. But when the number of objects to be ranked is large the process become unduly cumbersome.
See: Rating scale

MICRO ELECTRONICS (Computer): Electronic elements (for computers) manufactured in microscopic form. the miniaturization process has made it possible to make incredibly small switches and circuits of the processors and accessories of computers (Microprocessor). The microprocessors or chips, usually a quarter of an inch square may contain a million elements and their circuits. The microprocessors are manufactured by mass production methods and so they are comparatively very cheap.

MICRO FICHE: Transparent photographic film sheet containing matrix of micro-images or pages of texts.

MICRO WRITER: A device for entering text into a computer. It is a small device in which a number of high sensitive keys are positioned. Instructions (letters) can be produced by pressing the key in different combinations. There are only 6 keys in the microwriter but the number of possible combinations far exceed the letters of the English alphabet.

MICRO-TEACHING: A method used for training teachers in specific tasks – like questioning, class-room management, etc. Usually a ten minute session is provided and a small group of pupils 5-10 in nunber assigned for the trainee. He has to handle the class for the short period. His performance will be video-taped, which will be later subjected to a an analysis and discussion by the teacher-educators and fellow-trainees to see how far he has succeeded in mastering the specific skill.

MICROCOMPUTER: A computer system whose central processing unit is a microprocessor. Microprocessor is a small silicon chip in which all the CPU functions are incorporated. The microcomputer has all the four main components of a computer, viz., the input device, the output device, the central processing unit (CPU) and the memory unit. Microcomputers are cheaper, significantly smaller in size, still are reliable as conventional computers.

MICROFORM: An information storage device by which digital or iconic images as reduced photographically to microscopic proportions and recorded on films. It is possible to record about a hundred pages on a card size film.

They are stored as reduced images of graphic materials, pages of texts, etc. photographically or otherwise, like microfilms, microfiches (transparent sheets of photographic film carrying a matrix of images), microcards (ie. opaque sheets carrying matrices of microimages), etc. Special magnifying viewers or projectors are necessary to use them.

MID-POINT: The central value of a class interval in a frequency distribution. For example, in the step in a frequency distribution, '5-9' the mid point is 7, because the limits of the steps are 4.5 and 9.5 and so the class interval is 5. The mid-point in the step should therefore at 5/2 distance from 4.5 i.e. 4.5 + 2.5. In the step 10-12, the mid point is 11, because, the limits of the step are 9.5 and 12.5, and the class interval is 3. So the mid-point of the step is 9.5 + 1.5, i.e. 11.

The mid-point in the step is supposed to represent all values between the range of the scores in the step because it is the mean of the two limits. All computations for the scores in the step are based on the mid point. Illustration:

Class interval	*M.P. Frequency*
10-12	11 10

The total sum of the scores in the range 10-12 class interval is 11 x 10: 110.

See: Frequency distribution, Class interval

MINNESOTA MULTIPHASIC PERSONALITY INVENTORY (MMPI): A well known personality inventory. It is a non-projective test, and self administering inventory. MMPI consists of 550 items (statements) relating to physical conditions, moral and social attitudes, emotional stability, etc. The subject has to check those item (select) which apply to him by responding to 'True', 'False' or 'Cannot say'.

Sample items: I am easily embarrassed. I often feel as if things were not real.

It is mainly used for clinical purposes.

See: Inventories

MIXED-AGE GROUPING: Grouping children of different age groups in the same grade for instructional purposes. The class will be heterogeneous with regard to age but the scholastic level of the children in the class will be more or less similar.

See: Ability grouping

MOB: A large number of people assembled in a place who are under great emotional excitement. The term 'mob' is used in social psychology to describe a crowd in which emotion has been stirred up so that the people as a whole fail to see reason. The mob may indulge in antisocial acts like arson, looting, lynching, etc.

See: Crowd, Group behaviour

MOBILES: Three-dimensional wall charts used as teaching aid. It is called 'mobiles' because the components can be moved about. The items are cut out in card boards and hung independently from a horizontal bar using fine threads. The air current in the room make slight movements which makes it appear realistic. Word cards of basic vocabulary, names of a class of objects, etc. can be displayed with mobiles. Mobiles are suitable for young children.

MODE: An average or measure of central tendency indicated by the score that most frequently occurs in the distribution. It is the score with the maximum frequency in a set of observations. Example: The marks obtained by 20 pupils are given below:

7	10	13	13	16
7	11	13	14	17
8	11	13	14	17
9	13	13	15	18

The score 13 occurs 6 times, much in excess of any other score. The mode in the set of scores, therefore is 13.

It is used as a quick measure of central tendency. It is also used when the most frequently occurring value of the distribution is wanted. Approximately, the mode is equal to 3 Median – 2 Mean.

See: Central tendency

MODEL: A theoretic exposition of a phenomenon with the use of precise systematic verbal, mathematical or graphic symbols, which serves as the basis for interpretation of observed events, for prediction, for experimentation, etc.

Phenomenon that are not directly experimented upon or tested (like quantum theory, theory or evolution) are represented systematically by verbal (theory), graphic (two dimensional or three dimensional) or symbolic (mathematical equations) media. Such a representation is a model. The model is constructed out of the various evidences obtained about the phenomenon. The model helps in better understanding of the phenomenon and also in predicting events based on it. Testing of intelligence is based on the 'theory of intelligence'. The 'structure of intellect' proposed by Guilford is an example of a three dimensional model.

MODELLING: The social learning technique developed by Bandura for treating behaviour disorders. The principle involved is that learning can occur by witnessing the behaviour and the outcomes of behaviour experienced by other people; the experience need not be direct. To effect efficient learning in such a situation the subject should be exposed to the model and he should actively attend to it. The subject need not make any responses, he need only observe the model who displays the behaviour. Phobias and agressive behaviours can be treated in this manner.

Modelling can also occur in the negative direction; children may develop agressive tendencies by witnessing violent fighting scenes in films, TV, etc.

MODEM: A device that can convert digital signals into analogues capable of being transmitted through telephone wires and reconvert such messages back into digital form after transmission. 'Modem' is a contraction of Modulator–Demodulator.

MODIFIED FOG INDEX: Method used sometimes to determine the style of a text, in order to ascertain how far it is suitable for whom it is intended. It indicates the 'reading age' of the material.

To ditermine the index the following procedure is adopted. Take a random page and count upto 100 words. Find out also the number of sentences upto 100 words. Calculate the average sentence length (asl) by dividing the total number of words by the total number of sentences. From the sample, count the number of words with 3 or more syllables. Divide the number of words of 3 or more syllables by the total number of words and multiply it by 100. This will give the percentage of hard words (% hw).

The reading age of the passage can be calculated by using the formula for modified fog index = Reading age in years = 0.4 (asl + % hw) + 5.

MUDALIAR COMMISSION REPORT: The Secondary education commission Report 1952-53 (India). The Commission was headed by Dr. A. Lakshmana Swami Mudaliar, Vice-Chancellor of Madras University. The Commission recommended the reorganisation of secondary education, by diversifying it at the secondary stage. The main recommendations include: Starting of multi-purpose schools at higher secondary stage, introduction of vocational guidance programme in secondary schools, regional languages to become the media of instruction at the secondary stage, a Board of Secondary Education to be formed in each State, the first degree course should be of 3 years duration after the eleven year school stage in the pattern 4+3+4. The Commission also recommended reforming the examination system emphasizing the importance of continuous evaluation of pupil achievement.

See: Kothari Education Commission, Sargent Report

MODULARITY: 'Modularity', according to Chomsky and Fodor, is based on the structure of mind. The mind is conceived as 'modular', in the sense that 'different areas of knowledge and ability are qualitatively different from one another and not just special instance of a generalized notion 'knowledge''. The 'language module' therefore can be seen as a special knowledge or ability area obeying its special rules and principles which is not relevant to any other knowledge or ability (like mathematics). In Chomsky's view, grammar iteslef is modular and "what is grammatical and what is not grammatical in a language is not determined by a single set of global grammatical principles but by a number of quite different bodies of principles each of which takes care of a very specific aspect of grammar". Therefore one modular system can allow a particular structure, but that structure can be ruled out when the rules of another modular systems are applied.

MODULES: Subject matter of curriculum organised as modules. Each module will be organised around a central theme. In individualized learning, the learner works on each module at his own pace.

MONITORIAL SYSTEM: The system of pupil supervision by the 'monitor', prevalent in the indigenous elementary schools in pre-independent India. The institutions in which the monitorial system was practiced were mostly single-teacher (one-teacher) schools. The teacher was in overall charge of the class which was composed of 40 to 60 children of the age group 5-12 years. The teacher attended to the teaching of pupils individually or in groups and while he was engaged thus a senior pupil, the monitor, used to keep the others busy with some assignments. He was assigned a variety of duties like teaching the less able, teaching a particular topics, etc. Rev. Dr. Andrew Bell, Chaplain of Madras, who was convinced of its effectiveness, later introduced it in some schools in England. Later it was adopted in some European countries and Australia, New Zealand, etc. It is also known as the 'Madras System'. This method was adopted by America from England in the nineteenth century, where it was known as the 'Lancastrian System'. The system was developed by Joseph Lancaster in the U.K. and hence the name Lancasterian system.

The system disappeared with the single-teacher schools.

MONTESSORY, MARIA (1870-1952): The Italian doctor who became famous as the founder of the Montessory system of the pre-school education. She believed that mental deficiency posed more questions to education than to medicine and stressed the similarities in the development of the normal and sub-normal minds. She was first given the position of organizer of Infant Schools in Rome. She found that the main problem of the child was to adjust to the immediate environment. According to Montessory, the teachers' first task was to understand the children and feel her position as an observer. The liberty of the child has to be regulated and the teacher should employ activity methods. There should be provision of special materials designed to give the child practice in a variety of activities., which lead to sense training. Such didactic apparatuses should be given in a graded manner. It will develop the skills of manipulation and judgement through sense-training. The sense training toys should be attractive. For development of imagination, fairy tales, fables, etc., may be used. Learning will occur from the interesting activity in which the children engage. In 1936 all the activity schools (Nursery Schools) in Italy were abolished by a decree. Then she migrated to India in 1930 and continued her work in Madras.

See: Pre-school education

MORAL DEVELOPMENT: Acquisition of a set of rules of conduct appropriate for the age. It has two facets: first – the person has to learn the rules and second – socialization which implies that he, in his dealings with others conforms to the rules of conduct. Piaget identified three stages in moral development. At the first stage the child develops a respect for authority and an obligation to accept the rules. At the second stage the child begins to develop a morality of his own. At the third, the child gains full autonomy with regard to his social dealings and understands the reciprocity of social relations. According to Kohlberg also there are three stages. The pre-conventional,

conventional and post-conventional. In the pre-conventional stage there is a respect for authority and an orientation towards the avoidance of punishment. At the conventional stage there is the acceptance of the ethical values of the group and at the post-conventional stage the child develops his own conceptions of morality beyond those he has come across with. Conscience play the dominant role at this stage.

The child, in early infancy and childhood, is neither moral or immoral. It is non-moral, i.e., unconcerned with or oblivious of morals. As it grows, it imitates the moral values of the group to which it belongs. There are four essential components in moral development

1. learning what the group expects of its members according to customs, rules, laws, etc.
2. development of conscience
3. learning to feel guilty and ashamed of when behaviour falls short of social expectation and
4. enough opportunities to learn by social interactions the social norms and values.

Moral development and intellectual development are related. Most of the juvenile delinquents and criminals are found intellectually less able.

If the child belongs to two groups in which the moral codes and ethics differ widely (as in family and the gang) his moral development will be affected adversely. The exposure to this type of conflicts will possibly develop behaviour problems in the child.

See: Kohlberg Lawrence

MORALE: The confidence, satisfaction and coherence shown by the members of a group. In a group which has a high morale, the members feel one with the total group and are satisfied and so tend to uphold the values which the group possesses.

MORES: Social norms of behaviour which are of vital importance to society. Mores represent the basic values of the society, moral and ethical. Mores are actively enforced by the members of the society either through social pressure or legislation. Mores are often associated with the religious beliefs of the people. That the sons should look after their invalid aged parents is a more prevalent in many societies. It is enforced only by social pressure. Polygamy is forbidden in many societies. There are even legislation to prevent polygamy.

Mores relate to the customs observed by a group. Mores are norms of behaviour which have their origin in the basic moral values of the society. The mores are transmitted from generation to generation. They are resistant to change, but may be replaced as the values of the society change. Customs associated with 'decent' behaviour (like dress, habits, respect for elders) are usually described as mores.

MORON: A person whose I.Q. is between 50-70. At adulthood his mental age will be around that of a child of 6-7 years. Morons cannot benefit from ordinary type of instruction imparted in schools. Such children need special treatment in schools, like the schools for the sub-normal or feeble-minded.

MORRISON PLAN: A teaching method proposed by H.C. Morrison. The plan has five steps: (1) Exploration of pupil knowledge (apperception–i.e., finding their previous knowledge) (2) Lesson presentation (3) Assimilation of study, this should lead to a mastery test (4) Organisation of learning by the class (consolidation) and (5) Recitation or talk by pupils who have mastered the lesson.

See: Five steps

MOTIVATION: The process of arousing and maintaining specific behaviour by creating a need in the individual. The term implies the mental state that is characterized by biological needs (like food, water), social and psychological needs (like belonging, self-esteem, etc.) and interests, attitudes and values. Motivation is essential for good learning. Various psychologists have explained motivated behaviour in different ways. McDougall's view was that instinct (like curiosity, acquisition) is of prime importance in motivation. Hull saw it was drive reduction. Freud said a large proportion of our activities are unconsciously motivated. In teaching, 'motivate' means to create in the learner a need, which can be satisfied only by learning the task which the teacher wants. So, when motivated, the individual strives to satisfy the need which requires him to engage in the activity which leads to learning.

See: Drive reduction, Needs

MOTIVE: An urge to move towards some goal. It is the urge to engage in some activity that will lead to a goal, which consequently culminates in pleasurable experiences. Motive has an external goal. It is related to 'drive' which is also an urge– an urge to strive for an activity that will lead to the satisfaction of a physiological need (i.e., thirst, hunger, etc.). Motive, on the other hand, is an urge that is psychological in origin and the goal related to it is an incentive, reward, etc.

See: Interest

MOTOR AREA: The part of the brain (cerebral cortex) that is responsible for the control of motor activity. It is situated in front of the central fissure of the cortex. Control of all bodily motor functions, like movements of the hands, mouth, legs, etc. are localized in the motor area. Damage to this area of the brain (by blood-blockage as in thrombosis or physical damage) causes the muscles to remain immobile (paralysis). This area is also called the motor strip.

See: Cerebral cortex

MOTOR DEVELOPMENT: Level of control over body movements achieved through neuromuscular coordination at various age levels from birth to maturity. The sequence of motor development during the first year is:

4 weeks	:	Eyes move with moving objects
1 month	:	Thumb-sucking
2 months	:	Turning from side to back
3 months	:	Social smile
4 months	:	Eye coordination Holding head up in sitting position Turning from back to side Reaching and grasping
5 months	:	Sitting with support Grasping and holding
6 months	:	Trunk turning
7 months	:	Crawling
8 months	:	Picking up objects with opposed thumb. Standing with support.
9 months	:	Sitting without support Creeping on hands and knees

10 months	:	Creeping on all fours
11 months	:	Standing without support.
		Walking with support
12 months	:	Walking without support.
2 years	:	Bowel control.
2-4 years	:	Bladder control.

Fine coordinated activity is a function of growth, maturity and training. So precision in motor activities improves as the age increases.

See: Psychomotor abilities

MOTOR SET: Alerting the muscles to respond in a particular manner. The muscular readiness enables one to produce the appropriate reaction. The athlete who has been given the first signal for 'start' prepares his body for the action, i.e. he is in the proper motor set.

See: Set, Mental set

MOTOR SPEECH AREA: The area in the cerebral cortex which controls speech. It is situated in the left frontal lobe. The area is concerned with the control of vocal organs (organs of articulation). Damage to this part of the brain causes motor aphasia, i.e., total loss or partial loss of ability to communicate vocally, i.e., loss of ability to speak.

See: Cerebral cortex

MOTOR SKILLS: Proficiency in the use of muscles involving complex responses. It is also called psychomotor skills and perceptual motor skills–e.g. writing, cycling, etc.

See: Psychomotor abilities

MOUSE: A device for interacting with a microcomputer (Personal Computer). It is in the form a small control with two or three keys and a roller ball. In can be however, positioned to suit the convenience of the user whether sitting at a desk or at some distance away from the computer. With this, the user can manipulate the text which appears on the screen and also enter commands.

MUKTAB: The elementary schools in India during the Muslim period. The muktab was generally attached to the mosques and the children were taught to read and write Arabic. Most of the Muslim boys and girls of the locality around the mosque attended the muktab. The children were expected to develop the ability to read the Holy Koran.

See: Madrassah

MULLER-LYER ILLUSION: The apparent diminution in length by adding closing or opening arrow marks at the end of the lines.

This illusion, demonstrated by Muller and Lyer, shows the effect of 'field' in perceptual organisation. When closing arrows are added to the line it appears shorter and when opening arrows added the same line appears longer.

See: Gestalt, Illusion

MULTIPLE PERSONALITY (SPLIT PERSONALITY): Same person possessing two or more mutually exclusive personality patterns. This usually happens as a result of dissociation of personality. The splitting or dissociation of personality often follows severe emotional shocks. The person in the dissociated state may forget his previous identity (i.e., his name, job, etc.) and sometimes may be seen wandering aimlessly in places far away from his house (Fuge). When the original self is revived, he fails to recall the incidents during the dissociated state. Psychiatric or psychotherapeutic treatment is needed for restoring the normal personality. This is also called split personality.

See: Dissociation

MULTIPLE-CORRELATION: Correlation of a variable simultaneously with more than one variable. Multiple correlation (R) is the correlation between the criterion variable and two or more variables influencing it simultaneously. School success is often found to be influenced by both intelligence and study habits. Statistical processing of the two correlation coefficients gives an index of multiple correlation of the two variables (intelligence and study habits) to the criterion variable, school success.

See: Correlation

MULTIPLE-CHOICE ITEM: A guided response type of test item. The most widely used objective type item. The item requires the testee to choose the answer from among the several alternative answers provided (minimum four). Among the alternatives, only one will be correct or appropriate and the other alternatives serve as distractors or decoys. They are called distractors (decoys) because these are options that distract the persons who simply guess the answer, away from the correct one. The distractors are also carefully chosen (usually on the basis of a try-out of the test in the open-ended form) alternatives that appear as plausible answers. By increasing the number of alternatives the chance element is reduced considerably. With a multiple choice item, with 5 alternatives, the percentage of chance for hitting the correct answer by guessing is only 20. Multiple choice items are widely used in tests of intelligence, aptitude, achievement, etc. It can be used both in verbal and nonverbal tests. Answer sheets of multiple choice tests can be easily scored, manually or mechanically. So these items have a high level of objectivity.

The multiple choice item can be used for testing abilities at any level of difficulty and complexity, say from very simple items like mere recall of remembered facts to those that require a high level of reasoning.

A multiple choice item has two parts: the stem and the options or choices. Both parts have to be constructed with extreme care, to keep out all external cues that will lead the person to the correct answer.

See. Objective test

MYTH: Tales, part of the folk-lore of a people, handed down from generation to generation. The myths are often in the form of legends and the people generally consider them not as stories but as a living reality, which once happened. In primitive societies myths had a decisive role in expressing, reinforcing and codifying beliefs and values and in enforcing the morality of the tribe. All societies, both primitive and advanced have their own myths. There are myths about creation, life after death, etc. Myths are an integral part of the belief system of people.

Jung's contributions to the study of myths and their place in the development of the personality of the individual are well known.

N

N: Number of cases in a sample, distribution, etc. (statistics). 'N' is the symbol used in statistics for representing the number of cases of individuals, observations, etc. in a sample or population under consideration.

n ACH: D.C. Mc Clelland's 'need to achieve'. It is the urge in man to compete with standards of excellence. To find out n Ach, projective tests, like Thematic Apperception Tests (TAT) are used.

NAIK, J.P.: Noted Indian educationist. He was for many years Advisor in the Ministry of Education, Government of India. He served as Member Secretary of the Indian Education Commission, 1964 (Kothari Education Commission). He is the author of many books and monographs in Education, including 'History of Education in India' (with Nurullah), 'Elementary Education in India', etc. His contribution to the cause of universalization of primary education in India was immense.

NALANDA: Ancient Budhist, Centre of learning in India (Bihar). Nagarjuna and Aryadeva, the great scholars, were in Nalanda between AD 300 and 350. Hien Tsiang, the Chinese traveller, who visited Nalanda had recorded in his diary that the University had beautiful buildings and a well equipped library. The buildings were surrounded by a wall. Though it was a centre of Mahayana Budhism, Hinayana also was taught there. The curriculum included advanced studies of the Upanishads, Sankhya Vaiseshika, Nyaya and Jainism. Tantric form of Budhism was also taught, and also sculpture and architecture. Students lived there and the period of study extended upto 12 years. The number of students were between 3000 and 5000.

Many famous teachers like Dharmapala, who wrote treatises on logic and etymology, worked there during the early period.

The students were taught grammar and composition in prose

and poetry, logic and philosophy. Games were not allowed. The students from far off countries like China, Korea, Japan and Srilanka were enrolled in the University.

See: Thakshasila, Buddhist education

NATIONAL CLASSIFICATION OF OCCUPATIONS (N.C.O.): Classified list of occupations with definitions of occupations, published by the Ministry of Labour, Government of India. The N.C.O. has descriptions of about 10,000 jobs. New occupations appear every year, particularly as a result of the technological revolution (and some become obsolescent). So the N.C.O. undergoes revisions very frequently.

See: Dictionary of Occupational Titles

NATIONAL COUNCIL OF EDUCATIONAL RESERACH AND TRAINING (NCERT): The autonomous organisation under the Government of India, constituted 'to assist and advise the Ministry of Education in implementing policies and major programmes in the field of education, particularly school education'. It began to function in 1961. The main activities of the Council carried out by its various departments are: (1) developing programmes of edcuational research, organising pre-service and inservice training at advanced levels, educational extension work, dissemination of information about improved educational techniques, investigations and national surveys and assisting the NCERT's state counterparts viz. State Institutes of Education (SCERTs) to carry out their programmes. The important Departments under NCERT are: Department of (1) Psychological Foundations (2) Curriculum and Methods (3) Science Education (4) National Institute of Basic Education (5) National Fundamental Education Centre (6) National Institute of Audio-visual Education (7) Central Institute of Education (8) Department of Educational administration (9) Directorate of Extension Programme for Secondary Education, and (10) Centre for Educational Technology.

Associated with the NCERT are 4 Regional Colleges of Education and sixteen Field Offices.

NATURALISM: The school of philosophy, propounded mainly by Rousseau, which asserts the importance of nature in formulating the aims and values of life. Man should follow the laws of nature and education should be in harmony with natural development. So, education should be geared to the needs of children and methodology should be democratic.

See: Rousseau, J.J.

NATURAL SELECTION THEORY: Survival of the fittest. According to Darwin's theory of evolution, living things (plants and animals) that possess characteristics enabling them to adjust to the environment survive and reproduce, while those having weak adaptive mechanisms die out in the struggle for existence. Variations occur in the structure of the organism (mainly due to mutation) which may be better suited to adaptive behaviour. But survival is always based on the species' ability to make adaptive responses. By this process of natural selection, those which have shown greater adaptability survived, and others became extinct.

NATURALISTIC OBSERVATION: Observation of phenomena, events, etc. as they occur in nature. In naturalistic observation no experimental control is used. Many of the natural phenomena like the eclipse, storms, etc. can be observed only in this way. Ethology or study of animal behaviour largely depends on naturalistic observation. Naturalistic observation is also used for studying various types of child behaviour like play, expressive aggression, etc.

See: Controlled observation

NEEDS: A felt want. Need is aroused by the deprivation of a situation that is necessary for maintaining the individual in a state of mental equilibrium (homeostasis). When water is withheld for a fairly long time the cells of the body (particularly the throat) feels the effect of depletion and the need for water is felt. Primary needs or physiological needs are those needs the satiation of which is necessary for the maintenance of life. There are needs for air, water, food, warmth and elimination. Secondary needs are needs derived from the primary needs in the social context of existence. Secondary needs are therefore called psychological and social needs. They include needs for security, self expression, freedom, recognition, etc. Activity originates from need, because it is for satisfying a need that the individual acts. It is closely related to motivation (which means creating a need) which is a primary condition for learning. In the case of man, money can be used to procure satisfaction for practically any kind of need.

See: Driver, Motive

NEGATIVE TRANSFER: Mastery of one task hindering the learning of another task. This occurs in situations in which the new tasks requires habits and skills which are counter in nature to the skill already acquired. Shifting the positions of the key board of a gadget (eg., typewriter) will make learning the task with the new keys more difficult.

See: Transfer

NEGATIVE REINFORCER: The stimulus, the withdrawal of which, strengthens a response. Negative reinforcer aids avoidance learning–i.e., acquiring some response which will help the elimination of an unpleasant stimulus. This is called avoidance learning because the subject learns to do something to remove an unpleasant stimulus. Negative reinforcement differs from punishment in that in punishment the introduction of an unpleasant stimulus is involved while in negative reinforcement it is the removal of an unpleasant stimulus. The child who has learned to keep out of the presence of a bully has acquired this response by active avoidance learning. The unpleasant stimulus, which he wants to remove, is the aggressive bully.

See: Reinforcement

NEGATIVE DISCRIMINATION: An item of the test which correlates negatively with the whole test. In item analysis if the number of children doing an item correctly in the lower group is found to be greater than the number doing correctly in the upper group, then that item is said to discriminate negatively, because those whose ability is lower in the test as a whole get high scores in the individual item. Such items will be excluded.

See: Item analysis, Discrimination index

NEGLECTEE: An individual in a group who is neither chosen nor rejected by others. A sociometric test can be used to find out the neglectees in a group. The pupils of a class are required to write the names of those with whom they want to play, work, etc. and with whom they do not like to play or work with (2 or 3 names in order of rank). Analysis of the responses may reveal that in case of one or two pupils there are neither choices nor rejections, i.e., nobody chooses them or rejects them. They are just ignored. Such children in the social group are neglectees. It indicates that such children possess neither lovable qualities nor strong undesirable qualities. Their socialization (social development) process was inadequate. Such children may be helped by proper psychological counselling.

See: Isolate, Star

NEIGHBOURHOOD SCHOOL: A school catering to

the needs of all children in its catchment area. Neighbourhood schools are intended to serve the local area and so it normally does not admit students from other localities. Residents in the catchment area of the school normally have to enroll their children in the neighbourhood school.

NEILL, A.S. (1884-1973): The world famous teacher of Summer Hill, England. He has shown how school practices can be liberated from the clutches of the traditional formalized instruction and discipline. According to him, freedom' was the curative for many of the ills. Creation and self-expression were the only things that is of significance in education. Formal teaching was undertaken only marginally in Summer Hill. The pupils were to attend the morning class only if they wanted. Afternoons were free and after tea they could attend to a variety of crafts or other subjects. Evenings were set apart for dances, play production, visits, social gatherings, etc. According to him schools should be completely democratic and the pupils' role in managing them should be realistic.

NEURO TRANSMITTER: Chemical substance produced in the axon endings of the nerve cell and released at the synapse. It facilitates the transmission of impulses in the nerves by altering the permeability of the post-synaptic membrane eg. acetyl choline, dopamine, noradrenalin.

See: Acetyl Choline

NEURASTHENIA: Neurosis in which the characteristic symptom is extreme mental exhaustion. Literally, neurasthenia means weakness of the nerves. Neurasthenia is a functional disorder. The patient is emotionally disturbed and complaints frequently about fatigue and other symptoms of bodily weakness. Psychotherapy is applied in treating neurasthenics.

NEURON: The nerve cell. It is the basic unit of the nervous system, the entire nervous system is built up by tissues, predominantly consisting of neurons. It has a cell body with nerve fibres leading to it and going away from it. The incoming impulses travel through the fibres called 'dentrites' and they are transmitted to the next neuron through the fibres called 'axons'. There are three kinds of neurons: the sensory neurons (afferent neurons), the motor neurons (efferent neurons) and the connector neurons. The neurons that receive stimuli and transmit them to the brain are afferent neurons, the neurons that transmit impulses from brain and incite activity of the muscles are the efferent neurons. The connector neurons are in between the two.

NEUROSIS: A functional disorder of the mind characterized by anxiety, shyness, fear, etc. In neurosis there is an exaggerated reaction to emotion. Neurosis is a morbid state, but unlike psychosis, in neurotic condition the patient does not lose touch with reality. He is able to carry on his normal work even though he could not produce his best. In social situations, he will have problems of adjustments. In neurosis the person will be inwardly unhappy and generally in a state of anxiety. He is often unable to identify the reason for his anxiety. Neurosis has different forms. When conversion symptoms (like functional paralysis, loss of speech, etc.) predominate, it is called hysterical neurosis; when the patient is constantly under the fear of diseases, it is hypochondriacal neurosis: when the predominant symptoms are obsessions and compulsions, it is obsessive–compulsive neurosis. In the depressive neurosis the person is always in a state of melancholy mood. In neurasthenic neurosis mental exhaustion and fatigue are the dominant symptoms. All neurotics are emotionally disturbed. Usually they pass on as normal individuals.

Psychotherapy and counselling are effectively used in treating neurotic patients. Tranquilizers and anxiety reducers (like valium) are effective in symptomatic treatment.

NEUROTIC: Refers to neurotic behaviour. A person suffering from neurosis.

NEWSOM REPORT: Report of the UK Central Advisory Council (1964) entitled 'Half our Future'. It deals with the education of individuals of average and less average ability of the age group 13 to 16 years (England 1964). Evidence collected by the Commission showed that many children were handicapped by limitations of social environment in the poor areas. The Commission recommended that more funds should be allocated for the education of these children (Newsom children). Compensatory education should be given to such children; more boarding school facilities should be provided and proper link is to be made between school and work. The teachers should have industrial experience.

NOMINAL SCALE: The lowest in the four categories of scales viz. nominal scale, ordinal scale, interval scale and ratio scale. Nominal scale is the most primitive of the four, i.e., quantification component least. When we classify objects or people into categories and assign lables like Married- Unmarried, Urban-Rural, Low-Medium-High, etc. we assume that the division is made on the basis of some quality that exists. This process is a rudimentary step in quantification.

See: Ordinal Scale, Interval Scale, Ratio Scale

NOMOTHETIC APPROACH: The method of personality assessment which depends on hypothesis testing. The data is not based on only one individual (as in the case of ideographic approach). Hypothetico-deductive method is used to formulate generalizations. Personality dimensions like Extroversion–Introversion, and Neurotism were formulated in this manner.

See: Ideographic approach

NON-FORMAL EDUCATION: Systematic education organised outside the regular formal school system. Formal school system is so formalized with its rigours of rules for everything (like age of admission, school hours, courses of study, attendence, etc.) that it may not be suitable to the needs and conveniences of many people. So many people miss the school. Non formal education is mainly intended for those who have missed the regular schools.

In non-formal education the rigours of rules are almost non-existant. Orderlines that is necessary to carry out the programme alone is insisted. There are non-formal education programmes for adults (adult-education), for school drop-outs, disadvantaged groups, etc. Correspondence courses, Distance Education and Open Universities also offer non-formal type education.

NON-GRADED ELEMENTARY SCHOOL: School in which grades of the school are not organized on the basis of annual promotions or age; i.e., school which does not have grades. (Classes or standards, like standard 1, 2, etc.). In the nongraded system each student can progress at his own pace in each subject of the curriculum. Classes are not organized in a rigid manner on the basis of age, attainment, etc. and there are no annual promotions or failures. Children are grouped for the purpose of instruction as and when necessary, but most of the time they will be working on their own under the guidance of the teacher. When the child completes one unit of lesson he moves on to the next. This type of organization requires careful planning with plenty of self-learning materials for the children. The teacher will have to use individualized methods of instruction most of the time, as the heterogeneity in ability, interests, needs, etc. of the children in a non-graded class is likely to be wider than that in a graded class.

See: Individualization

NON-PARAMETRIC TEST: Statistical tests applied when the assumption of normality in a distribution is not tenable. Such distributions are not influenced by chance factors alone. When plotted graphically they will show gross deviation from a normal curve and so parameters like mean, standard deviations, etc. cannot be used to describe the distributions. They are also called 'distribution free tests'. Statistical tests (parametric tests) applicable to normal distributions are therefore unsuitable in the case of non-parametric distributions. Non-parametric tests are particularly appropriate for nominal and ordinal variables.

The branch of statistics dealing with distributions in which assumption of normality is not tenable is called non-parametric statistics.

See: Parametric test

NONDIRECTIVE THERAPY: The psychotherapy in which the therapist does not give any directions to the patients. The method was developed by Carl Rogers and is also known as client-centered therapy. The Rogerians assume that the patient has the potential to explore his own problems and find out the solutions himself. The therapist in the nondirective approach is to provide a free environment in which the patient speaks out his problems in an uninhibited manner. The therapist only encourages the patient with the minimum cues to gain insight into his problems. The therapist does not give prescriptive, or directive suggestions. The therapeutic sessions help the patient to gain a realistic view of the problems so that he could rebuild the proper self-concept which enables him to make successful adjustments.

See: Psychotherapy

NON-OPERATIONAL DEFINITION: A definition which employs concepts, which also need definitions to define it. A non-operational definition may be comprehensive enough to include all the essential characteristics of the concept. But as it depends also on concepts which characterize qualities that are not quantifiable, such a definition is not helpful in designing measurement instruments or tests. The definition of 'intelligence' for example as 'The allround innate intellectual efficiency' is non-operational; all the terms used in the definition also need definitions. But 'intelligence', if defined as the 'ability to solve new problems' becomes operational because no complex concepts are used in the definition and 'the ability to solve new problems' is quantifiable. In fact, most of the intelligence tests are constructed on the basis of this definition. But an operational definition cannot signify all the characteristics of the quality or entity defined. So comprehensive definitions are also needed. Such are non-operational definitions.

Non-operational definition is also called constitutive definition.

NONSENSE SYLLABLES: A combination of letters which makes no meaning. Ebbinghaus used nonsense syllables to study the importance of 'meaning' on memorization. Nonsense syllables convey no meaning but could be read out; e.g., LOF, MIFT, etc. So in learning to memorize nonsense syllables, meaning is of no help.

NONSTRUCTURED or UNSTRUCTURED: Structure not well defined. In non-structured situation the pattern and complexities of the stimuli situation remain merged with the surroundings so that its total shape and details are not discernible. An ink-blot is a totally non-structured stimuli situation since it can be explained in any subjective manner. A photograph taken out of focus is partially nonstructured as a lot of the details and complexities remain in confusion; whereas the sharp photograph of a dog is a well structured stimuli, because there will be total perceptual agreement among different viewers. An interview is said to be nonstructured when the interviewee is not given any direction which will help him to focus his thoughts or attention to any well defined topic. When unrestricted or uninhibited responses are required, unstructured stimuli situations are used.

NONVERBAL TESTS: Tests for answering which special verbal skills are not necessary. A test which uses non-language media for testing is called a nonverbal test. Pictures, geometrical drawings, symbols, etc. are used as test content in such tests instead of verbal materials. In answering nonverbal tests, knowledge of linguistic skills is supposed to give no additional advantage.

The term is usually applied to paper-pencil (printed) tests using non-verbal material. Nonverbal tests are used with advantage in the case of children of tender age groups, defectives, tribals, etc. When cross-cultural comparisons of abilities are required, non-verbal tests are widely used. Instructions for the test, however, will be given orally. Nonverbal tests can be administered individually or in groups. Raven's Progressive Matrices Test is a well-known Non-verbal test of Intelligence.

NORM: 1. The behaviour of people in a particular situation considered typical for that group of people.

2. The averages and other measures determined statistically in standardizing tests are also called norms. The norms thus obtained (e.g., arithmetic mean, percentiles, standard scores, etc.) represent actually the typical performance of the norming groups. So all other scores can be compared to the norms concerned in order to understand their real value.

3. The standards laid down as optimum required for a particular object or situation (e.g., norms for school buildings, laboratories, etc.) is also called a norm.

See: Standardized test

NORM-REFERENCED TESTING: Using tests which have norms or those that have been standardized. Norms are obtained from the performance of a representative population of the target groups and most of the norms are based on the average (arithmetic mean) obtained from the score distribution. The score obtained by a student is compared with the average in order to understand his position in the distribution. Results obtained from a norm-referenced test therefore can indicate the performance of individuals in relation to the norming group performance. It cannot indicate which objectives of the tests have been realized. To understand how the students have achieved in terms of objectives, criterion-referenced tests will have to be used.

See: Criterion-refrenced test

NORMAL PERSONALITY: A person who gets on well with people and is generally happy. The prominent characteristics of a normal personality are emotional maturity and the ability to make proper adjustment in social and vocational situations. The majority of people have normal personality. The normal personality is well-integrated and has little problems of adjustment. The normal person is mentally healthy, accepts reality without inhibitions, is effective in interpersonal relationships, is generally happy and is able to work up to capacity.

See: Adjustment

NORMAL CURVE: The bell shaped curve, also known as the Gaussian curve. When an event is caused by a large number of factors all of which are similar and independent, and the probability of the appearance or nonappearance of each factor is the same, the frequencies of occurrence of the various combinations of the factors when plotted, conform to the normal curve pattern. To illustrate with an example: If 10 coins of equal size, shape and weight are tossed, it is possible to get combinations like 10 heads; 9 Heads and 1 Tail; 8 Heads and 2 Tails; 7 Heads and 3 Tails; 6 Heads and 4 Tails; 5 Heads and 5 Tails; 4 Heads and 6 Tails; 3 Heads and 7 Tails; 2 Heads and 8 Tails; one Head and 9 Tails and 10 Tails.

When tossed many times it is seen that one Head and 9 Tails or 10 Tails occur very rarely as they are extreme combinations while combinations around 5 head and 5 Tails occur more often. So to get a combination 10 Heads or 10 Tails a very large number of tosses (many hundreds often) are needed, while it is easy to get a combination around 5 Head and 5 Tails with a smaller number of tossing. Theoretically the frequencies of the different combinations can be worked out from the binominal expansion $(H+T)^{10}$: (H standing for Head and T for Tail) as shown below:

Combination	*Probability*
H^{10} or T^{10}	1/1024
H^9T^1 or H^1T^9	10/1024
H^8T^2 or H^2T^8	45/1024
H^7T^3 or H^3T^7	120/1024
H^6T^4 or H^4T^6	210/1024
H^5T^5 or H^5T^5	252/1024

Theoretically, only once in 1024 tossing, there will be the frequency or occurrence for H^{10} or T^{10}, while the frequency will be 252 for H^5T^5. If a curve is drawn for these frequencies it will take the normal form, (the bell shape) or normal distribution form.

The development of physical characteristics like skeletal growth, colour of skin, distribution of hair, etc. and mental qualities like intelligence, aptitudes, mathematical ability, linguistic ability, etc. are influenced by myriads of genes (which have different functions) subject to the law of chance and so, the pattern of their combinations and the frequencies of the various combinations tend to conform to the normal distribution. Even common experience confirms this proposition. Individuals who are extremely tall or extremely short are very few in number, while the majority of people have height around the ordinary height (average). So, also is the distribution of skin colour or intelligence.

The concept of normality is pivotal in psychological and educational theory, because, as suggested earlier, practically most of the human qualities are found distributed in the population normally. The assumption of normality is basic in most of the measurement situations encountered is psychology and education.

The normal curve (also called normal probability curve) has the following properties:

1. The curve is symmetrical bilaterally.
2. The mean, median and mode coincide
3. The curve is asymptotic, i.e., it approaches horizontal axis but never meets it.
4. The points of inflection of the curve occur at ± 1 standard deviation unit above and below the mean. At this point the curve changes its shape from convex to concave.
5. Between the mean and ± 1 standard deviation there will be 68.26% of the cases, between ± 1.96 SD lies 95% of the cases and between ± 2.58 SD includes 99% of the cases.

The equation for the normal distribution curve is:

$$y = \frac{N}{\sigma\sqrt{2\pi}} e^{-\frac{x^2}{2\sigma^2}}$$

Where

y : is the frequency of a given X-value (the height of the curve above the X-axis).

N : Number of cases

σ : Standard deviation of the distribution.

p : 3.1416 (approx.)

e : 2.7183 (the base of the Napierian system of logarithm).

x : Deviation of a measurement from the mean.

See: Parametric Statistics

NORMAL: Typical, general or average. Behaviour that is close to the general or average behaviour of a group is normal behaviour. The adjective is used to signify qualities that tend towards the typical or general or most usual. Those cases that deviate from the normal are atypical to the extent they deviate from the normal. Marked deviation which results in undesirable qualities is designated by the term 'abnormal', deviation towards the lower side is 'subnormal' and extreme deviations on lower and higher sides are considered 'exceptional'.

See: Exceptional children

NORMALIZED SCALE SCORES: Raw scores converted into normal scaled scores, when the raw scores are not normally distributed. The statistical procedures render the new distribution normal by closing up the distribution in some regions and stretching it in others until normal distribution is obtained e.g. Mc Call's T-scores.

See: T-scale

NORMATIVE STUDY: Research study intended to establish norms. Normative studies are undertaken usually for determining developmental trends like the average age at which babies are able to pick up small objects with fingers, stand erect, climb staircase, etc. The level of development of an individual can be understood reliably if it is compared with the norms for his age group.

See: Norm

NORMING: Determining the typical scores, raw or reprocessed, for groups for population by the process of test standardization. Norming involves the process of standardization. By standardizing, the test's norms for the test population and its subgroups can be determined.

Norms are scores which typify the performance of a particular group (e.g. , age 9, 10, 11, etc. and grade III, IV, etc.). The performance of an individual becomes more meaningful when it is compared with the typical (average) performance of individuals of the group to which he belongs.

Norms are also represented as derived scores like T-scores, centiles, etc.

If the mean achievement in a standardized test for grades III, IV and V are 70, 85 and 100 respectively, the scores 70, 85 and 100 are the norms of the tests for those grades.

See: Standardized test

NORMS (TEST): A set of values representing performance of a group on a standardized test. The standardization of the test involves the preparation of norms. Norms are given in the form of a table containing the raw scores and their equivalent derived scores, like the percentiles, standard scores, etc. Norms are usually prepared for specific age-group, for the sexes, for separate grades, etc. National norms obtained from samples drawn from the entire country are available for some well-known tests.

For standardization, the test is administered on a large representative sample and the answer sheets are scored and from the raw scores obtained by the candidates, the means (the average) for the group and the subgroups, etc. are computed. The means with their standard deviations are given for each category. The score obtained by an individual in the standardized test is compared with its norms. The real 'value' of the score will be revealed when it is compared with the norm.

See: Standardized test

NORWOOD REPORT: The report of the Secondary School Examination Council (U.K.) under the Chairmanship of Sir Cyril Norwood (1943). The report was titled 'Curriculum and Examinations in Secondary Schools'. The report recommend changes in the secondary school curriculum and the school examinations. The report contains clear descriptions of the tripartite design of secondary education viz. the grammar, technical and modern schools. It recommends some kind of a diagnostic two year period in the lower school where the curriculum should be broadly similar in the various types of schools. It also recommend a school leaving examination at 18 for university entrance and for professional courses. There should be continued part-time education upto 18 for those who left schools earlier.

NULL HYPOTHESIS: A hypothesis in the negative form. If a teacher wants to determine the effectiveness of a particular method of teaching a topic–what he has to do is to prove or disprove his hypothesis with the help of an experiment. The hypothesis in this case is that 'the new method is superior to the traditional method'. If a person is tempted to see that his hypothesis should prove true, his approach is likely to be biased. So, as a precaution against this hazard in the drawing of inference, statisticians recommend that the hypothesis should be stated in the negative form, i.e., as a null hypothesis. The hypothesis in the example cited above, in the null form becomes, 'The new method is not superior to the traditional method'. Then the experimenter has to disprove this hypothesis by conclusive evidence, in order to prove that his method is superior. This rigour, makes the procedure more fool-proof.

The null hypothesis is written in the following form : Ho : $i_1 - i_2 = 0$, where Ho refers to the null hypothesis, i_1 and i_2 are the population means for which estimates are obtained from the experimental and control groups. $i_1 - i_2 = 0$ means that $i_1 = i_2$, which means that there is no difference between the means of the two samples. The null hypothesis can be compared to the legal assumption that a person has to be considered innocent until his guilt has been proved.

There are two types of errors likely to be committed in drawing inference from the testing of hypothesis: Type I error and Type II error.

Type I error : Rejecting Ho when it is actually true and accepting an alternative H_1 which is false.

Type II : Accepting Ho when actually it is false, and rejecting an alternative H_1 which is correct.

Precautions have to be taken to avoid these errors. Fixing a low level significance (above 50%) increases the possibility of Type I error and a high significance level (between 5% and 1%) for the possibility of Type II error.

See: Hypothesis

NUMERACY: First used in Crowther Report, U.K. (1959).

The concept includes according to the report, apart from number sense, ability to think quantitatively, observe, hypothesize, experiment and verify. But 1982 Crockroft Report proposed a simple appraoch which defined numeracy as the simple mathematical skills to cope with every day life and some understanding of mathematical terms, graphs, charts, etc.

See: Literacy, Oracy Skills

NUNN, SIR PERCY (1870-1944): A brilliant British teacher. His Book 'Education–Its data and first principles', which appeared in 1920, was a masterpiece. He stressed that the primary aim of all educational effort was to help all children to achieve the highest degree of individual development. This does not mean that social implications of education should be ignored. He also stressed the importance of interactions and the responsibility of man to his fellow beings.

O

OBJECTIVE TEST: A test which will yield the same scores when valued by different examiners. In other words it is a test which does not depend on subjective judgement. Responses to an objective test will be scored in the same manner by all the scorers, irrespective of their subjective inclinations. This is because the objective tests do not give room for subjective interpretations. The situation is well structured and there is no ambiguity and so there is no likelihood of the test being interpreted in different ways. An 'essay' is not an objective test because different scorers may evaluate the points in different ways according to their subjective inclinations. The testees taking an objective test interpret the items in the same way since there is no scope for different ways of interpreting the directions or the content of the test. The responses are usually provided in objective type tests (as multiple choice) and the testees are required to mark the responses that he finds appropriate. The responses are scored with a scoring key, which again rules out the possibility of any subjective influences. Standardized tests of intelligence, aptitudes, personality, interests, etc. are predominantly objective. As objectivity improves, both validity and reliability of the test tends to increase.

See: Test

OBJECTIVE: The purpose of education, stated in specific terms, so that procedures for achieving it can be planned and implemented. Then the outcomes also could be evaluated objectively. The terms 'Goal' and 'Aim' are used to denote the ideal purposes of education which are complex, abstract and comprehensive and so almost impossible to assess objectively.

Educationists now describe aims of education in terms of specific behavioural objectives. Extensive work has been done in the field and very useful taxonomies of educational objectives in

See: Taxonomy, Aim

OBJECTIVITY: The essential quality of the test that is necessary for ensuring its validity and reliability. It indicates that the test is uninfluenced by personal opinions and differing views of the scorer. An objective test is unambiguous with regard to the directions and test content. The test could be interpreted only in one manner, and only one predetermined response (or a set of responses) could be possible for the item. Whoever scores the test, it should give only the same values. As only objective tests can give consistent results, a test that lacks objectivity cannot have validity or reliability.

In all testing situations in which the questions have a fixed answer, the test can be made objective. In tests of general intelligence and the school subjects, the tests necessarily will have pre-determined responses.

To improve objectivity of a question, it has to be worded clearly and in unambiguous language. It should seek only predetermined answers. The key for scoring should be prepared before hand and made available for scoring.

Objective type tests consist of guided response items, like True-False, Yes-No, Matching, Multiple choice, etc. Multiple choice items are most widely used.

When flexible response pattern are possible for a test, then it is necessary to elicit unique responses of the individual. Such tests are intended to test qualities of creativity and imagination, where divergent thinking is the process involved and the responses are unique. such tests cannot use any guided response test items, as there are no right or wrong answers for them. Some personality tests, have to elicit unique responses (symptoms of mental illness and abnormal behaviour tendencies) also do not use guided response type items. In such situations other devices are used to improve objectivity of the tests.

See: Test

OBSERVATION: Focussing of the sensory system to an object or situation in order to maximize perceptual efficiency. Observation includes a number of characteristics or components like mental and body sets, selective attention and persistence. Motivation is a prerequisite for observation. Observation is the first step in all types of learning and for learning science it is particularly important. Experiments equipment, etc. are only means for amplifying and controlling observation. Observation leads to the discovery of similarities, differences, cause and effect and other relationships existing in the elements of the situation observed. So generalizations, concepts, principles and laws originate from them. In psychological and educational experimentation, practically, all data are to be derived directly from behaviour of individuals and so the place of observation in them is of paramount importance. Studies on child development solely depend on the method of observation.

Observation involves direct perception of the behaviour or phenomenon in question and its recording. It is the starting point for all measurement procedures. With proper precautions, it can be used as a method by itself for obtaining reliable data. In such 'controlled observation' the observer should focus attention only on pertinent aspects of the behaviour. In a scientific investigation, the observer should not have any emotional involvement with the subjects or the observed event (i.e., he should be unbiased and intellectually honest) and the data should be clearly recorded immediately on data cards or sheets.

OBSERVATION SCHEDULE: Forms designed for recording observation data. The forms contain direction for recording data, behaviours to be observed, etc. Rating scales, check lists, etc. also form parts of an observation schedule. The observation schedule helps the observer to focus his attention on pertinent behaviours and observe data objectively.

OBSTRUCTION METHOD: Method of obstructing motivated behaviour in order to assess the strength of motives. It is usually employed in animal experimentation. In one experiment, for example, a rat, deprived of water for known lengths of time, is kept in a box from where it can reach a dish placed on an electric grid. Everytime the rat's paw touches the grid it gets a mild electric shock and normally it avoids the grid. However, under strong motivation (resulting from longer hours of water deprivation) the rat persists in crossing over to the dish. The strength of motivation can be assessed in this method under varying conditions (i.e., by varying hours of deprivation) and for different drives (like food, sex, etc.).

See: Motive, Drive

OCCUPATIONAL THERAPY: A method of psychotherapy which employs work-involvement as a therapeutic factor. The patient is given some gainful employment, the job activities of which are quite interesting and well within his capacities. The social environment of the occupation will be also congenial. The experience in such a controlled occupational situation has a remedial effect on the patient. This method is recommended usually for patients with minor mental disorders and for physically and mentally handicapped.

See: Psychotherapy

OEDIPUS COMPLEX: The complex which originates from the son's intense attachment to the mother. According to Freud, this is a universal complex. The son, during infancy develops an intense desire for intimate attachment to the mother which is sexual in nature. This leads to the development of deep jealousy towards the father. As the 'love' towards the mother and hatred towards the father are strong taboos socially disapproved, the urges related to them are repressed. These form a complex in the unconscious. Oedipus complex will reappear in disguised (or socially approvable) forms during adult life as extreme irrational concern for the health of the mother (i.e., the son always worrying unnecessarily about mother's health) or his tendency to prefer older women as wife or to hate without reason any person resembling his father. According to Greek mythology, Oedipus killed his father in battle, married his own mother (of course, unwittingly) and had children with her.

See: Psychoanalysis

ONE-TEACHER SCHOOLS (SINGLE TEACHER SCHOOLS): A school in which there is only one teacher to look after children of more than one grade. A large number of schools in many parts of the world during the early decades of the last century were one-teacher schools. This was mainly due to low enrolment in the schools. One-teacher schools are in existence even now in some developing countries. When there is only one teacher to attend to children in different standards like 1, 2, 3, etc. the teacher has to resort to multiple-class teaching. He will be teaching all subjects in all the standards. Such schools are also known as single-teacher schools.

ONE-TWO-FOUR SNOWBALL TECHNIQUE: A snow ball technique of developing agreed responses: first an individual starts on a question followed by discussion in pairs leading to a final group discussion, each group with four members.

ON-LINE: Computer term which implies a terminal or peripheral under the control of the central processing unit (CPU) at a particular time. Opposite: Off-line.

ONTOGENETIC STUDY: The study of the development of the individual. In ontogenetic studies the individual's development is the subject of study, and so it gives stress to variations in individual development. In phytogenetic study on the other hand, it is the general characteristic of the species that is central.

OPEN ENDED (QUESTION): A situation in which the person exposed is free to respond in any manner he chooses. An open-ended question has no predetermined answer as in the case of a multiple choice question. Open-ended tests seek unrestricted responses, "What are the ways in which you can make use of a cigarette tin?", is an open-ended question because the number of answers are unlimited. The question: "Which word bears the same relationship to the word 'girl' as the word 'boy' bears to man?", is a closed question because it has only one correct answer 'woman'.

OPEN EDUCATION: An approach to education which emphasizes openness in everything connected with the educational process. This applies to the building (no specifications) time, curriculum and methods. The stress is on personal growth and learning (not teaching). The teacher serves as a guide and partner.

OPEN UNIVERSITY: University of non-formal type, which permits anybody to pursue any course at any age. The rigours of rules and regulations are almost absent in open universities. Those who have missed the opportunity to pursue higher education, are able to study the subject of their choice and obtain degrees by undergoing courses of the open universities.

OPERANT: A response that operates on the environment that results in certain consequences. In the well known experiment of Skinner, the rat in the Skinner box emitted a large variety of responses, (like running, rolling, scratching, etc.) but it got a food pellet only when it pressed its paw on the protruding lever. The food pellet served as the reinforcer because it reinforced 'the lever pressing' response. Subsequently the frequency of lever pressing increased. 'Lever pressing' was the behaviour that operated on the environment to produce the particular effect. So skinner called it 'operant'. The conditioning in this case was called operant conditioning. It is also called instrumental conditioning.

See: Skinner B.F.

OPERANT CONDITIONING: Conditioning of a response that operates on the environment to produce a particular effect. B.F. Skinner experimentally demonstrated this phenomenon. In his problem-box, the rat emitted a large number of random responses, but only one (i.e., pressing a bar) led to the release of a pellet of food. He called 'bar pressing' the operant. It produced the reward–the reinforcer. No particular stimulus could be ascribed to the response–the bar pressing. By repetition the rat learned to press the bar to get food when it felt hungry. As the bar pressing behaviour was instrumental for producing the desired effect, the procedure was also called 'instrumental conditioning.' By operant conditioning, Skinner showed that pigeons could discriminate shapes like triangles, circles, etc.

Skinner's experiments helped the psychotherapists to develop techniques in behaviour therapy like, aversion therapy, successive desensitization, etc.

See: Instrumental conditioning

OPINIONNAIRE: A series of questions or statements intended to obtain the written opinions of individuals on a specific subject or a group of related subjects. Opinionnaire contains only questions or statements which refer to opinions i.e., subjective views of the persons.

OPPORTUNITY COST: In the educational context, opportunity cost is the amount of money that the students would have earned had they not attended the school. This is also called the 'Income forgone'. It is both a private cost (by the student and parent) but it is also counted as a soul cost, because as the student remains unemployed, the potential contribution to the Gross National Product remains unrealized. Students beyond secondary schools could have secured employment suitable to their age and experience.

See: Cost of Education

OPTICAL VIDEO DISC: A kind of video disc on which information is stored. It is a device in which vast amount of data can be stored. Usually it is a 12 inch disc which can store more than 2000 pages, coded (digitally) in concentric grooves. The optical device, video disc player is used to playback the information. The discs are compatible with the computers. In this instrument the signal is read optically, usually using a laser.

OPTIONS: The alternatives given along with the correct answer in a multiple choice question. The words 'Options', 'Distractors', 'Decoys' and 'Alternatives' are used interchangeably.

See: Multiple choice item

ORACY SKILLS: Skills involved in speech. The skills involved in oral communication are listening, logical presentation of ideas, clear articulation and modulation of voice according to emotional tone and gestures.

ORDINAL SCALE: The scale of measurement that deals only with relative positions (ranks). In the scale of measurement, ordinal scales rank two in precision and comprehensiveness. The scales are nominal, ordinal, interval and ratio, scales. In ordinal scale, measurement is made in terms of comparison of the characteristic in the set of individuals in terms of order, that is, first, second, third, etc. If the characteristic to be considered is not directly measurable (like skin complexion) this type of scaling is often found suitable. In such cases, the individuals can be ranked with reference to the particular trait. In ordinal scaling, it should be remembered that the scale value (i.e., the rank) does not give any estimate of the absolute measure of the characteristic (in skin complexion for example, the degree of blackness).

See: Measurement, Nominal scale, Interval scale

ORGANIC: That which is related to the structure of the organism. An organic disorder is a disorder which originates from some structural problem, i.e., from some faulty condition of the body organ. Many mental diseases (like Psychosis) are caused by structural changes taking place in the nervous system (brain) and so are organic in origin. But in some cases of mental disorders, there will be no involvement of the structure of the nervous system, the brain structurally appears intact. Such disorders are called functional disorders.

See: Functional disorder

ORGANIZATION: Organizations are essentially groups of people who formulate policies, plan strategies, handle resources and initiate and operate programmes to achieve the pre-determined goals in keeping with their individual and collective values. The main features of an organization are that it has a well-defined pattern of authority, official body, rules and procedures and a net work of informal relationships and unofficial norms.

ORGANISMIC PSYCHOLOGY: The psychological system that stresses the importance of holistic approach in interpretation of human behaviour. The individual develops from a single cell, and this cell begins to multiply and rapid differentiation takes place as growth proceeds. Still the organism retains the integrity as at the beginning. The individual develops as an integrated whole. Kurt Goldstein said that analytical-synthetic approach in psychology is inappropriate. It should adopt holistic approach. The individual responds as a whole. The single comprehensive motive in life, according to him is the urge towards self-actualization. Development of personality is in accordance with the individual's striving towards the achievement of this goal. Maslow's view was also the same.

See: Maslow, A.H.

ORGANIZATIONAL CULTURE: The norms and values generally accepted which indicate how people in an organization should behave towards each other. The norms and values are often not recorded ones, but are taken for granted and are morally binding on all members. It reflects the general character, tone and strength of the organization.

OROM: A kind of digital optical disk: Acronym for Optical-Read-Only-Memory.

OVER-ACHIEVER: A student whose academic performance is consistently much higher than that is indicated by his scholastic aptitude (i.e., intelligence and other cognitive abilities). Over-achievement, generally is the result of hard work of highly motivated pupils whose overambitious parents set very high level of aspiration for their children which is not commensurate with their abilities. Often the advantages outweigh disadvantages. Such children are likely to develop emotional problems.

Under achievement, is, likewise, academic performance consistently lower than that can be expected from scholatic aptitude. Low motivation, parental neglect, etc. are some of the causes of underachievement.

See: Under achiever

OVERHEAD PROJECTOR (OHP): A versatile visual aid which can project the images of practically any kind of transparent material on to a screen. It can be used for all the purposes to which a black board is used. The teacher can use it, facing the class. Prepared materials, pages from a book, writings and sketches, etc. which are copied into transparency sheets can be easily projected and it requires no technical skill to operate it. Dark room is also not needed for using an OHP.

OVER-LEARNING: Learning activity extending beyond that is necessary for immediate reproduction. Overlearning aids in better retention of learnt materials. For mastering complex motor skills overlearning is recommended. Airline pilots, for example, are given training practices even after they are found to have mastered the skills.

OVERT BEHAVIOUR: Observable behaviour – like reflex actions, speaking, writing, etc. Though these actions are brain mediated they end in motor responses which are observable. There are other brain mediated activites which do not have observable outward motor activities – like thinking, imagining and phantasizing. Such behaviour are called covert behaviour.

See: Explicit

P

PAIRED-ASSOCIATE LEARNING: Learning to respond to the first item in a pair by giving the second. It is a form of sign learning (conditioning). Learning a Foreign language involves paired-associate learning. Learning of dates of events in history, capitals of countries, etc. also are examples of paired associate learning.

PARAMETER: Value (measures) obtained from a population–population values. Average (arithmetic mean) standard deviations, etc. of body weights of adult males in a district obtained from a complete demographic survey are population values–parameters. To obtain these values quickly and with less effort it is often computed from data collected for the same variables from a representative small sample. But values from samples are only approximations to the true population values. Values obtained from samples are called statistics.

PARAMETRIC TEST: Statistical tests that are applicable to distributions conforming to the normal pattern. If the values under considerations are influenced only by chance factors, their measures in the population, plotted graphically, will approximate the normal curve. Mean, standard deviation, variance, etc. can be used in that case to describe such distributions. The 'population values' (theoretical value that can be obtained if measurement is taken from all members in the population) of such measures are called parameters. So tests that are applicable to distributions that have parameters are called parametric tests. It can be applied only in situations where assumption of normality is tenable. The test can be applied to data obtained from nominal, ordinal, interval and ratio scales, provided their distribution can be assumed to be normal. The branch of statistics dealing with distributions that have parameters (i.e. values that describe the population) is called parametric statistics.

See: Non-parametric test

PARAMETRIC STATISTICS: Statistics applied to situations in which the assumption of normality (normal distribution of variables) is tenable. In parametric statistics a representative sample is also assumed to be normal, as the population from which it is drawn is normal. As most of the variables encountered in education (like intelligence, personality traits, scholastic achievement) are assumed to follow the normal distribution pattern, tests of parametric statistics are applied to analyse them.

PARANOIA: A mental disorder in which systematic delusion predominates.

In paranoia, the patient complaints of various types of problems such as 'people trying to poison me', or 'my enemies spying on me constantly'. All these fears will have no objective reference as nobody is particularly interested in him. He weaves around an imaginary idea (poisoning), details in a systematic manner so that the person who attends to his complaints often tends to believe him. The false convictions are persistent and make his life unendurable. Though the delusions are generally persecutory (delusions of persecution) in nature, there are also cases of delusions of grandeurs. In that case the patient may claim that he has discovered a new theory of light, etc.

In the normal persons also sometimes paranoic tendency exists (e.g., thinking that others on the street are watching him suspiciously). But in the case of patients in anxiety states, if paranoic tendencies are seen, therapeutic treatment will have to be given.

See: Delusion

PARANOID REACTION: Systematized recurrent delusions. A person with paranoid reaction, may otherwise appear normal, his intelligence will not be affected. The delusional ideas are persistent (e.g., complaining about his son's intention to poison him) and his emotional behaviour and general behaviour consistent with the delusions. There will be no visual hallucinations. The disorder can be cured by psychotherapy.

See: Paranoia

PARASYMPATHETIC NERVOUS SYSTEM: That part of the autonomic nervous system which controls the normal metabolic functions. The parasympathetic system is also involved in the general functioning of nutrition, reproduction, etc. It exercises

in some situations an inhibitory control against the excitation of the sympathetic system (e.g., sympathetic nervous system speeds up heart action while para-sympathetic system retards it).
. See: Autonomic Nervous System

PARETO PRINCIPLE: It is also known as the 80/20 percent rule. It is found that in every management procedure, some processes can be identified as critical. Improvement of these procedures (situations) can result in disproportionate improvement in quality of output. This is also called the 'critical process' and it is usually about 20% of the total activities. For school management this can be identified as class room activities and personal relationships.
See: Management Structure

PARKHURST, HELEN: The innovator of the Dalton Plan. Mrs. Parkhurst first tried the 'laboratory plan' in a class of crippled boys. Later, in 1920, the scheme was introduced as the 'Dalton Plan' in the Public High Schools of Dalton, Massachusetts. The basic assumptions of the Dalton Plan is that effective learning occurs, in an atmosphere of freedom and cooperation; freedom from interruptions and cooperation in interactions of group life. The stress is on the child and his activity.
See: Dalton Plan

PARTIAL CORRELATION: The correlation obtained between two variables, after the effects of other variable(s) influencing it have been eliminated, when two variables are found to influence a criterion simultaneously. The variables in question are said to have partial correlation with it. So to find the partial correlation of one variable with the criterion, the influence of the second variable has to be kept out. Appropriate statistical processing will help in eliminating (partialling out) the effect of one variable and find the correlation of the other, by itself, alone.

Example: Achievement of repeaters in elementary school grades shows some improvement in the repeating years. This better achievement may be due to the influence of both additional learning experiences in school during the repeating year and also due to growth and development resulting from the increase in mental age (because the candidate is one year older in the second year). Mental age and learning experiences, therefore, have multiple correlation with achievement in the second year. The influence of schooling singly is found out by partialling out the effect of mental age from the total correlation.

See: Correlation

PARTICIPANT OBSERVATION METHOD: The observer living with the group in the natural settings to obtain realistic recordings of data. This method is used to study the characteristics of natural groups. The observer participates with the group (as in a tribal group) in its different activities. The nature of contacts made between the members and various forms of their interactions are noted and records are made of every type of activity.

Usually in conducting experiments, the experimenter remains as an outside observer to collect data. But in certain situations it would be necessary for the researcher to remain unobtrusive and so he mixes with the group as a member of the group in order to observe the group or individual behaviour.

PASSIVE LEARNING: Learning that occurs simply as a result of passive listening. Passive learning is characterized by the absence of any kind of active participation on the part of the learner. Even when the student is not actively participating, some learning occurs because the learner is exposed to the stimuli. Passive learning is less effective than active learning. Teachers who depend much on books and who employ only lectures for teaching provide more opportunities for passive learning than active learning.

See: Active Learning

PASSIVE VOCABULARY: The number of words one knows but cannot use in speaking or writing. Possibly a person's passive vocabulary is fairly large. Even though the words may not come to his aid in using, he will not have any difficulty in comprehending it when heard spoken or when read. Unfamiliar words become familiar by contact. As the contacts become frequent, it passes through the stages of mere recognition to passive comprehension. By continued contact the word will become part of the active vocabulary. By long disuse active vocabulary may relapse into passive vocabulary.

See: Active vocabulary

PATHSALA: The Hindu school of higher learning prevalent in medieval India. The medium of instruction in Pathsalas was Sanskrit and the curriculum was restricted to the learning of the Sanskrit classical works. The pupils were mainly brahmins (top class in Hindu caste hierarchy) and they received stipends from the rulers. The teachers were also, essentially brahmins. The children of other upper class Hindus were taught in elementary schools, which also sprung up during the period. In the elementary schools instruction was provided in the mother-tongue in the three R's. The teachers were given gifts in cash and kind by the parents. Other than such casual gifts there was no source of regular payment for the teachers.

PAVLOV, IVAN PETROVICH: The famous Russian physiologist noted for the crucial discovery of the principle of 'conditioning' (1849-1936). Pavlov was the son of a village priest. After his early education he joined the natural history section of the university of St. Petersburg (Leningrad). His speciality was Physiology, but he also learned medicine for two years. He became professor of physiology at St. Petersburg University in 1890 at the Military medical academy where he began to study the digestive process. He concentrated on the glandular and cerebral processes involved in the physiology of digestion in dogs. This work led to the discovery of the 'conditioned reflexes', for which he was awarded the Nobel prize in 1904. He experimentally proved a number of phenomena related to conditioning viz. reinforcement, stimulus generalization, higher order conditioning, discrimination, experimental extinction, experimental neurosis, etc.

Pavlov's findings and the methodology he developed for producing conditioned reflexes had a tremendous impact on contemporary psychology. It provided later psychologists the strategy to study behaviour – both human and sub-human, objectively.

See: Classical Conditioning

PAYMENT BY RESULTS: The practice followed for many years after the implementation of the New Castle Report in 1861 (England) regarding school finance. The schools were provided funds (grant-in-aid) on the basis of annual examination results.

This practice was prevalent in India also during the British period. The system was in force in most of the provinces, during the early part of the last century. Grant-in-aid was stopped to a primary school if the Inspectors reported that the performance of the school was not satisfactory. The pupil achievement was judged by examination or tests. The practice was later abandoned.

PEDAGOGY: The theory and practice of teaching children, which includes the philosophy, sociology, psychology and methodology involved in teaching children as well as curriculum, school organisation and management.

PERCENTILE RANK: The value on the percentile scale corresponding to the percentile point or the person's rank expressed as a percentage of the group. If 50 is a raw score below which 70 percent of the total scores fall, then 70 is the corresponding percentile rank for the score 50.

PERCENTILE: The position in a series of scores below which a certain percentage falls. It is one of the methods used to convert raw-score distribution in terms of meaningful units. A cumulative frequency distribution and cumulative percentage distribution aids in calculating percentiles.

Tenth percentile in a distribution is the score below which 10% of the total score lies. Below the 50th percentile lie 50% of the scores in the distribution and so it is the median.

See: Raw Score

Cumulative Percentage Curve (Ogive)

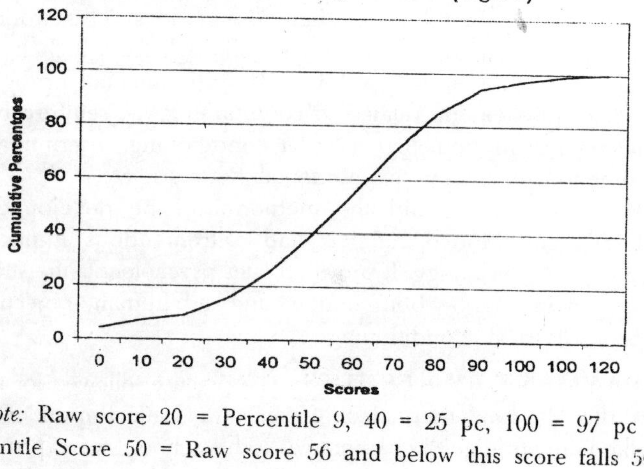

Note: Raw score 20 = Percentile 9, 40 = 25 pc, 100 = 97 pc
Percentile Score 50 = Raw score 56 and below this score falls 50% of the cases.

PERCEPTION: Mental process of ascribing meaning to sensory experience. It is on the basis of past experience that new incoming sensory signals are interpreted (apperception). To a savage who has never seen a book, a book would mean anything–a toy, a decorative object, etc.

Gestalt psychologists' major contribution was in the psychology of perception.

See: Gestalt

PERCEPTUAL LEARNING: Learning resulting from the sensory experience obtained from the environment. The environment offers vast and varied opportunities for the sense organs to receive perceptual experiences. The individual responds only to some stimuli with distinctive features. The learner distinguishes the differences in the set of stimuli and their discrimination facilitates the learning. The crucial part in perceptual learning is the learner's task to respond to certain distinctive features of the environment. The learner's ability to respond selectively to the mass of information available from the environment is very important in perceptual learning.

See: Perception

PERCEPTUAL CONSTANCY: Stability felt in shape, size, brightness, colour, etc. in perceiving objects in spite of the changes occurring in the retinal images (or stimuli). The size of a receding train appears to be constant upto a certain distance even though its retinal image gets diminishing every second. Likewise, colour of an object appears constant under varying degrees of brightness. The shape of an object appears constant even when the angles of vision are altered. Even though the quality of the stimuli varies within limits, objects are perceived to appear as constant.

PERENNIALISM: The philosophy of education which emphasizes the primacy of the past; the past represented by the great men and their writings. It advocates the unchanging nature of the universe, human nature, truth and knowledge. The perennialists have little respect for the achievements of the present era, like industrial revolution, scientific revolution, technological and electronic revolutions. Human nature is everywhere the same and so education must be the same for all. Education should aim to develop the rational man. Teaching is the art of stimulating and directing the development of individual's latent powers to think rationally. The perennialists emphasize the study of languages and mathematics.

PERFORMANCE TEST: Tests required to be solved by manipulating some special apparatus or three dimensional objects. Performance tests are usually used to test intelligence, aptitudes, etc. Since verbal skills are not needed for doing these tests and the testee is not required to handle pen or pencil for marking the answers, performance tests can be also administered to illiterates, culturally deprived and deaf or blind individuals; e.g., Block design, Form board, Pass along test, etc. are some of the types of performance test items commonly used in testing intelligence.

Form board contains some regular geometrical shapes cut out from a board and the cut out blocks placed outside in a jumbled order – The testee is to choose the blocks and insert them in the appropriate cavities as quickly as possible.

Performance tests are essentially individual tests (cannot be administered to groups) and can be made culture-fair to a large extent.

PERFORMANCE INDICATORS (PIs): The indices of effectiveness of an institution. Generally they are the components of cost-effectiveness.

PERIPHERAL: In a computer system (the equipment unit) the terminal or storing device that is connected to a central processing unit.

PERSONALITY: 'Personality is the more or less stable and enduring organization of a person's character, temperament, intellect and physique, which determines his unique adjustment to his environment' – Eysenck.

Personality is not simply an aggregate of behaviour traits, but a dynamic and unified organization of the traits which determines the characteristic and unique identity of the individual. The behaviour of a person in a particular situation is a function of his personality. The mode of adjustment adopted by the individual in a social situation is particulary dependent upon his personality. For example, an extrovert is likely to participate actively in a situation involving a large extent of social interaction, while an introvert is likely to withdraw from such a situation.

The most important aim of education, according to some educationists is the proper development of personality. This means that a well educated individual has the ability to make successful adjustment in any situation he is likely to be involved in. A person with a well-integrated personality is sociable, emotionally stable and inwardly happy. His attitudes and values are in agreement with the ethically approved norms of society. He has no unhealthy inhibitions that dissipate his energy. Personality development is dependent on early experiences of the individual (i.e., environmental influences). It is also, to a large extent, the product of learning. So schools have a decisive role in the development of the personality of children.

See: Personality Test

PERSONALITY TEST: Tests for the assessment of traits of personality. Personality tests are tests of typical performance, as opposed to tests of abilities which are tests of maximum performance. Personality tests are intended to draw out data on the typical ways in which the individual will react to social, personal and other environmental situations. So, for personality tests, there are no correct or incorrect answers. All responses provided by the individual are good and acceptable (if there is no cheating) and can be used to formulate conclusions about his personality.

There are personality tests designed to assess personality dimensions like Extraversion-Introversion, Ascendance-Submission, Neuroticism, Emotional stability, etc.

Most of the tests of personality are of the self-reporting type like questionnaires, inventories, check-lists, etc. Projective tests like Thematic Apperception Test (TAT), Rorschach Ink blot test, etc. are also available. Situational tests and sociometric tests are also used to assess personality.

Personality tests also should possess the essential qualities of tests, like validity, reliability and objectivity.

See: Tests, Personality

PERSONNEL ADMINISTRATION: The management of the staff of an institutions or organization. It includes matters regarding appointment, allocation of work, supervision, maintenance of discipline, assessment of work, promotions and punishments.

PESTALOZZI, JOHANN HEINRICH (1764-1827): The Swiss Educationist who was one of the pioneers in psychologizing education. Like Rousseau, he was also an advocate of naturalism. He believed in the equality of man. He said "Man is the same whether on the throne or in a hut ......" in his book "The evening hours of a hermit". His work and ideas were deeply rooted in this belief. The education of the child should be in agreement with its innermost nature, he said. Children should not be engaged in the thousand and odd confusion of verbal instructions, before having trained their minds for truth and wisdom through first hand knowledge. A person who has been educated in the "road of nature" only can understand other persons because he will have a sense of simplicity and uprightness. Even though everybody has to follow the road of nature, it is not the same road for every-body. He recognizes individual differences and also the need for catering to the gifted and other special categories. So differentiation is necessary, but if the variety is put above the unity, it will be reversing the order of nature. Pestalozzi has also emphasized the need for vocational education.

His famous works on education include “Leonard and Gertrude: How Gertrude teaches her children”, ‘Swan Song’ and the ‘Evening hours of the Hermit’, ‘Leonard and Gertrude’ is like ‘Emile’, written in the form of a novel. In ‘How Gertrude teaches her children’. Pestalozzi gives a systematic theory of psychological methods in education.

PHENOMENOLOGY: Study of the world as experienced by the individual. It is the approach in psychology that stresses the importance of the experiences of the individual as felt by him. Each individual has his own phenomenological world – the world as he sees and experiences. ‘Self concept’ of each individual is based on the experience the individual undergoes, and particularly on how he views these experiences. Husserl, who is the well known protagonist of phenomenology, says that to understand a person we have to see the world through his eyes. Each individual lives in his own subjective world and so the needs, desires, perceptions, etc. of each person are unique. Psychologists with phenomenological leanings stress the role of self-concept and ‘self actualization’ in the development of personality.

PHENOTYPE: Characteristics of the individual resulting from the interaction of the individual and the environment, beginning from conception. Genotype indicates the qualities developed from genes, and phenotype means all other qualities developed in the individual, excepting genotype.

See: Genotype

PHI-COEFFICIENT: The coefficient of corelation applicable when the two variables in questions are truly dichotomous. Phi-coefficient is sometimes used in the case of continuous variables also which have been dichotomized for convenience. The frequencies are given in the four-fold contingency table (as A, B, C and D).

The formula for phi-coefficient is

$$\phi = \frac{AD - BC}{\sqrt{(A + B)(C + D)(B + D)(A + C)}}$$

See: Coefficient of Correlation

PHILOSOPHY OF EDUCATION: The part of pedagogic theory that deals with the meaning, aims, and values of education. History, culture, religion and political ideologies often influence the formulation of educational philosophy.

PHOBIAS: Irrational fears. Phisychoanalysts believe phobias are caused by repressing painful experiences associated with objects or incidents. Behaviourists explain phobias as conditioned emotional reactions. Under phobic conditions intense fear reactions are evoked in the person when he encounters certain stimuli which others see as harmless. Psycho-analysis, Behaviour therapy (successive desensitization), etc. are applied to eliminate phobic reactions. Some common phobias are

Acrophobia
– fear of high places
Agoraphobia
– fear of open spaces
Claustrophobia
– fear of closed spaces
Haematophobia
– fear of blood
Zoophobia
– fear of animals

See: Behaviour therapy

PHONIC METHOD: In teaching language, a method used for the learning of reading. Reading practice is based on the sounds of letters and not on the names of letters.
See: Alphabetic method

PHOTOCOPYING: The term covers a wide range of different proceses, but they all make use of light of some sort to produce a copy or multiple copies of an original document. It makes use of electrostatic forces to transfer pigmented powder of some sort to the parts of the copy paper on which an image is to be produced and then using heat to fuse this powder to the surface of the paper in order to make the image permanent. Two main processes are used

1. direct electrostatic (when the pigment is deposited directly on to the surface of the copy paper) and

2. transfer electrostic (where the pigment is first deposited on the photosensitive surface of a rotating drum and them transferred on to the copy paper).

Transfer electrostatic photocopies have two advantages—they use ordinary paper as copy paper and can be made to operate much faster.

See: Electrostatic copying

PHYSICAL DEVELOPMENT: Changes occurring in body size, shape, and functions at different age levels from conception to maturity. There are four distinct stages of body growth. During pre-natal period growth rate is maximum. During the first 6 months also growth rate is high. From the end of first year growth rate becomes low and upto the time of puberty (i.e., upto 12 years) growth is at an even rate. Then there is a spurt in growth upto 15 to 16 years. Then again growth slows down upto adulthood.

Different parts of the body grow at different rates So body proportions change with age. At birth children have very large heads, short arms and legs, etc. Pubertal changes take place between 10-16 years; these include changes in size and proportion as well as the development of primary and secondary sex characteristics. There is very little growth after the individual reaches the adult size.

See: Growth cycle, Development

PHYSIOLOGICAL LIMIT: The maximum level of attainment in a task possible for an individual. The physiological make-up of the individual sets limits to his capabilities. Striving to attain beyond the physiological limits usually results in a breakdown. Ambitious parents sometimes set goals for children endowed with only average mental abilities to attain much beyond their abilities, i.e., attainments possible only for intellectually superior children. Such children work for attainments beyond their physiological limits. This is often the cause for some emotional problems seen among school children, otherwise normal.

PIAGET, JEAN: Swiss psychologist well known for his theory of child development. He was born in 1896. He began his career as a biologist and his first scientific paper was published when he was only ten years old. Later he studied psychology and psychiatry and in 1921 he went to Geneva where he conducted all his famous studies. His basic work was on the development of the concepts of space, time, number, causality and the process of reasoning. His primary work on cognitive development was based on the observation data collected from his own children. His contribution to genetic epistemology (i.e., the way in which individuals construct knowledge during development) is also very significant. He is the author of more than sixty books and a large number of articles.

The stages of development according to Piaget are summarised below:

Sl. No.	*Stage*	*Discount cognitive characteristics*
1.	Sensori-motor Stage Age–Range Upto 1½ years	Refinance and motor reactions to sensory experience
2.	Pre-operational stage 1½ years-7 years	Imitation learning by analogy, ego-centric thinking
3.	Concrete operation stage 8 years-12 years	Manipulation of number concepts, deductive thinking–all with concrete association
4.	Formal operation stage 12 years awards	Logical and symoblic thinking thinking from abstract premises

See: Sensori-Motor, Preoperational, Concrete operation, Formal operation

PICTURE FRUSTRATION TEST: A projective test in which the stimulus is a picture (usually a cartoon) with unfinished dialogue. The test is partly structured and elicits reactions of the testee to frustrating situations. Example: The stimulus picture contacting line drawings as in a cartoon – A mother and her small daughter have just arrived at the house of a friend. The child takes a flower vase which falls down from her hands and break. At that moment the host enters the room. She has not seen the child breaking the vase. The host says "Oh, it does not matter". The testee is required to write what the other would say on that occasion. The testee naturally will be projecting his or her own feelings and thoughts.

The test is usually applied to children: the well known test is Rosenzweig Picture Frustration Test. Picture frustration tests are also available for use with adults.

See: Projective tests

PIE GRAPH: Graphic representation of proportions of data in segments of a circle. It is a useful way to visually representing some type of data. The proportion of various religious groups in a population can be represented by a circle, the area of the whole circle representing the total population and segments (marked in proportion to the population of the religious people) to represent the particular sub-groups. It is also called Pie diagram.

PILOT STUDY: A short study undertaken before the planning of an investigation. It will be of the same kind, but on a small scale. The study will reveal the problems involved in the planning and implementation of the investigation proper and enable the investigator to take adequate precautions, to improve the tools, to estimate the duration of the study and its cost, etc. It is similar to a feasibility study.

PLACEBO: Something given to patients, as a pretence to medicine. The word means something to please. When some patients (like hypochondriacs) are to be convinced that they are given proper medicine, doctors administer sugar pills or simple saline injections to please them. Such a drug or therapy is called placebo. It has the desired effect simply because the patient believes that he has been properly treated. In educational and psychological experimentation, when the effect of a particular treatment on an experimental sample has to be studied, a control group is also taken for comparison. On this group is administered a treatment which is outwardly similar to the one given to the experimental group, but is known to have only neutral effect on the subjects. This is necessary to keep the effect of motivation similar in both groups. The treatment in the control sample in that case is a placebo treatment.

See: Experiment

PLATEAU: In a learning programme the stage at which the rate of improvement is very little or absent. When the rate of progress on a learning task (like typing) is plotted on a graph, initially, for a few weeks, the progress will be rapid. Then for a few weeks there will be very little progress, so the curve from this point will be horizontal for some distance. This is the plateau. Then there will be a spurt, and again the curve will show an ascending trend until the maximum (physiological limit) is reached. The reasons for occurrence of the plateau stage may be due to the unconscious transfer of one type of habit to another, lack of motivation, or the difficult nature of the task at that stage.

It may be also due to reactive inhibition. The same activity (or similar activity) continued for a long time, tends to build up an inhibition in the nervous tissues involved in the learning task. After a short rest period, the inhibition diminishes and the rate of performance improves. This is reactive inhibition.

Plateauś occur in a large number of the learning situations, particularly those involving motor activity (i.e., training of skills).

See: Learning, Motor skills

PLATO: The great Greek philosopher. His ideas on education are contained in his 'Republic' and the 'Laws'. According to Plato the division of classes is according to merit and ability. Both heredity and environment are important in the development of the individual. The education he proposed was for the different social classes. The classes consisted of the older and most experienced guardians meant for ruling, younger for army and law and the lowest, the merchants, employees or labourers. At the first stage the aim of education is to stimulate the love of the beautiful, the next stage love and acquisition of truth and at the highest state the realization of the good. The instrument to effect these changes are music and gymnastics. According to Plato, music included literature, music and arts. Systematic instruction in gymnastics was necessary during the last 3 years of adolescnce. Gymanstics has also importance in developing hardihood and alertness and also as training for military. For the rulers, who should have philosophic insight and practical experience, he recommended secondary education which is predominantly scientific to be given between the ages of 20 to 30 years. Mathematics was given a predominant place. This will be followed by higher education in dialectics. Rulers are to be chosen from among those who are successful. Rigorous tests and examinations are necessary to select the guardians. Women should receive the same kind of education (Aristotle differed in this). In the 'Laws', Plato gives more practical ideas on education. Education should start as early as possible. Boys and girls can be allowed to play together until the age of six. Boys are to be prepared for military and girls for motherhood. Education should be universal and it should be under the control of the Government. There should be separate secondary education for the very able. There should be also provision for vocational education, and early childhood education. The stress in higher education is mostly on pure mathematics. Teachers shoud be trained and should be paid regular salaries. . ,

See: Aristotle

PLEASURE PRINCIPLE: The natural inclination to seek and indulge in activities that give satisfaction or end in pleasant experience. Some psychologists from the early times believed that man is primarily motivated by his urge to seek pleasure. This 'pleasure seeking tendency' of men is also called Hedonism. Freudians believe that all urges that originate at the id level are guided by the pleasure principle. Pleasantness or pleasure is a subjective experience which cannot be observed by another individual; but its overt manifestations are characterized by the individual's persistence in seeking the object of activity, and to associate with it, indulge in it and resist when prevented from engaging in it. Pleasurable activities are interesting.

See: Id Interest

PLOWDEN REPORT: The report of the Central Advisory Council for Education (England) on Primary Education in U.K. (1967). The report reemphasized compensatory education which was earlier recommended in the Newsom Report. Further it recommended that special treatment should be provided for children of immigrants and that nursery education should be extended. Primary education should be extended upto cover, the age of 12 years. Streaming should be discouraged, and it is advocated that child-centered teaching methods should be adopted in primary schools. It also, suggested the abolition of corporal punishment.

POLYGRAPH: Mechanical recording of several responses in a graphical form. Polygraph is used to record simultaneously a number of reactions like rates of respiration, heart beats, galvanic skin response, etc. on a smoked paper attached to a revolving drum or moving tape. A pointer which magnifies the movements (reactions) records the reactions graphically in the tape. The Lie-detector record which contains recordings of pulse rate, blood pressure, GSR and ECG, EEG, etc. is a polygraph record.

See: Lie deterctor

POPULATION: Population is a group or aggregate having common characteristics based on which it is considered as one group. Based on nationality, an aggregate of people form a population, then we have the population of a nation. All the students in the secondary schools are considered a population. Likewise, there are populations of handicapped children, delinquent children, experimental animals, etc.

Inferential statistics is concerned with formulation of generalization about population characteristics based on samples drawn from the population. The statistics obtained from a sample is only an approximate value of the true population value. The true value of a dimension (characteristic) of a population is called a parameter. The average score obtained from a random sample of secondary school children in a standardized test is only the average for the particular sample, but it is a close approximation of population parameter (theoretical average obtained from all members of the population, if all students took the test). Broad generalizations are possible about trends in the population, from data obtained from representative samples.

The term 'universe' is also used to denote a population. Sometimes 'population' or universe is used to describe a set of observations; for example the universe of test items, etc.

See: Parameter, Sample

POST TEST: A test intended to appraise the changes resulting from a treatment (experimental procedure, etc). So the post-test has to be conducted at the end of the treatment procedure.

When the effectiveness of a new method of teaching is to be tried out, the experimenter first starts with a pre-test to ascertain the original status of the group and then introduces the treatment procedure (application of the new teaching method) and at the end applies the post-test.

See: Pre-test, Experiment

POWER TEST: A test intended to measure maximum performance in terms of difficulty rather than speed. The items in a power test are of increasing difficulty and it contains a good number of items at a higher levels of difficulty. Power tests are not timed, i.e., time is allowed liberally for such tests. Power tests measure the individual's depth of knowledge or skill rather than his ability to do a large number of problems in a short time. Power tests are better used for testing higher level cognitive abilities like 'application', 'analysis', 'synthesis', 'evaluation', etc.

PRACTICE EFFECT: The effect of prior trials on the scores attained at later administration of a test. Familiarization with intelligence and other ability test items, by giving opportunities to practice them was found to have little influence in improving the scores in subsequent testing unless the items were identical. Practice only helped the testees in familiarizing them to understand the strategy and approach in answering tests. Even when the same test was administered to the same candidates after a short period of interval (within a week) the improvement in scores was found to be marginal. (But coaching in the test, of course, will improve the results).

PRACTICE FRAME: In Programmed Instruction, it is used along with the teaching frame and test frame for drill and practice.

See: Programmed Instruction

PRAGMATISM: The philosophy that asserts that the meaning of a proposition is its consequences. To the pragmatists, 'ideas' have consequences. A meaningful idea is one which can be acted upon or tried out in practice. An idea that cannot be tested, or have no consequences, lacks meaning. Mind is such a concept, it cannot be tested and so it does not exist, brain and cognitive processes on the otherhand, exist. Moral and aesthetic values exist only to the extent they affect human behaviour. The universe is matter in motion. Change is continual and inevitable. Values are related to time, space and circumstances to the pragmatist. The curriculum should emphasize processes and methods of phenomena. Human beings create their world by continuous restructuring of their experiences, i.e., interactions with their environment. The curriculum is the focus of interest and should be seen as sources of problems and projects rather than as fixed collection of facts.

Pragmatism originated during the second half of the nineteenth century in America. Its origin can be traced back to Peirce. William James and John Dewey also are known protagonists of pragmatism.

See: James, William. Dewey, John.

PRAXIS: The exploration of the environment by the individual which produces real knowledge – rather than theoretical or second-hand. The term was used by Paulo Freire in 1972.

According to Freire, real education results from the individual's interaction with the environment. The teacher's task is not simply the handing over of second-hand knowledge to pupils, but to move with the pupils and explore the relationship between experience and knowledge.

The term was also used by Marxist educationists.

PRE-OPERATIONAL STAGE: The second stage in the development of children according to Piaget. This normally extends between the ages 2 to 7 years. In sequence, it follows the sensori-motor stage. At this stage the child is able to dissociate motor activity from an object and have a mental representation of it. He can represent the environment in symbolic form, but is still seriously handicapped, since his thought and language are egocentric. He is so self-centered that he is unable to comprehend the views of other people. He assumes that what is known to him is common knowledge for all. When he narrates his experience, he assumes that the listener also was present there.

Another characteristic of this stage is that the child is able to deal with only one attribute of an object at a time, like shape, size, colour, etc. For example, if 7 pencils are placed with 7 erasers, the child will say there is an equal number of erasers as pencils, but if erasers are spread out to extend beyond the pencils, the child tends to say there are more erasers. This is because he can handle only the attribute 'length' of the row at the time. The idea of 'conservation' (that is, the concept that the number of erasers remains the same unless more is added or some is taken away, is yet to develop; so also is the principle of reversibility (i.e., the shape of a given ball of plasticine can be changed and can be brought back to the original shape). So the style of thinking at this stage is based on a dominant physical attribute of the object, which of course is an abstraction.

See: Piaget Jean

PRE-SCHOOL EDUCATION: Kindergarten, Nursery edcuation, etc. for children below the age of 6 years. In most countries statutory compulsion does not exist for pre-school education.

PRE-TEST: A test administered before the introduction of a particular treatment in a controlled experiment. A pretest is given to ascertain the status of a group on a dimension (say mathematical achievement) before it receives a new treatment (say new learning experience). This information is necessary to know whether the experimental treatment has produced any new effect. For ascertaining the status of the group at the end of the experiment a post-test will be given. Pre-test and post-test are thus two important stages in educational experimentation, especially when one is interested in establishing the effect of a new method.

In an experiment involving two groups, one control and another experimental, a pretest is given to establish their equality. Suppose an experiment is planned to find out whether a new method of teaching a topic in mathematics is superior to a conventional one. A two group study is planned. Two equated groups with regard to their initial level of mathematics achievement is necessary for this purpose. So a pre-test in mathematics is given to both groups. This will help in establishing the equality of the groups. Only after this process will the new treatment (new method) is given to the experimental group.

See: Experiment

PRECONSCIOUS: A state of the mind between the conscious and the unconscious. Anything that can be brought readily to the conscious is called the pre-conscious. It is really a part of the 'conscious' which at the moment is not within the boundaries of awareness. The psychoanalysts divided the mind into three according to the level of awareness, the conscious, the pre-conscious and the unconscious.

PREDISPOSITION: Tendency to react in a particular manner. Predisposition may refer to the innate makeup of a person in terms of hereditary factors or his prior learning that determines his behaviour tendencies. Predisposition to mental diseases means: vulnerability to environmental stress to fall mentally ill owing to structural peculiarities of the nervous system. Attitudes are considered as predispositions to act in a particular manner (consistent) when confronted with certain situations.

PREJUDICE: Biased pre-disposition or attitude towards a person, group, thing or idea based on faulty generalization. Prejudice is more or less a stable predisposition to react in an unfavourable manner against people, races, institutions, etc.

Prejudices are formed by early conditioning and are usually faulty generalizations that have no rational basis. They are also resistant to change. Prejudices are considered as negative attitudes. Sometimes, some people develop prejudices against some other groups of people (racial for example) not as a result of any direct experience or contact with that people, but by conforming to the attitudes of others with whom they identify. Racial, religious and political prejudices are held not only by individuals, but often, by large groups of people.

PRENATAL: Prior to birth. Prenatal life or the period of life in the womb of the mother (intra-uterine). Development of the foetus during the intra-uterine period of its life has been extensively studied and the physiological characteristics and behaviour tendencies from fertilization upto birth have been recorded with the help of sophisticated instruments. So it is possible to identify many of the irregularities in development occurring at the prenatal period of life.

PRESSY SIDNEY: The educationist who devised the 'Teaching machine' in 1926 which is the fore-runner of all types of mechanised teaching. He first presented his Teaching machine in Washington DC at a meeting of American Psychological Association. The first prototype was of the size of a portable type-writer.

See: Computer-Assisted Learning

PRIMARY NEEDS: Needs directly related to survival. Primary needs are also called physiological needs. These are the needs for air, warmth, water, shelter, food and elimination. All other needs are derived from the primary needs. They are called secondary needs or psychological needs (like security, recognition, etc.,)

See: Secondary needs

PRIMARY MENTAL ABILITIES: The factors of intelligence isolated by L.L. Thurstone (1930). Thurstone's analysis revealed seven primary factors of intelligence. These factors were extracted by multiple factor analysis (technique which he perfected) from a large number of tests of intelligence. The Primary factors of intelligence (Primary mental abilities) (PMA) are:

1. Verbal comprehension (ability to derive meaning from spoken and written languages) (V)
2. Verbal Fluency (ability to speak out and think using a large number of words quickly) (W)
3. Numerical ability (ability to understand and manipulate numbers) (N)
4. Spatial ability (ability to perceive relationships of objects in space and to manipulate the relationship mentally) (S)
5. Perceptual speed (Ability to recognize quickly similarities and differences in things observed) (P)
6. Associative memory (the ability to remember and recall information) (M)
7. Reasoning (Ability to see relationships and invent basic rules for a task completion – both verbal and nonverbal) (R).

See: Factor analysis

PRIMARY GROUP: A small number of persons in close face to face association. Primary group consists of the small circle of people with whom the person has frequent direct association, like the family group, close friends and job colleagues. The influence of the primary group on the individual is decisive.

PROACTIVE INHIBITION: The inhibitory influence of previous learning on recall of new materials. Experiments in memory have shown that certain tasks learned previously interfere negatively with the learning of new tasks. As the inhibitory control is exerted from tasks learnt before it, it is called proactive inhibition. However, nonsense materials learned previously have no proactive inhibitory influence, only meaningful materials (with similar content) exert such inhibition.

See: Retroactive inhibition

PROBABILITY: The ratio of the number of cases in question to the total number of equally likely cases. If an event occurs r times in N number of times, r/N , the relative frequency may be considered an approximation to the probability p. Probability is the limit reached by the relative frequency as the number of times is increased. Probability, used in statistics, means, the relative frequency in the population. It is a parameter (population vaue). The relative frequency we obtain in an experiment is an estimate of the parameter. For example, the probability of proportion of heads when a coin is tossed is theoretically 1/2, but when a coin was actually tossed 1000 times heads were obtained only 485 times. So the relative frequency .485 is an estimate of parameter, the probability ratio 1/2.

PROBLEM BOX: The box designed for experimenting on the problem solving behaviour of animals. An earliest problem box was the one devised by Thorndike to study the problem-solving behaviour (and learning) of cats. It was a box in which a hungry cat was confined. Pieces of fish were placed outside, which the cat could see. The box could be opened only by lifting a latch. By trial and error the cat (after repeated trials) was able to learn the operation of lifting the latch for escape. Various modifications of this type of box have been designed subsequently to study different aspects of animal behaviour.

See: Operant conditioning

PROBLEM CHILDREN: Children who suffer from various handicaps–physical or mental. Their difficulties pose many problems, both for them and for others. The term is generally used for children who develop undesirable characteristics in behaviour, particularly in the emotional field. So children who consistently lie, pick up quarrels, bully others, avoid school, steal, remain withdrawn, etc. are characterized as problem children. Usually teachers and parents see them as offenders, really they are victims of faulty emotional development. What they need is not punishment but counselling leading to emotional security.

Children, likewise, with academic problems should be given remedial teaching.

See: Counselling, Punishment, Broken home

PROBLEM SOLVING: A problem is, psychologically, a partially structured situation in which there will be a gap, for the closure of which the elements of the situation (data) should be arranged according to the relationship existing among them. In other words problem solving involves (1) finding out the relationship existing among the elements of the data (2) rearranging them according to their relationship to the total situation. When this process is complete the situation becomes fully structured and clues for closure of the gap emerges–the problem is solved. Kohler's famous 'joint-stick' experiment has shown the nature of problem solving process.

According to Gagne, the highest category of intellectual skill is problem solving.

See: Insight, Gagne's model of Learning

PROFILE: A graphic representation of an individual's scores on a series of tests, usually tests in a battery. Marks in various school subjects, scores on adjustment inventories, ratings given by teachers, etc. may be presented on a profile. A profile is a good visual representation of the data which can very easily reveal the individual's weak and strong points.

The scores on each test are drawn as a bar diagram or all the scores points are connected by a straight line in a profile. If the profile is drawn on a graph paper the real position of the candidate in the various tests can be easily seen. Profiles are particularly useful when information on a variety of abilities and traits are required, to make important decisions about the individuals as for job selection, personal counselling, etc. A profile is sometimes called a Psychograph.

PROGNOSIS: 1. Predicting accomplishment from the current test results. Data on present level of ability obtained from systematic testing can indicate strength and weakness of an individual in specific areas of school subjects. The results will help in predicting future accomplishment. This is prognosis. The assumption underlying predictions in such situations is that a high level of achievement at present indicates a high level of ability and so in future also it will lead to high achievement. All tests of achievement have prognostic value. Promotion of pupils based on examinations relies on the assumption that the school tests have prognostic value. Intelligence tests and aptitude tests, achievement tests, etc. have prognostic value, hence they are used widely for selecting candidates for jobs or courses of studies. Personality tests are prognostic of social and personal adjustment of the individual.

2. Predicting recovery (improvement) of sick persons (bodily or mentally), i.e., on the basis of current symptoms and condition. A good prognosis means that the chances of recovery are good.

See: Diagnosis

PROGNOSTIC TEST: A measuring device that predicts future accomplishment in a particular area. Well constructed school achievement test can forecast success (or failure) in accomplishment. Intelligence and aptitude tests are used as prognostic tests. Personality tests are also used as prognostic tests. Practically all tests are supposed to have prognostic qualities.

See: Diagnostic tests

PROGRAM: Set of instructions for the computer. It is a set of coded signs that indicate the actions to be performed by the computer system in order to achieve its purpose (for example to carry out complex statistical analysis of the data).

PROGRAMMED INSTRUCTION: Teaching conducted with the aid of programmed textbooks and teaching machines. Programmed instruction is mainly based on Skinner's operant conditioning. Complex learning materials are broken down into a number of smaller units which are serially presented in the texts or machines. Directions are also given, but no teacher's help is available. As the steps are each very small, the learner will proceed from step to step (most likely) without failure. Knowledge of result is the reinforcement. The two important common types are, Serial programme (Skinner) and Branching Programme (Crowder).

PROGRESSIVISM: The philosophy of education that emphasizes the primacy of reform and change in both educational and social affairs. This philosophy emerged in America in the late nineteenth century, as a protest against essentialism. It is the individual who learns, but this learning takes place in an interactive mode. Individual differences should be accepted and education should be geared to meet its needs. Democratic approach should permeate all school activities. Individuals should have freedom but only within the constraint of a democratic social order. John Dewey is considered as the founder of this school of thought.

See: Philosophy of Education

PROJECT: An activity proposed for a student to be undertaken on his own effort to master a specific unit of study. Kilpatrick of Columbia University is the initiator of the 'Project method', in teaching.

See: Kilpatrick, W.H.

PROJECTION: 1. A psychological defence mechanism according to the psychoanalysts, to denote the process of transferring one's own faults, guilt and shortcomings to others. The process is to a large extent unconscious. By this mechanism the person tries to protect the security of his self (ego) by refusing to accept the responsibility for his shortcomings. He throws the responsibility of his failure as weakness on some others. Bad workmen complaining about the tools, is the classical example.

2. Projecting one's hidden or unconscious motives, ideas, etc. unwittingly when confronting an unstructured situation. Projective tests are intended to draw out such hidden aspects of the personality.

PROM: In· computer terminology, contraction for Programmable-Read-Only-Memory. A ROM (Read-Only-Memory) that can be programmed by the user if he has access to the appropriate specialized equipment.

See: ROM

PROMPT: In Programmed Instruction, a cue or a subdued suggestion used to lead the learner to the correct response.

See: Programmed Instruction

PROJECTIVE TEST: An unstructured or partially structured test of personality. The testee is presented with a vague picture, diagram, ink-blot, etc. to which he has to respond. As the stimuli is ambiguous, no objective explanation about it is possible. It stimulates his imagination and contents of unconscious. So the responses are only projections of his own inner life and experience. The stimuli shall also be a vaguely sketched picture, a hazy photograph taken with the lens out of focus, an ink-blot, etc. Just as the blotting paper absorbs water from ink, it is assumed that the stimulus provided by such tests draws out the inner aspects of the personality of the individual.

Projective tests are compared to X-ray testing in medicine which is used for diagnosing symptoms otherwise unnoticeable. It can be obtained without the patient being aware of the penetration of the rays through the body. Projective tests (particularly Rorschach) are supposed to carry out a similar function, i.e., make a diagnosis of symptoms and traits otherwise hidden deeply, without the person becoming suspicious or even aware of the fact that he is going to disclose his inner conflicts.

The response to projective tests will indicate the person's suppressed needs and desires, fears, anxieties, etc. Though these tests are generally validated on clinical samples, their interpretation unless done by an expert, is likely to be very subjective. Protective tests are widely used for clinical diagnosis (e.g. for psychiatric and psychotherapeutic diagnosis) research and counselling.

The important types of Projective tests are: the Ink-blot (Rorschach), Thematic Apperception Test (TAT), the Picture-Frustration Tests, the Incomplete Sentence Test and the Word Association test.

See: Personality Tests

PSI: Contraction for Personalized System of Instruction.

PSYCHOANALYSIS: The school of psychology developed by Sigmund Freud which deals with the dynamics of unconscious behaviour and the system of therapy used to cure mental disorders which originate from unconscious causation. The main contributions of Freud were the discovery of the unconscious and the psychoanalytic system of treatment. According to psychoanalytical theory, the mind has three strata: id, ego and superego. 'Id' is the most primitive, notionally deepest layer, from which all basic urges originate. Such urges are guided only by the pleasure principle. For example, when the urge of hunger is aroused id is concerned only with getting food and eating, for which the individual does not care if he has to steal it. At the 'ego' level the stress is on reality. The ego's main function is reality testing. If the urge that arises from the id can be satisfied without encountering environmental or other obstructions, action for it is motivated at the ego level. Superego is concerned with the fulfillment of urges in terms of rights and wrongs, i.e., against moral and ethical standards. A healthy personality has a harmonious combination of the three which enables him to lead a well adjusted happy life.

Many of the urges that originate in the id are unacceptable to the ego or superego. Such strong urges are repressed. As the repression also is an unconscious process, the person is not aware of these happenings and the repressed ideas around some common themes cling together forming 'clusters'. As time goes on, many such clusters form and these constitute the bulk of the unconscious. These clusters are called 'complexes'. Since the urges related to sex are the strongest and socially most unacceptable, most of the repressions occur in the area of sex. The repressed drives often come to the conscious level in disguised form, like slips of the tongue, 'compulsions', dreams, etc. Dreams are supposed to be attempts of the unconscious to fulfil repressed desires. The analysis of the contents of dreams provides clues to the repressed wishes and complexes. As repressions involve emotional strain and energy, they manifest outwardly in many behaviour forms with emotional contents which are maladaptive. They are the symptoms of mental disorders (like, anxiety, phobias, compulsions, etc.)

Psychoanalytical therapy attempts to bring up the repressed contents of the unconscious to conscious level by free association. Dream analysis is also used. Hypnosis is sometimes used for preliminary diagnosis and sometimes as a therapeutic technique. Psychoanalysis is used to treat anxieties, phobias and a variety of similar neurotic disorders.

See: Freud, Sigmund

PSYCHODRAMA: Acting roles in specially designed drama in order to aid the cure of behaviour disorders (like aggressive tendencies). The participants are required to act out roles specially designed for the purpose which give them ample scope for the release of restrained emotions and inhibitions through a healthy channel.

Psychodrama is also used as a useful method for personality development. Acting out roles (which are well planned) helps children develop an integrated personality, as in the case of role playing.

Psychodrama is sometimes used as a diagnostic method in vocational guidance.

PSYCHOGALVANIC RESPONSE (GALVANIC SKIN RESPONSE): Change in the electrical resistance of the skin. Human skin conducts electricity but the conductivity depends on various factors, the most important being wetness and salinity. So when sweat glands are activated electric response of the skin increases. When an emotion is aroused (fear, anger, etc.) sweat glands are activated which makes the skin more conductive. The skin resistance can be directly measured by attaching the electrodes of a psychogalvanometer to the skin. The change in conductivity of the skin brought about by bodily experiences is called psychogalvanic response (PGR) or galvanic skin reflex. It is used to detect emotional states in men. As it is an indicator of an emotional change, PGR forms a component of the Lie detector.

See: Lie detector

PSYCHOGRAPH: Representation of a set of Psychological characteristics in graphical form. Psychograph is a graphical representation of mental characteristics which are relevant for a particular purpose. A psychograph of a school student will usually comprise graphs showing his positions (in percentiles, standard scores, etc.) with regard to intelligence, aptitudes, interests, special abilities academic achievements, etc. A psychograph of an individual for job counselling will include his relative standing on qualities relevant for the job. A psychograph is also called a profile.

See: Profile

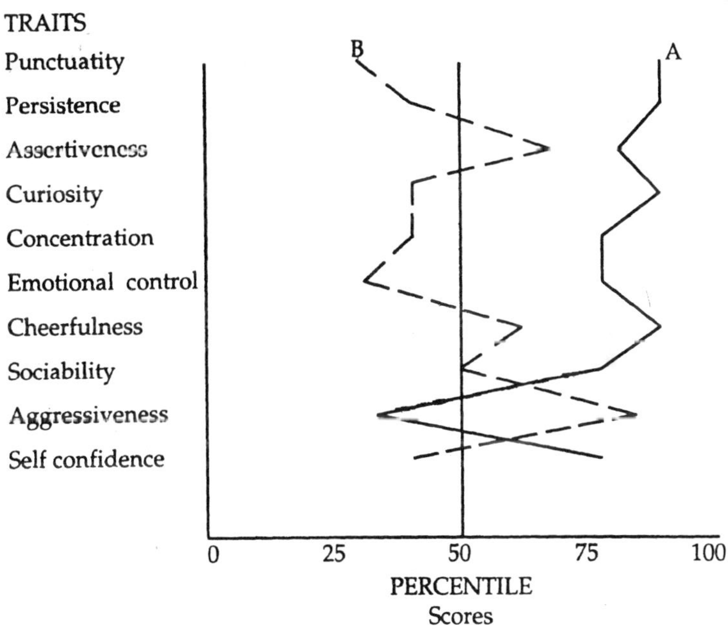

Psychograph (Profile) of two boys in ten Behaviour traits
Boy A (well adjusted)______
Boy B (not well adjusted)

PSYCHOLINGUISTICS: The study of psycholigcal processes involved in language acqusition, processing, usage, speech, reading, bilingualism and the relation between language and thought. According to Noam Chomsky, the linguist would be able to find out the child's innate language learning mechanism (language universals) by studying what is universal to all languages (universal grammar). Psycholinguistics has influenced the teaching of languages lately – both mother tongue and other languages.

See: Chomsky Noam, Universal grammar

PSYCHOLOGICAL ENVIRONMENT: The environment within which the individual responds. Psychological environment often corresponds with the physical environment but it need not necessarily be identical. The individual may be aware of and responding only to a part of the physical (geographical) environment at a particular time. The psychological environment comprises the physical space and objects and people surrounding a person. Sometimes this environment may narrow down to a small space and just one person, who is in intimate conversation with the individual. The elements of the psychological environment have a special significance for the individual because he will be responding only to them at that particular time.

PSYCHOMETRY: The measurement of psychological phenomena. The term covers the entire range of mental measurement including all testing procedures, but some scientists prefer to restrict the term to mean primarily the measurement of psychophysical phenomena, like reaction-time, conditioning–i.e., the measurement of mental phenomena made in psychological laboratories.

PSYCHOMOTOR TESTS: Tests designed to measure neuromuscular: coordination, strength, precision and speed. Psychomotor tests measure proficiencies in using coordinated muscular movements in order to perform specific tasks. Some tests of psychomotor abilities are:

Finger dexterity tests: Test used for measuring speed and accuracy in picking small objects with the finger.

Steadiness test: Ability to hold a stylus steadily for sometime stationary.

Pursuit-meter test: Ability to move the hands with a moving object.

Reaction time: Speed of eliciting a response.

Also there are tests designed to measure different psychomotor proficiencies, like the ability to tap a key, ability to operate the two hands at the same time to perform a complex task. Complex coordination tests are widely used in selecting persons for jobs which require a high degree of neuro-muscular coordination in operating complicated machines with the hands, legs, etc.

Other psychological processes like perceptual speed and sensory discrimination are also related to psychomotor efficiency (because correct muscular movement is possible only if the situation is objectively and speedily perceived). So such tests are sometimes called tests of eye-hand coordination.

PSYCHOMOTOR ABILITIES: Ability to perform tasks involving muscular movements. Fleishman and Hempel (1956) classified these abilities as follows:

1. Reaction time (speed with which the individual responds to a stimulus which he expects)
2. Tapping abilities (ability to make rapid movements as in tapping on a surface)
3. Psychomotor coordination (coordination of movements of hand and eyes)
4. Manual dexterity (controlled movements of the hand)
5. Finger dexterity (ability to manipulate the fingers to handle objects, particularly small objects at a rapid rate)
6. Psychomotor precision (precision and speed in eye hand coordination, as in aiming the finger at a rapidly moving object, etc.)
7. Steadiness (ability to keep fingers and hands steady)
8. Motor kinesthesis (ability to coordinate a series of movements by the help of incoming cues from body sensations as in the case of operating an aircraft in a simulated cockpit)
9. Psychomotor speed (ability to do simple tasks at a high speed, like marking dots in circles) and
10. Ambidexterity (Ability to use both right and left hands or legs) to perform tasks.

PSYCHOMOTOR DOMAIN: The hierarchy of objectives of learning skills involving coordinated muscular movements. Work in the field of psychomotor domain is not so well documented as in the case of cognitive and affective domains. However, A.J. Harrow produced a scheme in 1972 with six levels in the hierarchy of psychomotor domain. At levels 1 and 2 are reflex movements which are involuntary and involuntary motor responses to stimuli like crawling, walking and sliding. Level 3 is perceptual abilities, which involve more complex coordinated responses like catching, writing, drawing from memory and exploring. This stage is very crucial as basic school skills depend on it. At level 4 the skills in Level 3 become more coordinated and consolidated into more complex physical movements. At level 5 simpler skills are combined which results in the ability to manipulate tools and equipment. Smooth and well cordinated complex activities like typing, playing musical instruments, dancing and painting become possible at this level. At level 6, which is the topmost, most refined and subtle activities like ability to express emotions and thoughts facially and ability to communicate inner and creative feelings expressively develop.

According to another scheme, Simpson, E.J. classified the objectives of psychomotor domain as under:

(1) Perception: characterized by use of sense organ to obtain cues, guide motor activities, select task-relevant cues, translate use of perception into action. The motor activity can be described by the verbs: choose, describe, detect, differentiate, distinguish, identify, isolate, relate, select and separate.

(2) Set: characterized by readiness to take a particular type of action. It includes physical set, mental set emotional set. The activity can be described by the verbs: begin, display, explain, move, proceed, react, respond, show, start and volunteer.

(3) Guided response: concerned with early stages in learning complex skills. Includes translation and trial and error. The activity can be described by the verbs: assembles, direct, fix, manipulate, organize, sketch, etc.

(4) Mechanism: concerned with performance acts where learned responses become habitual performance skills at various levels The activity can be described by verbs: assemble, direct, fix, manipulate, measure as under – 2 and 3.

(5) Complex overt response: Connected with skillful performance of motor acts that involve complex movement patterns. Quick accurate performance, minimum energy used, automatic performance highly coordinated activity. The activity can be described by verbs; assemble, build, manipulate, direct, fix, sketch, organise as under 3 and 4.

See: Taxonomy of Educational objective

PSYCHONEUROTIC DISORDERS: Group of functional disorders in which the predominant symptom is persistent anxiety. The sufferer may try to control anxiety unsuccessfully with unconscious defence mechanisms. There will be no personality disorganization–so his sense of reality will be almost undisturbed. The common symptoms of the psychoneurotic disorders are–Anxiety reactions, Dissociation reactions (like amnesia, fuge), conversion reactions (like anesthesia, tremor), phobic reactions (like claustrophobia), Obsessive-Compulsive reactions (urge to do a meaningless thing repeatedly), Depressive reactions (extreme reaction to some loss) and all other symptoms associated with anxiety like sweating, palpitation, etc.

Psychoneurotic disorders are treated by different methods of psychotherapy–psychoanalysis, client-centered (non-directive) therapy, behaviour therapy, etc.

PSYCHOPATHIC PERSONALITY: A person with a disorder characterized by antisocial behaviour. A psychopathic personality, according to psychoanalysis, is one in whom the superego is very weak. He is guided dominantly by the pleasure principle. He could not restrain the impulsive urges of the id, and so he succumbs to them. He has no consideration for rules of conduct or ethics or morals. His reactions are impulsive. He may not show any remorse after committing a crime like murder, rape, burglary, dacoity, etc. as he is morally deprived. Many criminals are psychopaths who need psychiatric or psychotherapeutic treatment and rehabilitation, rather than penal punishment, which only aids in aggrevating their criminal tendencies.

See: Delinquent

PSYCHOPHYSICS: The branch of psychology that deals with the control and measurement of stimuli and responses and the variables relating to them. Psychophysics uses quantitative methods in studying mental phenomena, i.e., by the application of measurement. The first topics to be brought under a psychophysical experimentation were reaction-time and thresholds–the absolute and the differential. The name psychophysics was suggested by Fechner who argued that if we would measure the intensity of a stimulus and the strength of the sensation it produced, it would be possible to derive a formula relating physics and psychology to quantify and define the phenomenon.

PSYCHOSIS: Severe types of mental disorders known as lunacy and insanity. Most characteristic feature of psychosis is that the patient loses contact with reality. Schizophrenia is the most prevalent type of psychosis. The major symptoms of psychosis are delusions, hallucinations, regression, withdrawal, lack of emotional responsiveness and violence. Thought disorder often occurs and is very serious, the patient may say he was a contemporary of Shakespeare. In manic-depressive psychosis, the mood of the patient frequently drifts from elation to melancholia. In Paranoia, the predominant symptom is systematic delusions. The psychoses are mostly organic in origin.

Major methods of treatment apart from medication, are shock

therapy and psycho-surgery. Usually supportive psychotherapy is also given before rehabilitation.

PSYCHOSOMATIC: Disorders in which both body and mind are involved. Some physical diseases are caused by emotional problems. For example, continued anxiety or fear keeps the body in a state of emergency and tension characterized by heightened heart beat, suppression of stomach activities, excessive sweating, etc. This leads to the development of a lot of complications like chronic high blood pressure, allergic reactions, gastric ulcers, extreme fear of getting ill, etc. On the other hand, some physical diseases in which the patient feels himself hopeless, lead to the development of psychological symptoms of depression and anxiety. Psychosomatic diseases cannot be cured by drug alone, since symptoms originate from both organic and functional causes. Supportive psycho-therapy is also necessary for permanent cure.

PSYCHOSOMATIC DISEASES: Illness that has both mind and body involvement. Chronic pysical diseases may develop anxiety and depression in the patient and likewise neurotic conditions may cause the development of abnormal physiological conditions like hypertension, diarrhoea and constipation. Contined and severe psychological tension may lead to very serious cardiac problems.

PSYCHOTHERAPY: The therapeutic procedure based on psychological methods for the treatment of mental disorders. There are two major systems of treatment of mental disorders: psychiatry and psychotherapy. For treatment of those disease caused by organic changes in the nervous system, psychiatry is adopted which uses drugs, electro-shock, insulin shock and psycho-surgery. For those disorders caused as a result of faulty learning (i.e., by conditioning) in which the organic structure of the nervous system remains almost intact, psychological means are used to cure the diseases. The system used for treating such functional disorders is called psychotherapy. Psychotherapeutic methods actually aim at the elimination of the faulty habit systems and substituting them with the appropriate ones. For diagnosis and treatment, the therapist uses psychological methods, i.e., application of psychological tests, interviews, counselling, psychodrama, etc. Drugs are rarely used. The major forms of psychotherapeutical methods are: Psychoanalysis (Freudian and neo-Freudian), Non-directive therapy, behaviour therapy and yoga therapy.

PSYCHOTIC DISORDERS: Serious personality disorders characterized by the individual's loss of contact with reality. In psychotic state, the personality is severely disorganized and so all the congitive and affective functions like perception, thinking, emotional reactions, verbal and motor behaviour are seriously affected. The person has no insight into his own state of mind. Often there will be pronounced regressive tendencies, i.e., the individual behaving like an immature child.

The patient will need hospitalized treatment, psychiatric nursing and supportive psychotherapy.

See: Psychosis

PUBLIC LANGUAGE: The language in active use among the lower class of society, according to Bernstein. The language of the lower working class is characterized by its limited vocabulary in which individual selection and permutations are also restricted. They use simple structure with only a limited number of adjectives, adverbs and conjunctions. The sentences are short and grammar very simple. The tendency is to choose from a small stock of traditional and stereotyped phrases and words. The stress is on concrete, descriptive, material and visual symbolism and on emotive terms. Abstract symbolism rarely occur. This language is also called 'Restricted Code'.

PUNISHMENT: A stimulus which causes pain or unpleasantness, inflicted with the intention of eliminating an unwanted response. Punishments are supposed to curb the tendency to repeat mistakes. Punishments may be given either by inflicting pain or by subjecting the individual to unpleasant experience like restriction of freedom, denial of rights, disapproval, etc. The effectiveness of punishment, as they are usually administered in the schools as a means of eliminating undesirable behaviour, is controversial. The ill effects of punishments like anxiety, fear, etc. are often found to outweigh the advantages. The time lag between the occurrence of the offending behaviour and the punishment stimuli is the most important cause that reduces the effect of punishment as a correctional procedure. Because of this time lag, 'conditioning' effect of punishment is very weak.

Any aversive stimulus can be considered as a punishment, if it occurs as a result of an undesirable action. If the punishment (aversive stimulus) immediately follows the occurrence of the behaviour (to be eliminated), it is found to be effective. This method is adopted in Behaviour therapy in eliminating undesirable habits like smoking, drinking, bed-wetting, etc.

See: Negative reinforcement, Behaviour therapy

PUPIL-TEACHER RATIO (PTR): The number of pupils per teacher in a school. PTR = Total number of pupils/Total number of teachers. If the total number of personnel on the teaching staff of a school is 50 and the total number of pupils 1000, pupil teacher ratio is 20:1. Pupil teacher ratio should not be confused with class size.

PURPOSIVE SAMPLING: The process of selecting representative samples on the basis of the objectives. Sometimes we know definitely, on the basis of available evidence, a representative sample of a population with a specific characteristic is available within a particular area (geographic or otherwise). For example, journalists as a group can be taken to represent a larger section of people with regard to public opinion. Sometimes, required samples are purposively selected from among city dwellers, housewives, telephone subscribers, etc. Sampling done arbitrarily on the basis of specific evidence that it is representative of a particular population, is called purposive sampling.

See: Sampling

PYGMALION EFFECT: Also known as self-fulfilling prophecy or labelling. To classify a person in a category and give a name to him accordingly is a common tendency of social groups.

See: Labelling, Rosenthal effect

PYKNIC PHYSIQUE: A body type characterized by shortness and thickness of the body. Pyknic body build is found to be associated with manic-depressive type mental diseases, i.e., among mental patients larger number of short people are found to be manic-depressive, rather than patients who are long and thin.

Q

Q-SORT: A self-administering technique of personality assessment. The subject has to sort out from a large collection of statements concerning various traits, behaviour tendencies and situations those which are highly typical of him. Examples of such statements: 'I don't like to start conversation with a stranger', 'I feel sad most of the time'. The results are subjected to statistical analysis.

See: Personality tests

QUALITY IMPERATIVES: The motivating forces that operate in the institution that are necessary for ensuring quality. The main motivating forces are:

1. The moral imperative: the moral obligation of the school towards students, parents and community
2. The professional imperative: relates to the duties and responsibilities of all those concerned in the school's work
3. The competitive imperative: relates to the concern of the institution to maintain high standards vis-a-vis other institutions and
4. The accountability imperative: relates to the school's responsibility to prove the quality of its outcomes on the basis of objective and measurable methods.

QUALITY AUDIT: A component of accountability, quality audit in essential for accountability.

QUALITY ASSURANCE: The management system which by exercising control over activities at all stages ensures that only quality products reach the customers. The essential features of quality assurance are, efficient quality management system, periodic review and audit of the operation system, formalized systematic procedures, identification of customer requirements, well formulated quality policy, clearly defined roles and responsibilities, clear work instruction, correctional procedures and inspection.

QUALITY CONTROL: In the school situation quality control implies, maintenance of high standards in teaching and good student performance.

QUARTILE: The points that divide a distribution (scores) into 4 equal groups, the three points of the distribution showing the limit of the first quartile (25th percentile), the second quartile (50th percentile) and the third quartile (75th percentile).

QUARTILE DEVIATION: A measure of spread of scores in a distribution, given by the value of half the distance between the third and first quartiles (i.e., 75th and 25th percentiles), i.e., Q3 and Q1. Q1 is the point that indicates the score value below which ¼ (25%) of the scores fall, Q3, the point below which ¾ (75%) of the scores fall.

Q = (Q3-Q1)/2. Q is half the range of the middle 50% of the distribution, so it is called the semi-interquartile range.

Q gives a quick measure of the variability; it is particularly useful when there are scores of extreme values in the distribution.

QUASI-EXPERIMENTAL DESIGN: Design in which one or more of the requirements for an experimental design in wanting. Such a design is acceptable if other strong characteristic or practical necessity justifies its acceptance.

See: Design of Experiment

QUESTION BANK: Large pool of test items kept ready for easy reference. Questions, prepared by expert teachers for each subject are arranged according to objectives, levels of difficulty, etc. They will be indexed properly and stock-piled. Even on a single unit of the curriculum there will be a large number of questions, testing different objectives at various levels of difficulty.

QUESTIONNAIRE: A series of questions (or statements) intended to measure a particular dimension or group of related dimensions, widely used in personality testing, testing of attitudes, values, etc. Questionnaires are also used for obtaining information on social, personal and other types of data for surveys and investigations. Standardized questionnaires of personality developed for a variety of purposes are available now.

The questions in a personality questionnaire are based on

particular traits or symptoms of personality. The questions often refer to typical situations the individual has to encounter in life. He has to imagine himself in the situations and record the characteristic way in which he usually reacts to them. The responses to the questions or statements are given in the form of 'yes', 'no' or 'doubtful', 'can't decide', etc. Sometimes, the question directly refers to a characteristic of the person (e.g., Do you think you are a shy person?). The responses of the individuals are scored with the help of keys and interpretation of the results are made on the basis of norms obtained for the questionnaire. The questionnaires are often validated with the help of ratings obtained from external judges, or with clinical evidence. Norms are obtained for people with different problems of adjustment (i.e., introverts, extroverts, etc.). The number of questions in a questionnaire usually ranges from 20 to 100.

Since questionnaires depend on self-reports, apart from chance factors, faking or cheating is likely to upset the credibility. To check whether the testee has any tendency to fake, a few trap items (usually five) are also included sometimes in the questionnaire in a random order, like: 'I never tell lies' or 'Have you at any time hurt the feeling of some one. High scores for the trap questions (lie scores) indicate that the candidate has cheated

Personality questionnaires are also called adjustment inventories, emotional stability questionnaire, etc. Some personality questionnaires have items to test different dimensions of personality like, extroversion, introversion, ascendence, submission, neuroticism, anxiety, etc. Some questionnaires have separate forms for each category.

Questionnaires are fully structured tests (that is, the situation is given in clear terms and that there will be no ambiguity whatsoever). So the individual needs only identify the typical mode of his response. Some well known personality questionnaires are: Benreter personality questionnaire. 'Allport's 'Ascendance-Submission inventory', 'Allport-Vernon 'Study of values', Bell's 'Adjustment inventory', Eysenck's 'Personality questionnaire'.

QUINTILIAN: The great Roman thinker who was born in Spain around AD 35. In his book 'Institution Oratoria' he describes the Roman educational theory and the details of secondary and higher education. Elementary stage was of 5 years and around the age of 12 years the boy was transferred to the grammar schools. In grammar school, grammar was the main subject of study, other subjects like mathematics, geometry and astronomy were only subsidiary. The study of rhetoric began at 16 or 17 years. The boy was trained to become a perfect orator. According to Quintilian play should be the first method of instruction; children should be asked questions and should be praised for good answer. He preferred 'schools' to the practice of engaging private tutions. School is a society where there is healthy competition. He was against corporal punishments. The teacher should try to find out the boy's abilities and aptitudes. Individual differences should be taken into account in teaching. Though variety is necessary, curriculum should not be overcrowded. In grammar schools, education was of a general nature. The age of transition from the grammar school to the school of rhetoric was not rigidly fixed. The curriculum of the school of rhetoric emphasized advanced training in composition and style, study of prose and literary rhetoric. The pupils were given exercises and was to engage in a good deal of private reading in addition to attending lectures.

QWERTY KEY BOARD: In computer terminology, the key board in which alphanumerical (letters and numbers) and other standard control keys are provided as in a standard typewriter.

R

RADHAKRISHNAN COMMISSION REPORT: The report of the University Education Commission, 1948-49 (India). The Chairman of the Commission was Dr. S. Radhakrishnan the noted philosopher and educationist, who later became the President of India. The main recommendations can be summarised as follows.

- School course should cover 12 years and the university course, spread over 3 years.
- General education should form part of curriculum of both school and university stages.
- Facilities for research, both fundamental and applied should be expanded.
- Professional education in the fields of engineering, agriculture, medicine, commerce, etc. should be strengthened and expanded.
- All universities should be autonomous.
- Salary scales of teachers should not be inferior to those in central and state services.
- Examinations should be reformed, there should be continuous assessment; objective tests should be introduced. Scholarships and stipends to be awarded on a large scale.
- Teaching of English should continue along with Indian Languages and federal language (Hindi).
- A University Grants Commission should be set up to coordinate and maintain standards in universities.

RAM: A computing term, contraction for Random-Access-Memory. It is a fast random access store of the kind found in the Central Processing Unit of Computers.

RAMA SWAMI IYER, Dr. C.P.: Noted administrator, philosopher and educationist. He was the Dewan of the princely State of Travancore (which in 1956 formed part of Kerala) during the reign of the illustrious Maharajah Bala Rama Varma. He was one of the first administrators to try compulsory primary education in India. In spite of stiff oppostition, he started implementing compulsory primary education by late thirtees and early forties. The project was introduced in a phased manner in selected pockets in the State. Ancillary services like free noon-feeding, scholarships also were provided. To circumvent the problem of providing additional building and additional staff consequent on the sudden bulge in enrolment, he introduced double-shift in the primary classes, the same building and same staff serving both shifts. He had also served as Vice-chancellor in Annamali and Banaras Hindu Universities.

RAMACHANDRAN, Dr. G.: Gandhian philosopher and educationist. He devoted his life with a missionary zeal for the implementation of Mahatma Gandhi's ideas on education. He was the main architect of the Gandhigram Rural University near Madurai in Tamil Nadu where he successfully tried his ideas into practice.

RANDOMIZATION: Applying the random method for selection of subjects for the samples in an experiment in order to reduce the effects of systematic error. Randomization is intended to nullify or reduce the effects of extraneous variables which are concomitant with the dependent variable and so are likely to be correlated with it. To illustrate: In an experiment to study the effect of a new method of teaching a topic in mathematics, the experimenter has to select two samples, one for the experimental group and other for the control group. In this experiment, the dependent variable is mathematical achievement which will be measured at the end of the experimental instructional period. But the mathematical achievement cannot be isolated from the effect of other variables (i.e., variables other than the independent variable: the instruction) which are concomitant with it and correlated with it, like intelligence, previous level of mathematical efficiency, study habits, interests, etc. of the subjects. Their effects cannot be prevented, but can be equalized in both the groups. To balance these effects various methods are employed. If the subjects in the two groups are randomly selected and if the samples are sufficiently large the extraneous variables will be rendered less effective in introducing systematic bias. For example, if the selection was random there will be approximately equal number of subjects with similar IQ, interest pattern, previous achievement, etc. in both the groups so that one group will not be at an advantage or disadvantage when compared with the other. For randomization, different methods are used; one method is to prepare a numbered list of names of the subjects and assign the odd numbered subjects to one group and the even numbered to the other.

See: Experiment

RANGE: The basic measure of dispersion of different values of a variable in a distribution, given by the difference between the largest and smallest measurement.

Range is the simplest measure of variability or spread (dispersion) of a set of scores in a distribution. It gives only a crude measure of the variability as can be seen from the following example. Distribution of scores in two spelling tests for a sample of pupils:

Score in test I

0, 1, 3, 4, 6, 7, 8, 9, 10
(Range 10-0 = 10)

Score on test II

0, 5, 5, 6, 6, 6, 6, 6, 10
(Range 10-0 = 10)

It can be easily seen from this example that though the range is the same, in both set of scores, the manner of the spread of scores are not the same. So better measures are adopted for measuring variability.

See: Variability

RATE-TEST: A test which will help in finding out the ability to perform given tasks in unit time. Rate tests are therefore speed tests, that is, the speed at which the individual can perform the task. Such tests are needed to measure the speed at which a task can be done, when the individual has a complete mastery of the task elements. So reading tests are applied to children who have mastered the techniques of reading, to measure their speed (rate) of reading. Typing tests are, likewise rate tests.

See: Power test

RATING SCALE: A verbal or graphic scale used for rating individuals on the basis of behavior traits. A rating scale is usually a horizontal line with points noted 1, 2, 3, 4, 5, etc. often with verbal descriptions showing the degree of trait saturation at the points. The trait name will be noted at the top or on the left hand side. The rater is to mark the appropriate point on the scale for each trait given on the rating schedule, i.e., to assign position for the individual in the trait after observing him. According to the number of points (nodes in the rating scales) it is called a 3 point rating scale, 5 point scale 7 point scale, etc. Rating-scales are applicable for the recording of any kind of behavioural data which can be observed, and quantified on the basis of comparing each trait as distributed in the group. The rater has to do the rating without bias. Though a rating scale can be used for rating oneself it is often used for rating an individual by an external observer.

To enlighten the observer on rating a particular trait, it is better to give a list of type situations which gives the description of behavior in the natural setting. That will help the rater to observe the behavior properly and make the rating more accurately.

The rating scale represents a continuum with regard to the trait.

Example: Trait: Sociability (5 point scale)

1 2 3 4 5

|—|—|—|—|

RATING: The appraisal of a behavioral quality on a graphic scale with descriptions of the positions. It is employed for rating the behavior characteristics of individuals by a trained rater. In order to rate an individual the rater should know the characteristics to be rated and its behavior elements. He should also have acquaintance with the rating instrument. He should observe the individual for some time so that he gets an insight into the behavior characteristics of the individual. It is only then that he makes the rating. A rating card may contain usually 5 or more traits; he may be required to rate the individual on a 3 point, 5 point, 7 point, scale, etc. To avoid halo-effect it is advisable to consider one trait at a time and rate all the individuals in the group for it. That is, the order of rating should be trait-wise and not individual-wise. Assigning rank (ranking) for an individual on a particular criterion is also rating.

To reduce the effect of subjectivity in rating, it is better to take the pooled ratings of two or three raters for the same set of individuals, who make the ratings independently.

Rating though not as refined as standardized tests results, are easier to obtain. It is one of the best observational non-test techniques of collection of behavioural data. Rating also can be used as self-reports. In that case, the individual himself assigns his positions on the rating scale.

See: Halo effect

RATIO SCALE: In scales of measurement, the highest category which possesses a true zero point. Since there is a real zero (that is, the point designated by the absolute absence of the entity) in the ratio scale, not only the intervals between successive points are equal, but the ratios of equal intervals are also equal. Most of the physical quantities like length, weight, volume, etc. can be measured in ratio scales, since all of them have a true zero. Ratio scales possess all the qualities of the other three scales (nominal, ordinal and interval) and, in addition, possess a true zero, e.g., (1) 1 cm, 1.5 cm, 3 cm can be assigned ranks 1, 2 and 3 respectively (ordinal); (2) The interval between 1.2 cm and 2.5 cm is equal to the interval between 7.1 and 8.4 cm (interval); (3) 2 cm is half of 4 cm and two times 1 cm (ratio). '0' cm means absence of any length.

Measures obtained in ratio scales can be added, multiplied or divided. Ratio scales enable all kinds of comparison of measures.

See: Nominal Ordinal Interval

RATIONALISM: The doctrine that reason alone could reveal the truth. Rationalism arose as a revolt against the extreme bigotry of the aristocracy of the eighteenth century Europe. Wilhelm von Leibnitz (1646-1716). Baruch Spinoza (1632-1677) Rene Descartes (1596-1650) and Francois Voltaire (1694-1778) were the exponents of this doctrine. Denis Diderot later elaborated the rationalist theory. The aim of education according to the rationalists was to train those who are capable of thinking. As only a few were able to attain a high level of reasoning, the educational efforts should be concentrated on them. So, the masses were neglected. As intellectual training was considered as the sole aim of education, physical, aesthetic and vocational education were also neglected.

Manners were to replace models. The content of rationalistic education was dominated by philosophy, science, art, literature and mathematics. There was no place for religion. The method emphasized the reasoning processes like the inductive method recommended by Bacon. This trend was also responsible to encourage Rousseau to advocate an extreme view of education.

See: Philosophy of Education

RATIONALIZATION: Trying to give apparently satisfactory reasons and explanations for actions which lack justification. Rationalization is a defence mechanism, according to the psychoanalysts. It can be both a conscious or an unconscious process. To protect the ego, all kinds of reasons are advanced for covering up the weakness of the self. The purpose (conscious or unconscious) is to conceal the truth and make the action of the individual appear reasonable. A boy who has done badly in the examination may say, that he was sick during the week preceding the examination, or that the marking was not impartial, etc. Sometimes, the person may try to provide even far-fetched explanations to rationalize his motives.

See: Ego-defence mechanism

RAW SCORE: The total 'marks' or 'scores' directly obtained from the answer sheets of an individual, according to the directions given by the test constructor. Usually it is indicated by the total number of correct responses. Sometimes it is the total marks obtained by adding up those for individual items which may be numerically unequal owing to the difference in weightage given to each item. In some cases it is the time taken for answering the test. The raw score is the basic score obtained directly from the test sheet before subjecting it to any processing procedure.

Raw scores as such have limited meaning. Suppose in a test on mathematics a boy gets a score of 70 out of 100. Judging from the size of the raw score, it indicates a high level of proficiency. But if in the test, all the 1000 candidates who look the test have got scores ranging between 60 and 100, a score of 70 cannot represent a high value. In another test in which the scores spread from 0 to 80, a score of 70 necessarily indicates a high level of ability. This shows that raw scores by themselves convey only limited meaning. By subjecting the raw scores to appropriate statistical procedures, derived scores are obtained. Derived scores are more meaningful.

Different derived scores are computed from the raw scores which take into consideration the central tendency and the variability (spread) of the scores in the distribution; like the 'centiles', 'standard scores' (C-scores, T-score, etc.), various quotients like 'I.Q.', 'E.Q.', etc. But all operations are based on the raw scores and the raw score distribution, and so, they are the fundamental data for test measurement.

See: Derived scores

REACTANCE THEORY: The theory that states that there is a tendency on the part of the individual to engage in activities in the area in which his freedom is restricted. The child's persistence to do things which he is forbidden to do, is an example. Hostility and aggression also may be aroused as a result of restrictions of freedom. In social situations, when a person is pressurized to conform to a social norm he may develop reactance. The individual in that situation is likely to become hostile and behave in a manner opposed to the ways in which he feels pressurized.

REACTION-FORMATION: Unconsciously developing behaviour pattern which is just opposite of that which the subject wants to reject. This is a defence mechanism of the ego. An attitude of extreme tolerance displayed disproportionate to the situation; 'Don't care attitude' to hide feelings of being rejected, etc. are examples of reaction formation. These reactions are socially acceptable, while the real behaviour tendency which the individual hides is often socially abhorrent.

See: Ego-defence mechanism

READABILITY: The ease with which a passage can be read. The criteria of readability are length of words, length of sentences, the number of abstract words, examples and illustrations provided. Books for children are assessed for readability.

READINESS TEST: The test designed to find out whether a child is psychologically mature to start learning a new task, for example reading, number, etc. Reading requires recognition of forms, notions of horizontality, verticality, etc. Unless the child has developed the required ability in these areas, teaching of reading will produce only marginal results. So also children should have developed the ability to discriminate shape and size and largeness and smallness; the idea 'greater than' and 'less than', etc. before they start learning numbers. In other words, the children should be ready for learning the tasks.

The basic abilities resulting in readiness are developed as a result of maturation, i.e., sensory, psychomotor and other neural development for the appropriate stage. If the child has reached the stage of development appropriate for reading, he is said to have 'reading readiness' and if he has come to the stage of development appropriate for learning number he has 'number readiness'. Rich and varied experience the child gets at home early in life is also a factor that hastens the process of maturation.

See: Maturation

READINESS: The maturational level reached at which the child is psychologically or neuro-muscularly ready to profit from training. Teaching of reading, for example, can start only after the child has reached the reading readiness stage. The concept of readiness has been questioned by some psychologists and Bruner calls it 'a mischievous half-truth'.

READING AGE: A derived score which shows the reading ability of the child in terms of the typical reading performance of children of specific age-groups. A reading age of 6 means that the performance of the child in reading is almost like the average performance of 6 year old children, irrespective of his chronological age. Reading age is obtained by the administration of a standardised reading test. Reading age is the age equivalent of the respective raw-score. For example, if the average score in the standardized reading test for the age group 6 years is 30, a raw score of 30 will indicate a reading age of 6. If a child aged 5 years gets in this test a score of 30, his reading age is taken as 6. The child is accelerated by one year.

See: Derived scores

READING GRADE: A derived score which shows reading ability of the child in comparison to the average reading performance of children of specific school grade. A reading grade of 6 means the reading score obtained by the child on the particular standardized test is equal to the average reading score (mean) of the children in grade 6, irrespective of the grade in which the child is studying at present. If a child in grade 6 is capable of only getting the average score of children in grade 5, his reading grade is only 5. Reading grades are norms obtained from standardized reading tests in which raw scores are converted into grade equivalents.

See: Reading age

REALIA: The real thing used as an aid in teaching. Real articles, if can be obtained, are the best learning aids. Considering expense, safety matters, time to be spent, etc. teachers are constrained to make compromises. But specimens, as in the case of rock samples for geology, and plants for botany are good realia.

REALISM: The philosophy that asserts that 'reality' is a world of things and material existence. The external world exists independent of the mind. The external world is created and determined by laws that govern them. An idea can be considered true only if it corresponds with scientifically validated knowledge. Anything that exists possesses both quality and quantity. Everything can be known–the plan, order, structure and laws of nature. The rational realist finds no need for divine intervention for the creation of the universe or its maintenance. Neo-Realism advocated by Bertrand Russel and A.N. Whitehead attempts to apply the rigour of the methods of modern science and mathematics for philosophical problems. Education, according to the realists, should emphasize the natural laws. The curriculum should have a core of humanistic and scientific subjects. The students should master scientific and experimental methods. Values are available through reasons.

'Realism' can be traced back to Aristotle and Thomas Aquinas.

See: Aristotle, Whitehead, A.N.

RECALL: In memory, the retrieval of past experience. Memory, broadly has two stages–recognition and recall. All past experiences stored in the mind cannot be readily brought back. When the person is able to identify an old experience (stimuli) when presented again, he is said to be able to 'recognize' (i.e., the recognition). But certain experience stored in the mind can be retrieved without the presentation of the same experience. The process is called recall.

See: Memory

RECEPTOR: Specialized nerve cells which receive stimulation. Receptors are end organs situated at the terminals of nerve fibres (afferent fibres). They are distributed all over the skin and muscles. Receptors in the skin and muscles receive sensation of touch, pressure, temperature and change of position in space. Receptors of the inner ear are stimulated by sound waves. Nerve endings (receptors) of the eye are the 'rod' and 'cone' cells which are stimulated by light. On the surface of the tongue are distributed receptors which are sensitive to the taste of substances. So also are the receptors of the nose which are sensitive to different chemical substances. These cells enable us to recognize smells. It is the receptors that enable us to keep in touch with the environment and they are the gateways through which we receive all knowledge. A cluster of receptor cells receiving a particular type of stimuli is called a sense organ (like eye, ear, etc.).

See: Effectors

RECIPROCAL INHIBITION: A technique in Behaviour therapy (developed by Wolpe) for the treatment of anxiety neurosis. The principle states that if an antogonistic response (pleasurable) can be made to occur in the presence of the anxiety producing stimuli, so that a complete or partial supression of the anxiety response occurs, then the bond between the stimuli and anxiety response can be weakened.

See: Behaviour therapy

RECITATION: Speaking out what has been memorized. Performing orally, poems, theorems, etc., one has learnt by heart. Recitation is also a method of learning by heart effectively. It is more effective in learning a passage or poem by heart, than simply by reading it a number of times. Reading, interspersed with trials of recall (recitation) is found to be very effective in memorizing passages.

RECONSTRUCTIONISM: The philosophy of education that emphasizes the supremacy of the 'Society-centered' approach in education. This philosophy stresses social reform, and its chief concern is the future. Reform of Society is more important than the growth of the person. The image of an ideal society should determine the goal of education according to the reconstructionists. Schools should endeavour to educate the future citizens of the emerging society. Education is the instrument of social change. The teachers are committed to the creation of a new reconstructed progressive society. So group living and cooperative action should replace competition and individualistic leadership.

See: Philosophy of Education

REDUCTIONISM: The postulate that declares that all complex phenomena can be reduced to simpler ones. Explanation of complex human behaviour in terms of stimuli and responses, conditioning, 'programs' of the brain, etc. is based on this assumption.

REFLEX: Involuntary responses to a stimulus. It is the most fundamental type of behaviour. Reflex is an automatic response of a group of muscles (or glands) of the body to a specific stimulus. In reflex, the stimulus-response sequence is stereotyped. The reflexes function at the spinal cord level of the nervous system and that is why they are not subjected to conscious control. A common example of a reflex is the eye-wink reflex. Any object moving towards the eye (a hand, puff of air, etc.) makes the eyelids close automatically. This sequence of actions (i.e., involved in eye wink reflex) persists throughout life from first day of life to the end. Some reflexes exist almost from the intra-uterine period of existence. The reflexes function as an inbuilt self-preservation device.

The most common reflexes are involuntary withdrawal of the body parts (e.g., hand) when suddenly subjected to harmful stimuli (like pin prick, fire, chemicals, etc.) and cough produced automatically when something gets struck up in the throat. Salivation, sneezing, vomitting, etc. are caused by reflexes.

Reflexes are conditionable. A stimulus linked to the original stimulus by conditioning can also elicit the old responses. Even a bell ring can produce salivation in a dog, if the animal has been experiencing the bell ring paired with the natural stimulus (meat) a number of times.

See: Classical conditioning

REGRESSION: Retracing or going backwards. Regression is a defence mechanism. In regression an individual adopts an earlier mode of behaviour (less mature form of response). In some mental disorders adults behave like children. In some cases of psychoses, the patients regress to the most early stages of their lives, i.e., they behave like babies.

Normal adults under severe stress and frustration are seen to show behaviour which are regressive (crying like children, showing temper tantrums, etc.)

In psychoanalysis, it means an individual reverting back to an earlier stage of development, such as an young adult showing the characteristic behaviour of a five year old – thumb-sucking, bed wetting, etc.

REINFORCEMENT: An event that will strengthen the bond between a stimulus and a response. In this sense all rewards are reinforcers. A negative reinforcement is an event (or condition) the withdrawal of which will strengthen the bond between stimulus and response.

In operant conditioning (Skinner) it is the event (or condition) that tends to increase the probability of the emitting of a particular response to a stimulus again under similar circumstances. In the Skinner box experiment the rat emits a large number of random responses and one such random response accidently pushes down the lever which releases the food pellet. The response (i.e., the one random response which released the food) is immediately reinforced (by food). The reinforcement event is the food and it tends to increase the probability of lever pressing.

See: Rewards, Contingency

REJECTEE: A pupil (boy or girl) whom all his classmates refuse to accept as a playmate or as a companion. Rejectees are objectively found out by administering a sociometric test. The test requires all the children in the group to write down the names, 3 usually, of his classmates with whom he does not like to play, work with, etc. in order of rank. The pupils who receive large number of choices (i.e., rejections) are rejectees. A rejectee may possess behavior traits which others consider aversive. He may be having problems of adjustment, which can be resolved by prompt psychological treatment (counselling).

See: Star, Isolate, Neglectee

RELEARNING: Attempting to learn once again what has been previously learnt and forgotten. Partially or completely forgotten knowledge can be regained by relearning. The effort (repetition) required for relearning is considerably less than that was originally required for the first learning. 'Relearning' is used for measuring the degree of retention. The 'savings' in relearning gives an index of retention.

See: Saving method

RELIABILITY: The consistency with which a test measures the dimension it intends to measure. So, it refers to the accuracy of measurement of the tests in terms of repeated measurements. A reliable test gives almost the same values when repeated measurements are taken with it on the same individual under the same set of conditions. As the effect of various chance factors that affect test performance changes from administration to administration, it is not likely to get exactly the same scores on repeated applications on the same individuals even if the test is an ideal one. But a good test should provide values which are approximately the same. To illustrate: If in a test of intelligence a boy gets a score of 70 on one day and 45 and 55 on subsequent applications after intervals of one week each, the test does not yield consistent result, and so is not reliable. If it gives values like 70, 69 and 72 the test can be assumed to be very reliable. An unreliable test is like a measuring tape calibrated on an elastic material. As all educational and psychological tests are influenced by chance factors, their reliability can never be perfect. So it is necessary to ascertain the reliability of a test before it is used. The principle involved in obtaining the reliability is based on the characteristics of the test – i.e., it should give consistent results on repeated administrations. The methods commonly used are:

1. *Test-retest method:* The correlation of the score on the same test on the same sample of populations on two administration with a time interval, say one to 2 weeks, provides the index of reliability. This is called Test-retest reliability.

2. *Alternate forms method:* If two tests of the same kind measuring the same dimension can be assumed to be equivalent, correlation between the scores of the two forms also yields the index of reliability. This is Alternate Test Form Reliability.

3. *Split-Half Method:* The same test can be split into two parallel forms (also equivalent). The usual method is to obtain scores separately for the odd-numbered items and even-numbered items and compute the correlation between the two. This is split-half reliability. For example, a test of 100 items will be considered as two tests, with item number 1, 3, 5, 7....99 as Test A and that with item numbers 2, 4, 6, 8,....100 as Test B. Scores for A and B for all candidates will be obtained separately. Their correlation coefficient will be worked out. This correlation coefficient will be

actually lower than the complete test of 100 items because it gives the value for only half the test. The reliability of the whole test can then be obtained from it by the Spearman-Brown formula.

$$r_{11} = \frac{2r_{hh}}{1 + r_{hh}}$$

where r_{11}: reliability coefficient of the whole test

r^{hh} : reliability coefficient of one half the test obtained experimentally.

4. The method of rational equivalence or internal consistency. This is also obtained by a single administration of the test. The assumption underlying this method is that in a reliable test, there is equivalence between the intercorrelations of items in the test and the correlation of the items with the whole test (rational equivalence). To find out the reliability coefficient according to this method, the Kuder-Richardson formula is used.

For a test of maximum performance (ability tests, like intelligence tests, scholastic tests), reliability coefficient above 0.8 are recommended while for tests of typical performance (personality tests, attitude scales, etc.) reliability coefficients above 0.7 are considered acceptable.

Reliability is dependent on the length of the test; lengthening the test increases its reliability.

See: Validity, Kuder-Richardson formulas

REMEDIAL EDUCATION: Special teaching provided for backward children in subject areas in which they are deficient. Both normal and dull children experience difficulties in learning some concepts or skills. They may skip the portion and proceed. This practice leads to further difficulties and when such deficiencies accumulate, at a later stage the child will be seriously handicapped in learning more complex concepts. This is particularly true in the learning of the basic skills and concepts, like the fundamental operations in mathematics. Many skills develop in a hierarchical manner and so deficiency at a lower level will be a hindrance in learning the skill at the higher level. If the areas in which the children are deficient can be identified and suitable programmes are provided for them, they will catch up. Teaching programmes meant for remedying such defects in learning is called remedial education. Remedial education has, as pointed out, two steps (1)

Identification of the exact area of difficulty. Diagnostic tests or achievement tests can be used for diagnosis. (2) Remedial work. This involves individualized instruction with the use of suitable teaching learning-materials.

For dull children (slow-learners) a continuous programme of remedial education will be necessary.

See: Diagnostic tests

REMEDIAL FRAME: In Programmed Instruction, a frame which requires repetition of a previously covered concept (in some altered simplified form) for proper mastery.

See: Programmed Instruction

REMINISCENCE: The improvement in performance that occurs as latent learning taking place during the rest period after learning. This phenomenon was first demonstrated by Ballard in 1913. He gave a short poem to a class of young children for memorization. He tested the amount memorized by the children immediately after the memorization period and on the following day. He found that the children remembered more the next day than at the end of the learning session.

See: Latent learning

REPRESSION: The fundamental defence mechanism postulated by Freud, by means of which painful and traumatic expriences are pushed down from the conscious to the unconscious. As it is an unconscious process the subject is not aware of what is happening. The repressed ideas and thoughts are not really forgotten, they remain in the unconscious and reappear, often in disguise, in jokes, dreams, slips of the tongue psyhological symptoms, etc. It is a protective mechanism as it shields the ego from the pangs of traumatic and distressful suffering.

Many psychoneurotic symptoms of anxiety, phobia, obsession, delusion, hallucinations, etc. have their origin in repressed experiences.

See: Ego-defence mechanism

RESPONSE FRAME: In computer terminology an Interactive video text system that is intended to elicit a response and in Programmed Instruction a frame which follows a branching program.

See: Computer-Assisted-Learning, Programmed Instruction

RESPONSE SET: Tendency to react under the influence of factors other than those which exist in the stimulus situation. When required to give a response in a social situation, individuals tend to produce socially desirable responses. The proneness to respond in this manner, in other words, is the response set.

RESPONSE: Reaction an individual makes to a stimulus. Voluntary or involuntary (reflexes) reactions the organism makes to a stimulus is a response. A response can be either overt (like speaking out the answer to a question) or covert (like thinking about a problem posed by the teacher). Adjustment to the environment depends on the individual's ability to make appropriate responses in the situation. Education is concerned with the development of the capability to produce appropriate responses that lead to successful adjustment in various situations the individual is likely to encounter with. Withdrawal of the hand when the finger touches a hot object, finding out solutions to a complex mathematical problem, marking the answer to a question in the frame of a programmed learning unit are all responses. 'Learning' is the process of acquisition of proper response systems. This is possible because behaviour (response) is modifiable. By the management and control of appropriate stimuli (teaching) expected responses system can be developed in the individuals (learning).

It is also used to denote the reactions of the individual to stimulations presented by the teacher, like answers to questions, responses made by students in programmed learning, etc.

See: Conditioned response

RESPONSE FRAME: In CAL the frame which requires the learner to make a response. Usually when the frame is presented, after reading it (or seeing it) the learner types the word required (response). This is one of the most important feature of the CAL, it ensures active participation of the learner.

See: Computer-Assisted-Learning

RETARDATION: 1. Arrested growth. Retardation is either physical or mental. Physical retardation is marked by stunted bodily growth. It may be due to hereditary causes or due to malnutrition. The ill-effects of the deficiency apparently increases as chronological age increases. Glandular (pituitary and thyroid) malfunctioning and lack of proper nutrition at the early stages of development are contributory causes of physical retardation. A physically retarded child has ill-developed skeletal and muscular systems.

2. Mental retardation is considered to be largely hereditary in origin aggravated by environmental deprivation. A mentally retarded child's mental age fails to catch up with his chronological age. When the mental age of a child equals that of his chronological age, his development is normal. But when the mental age is considerably below that of his chronological age there is retardation. The degree of retardation is reckoned in terms of the disparity between the two. Based on the degree of retardation, mentally defective children are classified as 'border line', 'morons', 'imbeciles' and 'idiots'. All these children have I.Q. below 70 (idiots have I.Q. below 20). A 14 year old idiot has only a mental age of a child around 3 years.

3. Retardation is also used to denote the lack of progress of pupils in schools in terms of their capacity. A bright child whose attainment is consistently low in school subjects is considered as a retarded child. This is scholastic retardation. It is also called underachievement.

See: Backwardness, Mental deficiency

RETICULAR FORMATION: The diffuse network of nerve cells running through the brain-stem up to the thalamus. It receives message from all sensory pathways. It is closely connected with the spinal cord, thalamus and cerebral cortex. It has an important role in the arousal of the cortex and is involved in selective attention. Sleeping pills act by inhibiting reticular formation.

See: Hypothalamus

RETRIEVAL: The mental process involved in drawing out information from the Long Term Memory (LTM) system. It is a process of search. In certain cases it is a spontaneous identification process (recognition) and in some other cases it involves active search resulting in recall. The 'Context' is very important in retrieval process.

See: Memory

RETROACTIVE INHIBITION: The inhibitory interference of a new learning on a thing previously learnt. Attempting to learn something (which is similar in content) immediately after learning another item before it is recalled, tends to weaken the retention of the thing first learned. This is because the second activity is supposed to exert some inhibitory influence on the retention of the first. Learning followed by rest periods (or sleep) are found to be better retained considerably than a learning followed by other learning activities.

See: Proactive inhibition

RETROGRADE AMNESIA: Forgetting that occurs backwards from an event. After suffering a traumatic experience (may be a severe blow causing brain injury, or severe emotional shock) an individual tends to develop partial or total forgetfulness of experiences he had before the occurrence of the trauma. In severe cases he may even fail to remember his identify. The memory is often brought back by chemotherapy and/or psychotherapy.

See: Anterograde Amnesia

REWARDS: Pleasant stimuli given for producing a desired response. Rewards can be material (as sweets, coins, medals, tokens, etc.) or psychological (like praise, positions of honour, etc.) Rewards are in recognition of good work. They are believed to strengthen the characteristics for which they are given. In schools, they are also offered as an incentive for good work and exemplary behaviour.

Rewards are positive reinforcements. A reward satisfies a need. To be effective, rewards will have to be administered judiciously. They will lose their significance if given indiscriminately. Variable interval schedules or variable ratio schedules for the award of the rewards are found to be the most effective in producing good results. Psychological rewards (like recognition, approval, praise of knowledge of results of work done, etc.) prove very useful in human learning.

See: Punishment

RIGMAROLE: A language game played in groups. Each student is given a sheet of paper in which is given the opening sentence of a story. The student is to read the sentence and add another sentence of his own. The papers are then circulated among the members of the group and each student is required to add a sentence to each story. The last student in each case writes the concluding sentence and gives a title for the story.

RIPPLE EFFECT: The effect of censure and reprimand administered on high prestige pupils for misbehaviour, on other pupils. Mild punishment imposed on pupils who are popular in sociometric status, for elimination of misbehaviour is found to have beneficial effects on others with similar problems. The reprimand to be effective has to be administered in a social situation.

RITALIN: A drug which is believed to suppress unruly behaviour. The drug, when taken, reduces physical activity in children. It is a form of amphetamine. Child specialists sometimes prescribe the drug in the case of hyperactive children.

ROBINS REPORT: The Report on Higher Education, England, 1963. The committee was headed by Lord Robins. The main recommendations of the Report were that: the number of students in higher education should be doubled, that nobody should be prevented from pursuing higher studies for lack of money, that new universities should be set up, training colleges should be transformed to colleges of education providing degree course, etc.

ROGERS, CARL: American psychologist who popularised client-centered psychotherapy and counselling. It is also called Non-directive counselling since the psychologist's role is minimal, only to encourage the client to talk out his problems.

ROLE PLAYING: Acting out certain roles under simulated conditions. Role playing is a technique used for training people for jobs. A group of trainees are assigned various positions in the job and each one is required to act out his part under simulated conditions. This gives the trainees a real grasp of the job activities, work situation, etc. Sometimes, it is also used for identifying the aptitudes and interests of the trainees. Role playing is also used for the elimination of the undesirable behaviour tendencies like aggression, shyness, etc. Then its effect is similar to a psychodrama.

See: Psychodrama

ROLE CONFLICT: Conflict arousing out of the situation in which the individual is expected to play two roles that have opposing qualities.

When the individuals in their dual role require to respond in two opposing ways they face role conflict. This happens when they have to occupy two positions simultaneously whose roles are antagonistic. The housewife who takes up a career experiences role conflict. As housewife she has to devote most of her time in home management, care of children, etc. The job, likewise requires her full devotion to her duties. The demands from the two are opposing and that cannot be easily compromised.

ROLE: Pattern of behavior expected of a person in a particular position. The members of a group expect a specific pattern of behavior qualities in a person occupying a position. The role prescribes the pattern of needs, abilities, attitudes, interests and values of the person in a position. The role has its typical pattern of behavior which the people expect in standard situations. i.e., person's duties and obligations.

ROM: In computer terminology, a term used for a store from which information can be retrieved as and when required. When once entered in the store, normally it is not easy to be altered. A contraction for Read-Only-Memory.

ROMAN EDUCATION (ANCIENT): The education prevalent in Rome during the pre-Christian centuries. Ancient Romans were practical people whose main concern was utilitarianism. The aim of education emphasized the subordination of the freedom of the individual to the interest of the state. The state required a nation of brave soldiers and good citizens. So the training was for producing good citizens, brave warriors and hard workers. Piety, honesty, dignity, manliness and industry were important qualities that the citizens were expected to develop. Education therefore emphasized ethics and religion. Intellectual and aesthetic education received little attention. Vocational education, was however, considered important. The children were taught homelife, tradition and citizenship. 'The Laws of the Twelve Tables' was a part of early education. Games were encouraged. There were separate educational programmes for the patricians (nobles) and plebians (commoners). Girls were trained at home, particularly in weaving and spinning. Family was the first agency involved in teaching the children. Formal schools played an insignificant role, while in the farm, work shop and military campus the pupils received most of their training. The method of learning was direct imitation and their discipline was very rigorous.

ROSENTHAL EFFECT: Same as PYGMALION EFFECT.

ROSMINI-SERBATI, ANTONIO (1797-1855): Italian Educational thinker whose views on teaching were far ahead of his times. His ideas on pedagogy are contained in his book 'Ruling principles of Methods in Education'. According to him, the place of the child in education is central. Teaching should be undertaken only according to the principles of mental development. His view was that the mind first conceives the general and then the particular. The child should be presented first with objects which belongs to the first order of cognition (concrete) then only proceed to the second order (abstract). The child first sees the world as an unanalysed whole and later acquires knowledge of details. The child should be provided with ample opportunities for looking at, touching, smelling and experimenting upon with objects. Imaginative play is an effective way of learning.

ROUSSEAU, JEAN JACQUES (1712-1778): The great eighteenth century thinker whose contribution to political, social and educational ideologies had great impact all over the world. Rousseau was born in 1712 in Geneva. His thoughts were based on his firm belief in his naturalistic philosophy. His revolutionary political treatise 'The Social Contract' and his educational masterpiece 'Emile' both declare man to return to nature. In 'Social Contract' he says "Man is born free and everywhere he is in chains, one thinks himself the master of others and still remains a greater slave ....." Since no man has a natural authority over his fellow beings and force creates no right, we must conclude that conventions form the basis of all legitimate authority among men. The first paragraph of "Emile" opens like this "All things are good as they come out of the hands of their creator but everything degenerates in the hands of man..... He is not content with anything in its natural state not even with his species." 'Emile' deals with the education of boys, written in the form of a novel. It was published in 1762. Education should be "negative" upto the age of twelve and should allow free play of nature. The teacher should see that the experience of the child should be in harmony with his physical and mental development. He says that in the first year of his life the child is not clearly conscious of his experiences. In infancy the child learns to develop his senses through contact with environment. Books and abstract concepts should be avoided at this stage. After the eleventh year of life education can become more intellectual. The child learns to form concepts with the help of the tutor who should improvise devices required for instruction. In this way he develops a sense of utility. At about the age of fourteen the child is a thinking, acting individual. Now history and natural theology must be used for leading the child to adulthood. Rousseau's call to "return to nature" was forceful enough to make people think about the urgency of revamping education and to change the view of the parents that children are 'mere inferior adults'. It focussed the attention to the need for psychologizing education. His views were apparently extreme, for instance, he said that 'the only habit he would like Emile to develop was the habit of forming no habits'. Roussau died in 1778.

Rousseian ideas on girl's education, however, were retrograde. This is apparent in his discussion in the 'Education of Sophie', Emile's future wife. Every principle advocated for Emile is reversed for Sophie. The educated woman was only to be a shadow of the husband, her responsibilities were only to be useful to him, to please him to make herself look and honoured by him, to console him to render his life agreeable, sweet ...."

RULEG: A teaching technique – 'rule given first', followed by 'examples'. (Rule – eg).

RUSSELL, BERTRAND: Russell (1872-1970) is one of the greatest thinkers of the twentieth century. He published more than fifty books and was awarded the Nobel Prize for literature in 1950. He was a philosopher, mathematician, political thinker and a literary genius. He started a private school, in Sussex, in order to try out his ideas in education. His books 'On Education' (1926) and 'Education and Social Order'(1932), 'Human Knowledge, its scopes and limits' (1948) have greatly contributed to the educational thinking in the modern era.

S

SACCADIC MOVEMENTS: Movements of the eye when it fixates in reading. When reading, the eye appears to fixate at points along the print. But these are not motionless steps; the eye continues to make slight movement (though very rapid) like slight vibrations. These movements are called saccadic movements–and are essential for perception.

SAMPLE: Representative fraction of a population. Populations about which generalizations are to be made are so large in many cases that it is almost impossible to collect data based on all members. For example, to draw conclusions about the general level of mathematical achievement of students in secondary schools in a State (based on the population of students) it would be necessary to test tens of thousands of students under standardized conditions. This is impractical; so the experimenters are constrained to choose a small workable proportion of students from the population, which should preserve all the characteristics of the total population (as far as possible). Such a small segment of the population drawn for a particular treatment is called a sample. The sample, if well chosen, will preserve almost all the characteristics of the whole population. The method of selecting such samples is called sampling.

In order to make useful conclusions from sample statistics, it is necessary that the sample should be sufficiently large. How large it should be, is dependent on the size of the population, the complexity in the characteristics of the members of the population and practical convenience. The unavoidable error component in a single value obtained from a sample is inversely proportional to the square root of the size of the sample.

See: Parameter, Population

SAMPLING STATISTICS: Statistics obtained from samples as estimates of the population parameters. Sample statistics help us in drawing conclusions about the properties of the population, from a single sample. The value obtained from the sample will only be an estimate of the population value and it will incorporate an error component also. But the range of the error component also can be estimated. Sampling statistics enables us to estimate the accuracy of the values obtained from the samples. For educational and psychological experimentation samples only are used unless there is a specific need for a survey data on the entire population.

SAMPLING ERROR: The error component in the sample values. Generalizations in education and psychology are often based on statistics obtained from samples of populations. Even if the samples are selected with utmost care to make it random, it may still have an error component, caused by chance factors. So the mean (M) on a dimension (e.g., intelligence) derived from a number of random samples drawn from the same population vary. So the sample value is only an approximation of the population value. The errors due to chance factors inherent in the values obtained from samples is called Sampling error.

The sampling error of a value can be estimated.

If we obtain a large number (more than 30) of values for a variable obtained from different samples of population and plot them on a graph we will find that it takes approximately the form of a normal curve. Such a distribution is called a sampling distribution. The means and standard deviations in this distribution can also be worked out. From this the standard error for each statistic can be calculated by the application of appropriate formula.

See: Standard error

SAMPLING: The process of selecting representative samples. If the sample is to be representative of the population, the sampling procedure should ensure that every individual in the population has an equal chance of being selected. Suppose that 1000 students are decided to be selected from a population of 10,000 students. Every member in the total population should have equal chance of being selected, i.e., nobody gets advantage of favour or disadvantage of disfavour. A sample so selected is a random sample. As all candidates have been equally considered for the selection (i.e., every 10th student selected starting from any random number in the roll) the sample will be approximately similar in character to the population. It will be a representative sample. Inferences drawn on data obtained from the sample can be accepted as applicable to the entire population.

There are different methods of selecting a sample randomly. After deciding the size of the sample, members may be selected with the help of a Table of random numbers or by taking every 10th, 20th, etc. member of the population.

When the population consists of well defined sub-groups sometimes stratified random sampling method is adopted. Suppose the children to be tested consist of different sub-groups which are found in concentration in particular geographical locations, like children of culturally disadvantaged people, or factory workers, or urban dwellers, etc. each sub-population is considered separately to select the sample at random from them in proportion to their number in the total population. Such a sample also will be representative. This is also called quota sampling.

See: Sample

SARGENT REPORT: The report of the Committee constituted for guiding post-war educational development in India. The report is also called "Post-war Educational Development in India, 1944". The committee was headed by Sir John Sargent. The recommendations outlined in the report were intended: "to create in India in a period of not less than 40 years the same standard of educational attainments as has already attained in England". The committee suggested: provision for pre-primary education between the ages 3-6, primary or basic education for all children between 6-14 years, a high school education of 6 years for selected children between 11-17 years, and a university course of 3 years after the intermediate examination; for selected students Technical, Commercial and Art education for full time and part-time; adult literacy programmes; development of public library system; full provision for proper training of teachers; compulsory physical education in schools; schools for physically and mentally handicapped; creation of employment bureaus, etc. It also recommended that the medium of instruction in all high schools should be the regional language, but English should be compulsory and that frequent refresher courses should be held for teachers and routine medical check-up for school children as often as needed. The report is also known as 'Sarjent plan' and 'Report of the Central Advisory Board of Education 1944'.

See: Radhakrishnan Report, Mudaliar Report, Kothari Report

SAVING METHOD: A method used for determining the degree of retention of learned materials. The number of trials (and time) required for the original learning. The difference between the two or savings gives an index of retention of the learnt material (i.e., degree of retention in memory).

See: Relearning

SCALE VALUE: The median value obtained from the scale positions assigned by the judges for a statement, according to the Thurstone's method of attitude scale construction. In this method a large number of statements relating to the expression of the attitude in question (e.g., attitude toward nuclear war) are collected and a panel of judges (usually 50) scrutinize the items and assign each item a scale value from extreme 'unfavourable' (0.0) to extreme 'favourable' (11.0). The scale is supposed to spread in a continuum with 11 divisions with equal intervals. For each item the judges may assign different scale values. From these the median value is computed, which is taken as the scale value of the statement.

See: Attitude scale

SCALING: Observation data or test data converted into a scale. 'Scaling' is the method of representating obtained data in some understandable unit after converting the distribution into a scale.

The marks obtained by children in a school may be scaled on this basis. For scaling of school marks, often the teacher's ratings are also considered. According to the level of performance the score may be scaled from 0 to 5, 0 to 7 or 0 to 9 points. In a scale with 9 points, 9 represents the highest level of performance. Each scale division (e.g., 0-1, 1-2, etc) will represent a range in the marks. (e.g., from 0-10, 11 to 25, etc.).

SCAPE-GOATING: The practice of shifting blame to an innocent person or group, to cover up one's involvement in one's misdeeds or to victimize an innocent person or group. The person in superior positions sometimes play this trick on their subordinates, by shifting the responsibility of their lapses on them, i.e., making them scape-goats.

SCATTER DIAGRAM: A chart showing two paired variables with one variable on the x-axis and the other on the y-axis. It is also called a Scattergram. It is prepared for the computation of the Pearson Correlation Coefficient. So it is also called a correlation table.

See: Correlation coefficient

SCHEMA: Also 'schemata'. The Piagetian concept which is used to explain how new information perceived by the senses (from external world) is received in the mind. The conceptual (schema) structure already existing in the mind enables the itnerpretation possible, i.e., if it is compatible, it will be accommodated or assimilated, otherwise, rejected.

See: Adaptation Piaget J.

SCHIZOPHRENIA: A severe form of mental disorder, the most remarkable symptom being extreme withdrawal. The word means split-brain. The symptoms of schizophrenia are: thought disorder, inappropriate emotional responsiveness, delusions, withdrawal and regression to a very early stage (behaving like small children). Complete cure is difficult in the case of schizophrenia, but improvement is possible with hospitalized psychiatric treatment.

See: Psychosis

SCHOOL RETENTION POWER: The efficiency of the school in keeping all the children admitted in it till they complete the specified course. The 'retention power' of the school is high if almost all of the children admitted in its lowest standard complete all the standards of that school before leaving it. In other words, the rate of premature leaving (droppage) will be low in schools which have high retention power. This is also called 'holding power' of the school.

See: Holding power

SCHOOL COMPLEX: A net-work of primary schools organised around a secondary school for the purpose of quality improvement of both. The main objectives of school complexes are the sharing of resoucres, human and material and the breaking of isolation existing among various types of educational institutions. The activities proposed for the complexes are: conducting conferences, seminars, model classes, etc. in the nucleus secondary school for the benefit of primary teachers, lending of teaching aids and scientific apparatus to the primary schools and secondary shool teachers taking demonstration classes in primary schools.

The primary school teachers can visit the secondary schools as often as necessary. The secondary school teachers, by their contact with the primary schools, gain direct experience of the programmes of the primary school, and so will be in a better position to gear their activities to synchronize with it.

SCHOOL INSPECTION: One of the most important and managerial procedure in education necessary for quality assurance. It is intimately linked with the accountability of the institution.

The purpose of school inspections should be development-oriented. It should neither be ritualistic nor directed simply towards fault detection. The inspecting agency should consist of a team of experts and the inspection should be regular and thorough. The area of inspection is mainly two–the teaching-learning aspect and the management aspect (administration and finance). Detailed examination by an external agency can find out both the weakness and lacuna in the system as well as the strengths and achievements, objectively. Institutions in their turn can remedy their defects, take precautions to avoid failure, utilize their resources fully and plan progress in all directions. This will also help in standardizing quality of education in a region or state.

See: Accountability, Quality control

SCHOOL LEAVING AGE: The upper age-limit fixed statutorily for compulsory education.

SCHOOL PHOBIA: Abnormal fear of school experienced by some children. The school's inability to provide pleasurable experience to children is a conducive condition for the development of intense fright in young children. Generally, the phobia develops by emotional conditioning. Many children overcome the fear spontaneously, but for some psychological treatment may become necessary.

SCHOOL REFUSAL: Premature voluntary leaving of school. Also known as 'droppage' and 'wastage'. The reason, for school refusal is very complex, the origin of the trouble can be traced back to the individual, home, school or society, singly or collectively. Retrieval will be possible only after identification of the causes and effecting remedial measures.

See: Droppage, Wastage

SCHOOLS OF PSYCHOLOGY: Different systems of psychology based on different approaches. Down from the time of recorded history, thinkers and philosophers held their own views of mental behavior. The explanations of human behavior differed according to the basic approach adopted by the thinker. The most important Schools of psychology are:

1. Structural psychology which developed around 1879 in Germany
2. Functional psychology which originated in USA around 1898
3. Associationism around 1898 in UK, USA, Russia
4. Psychoanalysis in Austria in 1900
5. Personalistic and organismic psychology in Germany, USA in 1900,
6. Purposive or Hormic psychology in 1908 in UK
7. Behaviorism in USA in 1912 and (8) Gestalt psychology in Germany in 1912.

SCORING: Marking the responses, or assigning marks according to the key prepared for the test. Scoring is done manually by comparing the answer sheet with the keys (manual scoring) or by using stencil keys (stencil scoring) or by machines (electronic test scoring machines). After scoring each correct response, the total will be taken. The total score will be in terms of the number of correct responses (or significant responses) made by a candidate, or the total time taken by him to complete the test or the total of marks assigned for each item, as in the case of school and college examinations.

See: Tests

SCORING STENCIL: A mechanical device for scoring tests. A scoring key is made of stencils with windows cut out at the position of correct answers. It is usually a transparent thin plastic sheet which is of the same size of answer sheet. Punched windows are made at the positions of the correct answers. The stencil is placed flatly on the answer sheet so that its edges coincide with the corresponding edges of the answer sheet. Then the position of correct responses will be exposed through the windows. The candidate's markings can be seen through the window if he has chosen the correct answer.

The stencil key for a test is prepared beforehand and copies of the same will be made available so that a number of persons can do the scoring at a time. It is not only economical but also more fool proof (objective).

See: Machine scoring

SCRAMBLED TEXT: The text book used in programmed learning in which the pages are not numbered sequentially. To find out the correct responses for a frame the student has to look into the page he is instructured to. So the order of use is determined by the response of the learner and he has to move from forward and backward alternating as often as needed. This method is needed particularly for programmed text books using branching programmes.

See: Programmed learning

SCREENING TESTS: Test used to select suitable individuals for some purpose (job, training course, etc.) and to eliminate the unsuitables.

Screening tests are criterion-oriented, i.e., such tests are prepared specifically to find out whether the person possess particular set of qualities. For example, for selection to the post of air-line pilots, the candidates are given tests under simulalated conditions (as in the cockpit of a fighter plane) that can measure the degree of concentration, complex psycho-motor coordination, alertness, etc. For the selection of candidates for the post of typists, a test to obtain data on speed and accuracy in typing is given. For professional courses like engineering and medicine, special aptitude tests are used as screening tests. Screening tests are believed to be prognostic, meaning that those who do well in them are likely to succeed in the specific job in future.

SECOND ORDER CONDITIONING: Conditioning a new stimulus with a previously conditioned stimulus. In the conditioning experiment on conditioned reflexes, it was possible to elicit saliva (conditioned reflex) at the sound of a bell (conditioned stimulus). After establishing this conditioning, if another stimulus (say the glow of an electric bulb) is paired with the conditioned stimulus i.e., with the bell a number of times, the glow of the bulbs also succeed in eliciting the conditioned reflex (salivation). This is second order conditioning. Second order conditioning is less strong than the first order conditioning (i.e., in terms of the quantity of saliva secreted). The translation method of learning a new language corresponds roughly to second order conditioning (i.e., the real object is paired with the word in the mother tongue first, and the word in the mother language is paired with the word in the new language at the second stage).

See: Classical conditioning

SECONDARY NEEDS: Needs derived from primary needs or needs not directly connected with survival. Secondary needs are derived from the basic (primary) physiological needs for oxygen, water, elimination, warmth, etc. For satisfying the physiological need of hunger raw vegetables and raw meat would be adequate. But man wants delicacies according to his own tastes for food. The need for such delicacies are derived needs, the need derived from the primary need for food. Similarly from the primary needs for warmth and support a variety of secondary needs are derived (like the need for magnificent houses, air conditioners, etc.). The needs like, security, comfort, recognition, approval, love, etc. are derived secondary needs. Secondary needs are psychological needs. Motivation is strongly related to need satisfaction.

See: Needs

SELF: The core of the personality, otherwise called the ego. It is the sum total of the personal awareness of the person himself. The interests and values with which he identifies himself along with his social perceptions are central to the self of the person.

See: Personality

SELF CONCEPT: The image of a person as he believes he has. The development of self-concept, takes place as the child grows and by adulthood, it normally stabilizes. If his self-concept does not agree with reality, problems of adjustment in social situations may arise. Severe distortion of self-concept will have to be treated by counselling or psychotherapy.

SELF FULFILLING PROPHECY: Also known as 'Labelling' and Pygmalion effect.

See: Labelling

SEMANTIC GENERALIZATIONS: Stimulus generalization that occurs when a conditioned verbal response is elicited by other words (or abstract symbols) which are similar in meaning to the original word. The principle was first demonstrated by Ivanov Smolensky. If a response was conditioned to a particular word, he showed that the same response would be elicited by other words similar in meaning to the conditioned word. The strength of the conditioning depends on the extent to which the words are similar. When the degree of similarity is low, the strength of the bond is weak. A response conditioned to a word, thus generalizes to a set of words (with different degrees of strength) that are semantically similar. A human subject conditioned to respond in a particular way in the presence of an object would make the same response on hearing the 'word' representing the object or to the words which are similar in meaning. The generalization sometimes extend even towards that sound similar or appear similar in written form (visually). But in that case the generalization effected is very weak.

See: Classical conditioning

SEMANTIC DIFFERENTIAL RATING INSTRUMENT: The method of measuring the meanings of concepts by analyzing ratings on a number of bipolar adjectives.

The underlying principle of semantic differential rating method, developed principally by Osgood, is that the meaning of an object for an individual includes two components-denotative meaning and connotative meaning. Denotative meaning is obvious; it is the objects, events, etc. the word represents. But connotative meaning is more subtle and varies from individual to individual. It refers to the feelings and attitudes associated with the word. So to measure the important connotative meaning of a concept or object, ratings of the object/concept on a number of bipolar adjectives are obtained from the individual. The meaning of the object for the person can be understood from the profile of his ratings.

The ratings are obtained on each concept from a number of persons and the profiles based on their means indicate the connotative meaning of the word.

Semantic differential methods is also used for the measurement of attitudes.

SEMIOTICS: The study of signs and symbols. It involves the study of symbols as means of communication, whether transmitted as language or gesture, touch or in any other manner. Also 'semiology'. This branch of study is currently assuming high significance in the context of communication revolution.

SENSE REALISM: The view point that the basic reality is the reality found in the forces and laws of nature. It is also called scientific realism. The proponents of this philosophical approach were Wolfang Ratke (1571-1635), and John Amos Cominius (1592-1670). The aim of education according to the sense realists were 'to help nature to her perfection, learn nature's laws and control nature for the benefit of man'. So good education should aim at teaching all good things to all men. The teaching methods also should be related to the laws of nature. Education should be liberal and democratic. There should be elementary education of six years for both sexes. The contents of curriculum should be drawn from the various areas of interest of children. Teachers should be trained for the job. The structure of schools should be in agreement with the capacities of children and so a ladder system of grading was necessary. Each class should have a separate classroom and a teacher. Younger children needed only four hours of instruction and older, six hours. The most important impact of this approach was that it initiated studies and investigations on child development and teaching methodology. Ratke formulated the following principles of teaching: Everything to be introduced in its natural order, Teach only one thing at a time, Repeat as often as necessary, First teach in the vernacular, Do not compel, there should be no rote learning, Similar subjects taught in the same way, Concrete ideas first, explanation afterwards and Use induction and experimentation.

SENSORI-MOTOR: Behavior comprising afferent (stimulus) and efferent (response) elements. A response elicited by a sense stimulation is a sensori-motor act. The sense impression is conveyed to the spinal cord or brain as electrical impulses through afferent nerves (sensory) and the resulting signals from the brain are also likewise transmitted through the efferent nerves (motor) to the effectors (muscles or glands, etc.) which results in an overt activity like withdrawal of the hand, or moving towards a person, etc.

See: Stimulus, Response

SENSORY-MOTOR STAGE: The first stage of cognitive development in children, according to Piaget. The stage extends from the period from birth to 2 years, approximately. At this stage, the child's activities are limited to motor reactions.

Manipulation of the environment is solely by physical actions. The child is unable to internalize the representation of an object, but he can symbolize it in the form of physical action (e.g., shaking the hand in imitation of shaking a rattle). The idea of permanence of an object develops only towards the later phase of this stage. The child then tries to seek objects hidden from view. At the sensory motor stage, the child cannot think about an object without manipulating it. Towards the end of the second year the child shows some evidence of internal representation of objects.

See: Development, Piaget. J

SERIAL LEARNING: Learning involved when the elements of the learning task is to be learned in a specific sequence. In serial learning, the items occurring in the beginning and end are more easily learned than those occurring in the middle. This is called the 'serial position effect'. Omissions and errors are more frequent in the middle of the series. Meaningful words are more easy to learn than words the meanings of which are not familiar. Serial learning is involved in the case of learning number, the names of the rulers of a country, etc. Learning the lines in a poem by heart also involves serial learning. In this case the learning task is easier than learning a list of the names of prime ministers or presidents of a country in the proper chronological order, because in poetry meaningful words occur in a meaningful sequence.

SET: Preparedness for learning a new task or for perceiving a situation. It is characterized by preparedness to increase the likelihood of attending to certain stimuli. An athlete for a running race in a competition standing on the track waiting for the signal shot, is a good example of a person in the proper set. All his attention is focussed on the shot and the subsequent dash forward. Set has thus two phases, viz., expectation to wait for certain stimuli and then to proceed to an action. Attitudes, in a way, are closely related to set.

See: Attending

SHAPING (BEHAVIOR): Attempting to perfect responses successively. It is a method developed by the principle of operant conditioning. The process of shaping involves: first reinforcement of a response close to the desired response, and then another and so on. Thus by following the principle of successive approximations, finally it will be possible to effect the conditioning of the desired response. By this method, it was shown that a pigeon could be conditioned to pick at a circular disc mounted on a stand on giving a particular signal (Stimulus). This procedure is also applied as a method of treating behavior disorders under the system 'Behavior therapy'.

See: Behaviour Therapy, Successive approximations

SHOCK THERAPY: Treating mental patients by passing low voltage electric current through the brain or by injecting large doses of insulin which also produces convulsions. The first method is called Electro-Shock therapy and the second 'Insulin-shock therapy'.

In shock therapy the principle involved is the production of convulsions which is found to have effect in reducing the intensity of certain symptoms. Electro-shock is usually applied in the case of patients with severe depressive episodes. Electrodes are applied to the scalp and a current of required voltage is passed through them for about 2 secs. This produces violent convulsions. Usually there is remarkable improvement after the treatment.

In insulin shock therapy, the patient is injected with large doses of insulin. This also produces convulsive reactions.

Shock therapies are found useful in cases of epilepsy also.

See: Psychosis

SHOLASTIC APTITUDE TESTS (SAT): Battery of a variety of Tests used primarily for selection of students for colleges and universities.

See: Aptitude test, Screening tests

SHORT-ANSWER ITEMS: Types of questions for which the pupils have to give answers (in writing) in a word or two (or a few words). The possible answers for the questions will have been predetermined and so can be scored objectively to a fair degree. They are not fully objective, as the candidates are required to write their answers; illegibility or ambiguity in writing gives room for subjective decisions.

See: Objective test

SHORT-TERM MEMORY (STM): Memory that persists for only a very short time. Retention is very limited, say a few minutes, as in remembering a telephone number just before dialling.

See: Long-term memory

SIGNIFICANCE, STATISTICAL: The statistical quality of an obtained value that has been proved by ruling out the probability of chance factors for its occurrence. For example: in a test of mathematics, the average for class A was 70 and class B, 75. In class A, there were 45 pupils and in class B, 35. Is the performance of class B better than class A? There is a difference of 5 scores in favour of class B. This difference may represent the superiority of class B to A, but it may also contain the effect of some chance factors that might have worked in favour of class B. In all such situations there is an element of chance working in one direction or other or both. If this can be found out, (that is, the difference that can occur due simply to chance alone), it can be concluded whether the obtained difference is real. The statistical test applied to find out whether the value is a real one and that it has not been produced by chance, is called the test of significance. A difference is statistically significant, if its occurrence cannot be proved to be due to chance; nonsignificant if it can occur due to the operation of chance factors resulting from sampling errors. As the values obtained in educational measures are generally from 'samples' the probability of the influence of chance factors cannot be ruled out. So, for all such measures, the significance has to be ascertained. There are procedures for finding out the significance of differences between means, differences between variances, proportions, percentages, correlation coefficients, and so on.

See: Sampling statistics

SIMULATION: Activities representing a real process. In educational training and research, simulation is often used as an effective method of instruction. The trainees are expected to play the role in the same manner as done by the persons in real situtions.

SIMULATIONS (COMPUTER): Teaching technique, using life-like situations presented as animated examples for the effective learning of ideas. It is either used as complete simulation package (e.g. for teaching the topic: working of a Parliament) or as short animated examples in conjuction with normal CAL program. It can be run in real time or fast-time. In real time it can be used, for example, to learn the control of a manufacturing process. In fast-time, activities spread over a long period of time can be condensed into short periods, for example, to show the planning and control operations, etc. in a ship building yard for a period of a few years. A large number of variables can be handled in simulations. Simulation are very useful for learning complex processes.

SIGN LEARNING: A principle formulated by Mowrer, on the basis of classical conditioning theory. It states that a classical conditioned stimulus to an emotional response, becomes a signal for coming events.

See: Classical conditioning

SKEWNESS: A distribution in which the mean, median and mode fall at different points is a skewed distribution. Skewness of a curve can be easily seen from its appearance. The curve will not be symmetrical, i.e., its shape on the left and right sides are different. The skewness may be negative or positive. In a negatively skewed distribution the cases are seen concentrated at the high end of the scale and in the positively skewed distribution the concentration is at the low end of the scale. In a normal distribution the mean, median and mode fall at the same point and so skewness is 0. To measure the skewness of a distribution the following formula is used:

$$Sk = \frac{3(mean - median}{\sigma}$$

where Sk is the skewness

s is the standard deviation of the scores.

See: Normal Curve

SKILL: Proficiency resulting from repeated practice. Skills are developed by training. Skills are habituated behavior which consist of normally repetitive type of activity. Skills may be very simple, involving only simple action as in washing a dish or very complex consisting of a number of coordinated precision movements as in operating on anti-aircraft gun against fast moving jet fighters. Skills may be motor, like writing, riding bicycle or verbal like reciting, speaking or numerical like computing, etc. As all skills essentially involve motor and mental components, they are also called psychomotor proficiencies.

See: Psychomotor abilities

SKINNER, BURRHUS FREDERIC: Famous American behavioural psychologist (born 1904). He worked extensively on learning (using rats in problem boxes) on behaviouristic lines and developed his theory of learning: Operant conditioning (instrumental conditioning). According to him, if an emitted behaviour (bar pressing by rat) is immediately followed by reinforcement (a pellet of food), they tended to be connected– and learning occurs.

Programmed instruction and CAL owe to a large extent to the work of Skinner.

Skinner's important works are: 'Behaviour of organisms' (1938) and 'Science and Human Behaviour' (1953). 'Technology of Teaching' (1969) and 'About Behaviourism'.

See: Operant conditioning

SOCIAL INTELLIGENCE: Ability to adjust in social situations. It comprises the ability to perceive social situations realistically in addition to the possession of a number of social traits like cooperativeness, emotional stability, communicability, and an interest in mixing with people. Social intelligence is essential for being liked by people and for being accepted socially.

See: Socialization

SOCIAL DEVELOPMENT: Changes occurring in children from birth to maturity in the ability to respond in conformity with social norms. The main characteristics of social reactions in babyhood are imitation (baby imitating others), shyness, likes and dislikes. Attachment, dependency, rivalry, attention-seeking, social cooperation (playing with adults) are also early social responses. From 2 to 6 years children learn to get along with other persons outside the home. The pattern of behavior developed during the pre-gang period (6 to 8 years) forms the foundation for the development of social qualities like sportsmanship, cooperativeness, responsibility, etc. During early adolescence (puberty) unsocial or antisocial trends may develop. But usually it is a transitory phase.

See: Development

SOCIAL CLASS: A division of society comprising members of equal status and possessing common social characteristics. In a social class the members enjoy intimate equal status relation with one another. It is a constituent of a large society but have only restricted interactions with members of other social class, groups. The people of a social class prefer to live in their own social environments. The terms 'upper class', 'middle class', 'lower class', etc. roughly indicate the social class stratification.

SOCIAL MATURITY: Social development level characterized by independence from parental and adult control in social situations. It is characterized by the individual's ability to mix with people in social situations and manage social dealings without anybody's assistance. In other words, it is the attainment of the adult level social behavior, after undergoing the natural process of socialization.

See: Development, Socialization

SOCIAL MOBILITY (VERTICAL): The movement of persons upward or downward, in the vertical social status systems. A person in the lower social class may move upward to upper class if he acquires the status and prestige to qualify him to be a member of that class. Likewise, a person may move down in the status scale if he loses his social status in that class.

See: Social Class

SOCIAL SKILLS: Personal traits that enables one to mix well with people. These include qualities like cooperativeness, extroversion, communicativeness, tolerance, etc.

See: Social Intelligence

SOCIAL DISTANCE SCALE: Scales used to measure an individual's attitude towards social groups in terms of degree of kinship. The method was developed by Bogardus to measure attitude towards different nationalities. The social distance scale consists of a number of statements to which the individual has to respond: Illustration: The individual has to mark his response to items like this: "I would willingly admit members of (race, nationality, etc.) to one or more of the classifications under which I have placed a cross:

1. To close kinship by marriage
2. To my club as personal friend
3. To my street as neighbours
4. To employment in my occupation
5. To citizenship in my country
6. As visitors only in my country
7. Would exclude from my country."

SOCIAL REALISM: The ideology that education should effect in developing the qualities of the gentleman, the man in direct contact with people. The aim according to this view point is to prepare individuals as 'aristocratic youths' and not to produce scholars and professionals. The individual's efficiency is important in social life. So they recommended a practical type of education– not merely aiming at vocational efficiency. A broad moral and intellectual training, based on an activity curriculum was needed to achieve it. Experience is more important than words in the text books. Memorization was discouraged, teaching should result in the assimilation of knowledge. Learning should be attractive and pleasurable.

SOCIAL REINFORCER: Teacher's approval or disapproval in class or group situations that functions as reinforcers for the elimination of undesirable behaviours. This is a technique used in behaviour modification. The teacher has to be very careful in praising or reprimanding, as undue attention given to misbehaviour may even reinforce it. Attention-seeking behaviour should be ignored and a desirable behaviour from a misbehaving child should be recognised and rewarded by the teacher immediately and openly.

SOCIALIZATION: The process of developing all behavior qualities essential for adjustment in society. It is a normal process that takes place from birth. At birth the child is asocial, i.e., neither social nor unsocial. As it grows it begins to like the mother, and develops non-verbal means of responding to her. Gradually his social circle enlarges with the inclusion of more and more members. The child naturally learns the skills necessary for dealing with people who meet him in various different roles. The child is thus able to identify with the group. He acquires and adopts the mode of behavior of the people to whom he belongs. This makes him adjust successfully in the social situation. Inadequate socialization leads to adjustment problems in social groups i.e., the individual finds it difficult to deal with social situations to his and other's satisfaction. After the home, it is the school that has the most decisive influence in the socialization of the individual.

Socialization results in the child's gradual acquisition of knowledge of values, norms and skills necessary for adjustment in the group to which he belongs. By socialization, he becomes socially sensitive and he gets integrated into the group. He can very easily adapt himself to differing social situations and will be able to mix with people easily and derive satisfaction from group life. Socialization is an important function of the school and it forms an essential part of the hidden curriculum.

See: Social development

SOCIALLY USEFUL PRODUCTIVE WORK (SUPW): Work experience programme of schools. In socially useful productive work, the work experience should be based on activities which lead to some socially useful results either as products (goods) or as service. The main objective is to develop in children the proper attitude towards work. The activity helps the students to discover their own vocational aptitudes and at the same time develop respect for manual work. The work should be meaningful and with stress on production. The children will also understand the significance of working hard systematically. Agriculture, wood work and carpentry, metal sheet working, sewing, electronics, etc. are some of the items that are undertaken under this programme. Makarenko, the Soviet educational innovator, developed 'socially useful productive labour' as an integral part of education, early in the nineteen twenties.

See: Basic education, Makarenko A.S.

SOCIETY: A collectivity of persons organized by itself on the basis of common culture. The unique characteristic of a society is that it is an organized collectivity of interacting members who have similar goals and who share common beliefs, attitudes, values and standards of action. A society may be composed of many communities and smaller groups, but they have an internal structure that pulls them all together.

SOCIOGRAM: The diagram drawn from sociometric data. In sociometric tests the student is required to write the names of fellow students with whom he likes to play, work, etc. and with whom he does not like to work or play. From the data a diagram for the group can be constructed showing by lines and arow marks the childrens' choices and rejections. A sociogram clearly reveals the structure of the group. 'Populars', 'isolates', 'neglectees' and 'rejectees' among the group also can be easily found out from a sociogram.

See: Sociometry

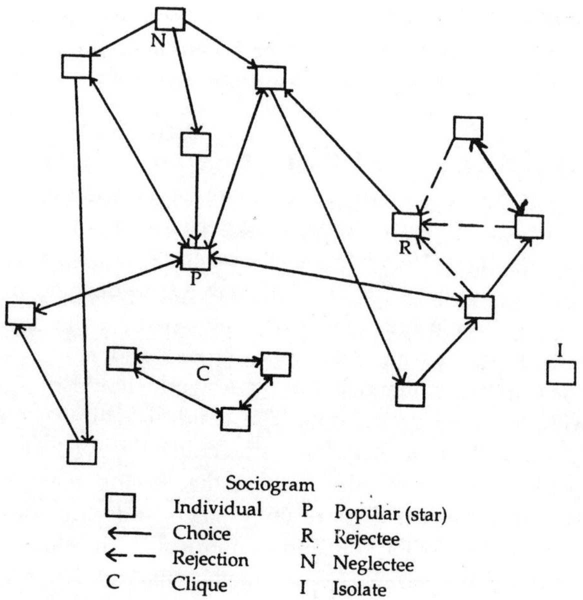

SOCIOMETRY: The technique developed by J.L. Moreno for the measurement of social relationship. A sociometric test is administered and a sociogram is constructed from its data. It will reveal various social characteristics of people in a group, like leadership, friendship, rejection, isolation and withdrawl.

See: Sociogram

SOCIOPATHIC DISORDERS: Behavior disorders characterized by serious deviation from prevailing social and ethical norms. A person with sociopathic disorder has a disturbed personality. He is impulsive, ego-centred, pleasure seeking and is unmindful of his responsibility to society. The marked reaction tendency of the sociopath is called 'dyssocial reaction'. Usually such individuals have an unhappy childhood brought up mostly in an abnormal environment. Though they have no regard for social norms, they seem to be loyal to their own group (criminal gang). Sex deviants and drug addicts also sometimes become sociopaths. A sizeable percentage among the law-breakers like dacoits, murderers and rapists are sociopaths.

See: Psychopathic personality

SOCRATES: The great Greek philosopher (470 BC–399 BC). According to Socrates 'virtue' was the main aim of education. He postulated the existence of universal concepts like goodness, temperance and justice. His contention was that the rudiments of these concepts exist in the minds of all men and can be clearly understood by reasoning.

Socrates said that knowledge should be acquired through direct contact with people and nature. The contribution of Socrates to the development of a theory of teaching method–which is known as 'socratic method'–was acknowledged by all later thinkers as epoch making. The conversation or question answer method. It has two stages–first, the ironic or destructive stage in which by questioning, the ignorance of the pupil is brought to consciousness and second, the constructive, in which again by questioning the pupil is led from ignorance to clear logical truth. To achieve this, a teacher has to be critical, sympathetic, patient, honest and understanding. The teacher's duty was mainly the stimulation of the mental activity of the pupil.

Socrates's closest disciple Plato also helped in developing the Socratic method.

SOFT COPY: In computer terminology, the output presented on video display unit or fed into a medium for storage.

See: Hard Copy.

SOMATIC APPERCEPTION TEST: Performance type projective test of personality used for children, designed by Caldwell (1963). The Somatic Apperception Test consists of ten wooden model bodies and model spare parts of human bodies. The child is required to select the model which he thinks he resembles most and then to select one model which best corresponds to the body he would like to possess. Then the child is required to construct his ideal body with the spare parts. From the responses of the child, inferences can be made about the characteristics of his 'perceived self', 'ideal self', etc.

See: Thematic Apperception Test

SOMATIC: Concerning the body. Mental disorders originate either from psychological causes (functional) or from bodily causes (somatic i.e., organic in origin) or from a combination of both (psychosomatic). Soma means body.

SOMATOTONIA: Personality type characterized by

assertiveness. This is a classification based on temperamental analysis. Somatotonia is a cluster of traits, the chief characteristics of which are general assertiveness, well controlled body movements, energy, craving for power, courage, straight forwardness, showing preference for action in troubled situations and love of power.

SOVIET EDUCATION: The communist educational system and practices of the former U.S.S.R. The basic aim of the rulers was the conversion of the educational system as the primary instrument of potential socialization of the youth. The system was centrally controlled by the Department of schools of the Party Central Committee. Each unit of the system was subject to tight control by local party organization. There was only a single basic pattern of school organization for the whole country. Law enforced universal seven year education beginning at age 7 and seven year secondary education. After completing the seven year programme there was a 3 year course for workforce or technicians where they received a complete middle level technical education. Those who obtained high scores on a rigorous screening examination were admitted to complete secondary education (3 years secondary). The core-curriculum was uniform. Socially useful labour was an integral component of the curriculum. The 1958 reform introduced 8 year primary education instead of 7 years and 11 year secondary education instead of 10 years. The great majority of the secondary school graduates were to enter the work force and stay there for at least two years. Eighty percent of all places in institutions of higher education were reserved for youth with the two years experience in work force. Polytechnical training offered a wide range of technical subjects in the curricula. At lower and middle levels polytechnicalization emphasized 'shop courses' while in secondary, students had to spend one third of the time in industry or agriculture.

SPAN OF APPREHENSION: The maximum breadth of items that can be held mentally at a time. It is tested with a tachistoscope using digits, letters, nonsense syllables, etc. When visually presented, individuals can apprehend from 6 to 11 items (number, digits, etc. simultaneously). A span of apprehension of 7 in the visual mode, means that the individual can apprehend 7 digits or letters simultaneously (4, 2, 6, 3, 7, 9, 4, etc.).

SPARTAN EDUCATION ANCIENT: The educational practices prevalent in ancient Sparta (in Greece) around 1000 BC. The Spartan city states at those times comprised the ruling class surrounded by a huge population of subjugated people. A firm administration was the prime concern in such a situation. So their constitution aimed at training strong and brave soldiers in large numbers. A strong spartan state was the ideal. So all education was controlled by the state – Only the able and fit were allowed to survive. Moral and social education was emphasized. The boy was put under the charge of a trainer. The pupils ate and slept in a common building. Severe discipline was enforced to develop the qualities of hardihood. Gymnastics and dancing were necessary, but intellectual education received little attention. Youths above fifteen years were given practical training in warfare. Citizenship training was also given. Women received practically very little education.

See: Athenian Education

SPATIAL ABILITY: Ability to visualize space and manipulate three-dimensional objects in concrete situations and in imagination.

SPEARMAN, C.: British psychologist (1867-1945) who was one of the pioneers to apply factor analysis to explain the nature of intelligence. He propounded the two-factor theory of intelligence on the basis of his findings. There are two factors of intelligence– one general factor G – which pervades almost all intellectual activities and some specific factors 's' which are specific only to particular activities, like spatial ability. Spearman's principal works are: 'The Nature of Intelligence', 'Principles of Cognition' and 'Abilities of Man'.

See: Factor analysis

SPEARMAN-BROWN PROPHECY FORMULA: The formula used for predicting the reliability coefficient of a test when its length is increased. Reliability of a test is related to its length. Shorter the test, less is the reliability. How much should the test be lengthened (i.e., by adding items) in order to get a desired level of reliability? Spearman-Brown prophecy formula helps to find out the answer. The formula is:

$$r_{kk} = \frac{kr_{xx}}{1 + (k - 1)r_{xx}}$$

where r_{xx} is the reliability coefficient of a test of unit length, and r_{kk} is the reliability of the test made k times long.

See: Reliability

SPEED TEST: A test which has to be completed within a specified time. Usually speed tests contain only items of medium difficulty. The test will contain a few more items over and above than that can be done by any testee, i.e., it should have enough head-room.

See: Power test

SPENCER, HERBERT: British philosopher (1820-1903). He defined education as a preparation, for complete living. According to him activities of life comprised either those directly related to self-preservation and those indirectly related to it. Those concerning life preservation directly should come first in the curriculum and others, later. Literacy studies, he placed at the bottom. History should include descriptive sociology and leisure time activities. He discouraged the practice of learning by rote. It is the harmonious development of all human potentials that he emphasized. Education should, therefore consist of all the domains of development: physical, intellectual and moral. The maxims that he propounded for teaching were: proceed from the simple to the abstract, from the concrete to the complex, from the empirical to the rational. These are in good agreement with sound psychological principles. He also said that the education of the child should agree with the mode and order of development of mankind considered historically (culture-epoch theory). Moral education should receive a prominent role. Discipline should be on the basis of rational consequences. Physical education should be an integral part of the school curriculum.

SPONTANEOUS RECOVERY: Automatic revival of an extinct conditioned response. A conditioned response tends to disappear if not reinforced repeatedly for some time. Then the conditioned stimulus fails to elicit the conditioned response i.e., it becomes extinct. But later, i.e., after the lapse of sometime, in some cases, the presentation of the conditioned stimulus is found to elicit the response which was extinct, and the conditioned stimulus CS, continues to elicit the conditioned responses. This phenomenon is called spontaneous recovery.

See: Classical conditioning

SPRITE: In computer terminology, a small graphic unit (e.g. picture of a fruit) which can be moved or controlled.

SQ3R-METHOD: An effective method of studying materials available in written form. The expansion of the abbreviation is: Survey-Questioning-Reading-Reciting-Reviewing.

STANDARD ERROR: The systematic error in sample statistics. If values for an attribute (e.g., means in an intelligence test) obtained from a number of mutually exclusive random samples drawn from the same population are plotted graphically, the curve will conform to the normal form. The standard deviation of this distribution is the standard error of the values. If the mean for a science test is 30 and its standard deviation is 6, it means, that theoretically if 100 separate samples are taken from the population and measurements are made, the means obtained will fall approximately two thirds of times within 6 points of the true mean (parameter) that is between 24 and 36, and between 1.96 x 6 or 11.76 score points above and below the mean in 95 times, and between + 2.58 x 6 i.e., 15.48 points above and below the mean is 99 times. Standard error, thus, indicate the probable deviation of the obtained mean from the true mean. As all measures in educational and psychological dimensions are obtained from samples, they only approximate the true values: viz., mean, standard deviation, correlation efficient, etc. To estimate their accuracy, the respective standard errors also should be known. Standard errors of mean, SD, etc. can be calculated by the formulae:

1. Standard error of a mean:

$$SE_{mean} = \frac{\sigma}{\sqrt{N}}$$

2. Standard error of SD =

$$SE\,\sigma\ or\ \sigma_{\sigma} = \frac{.71\sigma}{\sqrt{N}}$$

3. Standard error of a proportion where p is proportion of one category and q = 1–p

$$\sqrt{\frac{pq}{N}}$$

STANDARD DEVIATION: The sensitive measure of dispersion (spread) of a set of scores. It is the root-mean-squared deviations of the distribution. It is represented by the Greek letter s

$$SD \text{ or } \sigma = \sqrt{\frac{\Sigma X^2}{N}}$$

Where åX² = total sum of the variance.

N is the total number of cases.

SD (s) is the Standard Deviation

STANDARD SCORES: Scores in distributions transformed (from raw score distributions) to have mean and standard deviation of standard value. Raw scores as such have limited meaning, unless they are interpreted in terms of the distributions to which they belong. The interpretation is usually done by fixing the position of the scores in the distributions by finding out the number of cases in percentage falling below the score. This is a percentile equivalent ot the score. Another method is to compare the score in relation to the mean of the distribution. A sensitive procedure to effect this transformation is to indicate the position of the score in terms of standard deviations above or below the mean. A score obtained in this manner is called a standard score. It is obtained by using the formula

$$Z = \frac{X - M}{\sigma}$$

(Z is the standard score, X is the obtained score, M is the mean of the distribution and σ is the SD of the distribution.)

The mean of this new distribution is zero and values below that mean have negative signs and values above mean have positive signs. To avoid this inconvenience, other standard scores like T-scores, and Stanines are derived from Z-scores.

One main advantage of the standard scores is that scores obtained from different distributions can be added together (like marks for different school subjects of a pupil) to get a composite score as all the distributions have been converted into the same scale units (i.e. SD unit). This procedure is not permissible with regard to raw scores (though this is often done) as they belong to different scale units, (i.e. with different means and SD's).

Some standard score scales are given below:

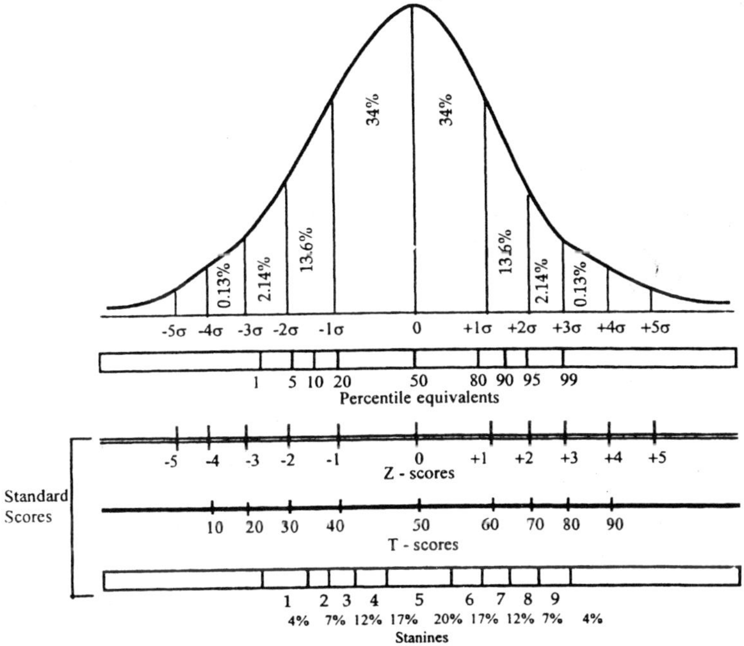

STANDARD SCORES

See: Percentiles, Stanine, T-score and Z-score

STANDARDIZATION: The process of preparing norms for a test, for a population.

See: Standardized Test

STANDARDIZED TEST: A test for which norms have been established on a representative sample of population and which have been prepared under standard procedures. The standardization process consists of the following steps: (1) Deciding the purpose and objectives of the test (2) Preparation of test items (3) Scrutiny of items by experts (4) Try-out administrations (5) Item analysis (6) Preparation of final forms (7) Selection of sample for standardization and administration of the test on the sample (8) Reliability and validity studies (9) Statistical analysis and development of norms (10) Preparation of reports.

1. Deciding the purpose: The question to be answered under this are: (a) What are the dimensions to be measured (intelligence test, verbal, nonverbal, etc.)? (b) To whom is the test intended? (Age group 6-10 grades 5-8, etc. in a particular districts, state, nation, etc.) (c) How many forms of the test are intended, one, two or three?

2. Preparation of test items. The questions to be considered are (a) What types of items are to be included. True-false, multiple choice, matching, etc. How many items are needed to test each objective? (e.g., in achievement tests, like knowledge, comprehension, application, analysis, appreciation, etc.). Accordingly items are constructed two or three times in excess of the needed number.

3. Scrutiny of test items. This is done by a panel of experts, who select each item after examining the qualities which ensure validity of the test (face-validity, construct validity, etc.). Ambiguous wording is eliminated and distractors are improved. This procedure will lead to the selection of items.

4. Try-out administration. The purpose of try-outs is to find out the general reaction of the testees to the test and to obtain data on the discriminative power and difficulty level of each item, the functioning of the alternatives as distractors and to determine the optimum time needed to complete the test.

The try-out forms of the test are prepared and printed and administered on a representative sample of children (usually around 500) under conditions similar to those contemplated for the final test. The try-out forms are then scored and the test is then ready for item analysis.

5. Item analysis will lead to the determination of discrimination and difficulty indices for each item. The distributions of responses among the distractors are found out. Those distractors which fail to get a fair proportion of the wrong responses are non-functional and so have to be rejected. Items for the final tests are selected from among those which satisfy all the requirements.

6. Preparation of final forms of test. The final forms of the test are then prepared. The manual of instructions which contains the procedure for administration, scoring, etc. is also prepared.

In the final test form, the items are arranged in increasing order of difficulty. If sufficient number of good items are available, the test may be prepared in parallel forms (alternate forms, equivalent forms). The test is then printed.

7. Selection of sample for administration for standardization. A random sample, the number depending on the size of the population (may be 5000, 10,000, etc.) is selected. For obtaining national norms, large samples will be necessary. The test is then administered on the sample under standardized conditions (i.e., the conditions prescribed in the manual with regard, to the physical conditions of testing like seating, ventilation, etc., timing, instructions to be given (oral and otherwise), etc.

8. Reliability and validity data are also obtained along with the standardization administration. For establishing validity, scores for the same individuals or a small sample from the standardization sample, on a well established test measuring the same ability are usually obtained i.e., for finding the correlation of the test with the criterion.

9. Statistical analysis: First, the test is scored. The scores for the questions with odd numbers and even numbers for each candidate are taken separately. The total for the 'odd and even' items will give the actual score for the individual. The score for 'odd and even' items are necessary only for computation of reliability by split-half method. From the distribution of scores the following are computed.

(*a*) Arithmetic mean for the whole group and sub-groups (for the state, district, boys-girls, etc.)

(*b*) Standard deviation of the distributions.

(*c*) Correlation between the scores obtained for the 'odd' item and 'even' items and the correlation for the whole test.

(*d*) Correlation between the test and the criterion (for establishing validity). (A test which contains only items of good discriminative indices, will be valid.) In the case of an achievement test, the criterion will be school marks of grades. The correlation between the two will give the index of validity of the test.

(*e*) From the mean of the raw scores and standard deviations, 'derived scores' are prepared. These may be represented as I.Q. scores, centiles, standard scores like T-score, etc. They are the norms for the test.

10. Preparation of reports: This is mainly a technical report containing facts about the preparation and standardization of test, test statistics, like mean, SD, norms, validity, reliability, etc.

Standardized test can be considered as a calibrated instrument. It can be used as a valid and reliable instrument for measuring the dimension. Scores obtained by a candidate in the test is compared with the norm for his group. Standardized tests are also useful in comparing the performance of groups of populations (like people in different districts). Standardized tests can be used for a fairly long period of time, say 20 years or more.

See: Test, Norm

STANINE: A normalized standard score, with nine score categories from 1 to 9 with a mean 5. Stanine is an abbreviation for 'Standard Nine'. The Stanine divides the normal curve area into 9 units, i.e., 1 unit equals to one standard deviation. As the base-line of the normal curve is divided into 9 standard deviations, the mean is 5 and the standard deviation is 1.96. So the percentage covered by each unit is:

Stanine		*Percent covered*
1	—	4
2	—	7
3	—	12
4	—	17
5	—	20
6	—	17
7	—	12
8	—	7
9	—	4

Stanine is a simple method of transforming a distribution in the normal form. Though the scale is not a very refined one it has practical applications.

See: C-Score, T-Scale

STAR: The person chosen by a large number (or majority) of people in a group. In a sociometric diagram the star can be clearly seen. It is the circle (for denoting the person) towards which the lines of choice (arrows) reach from other circles. The star is the person who receives most of the preferential choices of the members in the group. Obviously, the 'star' is highly sociable and likeable and may possess some leadership qualities.

See: Sociogram

STATIC SENSE: The sense of maintaining bodily balance. Body equilibrium (like vertical posture) is regulated by the sensations originating in the non-auditory labyrinth of the inner ear. The three semicircular canals lie almost at right angles to each other. Any tilt in the body produces movements in the head, and the spatial variations of body positions stimulate the receptors of the non-auditory labyrinth which transmit impulses to the brain. The body muscles directly involved in static balance of the body receive impulses through the efferent nerves from the brain which results in the restoration of the balance. The static sense mechanism thus maintains the balance of the body in its different positions (like standing, sitting, etc.)

STATISTICS: The branch of mathematics dealing with the collection, processing and interpretation of data obtained from surveys and experimentation. The word 'statistics' refers to the methodology of collection, classification, description and interpretation of data obtained from population or samples of population as well as the measurements obtained from the population, or samples, like total number in category, percentages, mean (average) standard deviation, etc. More accurately, population measures are called parameters and their estimates obtained from representative samples are called 'statistics'.

The measures obtained for most of the quantifiable qualities that are encountered in education are of the nominal, ordinal and interval scales which have no true zeros and so the measures as such have only limited meaning. The statements that the score obtained by a boy in a test is 70 out of 100 does not carry much meaning, if the distribution of scores to which the particular score belongs is not known. The score '70' has not got the meaning similar to '70 centimeters' because '0 cm' means absolute nonexistence of length while score '0' does not mean absolute non-existence of the ability. So in this case there is no reference point to compare its real magnitude. But the raw score becomes meaningful when we know the total number of children who have taken the test, the mean (average) of the test and its standard deviation (i.e., measure of the spread of the scores) because it enables us to compare the score with the group values. Statistical analysis enables to churn up the hidden meanings and relationships in an array of data. For finding out whether two or more variables are related, whether they are different, to what extent an occurrence can be ascribed to chance factors, etc. statistical procedures are used.

STEM: In a multiple-choice item, the introductory part. eg. The city situated closest to the North Pole is–

A. London
B. Tokyo
C. Helsinki
D. Montreal

In this question: "The city situated closest to the North Pole is", is the stem.

See: Multiple choice item

STEREOTYPE: An idea (belief) held by practically all the members of a social group about other social groups. Stereotypes are cognitions shared widely by the members of a society. The stereotypes are oversimplified beliefs unaffected by objective facts. Black people are 'unclean', 'superstitious', 'are ugly', etc. are stereotypes. When a person holds a stereotype about a particular group, his judgement about an individual belonging to that group is likely to be biased by the stereotype.

STEROIDS: A naturally occurring group of fatty substances allied to cholesterol. Sex hormones, adrenal cortical hormones, bile acids, vitamin D, etc. are steroids.

STIMULUS: Energy changes that start impulses through nerves. Stimulus is actually a change in energy that affects the sense organs. The energy change may be in different modalities like light, sound, heat, pressure, etc. The stimulus may originate either from the external environment or from the internal environment (that is from within the body).

The sense organs are specialized groups of cells which are receptive to changes in certain types of energy forms and not sensitive to others. Our sense organs are sensitive to light, sound, heat, pressure smell, etc. But no human sense organ is sensitive to radio waves or ultrasonic sound waves.

Our awareness of the environment, and in fact all knowledge we acquire, start with stimuli. The stimuli also evoke responses. Responses are what the organisms do and stimuli are the variables in the environment which elicit them. Education is concerned with the production of desirable response patterns in the individual. It can be achieved only by the manipulation of proper stimuli. Teaching is often seen as the process of manipulating the stimuli in order to produce sustaining desirable behavior in the pupils.

The study of behavior essentially begins with the study of stimuli.

See: Response

STRADAPTIVE TEST: A test containing items at different difficulty levels, with items of homogeneous difficulty assigned to one stratum of the test. The term was coined by Weiss in 1973. The test may have a number of strata, say 4,5,6 as required. Within each stratum, the items are homogeneous in difficulty, but are arranged in decreasing order of discriminative power. The testee starts with the stratum appropriate for his age, grade, etc. When he completes the items in the stratum he moves up to the next, and when he fails in the items, moves down. Usually the testee's attempt is seen confined to two or three strata closer to his ability level.

STRESS: A severe state of tension resulting from conflict. A conflict is a situation in which the individual has to make a choice out of alternatives, the choice of any one alternative leading to undesirable consequences. A person in such a situation may develop stress. When an individual is required to work far beyond his capacity for a considerable period, then also he is likely to develop stress. Remaining continuously for a long time in a state of fear, threat, etc. also produces stress.

Under stress, the capacity of the individual to work will be lowered and he will be in a state of anxiety. Other common symptoms of stress are hypertension and irritability. Continuous stress may lead to psychosomatic complications, causing diseases of the digestive system (like gastric ulcers) and circulatory system (like hypertension).

Minor stress is a spur for energetic action, but existence in severe and continued stressful situation will even lead the person to a mental break-down.

Counselling and psychotherapy will help to lessen the severity of stress.

STRIP KEY: A scoring aid, in which the correct answers recorded on a strip, which when placed alongside the answers in the test sheet makes scoring easy. It is usually made out of a test sheet by cutting out the edge strip in which the alternatives or answers are printed. The correct response for each item is marked on this strip. This is the strip key. For scoring, it is placed alongside the answers given in the test sheet of the candidates. As the key and the marked response come close together it is very easy to score the test with a strip key.

See: Scoring, Scoring stencil

STRUCTURAL PSYCHOLOGY: The approach that explains behavior in terms of the characteristics of the elements (which the proponents thought to be the elements) of consciousness. Titchner, Wundt and James were protagonists of this school of psychology. The internal experiences (consciousness) are analyzed into sensations, feelings, thought, volition, perception, memories, etc. and mental activities are interpreted in terms of them. The prime concern of the structuralists was to describe the elements, unlike the functionalist whose emphasize was on the function.

See: Functionalism

STUDENT COST: The total expenditure incurred by a student for his education, for a specified period. It includes, tuition and other fees, equipment and stationery cost, and other extra cost needed for his maintenance, like hostel expenditure, conveyance charges, etc. Usually, 'opportunity cost' or 'income foregone' is also included under student cost.

See: Opportunity cost

SUBCONSCIOUS: The 'stratum' of the mind below the level of awareness. It is also used interchangeably with unconscious. It is the store house of all repressed desires, and experiences that remain submerged in the mind about which the individual is not aware of. Such repressed ideas seldom come to the mind in their real form.

'Subconscious' should not be confused with 'pre-conscious', which means those experiences that are, though out of the awareness level at the time, can be readily brought into awareness.

See: Pre-conscious

SUBJECT: 1. The organisms experimented on. Psychology employs both human and animal subjects. The experiments in psychology involve the manipulation of independent variables and the study of their effects on the subjects, i.e., their behavior which are the dependent variables.

2. Separate disciplines in the curriculum, like mathematics, physics, chemistry, etc. A subject is a wide unit of knowledge the parts of which are logically related.

SUBJECTIVE: Based completely on the experience of the individual, which cannot be observed and measured. Experiences are subjective and objective. Experiences, like 'pain', 'feeling of pleasantness', etc. are subjective, while withdrawal of the hand on touching fire or saying that the individual wants to have more of the experience (liking) are objective. Subjective experience is not observable and measurable and so are not considered valuable evidence in the study of behavior. 'Subjectivity' is difficult to be kept away from interpreting psychological phenomena, but scientists are always alert in making observations and giving explanations, etc. only objectively, keeping out subjective impressions. Subjective impressions of various people on the same observations are seen to vary widely. As subjective experience is also a reality to be reckoned with in scientific investigations, psychologists try to devise procedures that reduce the effect of subjectivity in such data.

See: Objectivity

SUBJECTIVE TEST: A test which is liable to be interpreted differently by different persons and/or for which the responses are also liable to be interpreted differently by different scorers. In the case of such tests personal impressions, opinions and biassed judgements operate in test answering and scoring. So both 'validity' and 'reliability' of such tests are always at risk. A good example is the old essay type examination. The same questions can be understood in different ways by the examinees. Most of such questions have no specific responses. Different examiners may assign different scores to the same response. Subjectivity will vitiate not only the responses but also scoring and interpretation.

When unique and original responses are required from the individuals, tests which permit subjective interpretations will have to be used. In that case, to improve reliability and validity, appropriate precautions are taken. The projective tests and tests of creativity are examples of such tests.

See: Objective test

SUBLIMATION: The mechanism of adjustment (according to Freudians) by which the individual unconsciously transforms a socially unacceptable urge into a desirable activity. Certain urges and motives like sex, aggression, hatred, etc. are considered socially undesirable. Unconsciously these urges are 'lifted up' (sublimated) in the case of some individuals. Sublimation of sex urge may appear in the form of the person leading a celebate life and devoting his entire time to religious activities. Sublimation of aggressive tendencies may appear as excellent performance in boxing, football and other games. Extreme interests in social work, art, philanthropy, etc. are often sublimated urges and can be traced back to urges and ideas at the unconscious level which are basically opposites of the sublimated activities.

See: Ego-defence mechanisms

SUBLIMINAL: Below threshold. An optimum intensity is needed for a stimulus to elicit a response or to become noticeable. This is true of all sense modalities like seeing, hearing, etc. A stimulus below the intensity (energy) level needed for arousing response is a subliminal stimulus. A subliminal sound is that sound which will not arouse auditory awareness.

See: Just-Noticeable-Defference

SUBSTITUTE TUTOR PACKAGE: Computer as a vehicle for administering individualized learning. The computer has potential to provide a degree of interaction and feed-back that no other system provides. The Substitute-Tutor computer-based learning package is one of the most important available tools for teachers.

See: Computer-Assisted-Learning

SUBSTITUTION LEARNING: Learning to replace one symbol with another. Deciphering a code involves substitution learning. In language teaching 'substitution method' is used as an effective drill procedure for mastering sentence patterns. Substitution tables like the following are constructed by the students.

He bought a new pen
She .... Pencil
We .... Book
They .... Watch

SUBVOCAL SPEECH: Inaudible speech. According to

the behaviourists, 'thinking' largely consists of sub-vocal speech. The vocal apparatus (larynx) is active when one is engaged in thinking and the vocal cords make appropriate vibrations that are not strong enough to produce audible sounds. Any form of speech like talking silently to oneself, which others cannot hear, is also sub-vocal speech.

SUCCESSIVE APPROXIMATION METHOD: In operant conditioning, the method of reinforcing a response closer to the correct one in successive stages. In an experiment, the purpose of which was to develop in a pigeon a conditioned response to pick at a triangular disc, the bird was rewarded only when it emitted responses which were closer to the correct response, successively. When the bird made a pick at a point close to the disc it was rewarded and the next response was rewarded only if it was closer to the correct response than the first one. The next response was rewarded only if it was still closer. Thus by successive steps the conditioning progressed. This method of operant conditioning is called the method of successive approximation. This method operates in many human learning situations–e.g., in speech development in young children (vocalization). Whenever the child utters more correctly, the parents use to reinforce positively with verbal approval. Writing skills also develop more or less in this manner.

See: Operant conditioning

SUCHMAN INQUIRY MODEL: A class room model of teaching making use of thinking skills, designed by J. Suchman– This is an 'inquiry model' and it uses both inductive and deductive methods. It is similar to the hypothesis testing approach employed in problem solving. As in any lesson, in this case also, there are three basic stages–Planning, Implementation and Evaluation. Planning is concerned with the identification of goals, formulation of the problem and the preparation of the media for presentation of the problem. The problem is usually posed by the teacher (e.g., on losing support why does a piece of stone fall down to the ground?) The media for presenting the problem may be pictures, diagrams, maps, films, etc. Implementation of Suchman Inquiry model consists of three stages. Presentation of the problem, hypothesizing and data gathering and closure. At the presentation stage the teachers should ensure that the pupils have understood the problem well. Hypothesizing stage may also involve data gathering. The data are intended for testing the hypothesis. If the data support the hypothesis, it is retained and if it does not support the hypothesis it is rejected or revised. The last stage of the implementation is closure. Here the pupils formulate the conclusions. The final stage of evaluation includes both testing of content acquisition and process skills in observation, collection of relevant data, organizing data, etc.

SUGGESTION: Uncritical acceptance of an idea suggested by some person; Uncritical acceptance of an idea on the basis of some cues: visual, auditory, verbal, etc. A person who has not developed proper scientific attitudes in facing a situation, is found more prone to suggestion. So also is a person who is deprived of a need (say food) for a long time, is prone to perceive the objects connected with the need (food articles) more frequently than a normal person. The most important extrinsic factor of suggestion is the ambiguity of the situation perceived. When the situation is unstructured (lacks clarity) the individual is more susceptible to suggestion. 'Authority' is also a determinant of suggestion. Those whom the individual consider 'authorities' also have the power to exert suggestion. This is called 'prestige suggestion'. A person who easily submits to suggestion is said to be highly suggestible. A person's proneness to suggestion is called 'suggestibility'.

In hypnotic suggestion, the individual's conscious thinking capacity is at a low ebb. In the hypnotised state the individual is in an induced state of uncriticalness and so is highly suggestible. The proneness of individual to hypnotic suggestion varies widely.

See: Hypnosis

SUMERIAN EDUCATION (ANCIENT): The education that flourished in Sumaria during the pre-Christian centuries. Sumeria included the plain of shinar and the lower basis of the rivers Tigris and Euphrates. Indo-European clans migrated to the plains from interior Asia, and the people developed a civilization in which agriculture and trade dominated. They developed the cuneiform system of writing (wedge shaped characters pressed into clay and dried in the sun).

Sumerian education was accessible only to the wealthy. Training was mainly meant for the preparation of scribes (for writing and account keeping) for commercial and temple duties. Vocational education was considered essential. Reading and writing were emphasized at the early stage. Arithmetic was also taught. At higher stages astronomy, medicine, architecture and hydraulics formed part of the curriculum. Schools were usually conducted in the temple buildings. The method used for teaching was largely imitation. The pupils copied the characters and memorized. Teacher-pupil relationship was like father-son relationship and discipline was very rigorous. Flogging was common for violation of rules. Handicrafts (jewellery) art, poetry, music and law flourished during the period.

SUMMATIVE ASSESSMENTS: Assessment conducted at the end of the course to determine students' progress. Usually the purpose is to decide promotional policies. As there is no feed-back, this assessment does not help pupils to remedy deficiences.

Formative assessment on the other hand is a continuous process and there is regular feed back of results to the children.

See: Formative assessment

SUPEREGO: The stratum of the 'self' that approximately corresponds to the 'conscience', according to Freudian psychology. According to psychoanalytic theory, the 'psyche' consists of three strata; the 'id', 'ego' and 'super ego'. The id is concerned with the fulfillment of urges, whether or not they are attainable, or socially acceptable. The ego is concerned only with the reality and consequences in the fulfillment of the urge. The superego's concern is the moral and ethical considerations involved in the fulfillment of the drives and urges. At the super-ego level, the drives and their mode of fulfillment are judged against moral and ethical principles (i.e., values and rights and wrongs). Actions that are in conflict with the accepted values are avoided. So, in a way this part of the psyche corresponds to the conscience. A part of superego is unconscious and so in many cases the individual does not know from where the urge to curb certain action tendencies emerge.

The internal control that results from superego develops as a result of the various experiences one undergoes during childhood. Parental control, commands of dos and don'ts, imposition of things considered good and moral, punishment for wrongs and misdeeds, religious practices, etc. have a strong role in the structuring of one's superego. Overstrictness in the parent's behaviour, and the imposition of too many don'ts for the child, tends to develop in him an abnormal superego. A person with a weak superego tends to do things without much consideration for other's rights, moral or ethical principles. A person with a disproportionately over-developed superego tends to be internally inhibited, because he is over-concerned with the rights and wrongs of each and every action in an unrealistic manner.

See: Moral Development

SWOT ANALYSIS: The method of identifying the key areas of the institutions' potential. SWOT is the acronym for Strengths-Weaknesses-Opportunities-Threats. A detailed analysis of the problems that affect the effective working of the institution will enable us to list them under the four SWOT heads. For example:

High percentage of pass in examinations can be listed under 'strengths'.

Inadequate laboratory facilities to be under 'weaknesses'.

Excellent infrastructure for sports activities to be under 'opportunities'.

Decreasing trend in enrolment to be under 'Threats'.

In this manner all the individual items which are relevant can be listed. SWOT analysis leads to the formulation of appropriate strategies for development.

See: Management

SYLLABUS: Guidelines of a course of study indicating the objectives, content units and topic coverage. Usually it is obligatory for all the schools in the state to implement the syllabi prescribed for all the grades of the school system. The syllabus for each subject aides in the preparation of text books, lesson planning for teachers and in planning evaluation procedures and examinations. In some countries, the teachers of the schools themselves prepare syllabi for their schools; but the general practice is that syllabi of a state are constructed by a committee of experts appointed by the governments.

See: Curriculum

SYNAPSE: The junction of an axon of one nerve cell and the dendrite of another nerve cell. The transmitter substance (neuro transmitter) released at this terminal knobs (synapse) enables the nerve impulse to pass over the synaptic space.

See: Neuron

SYNDROME: The group of symptoms that is specific to a disorder. Symptoms are signs which indicate a disorder (bodily or mental), for example, high body temperature is a symptom which indicates some disorder. So also is headache. But these symptoms can appear due to a number of causes. So for making a correct diagnosis, just one symptom like erratic pulse or fever is quite inadequate. A disease has a specific cluster of symptoms. All these symptoms have to be identified for making any judgement on diagnosis. The symptom cluster specific to a disorder is called a syndrome. High temperature thus forms only one of the symptoms of the diseases, like typhoid, influenza, meningitis or any kind of infection.

Likewise, mental disorders like anxiety, hysteria, neurasthenia, paranoia, etc. have their peculiar syndromes.

See: Diagnosis

SYSTEMS APPROACH: In educational context, systems approach means the application of management techniques like systems analysis to solve problems in school adminstration and teaching-learning processes. To achieve this, the analysis should start with the input (entry behaviour) and proceed to the output (terminal behaviour) which will show the progress achieved during the period

T

T-MAZE: A maze used for experimentation, the unit of which is in the form of letter T. Mazes are used for studying animal behavior, primarily learning in primitive organisms. T-maze (tubular) for example is used to study learning in earthworms.

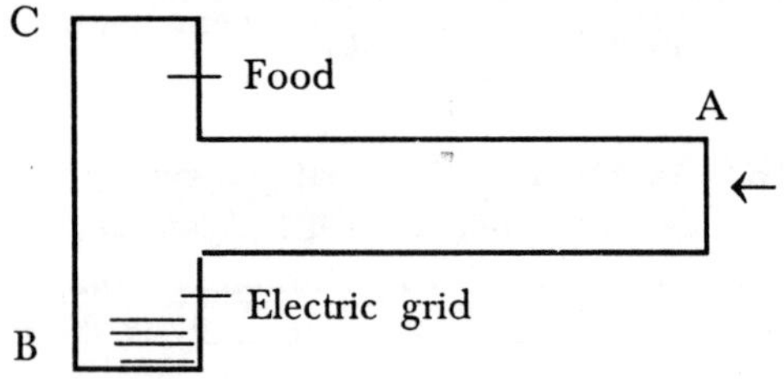

The earthworm is introduced into the maze at A, B is an electic grid, which gives a mild shock, C is food.

The worm crawls quickly as it is wet and dark inside. As it is blind it is guided only by touch; when it touches the obstruction it turns to the left or right at random. If it turns to the left it gets the shock and suddenly withdraws. If it moves to the right it gets food and comfort. The same organism undergoes the trial hundreds of times and finally it learns to turn to the right only when it touches an obstruction. T-maze in this case is used to study how a primitive organism can learn a simple task, and the conditions under which the learning occurs.

Multiple T-mazes are also used to study learning behavior of more complex organisms like fish, mammals, etc. In that case the maze is formed by the combination of a number of T-mazes. Finger mazes used for testing children are multiple T-maze.

T-SCALE: A standard scale with a mean of 50 and standard deviation of 10. T-scale is closely related to the Z-scale. In Z-scale, one disadvantage is that its effective range is only from 3 to 13. It has also negative scores. In T-scale, these difficulties are overcome. Its effective range is from 5 to 65 and it has no negative scores.

A raw score can be converted into its corresponding T-score by the following formula

$$T = 50 + \frac{10(X - M)}{\sigma}$$

in which X is the raw score.

M: is the mean of the distribution of scores containing X.

s: is the standard deviation of the distribution of score containing X.

The T-scores obtained from different distributions can be added and averaged, as after conversion to T-scale all of them belong to the same scale.

See: Standard scores

t-TEST: A statistical test applied to determine the significance of the difference in means when the sample size is small (i.e., below 20). It is applicable only when the distribution is approximately normal.

$$t = \frac{\text{Difference in means}}{\text{SE of Difference in means}}$$

Standard error of the difference in means for a t value to be statistically significant at 5% level, it should be 2.262, and at 1% level it should be 3.250, when the number of cases is 10.

See: Critical Ratio

TABA MODEL: A class room model for the teaching of generalizations. The processes involved in this model are to some extent similar to 'the concept attainment model'. The emphasis is on the process-approach to teaching. It aids in the process of skill development since the students actively involve themselves in making generalizations, explanations and predictions. The model was designed by H. Taba. It has the three basic stages: Planning, Implementation and Evaluation as in any lesson. The details of each stage: Planning has two steps: Identification of goals and the construction of a data retrieval chart. Data retrieval chart consists of examples, situations, etc. and it is designed to display materials in a manner that aids generalizing, making comparisons and predictions.

Implementation has four phases: Listing, Grouping, Labelling and Generalization. Listing means listing all examples, situations, etc. given by the pupils; grouping involves bringing together similar items from the list and at the labelling stage the students give a name to the group like 'mammals' 'nonmetals', etc. At this stage the pupils revert to the data retrieval chart and complete the chart using the samples enumerated in the class. The final phase in implementation is 'Generalizing'. The pupils study the charts and form generalizations including comparisons and predictions. At the evaluation stage, outcomes of learning in both 'content' and 'processes' are tested.

See: Concept Attainment Model

TABOO: A social prohibition based on deep-seated fear. The enforcement of the taboo is dependent on the fear in the person related to the taboo. In primitive societies people believed that the violation of a taboo by an individual would lead to the collective punishment of all the members. Unlike phobias (which are also irrational fears) taboos are not individualistic; all the members of the society posses them. Eg: food taboos: forbidden food items like pork, beef, etc. Freud explained taboos in terms of repressed unconscious wishes – and so there is a strong ambivalent attitude towards the object of taboo: Both attraction and repulsion.

See: Mores, Stereotypes

TABULA RASA: A blank slate. Mind was considered analogous to a blank slate at birth, on which gradually experiences make their impression as the child grows, just as writings on the slate. This was the view of the early philosopher Locke about mind and its functions. Mind is simply conceived of as a passive receiving store house for knowledge and so the early teachers thought that the aim of teaching was to fill it efficiently by memorizing and rote learning.

See: Locke, John

TACHISTOSCOPE: A device for exposing materials for short time intervals, in psychological experiments. Pictures, words, nonsense syllables, digits, etc. are presented for short intervals for the individuals to respond. It is an apparatus with an opening at the front for fixing the stimulus object. A sliding door can be operated, so that the door opens and shuts within the specified time (say 5 sec. 10 sec., etc.). The stimulus is exposed for a short interval. The subject will have to identify the objects seen in the picture, repeat the digits or letters in the correct order, etc. It is used for determining the digit span, attention span, etc.

See: Digit span

TAGORE, RABINDRANATH: Indian poet, philosopher and educationist (1861-1941). He was awarded Nobel Prize for literature in 1913. According to Tagore, the traditional schools very much resembled prisons, and were dissociated from the context of life. He said that education should be a process of creative joy. The ultimate aim of education is to help men realize the inner principle of unity of all knowledge. Education is the harmonizing element of man's various capacities. Real education should strive to realize the problems of life of the universal man. For the attainment of the wholesome personality, man should be in sympathy with all forms of life. So nature is of prime importance in education. Education should therefore take place in the natural environment, free and open. The first seven years should be completely left to nature. All the children should engage in activities experimenting with whatever things available to them. The school should resemble the family. National education should be in full agreement with the social needs of the people and in harmony with international fellowship. For a total education, creative activity is necessary. So art should be an integral part of education. Education according to Tagore, should begin with the training of instincts, emotions and should lead to self-reliance and communal cooperation. Art, music and play can be used to realize the aim. National and international culture should receive proper recognition. Curriculum will have to be activity-oriented. The teacher's primary duty is to provide an atmosphere of creative activity within the school. Tagore implemented his ideas in the Ashram he established in 1901 near Calcutta–Shanti Niketan (Abode of Peace). The Viswabharathi University was founded by the poet in 1922.

Tagore has the unique honour of being the author of the National Anthem of two nations – India and Bangladesh.

See: Viswabharathi

TAKSHASILA: Ancient Hindu Centre of learning in Gandhara (now in Pakistan). Even as early as Seventh century BC, scholars from all over the Indian sub-continent attended the centre. It was destroyed for more than once by foreign invasions. It was occupied in turn by Persians, Bakhtrians Scythians and Kushans. Famous teachers and scholars worked there. The great grammarian scholar Panini was a student of Takshasila.

Study of Vedas and Vedanta and the arts formed the core of the curriculum. But other subjects like Ayurveda, commerce, agriculture, archery, accountancy, magic, etc. were also taught.

Takshashila was at the zenith of its glory till the middle of the third century A.D. It was totally destroyed by the invasion of the Huns.

TASK ANALYSIS: In the planning of an instructional programme, identifying the component skills of complex skills is necessary to formulate a strategy. Task analysis involves the process of analysing the components of complex skills and arranging them in hierarchical order.

TAXONOMY (OF EDUCATIONAL OBJECTIVES): Classification of objectives of education. The term now refers to the system of classification of educational objectives as drawn by the Taxonomy group constituted under the leadership of Benjamin S. Bloom of Chicago University. The aim of the group was to identify the objectives and describe them in behavioural terms, so that learning activities could be clearly directed and evaluated, in the place of the conventional 'aims' previously enumerated by teachers like 'to develop knowledge', 'to develop appreciation of aesthetic experiences', 'to develop moral values', etc. which were vague and immeasurable.

The taxonomy group found that all the objectives of education could be broadly placed under three major domains:

1. **Cognitive**: Objectives relating to remembering and recalling something learned (knowledge), applying knowledge in new situations, analyzing, combining and synthesizing of ideas and critical examination of ideas (evaluation).

2. **Affective**: The objectives under this group have emphasis on the feeling tone and emotions. Interests, attitudes, appreciations and values, fall under the category.

3. **Psychomotor**: The objectives in this domain relate to muscular or motor skills, manipulation of materials and objectives, i.e., acts which require neuro-muscular coordination like writing, speaking, dancing, operating machines, etc.

The three-fold classification of mental activities used by ancient philosophers, viz., cognition, conation and volition (i.e., knowing, feeling, willing) roughly coincide with the classification under the new Taxonomy.

See: Bloom, B.S.

TEACHING STYLES: Specific methodology of teaching and teacher attitude adopted by the teacher in teaching situations. Authoritarian, informal, democratic, laissez-faire, didactic, child-centred, book-centred, subject-centred, enquiry based, heuristic are some of the terms used to describe teaching styles.

TEACHER: Literally, one who teaches. The professional personel employed in schools for implementation of the curriculum. Teaching is a profession which requires its practitioners to possess specialized knowledge and specific skills acquired through intensive training. They are also bound by a set of ethical rules and code of conduct specific to the profession.

The teacher's job is not simply the transmission of knowledge to the pupils; instead they are expected to help in developing the competencies of the child to the optimum and in making him fit for well adjusted life in society. For this the pupil has to posess a well-integrated personality and sound moral and ethical values.

In summary, the children have to be prepared for taking up the challenges of life. School is the agency to achieve this ideal and society maintains the school on the basis of this hope.

So the teacher has to equip himself with the essential theoretical knowledge and practical skills as well as develop an integrated personality himself. He should work with the belief that he is accountable to the children and to the society. As quantification of the results of teacher's work is not possible objectively as can be done as in the case of manufacturing units which produce commodities that can be assessed by quality control measures, many teachers who do very badly, escape unhurt easily.

The most reliable means of building up an eficient system of education is by maintaining a team of competent and devoted teachers. It is in recognition of this fact that the Crowther Report remarks that 'the most potent single factor in education is the teacher'. Many of the deficiencies in the other components of the educational machinary can be made up by the efforts of the teachers, to a considerable degree.

See: Education

TEACHING: The process of providing learning experiences. 'Teaching' has undergone revolutionary changes since its emergence in prehistoric times. Originally it was concerned with the transference of skills from the parents to the child. When society became complex, it became necessary to provide for the training of the child in order to enable him to cope with the different roles he would have to play, on becoming an adult. Methods have been improvised to meet this demand. Imitation, memorization, etc. were the methods largely employed initially to achieve the last end. Till recently this trend continued and teaching has been largely directed to produce rote learning. The teacher's techniques were mostly concerned with lecturing and giving drill works to children. Vast research carried out during the early part of the last century in psychology and education has led to a metamorphosis in 'teaching'. At present the child is at the centre of the teaching-learning process; the teacher's job is to plan the activities beforehand (that would produce the desirable behavior changes in the children) and provide them in the proper sequence. Learning is the activity of the child and the teacher only plans and provides the situations in which appropriate learning takes place. The teacher is not to explain everything. He gives the directions and guidelines whenever necessary. He is active in supervising and controlling the entire progress. The teacher has to make comprehensive preparations for implementing a lesson. He seeks answers to the following questions in his planning:

1. What are the objectives to be achieved by learning this unit?
2. "What type of pupil activity will be needed to achieve them?"
3. What accessory material and aids would be necessary for the acquisition of the knowledge, skills, attitudes, etc.?
4. How can the children get interested in pursuing the learning activity?
5. How can the outcomes of learning measured in terms of the objectives?

All good lessons will have a preparation stage (for motivating pupils), a development stage (activities for mastering the knowledge, skills, etc.), a consolidation stage and an evaluation stage. The teacher may employ a variety of methods as needed: explanation, lecture, demonstration, drawing, dramatising, etc. but the main activity will be for the pupils viz. observing, reading, discussing, calculating, answering, recording, experimenting, drawing inferences, collecting data, creating, writing reports, working out projects, etc. A good teacher helps the children to learn and also helps them learn to learn.

See: Education, Teacher

TEACHING FRAME: The frame used in Programmed Instruction to provide new concepts, ideas, etc. that help to restructure existing knowledge. It is followed by practice frames and test frames.

See: Programmed Instruction

TELEOLOGY: The study of the directional character of living beings. Organisms behave in a way as if their actions are directed towards a goal or end purpose. The study of this characteristics is also called Telenomy.

TEMPERAMENT: Basic emotional nature of a person. Temperament is a term used to denote the general emotional characteristic of the person, such as the quality of his moods, cheerfulness, tenseness and the emotional nature of his motivation. Sheldon's classification of personality (as Viscerotonia, Somatotonia and Cerebrotonia) is based on temperament.

See: Emotions

TENSION: A heightened mental state characterized by muscular and visceral strain. Tension is felt when one is under pressure, or is expected to work beyond capacity, or when faced with a conflicting situation, or when anticipating the outcome of some critical events. When an individual is in tension, he is in a heightened emotional state, apart from being tormented by distressing thoughts. He may also have discomforting physical symptoms.

When a person faces a challenging situation and is motivated to react to the situation, normally, some tension is built up in his system. Reduction of this tension is also necessary for restoration of a normal mental state. So the tension under normal situation is a condition that energizes the individual for better and speedy performance. But when the person perceives the demands of the situation as insurmountable, heightened tension is built up, which has a deleterious effect on performance. Threats of failure or low performance also leave the person in a state of tension. In short, mild tension energizes action, while severe tension pulls down efficiency.

See: Conflict

TERMAN, LEWIS M.: The American Psychologist (1877-1956) who adapted and revised the Binet scale (intelligence test) with the help of his assistants at Standford University (Standford Revision, published in Terman's 'Measurement of Intelligence') for use in U.S.A.

See: Binet A. Binet-Simon scale

TERMINAL FRAME: In Programmed Instruction, the frame used to revise, recapitulate or summarise materials presented in earlier frames.

See: Programmed Instruction

TEST FRAME: In CAL, a frame that elicits evidence of learning from the student. The student, by this frame is required to make a response to an item already learned. Also called T-frame.

See: Computer-Assisted-Learning

TEST: Systematic procedure for obtaining data or measurements on a particular behaviour. A test is a standard or standardized situation to which the individual has to respond. The items of a test are supposed to be a representative sample of the universe of items (i.e., all the items that are possible). So it can be assumed that the measure obtained from a test is approximately equal to the measure that can be theoretically obtained if the test contained the universe of items.

An intelligence tests calls for the mental activity which is considered to be intellectual and so a test item in it is a typical situation to respond intelligently. In other words, a test item represents a bit or unit of the dimension it is expected to measure. As all the items in a test are such units, the test as a whole is considered as a measuring instrument, capable of measuring that particular dimension.

The two essential qualities of a test are 'validity' and 'reliability'.

If the test measures actually what it claims to measure, it is valid. If the test gives consistent values from an individual on repeated administrations, it is reliable. A test can be reliable without being valid, but a valid test essentially has to be reliable.

A good test is also objective, i.e., it is uninfluenced by subjective opinions of the testee or scorer. All the testees taking the test should interpret the instructions in the same manner. Answers of an objective test can be machine-scored if necessary. Objectivity is an essential component of validity and reliability.

Psychological and scholastic tests are broadly classified into two categories: according to the nature of the behavior tested– 'Tests of maximum performance' and 'Test of typical performance'. Tests of maximum performance are tests of abilities and proficiencies (like intelligence and achievement) in which what is needed is the information about the maximum level of achievement possible for the individual, as indicated by the highest score possible for him. Tests of typical performance, on the other hand, are meant to obtain data on habitual characteristics of the individual: like attitude scales, personality tests, sociometric tests, interest inventories, etc. For these tests, there is no maximum performance as in the case of ability tests.

Tests are used for a variety or purposes, including selection and screening for posts and educational courses, guidance and counselling (vocational, personal) and in therapy, research and experimentation, etc.

See: Standardized tests

TEST PROTOCOL: Set of complete instructions for administration, scoring and interpreting individual tests. Individual tests (individually administered test like the original Binet-Simon test) need a detailed set of standardized instructions and directions for administering the test, for grouping, classifying and interpreting data. Thematic Apperception Test (TAT), Rorschach Test (Ink-blot) are tests that have test protocols.

TEST CEILING: The highest level of the dimension measured by the test. An important property of a good test is that the maximum score indicated in the test could not be attained by anyone. For example, an intelligence test may have a maximum possible score of 100, but nobody in the particular age would be able to reach it. A high ceiling is necessary for a good test of ability, since it should be able to accommodate anyone at the highest level.

See: Floor

TESTOSTERONE: Male sex hormone (androgen). It controls the growth and development of reproductive organs and secondary sex characteristics. It also influences sex-drive.

See: Estrogen

TETRACHORIC CORRELATION: The correlation coefficient applicable in the case of the normally distributed continuous variables, for which data have been artificially reduced to two categories. The tetrachoric correlation gives a value approximate to Pearson's. The equation for computing tetrachoric correlation is long and complicated and so, usually short cut methods are used. The formula that can be used to obtain an approximate value of tetrachoric correlation (r_t) is

$$r_{cos-pi} = \cos\left(\frac{180°}{1+\sqrt{ad/bc}}\right)$$

a, b, c and d are the cell frequencies in the contingency table.

To illustrate by an example:

To find out the relationship between the economic status of the parents and the educational achievement of pupils in primary classes, data were obtained on both the variables. Both variables are continuous but the distributions were dichotomised: achievement into Normal and Backward and Economic status criterion dichotomised at the median (i.e., as parents whose economic status was above median and those below median). From the data tetrachoric correlation was computed. (In the cells are given the numbers of children in each category)

r_{cos-pi} in this case worked out to .5, suggesting that there is a fair degree of correlation between the two variables. Backwardness is associated with low economic status of the parents.

See: Correlation

THEMATIC APPERCEPTION TEST: A projective test of personality using hazy pictures, developed by H.A. Murray.

The original test designed by Murray consists of 31 picture cards, which depict various social and emotional situations. The pictures are hazy and almost ambiguous. The testee is shown each card and is asked to respond to questions relating to each card, like: What does this picture show? What has led to the situation shown in the picture? What will happen next? As the picture is not clear, the testee has to project his self (unwittingly or unconsciously) to interpret the situation. As the pictures have been standardized the responses of the testee can be interpreted in terms of the typical responses of the norming group. From this, his personality can be assessed–particularly his thwarted needs, aspirations, past experiences, traumatic experiences, etc.

Various adaptations of Thematic Apperception Tests (TAT) (like 'Children's Apperception Test') are also available.

See: Projective tests

THEMATIC APPROACH: A strategy used in class teaching. It can be adopted for teaching a topic or for implementing a project, either individually or in groups. The starting point for the lesson is a theme like power generation. The students may view the theme in different ways. Each may choose an aspect of the theme and proceed with the project.

See: Project

THORNDIKE, EDWARD L.: Famous American educational psychologist (1874-1949). His 'laws of learning' based on Stimulus-Response hypothesis had been very popular with teachers. The three laws are: 'The law of readiness', 'the law of exercise', and 'the law of effect'. The cardinal principle is that 'when a given stimulus has been followed by a response which leads to satisfying conditions, a bond is formed between the two.

Thorndike's name is also associated with 'Thorndike's Hand Writing Scale' (1909). He authored several books of which the following became popular: Principles of Teaching (1905), Elements of Psychology (1905) and Educational Psychology (1914).

THOUGHT QUESTION: Questions that provoke reasoning. The term is loosely applied to some questions of the essay type that require extended answers. The questions are expected to test higher abilities in thought organization. The implication is that the test, instead of requiring the candidates to reproduce memorized facts, makes them produce answers that are the results of reasoning, analytical thinking, critical analysis, etc.

THWARTING: Obstructing a person's progress towards a goal. The barriers that occur on his way results in thwarting. If his motive is strong and the barrier is insurmountable or too difficult to overcome, the situation may lead to frustration.
See: Frustration

TIME SAMPLING: The method of child study based on recording of behavior of children at definite periods of time. According to this method, a child is observed, say, for 5 minutes and the behaviours occurring at that time are duly recorded. The child may be observed for the 5 minute period, two or more times during a day at different intervals like, between 9-10 am, 10-11 am, 1-2 pm, etc. Samples of behaviour like this will be obtained from the child for the period planned: One month, three months, etc.

TIMED TEST: The test that allows only a prescribed time for completing it. Timed tests require the candidates to complete the items within the specified time. The optimum time required for the majority of candidates (75% usually) to complete the test during the standardization process is usually fixed as the time allowed for the test, in its application in future. A standardized test, in its instructions, will indicate this time. The candidates will not be allowed additional time. Timed test often contains a large number of items around 50% level of difficulty. When a general survey of an ability in a particular dimension among a sample of population is required, the choice is a timed test.
See: Power Test

TOKEN REWARDS: Symbolic rewards which can function as a real reward. Rewards are reinforcers, because they strengthen the response. A food-deprived chimpanzee housed in an experimental cage, learns to press a bar to release pellets of food. Whenever it presses the lever in the right manner it receives a pellet of food. At the second stage the animal is made to learn to put a coin in the slot in the cage to release the food pellet. The lever pressing thereafter releases only the coin. The chimpanzee then has to press the lever, get the coin and put the coin in the slot and get the food. The animal soon learns to press the bar, take the coin and put it in the slot. Animals which have mastered this, is seen to press the lever repeatedly even when not hungry and keep the coins, using them later when they feel hungary. The coin in this case, functions as a reward in the place of food which is the primary reinforcement. The coin is a secondary reinforcer which stands for the primary reinforcer. Such secondary reinforcers are token rewards. Money in the case of man functions as a token reward because it is the unique symbol of the real reward (like food, clothing, prestige, etc.) that satisfies his needs.

See: Rewards

TOLSTOY, LEO (1828-1910): World famous Russian writer and thinker. He studied in Germany, Switzerland and France. Tolstoy began to try out his principles of education in an elementary school of his native village, Yasnaya Polyana from 1861. In this school, pupils were given complete freedom – even freedom to attend or stay away, learn or not learn. He emphasized 'experience' as the basic need in education and discouraged mere book-learning. The importance of the world outside the school was stressed and he advocated the method of teaching by 'incitement' – i.e., initiating discussion in real situations.

TOOLS: Devices which help to increase the range and efficiency of work. In psychology and education 'tool' refers to devices constructed to gather behavioural data, which help in measurements and classifications. Tests of various kinds, rating scales, behavior data schedules, etc. are therefore, tools. Tools are also called instruments. Tools are also used for collecting qualitative information about the individual, for example, study habits, interests, etc. of students. They are also used for guidance and counselling.

TOPOLOGICAL PSYCHOLOGY: The system of psychology that interprets behavior as the resultant of positive and negative forces in the environment. Under this system, the behavior at a moment is likened to a magnetic needle placed in a magnetic field. The position at rest ultimately arrived at by the needle, depends on the strength, direction and polarity of magnetic field affecting the needle. In the same manner the psychological forces resulting from needs, knowledge, attitude, interests, etc. within the individual are influenced by negative (repelling) and positive (attracting) forces in the environment (like objects that are accessible for need satisfaction and situations that threaten the approach towards need satisfaction). The resulting behavior is a balance of all these forces. The space within which the forces originate in the environment, including the individual, is called the 'life space' at the moment. It need not coincide with the geographical space. For example, in a large congregation of people, an individual may be concerned with only a few at the time. As the forces influencing the individual change, the life space also changes. Topological psychology is so concerned with the 'structuring of self' which is characterized by personality needs, field forces (which are called negative and positive valences) and the resultant behaviour.

This branch of psychology is also known as Field Theory.

Kurt Lewin and Tolman contributed largely to the development of this theory.

See: Field theory

TOTAL QUALITY MANAGEMENT (TQM): A customer is one to whom a product or service is provided. In education the parent (or the public) is the customer (client). So their expectations, values, attitudes, socio-cultural situations and commitments have to be understood in order to know their demands. T.Q.M. provides information on these items and the processes to enable the school, to work harmoniously. The pupil is central and TQM foresees all aspects of the organization vis-a-vis its aims. The main features of TQM are – 'Quality' and implies the fulfilment of the needs and requirements stated by the customer. Continous improvement is effected through prevention and not by correction. Senior management is concerned with the direction, but responsibility is equal for all. Quality is to be measured in realistic terms. Quality can be achieved only by a competent team of workers. Education, training and personal growth are essential components of success. Quality has to be used as criterion for reviewing decision, actions, processes and outcomes. Accountability is a prime factor in quality management.

TRANSCEIVER: Device used (like teleprinter), to transmit and receive information.

TRANSDUCER: A term in information technology used

to signify any device used to convert signals from one form to another, like electrical signals into mechanical vibrations.

TRANSFER: Mastery of one task facilitating the learning of another task. Transfer is dependent on the degree of similarity between the two tasks, i.e., when the two tasks possess 'identical elements'. Mastering the skill of driving light vehicles like motor cars, makes it easier to learn driving heavy vehicles like trucks. This kind of transfer is called positive transfer. In some cases mastery of one skill may adversely interfere with the learning of another task. Mastery in the skill in typing in a specially designed typewriter with a keyboard different from the standard typewriter, will make learning in the standard keyboard more difficult. This type of transfer is called negative transfer. Mastery of learning tasks with organs on one side of the body (hand, foot) is seen to transfer to the other side. This is bilateral transfer. Education is assumed, to have the greatest 'transfer value' as the skills and proficiencies acquired in schools and colleges facilitate all learning (active or passive) that occurs in future.

See: Learning

TRANSMITTER: Also neuro-transmitter. The chemical substances contained in the small vesicles (sags) at the synaptic nerve spaces, released when a nerve impulse reaches the synaptic end of the axon of a nerve cell. The transmitters either excite or inhibit the impulse at the synaptic dendrite of the neuron. It thus facilitates or obstructs the flow of impulses along the nerve fibres. Transmitters are molecules of acetylecholine noradrenaline.

See: Neurotransmitter

TRAUMA: A physical or mental shock that has damaging effects. Involvement in an accident is a traumatic condition, both physically and mentally.

TREATMENT VARIABLE: An independent variable of an experiment which is intended to modify the behavior of the experimental subjects and which is controlled by the experimenter. The subjects are treated in some manner by the experimenter in an experiment. For example, in an experiment to establish the effectiveness of a particular method of teaching, the teacher tries out the new method on a sample of students. This treatment is expected to produce behaviour modification. The teacher controls the treatment procedures (which involves the treatment variable). The new method of teaching in this experiment is the treatment variable.

See: Experiment

TREMOR: A muscular spasm on limited muscle tissue. Tremor may occur due to organic or functional disorder. It may occur as a conversion symptom in some cases of hysteria, like trembling of the hand, fingers, etc.

TRIAL-AND-ERROR: The method of learning by which the successful response is hit by trying out a number of random or plausible responses. Trial and error learning is supposed to occur when the 'field' is unstructured, i.e., the learner is not in a position to perceive all the components of the situation. Under strong motivation, in such a situation, a subject is forced to try 'the hit and miss' method. Various possibilities are tried (randomly) and finally he may hit the correct response. As this leads to 'satisfaction' the response tends to be fixed. Even when the situation is structured, if individuals fail to perceive the total field in relation to its elements, he resorts to trial and error.

It was E.L. Thorndike with his famous 'problem box' experiment who demonstrated trial and error learning in cats. A cat (which was hungry) was locked in a problem box, with a fish outside. The box could be opened from inside by moving a latch. The cat made all types of random movements. Sometimes it accidently pressed its paw on the latch, which resulted in the opening of the door of the box. This action has resulted in satisfying the need (hunger) and also helped in escaping from the box. So the latch pressing response tended to be learned, when the cat was placed in the experimental situation repeatedly. The number of trials became less and less and finally the animal made no wrong responses. The cat has learned to open the box. This is 'trial and error' learning (problem solving by trial and error).

When the subject (human) in a problematic situation fails to structure the field properly, in abstract and symbolic thinking also he resorts to trial and error approach. He thinks of different possibilities of coping with a situation and may put each to trial until he gets the correct one.

See: Problem Solving, Operant conditioning

TRIANGULATION: Using two or more methods for collection of data for studying some phenomena of complex human behaviour. Instead of depending upon one method (single method approach) the researcher makes use of two or more methods (multi-method approach) for data collection. Data are collected both qualitatively and quantitatively. There are four main types of triangulation, viz. time triangulation, space triangulation, investigator triangulation and methodological triangulation. In time triangulation, for example, data can be collected for cross-sectional and longitudinal studies; in space triangulation data can be collected from samples in two or three separate geographical areas or samples cross-culturally; in investigator triangulation more than one observer can be engaged for the investigation; and in methodological triangulation different methods of data collection can be adopted or the study can be replicated.

TROPISM: The unlearned ability to orient and move towards a natural stimulus. Organisms at the primitive stage of evolution possessed this type of response tendency which helped them to move away from or towards certain class of stimuli. This reaction was basic to survival. Phototropism is the tendency to orient and fly towards light found in moths and the tendency of cockroaches to take refuge in dark corners. Earthworms display a tendency to move away from dry earth towards wetness (hydrotropism). Tropism is one of the earliest types of reflexive behavior that appeared in the organism. The common tropisms are: phototropism (orientation towards light), geotropism (orientation to move downwards), stereotropism (orientation towards solid surfaces), etc.

See: Reflex

TRUANCY: Running away from school. The truant child is a problem child, who often suffers from deep seated emotional disturbance. Contributing cause can be traced back to home and parents, peer group, school situations, etc. Broken-home condition is often found to be the most common cause for driving out the child from home and school. A truant child is likely to slip into delinquency. Prompt counselling will restore normalcy.

TYPOLOGY: Classifying people into types. The early attempts to study the characteristics of man in many cultures resulted in the development of systems for classification of man into types.

Principle of classification differed with the various cultures. Some used body build for classification (physique) like endomorphy, ectomorphy, etc. (Sheldon). Some were based on temperament, e.g. pyknic and leptosome (Kretchmer). Vatsyana, the ancient Indian scholar, classified men into three categories: bull, horse and hare, and women into mare, elephant and deer. Current personality theories also use typology to describe people who possess specific definable trait constellations like, cyclothymic, paranoic, extroverted, introverted, etc.

See: Personality

TUTOR-MODE CAL: A sophisticated type of Computer-Assisted-Learning (CAL) in which interaction is possible between the computer and the learner, as in the case with a live tutor. The learner can engage in a dialogue, with the computer, based on the responses of the learner.

See: Computer Assisted Learning

U

UNCONSCIOUS MOTIVATION: The urge that impels the individual to action, about which he is not aware of. Unconscious motivation has its origin in the unconscious and so the individual does not know why he tends to act in a particular manner. The irresistible urge to touch every lamppost when one walks along the street, or to steal things that one does not require has their origin in the unconscious. Actions that are motivated by the unconscious are acceptable forms of expressions of repressed wishes, appearing in a disguised form. The meaning of such seemingly irrelevant actions can be brought to light by psychoanalysis. Freud claimed that many of our actions are motivated at the unconscious level.

See: Repression

UNDER-ACHIEVER: The students whose sholastic performance is far below than that can be predicted from his intelligence, i.e., a student who does not work up to capacity. This may be due to lack of motivation, poor study habits, etc.

See: Backwardness, Over-achiever

UNIDIMENSIONAL SCALE: A scale which measures a non-composite dimension. A test which measures only one dimension (one factor) at a time is a unidimensional test. Attitude scales can be constructed to measure a person's attitude towards a variety of social dimensions or to simply one: like, 'attitude towards democracy'. Personality tests are usually multidimensional, while a test of introversion-extroversion is unidimensional. Achievement tests can be considered unidimensional when it tests ability in only one particular content area.

UNIT COST: In education it means the total amount of money needed for (1) educating a student, (2) providing a class extra, and (3) opening or running a new school. To calculate unit cost all direct and indirect expenditure incurred are to be reckoned with. The broad area of expenditure to be included are: institutional costs, Student cost, cost of administration and supervision, and Opportunity cost.

See: Cost of Education, Institutional Cost

UNIVERSAL EDUCATION: Education for all. Education open (and compulsory) to all the citizens of a country, where no discrimination based on religion, race, language, etc. exists, or in other words, opportunity for pursuing education has been totally equalized. It presupposes schools within reasonable distance from the home of every child and school attendance compulsory for all eligible children.

UNIVERSAL GRAMMAR: As proposed by Chomsky, children everywhere are endowed with 'a system of analysing speech sounds' which he calls universal grammar. Based on the similarity of structure of all languages there is a universal grammar and this is possibly built into the brain of every child.

See: Chomsky. N.A.

UNIVERSALIZATION OF EDUCATION: Ensuring education for all the citizens of the country. Usually, universalization is insisted upon for the stage upto which education is compulsory for a country (i.e., for primary stage or for the age group 6-16 years, etc.). Universalization implies that all children of the specific age group are enrolled in schools at the appropriate age and they complete the education, till they complete the age prescribed. To achieve this (1) schools should be provided within a reasonable distance from the home of every child. This is 'universal provision of facilities' (2) all the children within the age range are enrolled in schools. This is 'universal enrolment' and (3) all the children enrolled should complete the education till they attain the specific age. This is 'universal retention'. So universalization can be achieved only if these conditions of universal provision, universal enrolment and universal retention are ensured.

UNIVERSE: In statistics, the totality of the members of which a particular sample is a part. It is often interchangeably used with 'population'. Universe is used also to include the totality of members of any type of objects, observations, etc. (other than people, animals, etc.). For example, a standardized test is supposed to contain items (questions) which are representative of a universe of items, which means, theoretically, that the items of the test are drawn at random from a group of all possible and conceivable number of items.

See: Statistics

UNLEARNED RESPONSE: A response which has not been produced by learning. 'Unlearned responses' is used to denote those responses that are believed to be inherited for the whole species. Tropism, reflexes, and instincts (a term which is now used only by few) are known to be not due to learning. They appear at the appropriate stage like the sucking reflex in the new baby and the migratory instinct found in birds, fishes, etc. These response patterns are essential for the survival of the species.

See: Tropism, Reflex, Maturation

V

VALENCES: The forces of the environment that attract and repel the individual. According to the Field Theorists, the behavior of the individual at a particular moment is dependent on the resultant of the internal forces within the individual interacting with the forces of the environment. The forces of the environment may be either positive or negative. The positive force pulls the individual towards the environmental object (resulting in approach) and negative force repels (avoidance, withdrawal). The positive and negative forces that ultimately decide the behavior of the individual are called the valences.

See: Field theory

VALIDATION: The process of establishing the validity of a test. Validation process is a stage in the standardization of a test. The data for validation are obtained by administering tests of the same kind (i.e. measuring the same dimension) whose validity is well known, to the same sample of persons who have taken the test for which validity has to be established. The correlation between the two test scores is the index of validity of the test. A correlation coefficient above the value 0.7 is considered acceptable.

For validation, correlation with another criterion which is highly correlated with the test dimension also is acceptable. Many intelligence tests have been validated in this manner. In this case, the correlation between intelligence tests scores and scholastic test scores are taken (Intelligence is considered to be most powerful single factor influencing school achievement). If the correlation coefficient is above .5, the test is considered fairly valid.

In some cases, the test scores are correlated with objective data obtained from performance in social situations, jobs, etc. at a later date. Some aptitude tests, psychometric tests and tests of personality are validated in this manner. For example, a high score in a mechanical aptitude test is theoretically, predictive of a high degree of success in the engineering profession. So scores obtained by candidates in the aptitude test are correlated with the performance index obtained for the same individuals in the job. A high value of correlation shows that the test is valid.

See: Standardization

VALIDITY: The fidelity of the test in terms of the quality it intends to measure. A test is valid if it truthfully measures the criterion it claims to meausre. An intelligence test is valid if it actually measures the quality, 'intelligence'. If it is only partially effective in measuring intelligence, it is valid only to that degree.

Measurement involves the comparison of the like with the like (i.e. quantification). When we measure length, we compare the distance between two given points with a small 'segment' of length which we call the unit: 1 cm , 1 inch, etc. The value is given as multiples or fractions of the unit. There is no question of validity in the case of a metre scale as the measuring instrument of length – its validity is self-evident. So also in the case of most of the physical measurements like mass, time, temperature, electrical resistance, etc. validity is self-evident. In the case of qualities to be measured in education and psychology, generally, it is not possible to devise a unit to measure it, which has self-evident validity. Take for example: intelligence. The quality 'intelligence' does not easily lend itself to a definition, on the basis of which a test can be constructed. So psychologists were constrained to propose an operational definition to enable them to construct the test. When intelligence is defined as 'the ability to solve new problems', it becomes easier to design a test which measures the ability to solve new problems. Then theoretically, it becomes possible, to claim that we compare the like with the like. The mental dimension 'ability to solve new problem' can be compared with bits of the same dimension, i.e., solving individual items. A test constructed like that, will be fairly truthful to the criterion. Still it is possible that other factors may get mixed up with the test and pull down its validity, like the language factor, previous learning, etc. If a test in history needs knowledge in other areas like language, statistics, etc. to answer it, its validity will get vitiated. So it is necessary that the validity of tests of mental abilities – aptitudes, interests, attitudes, personality, scholastic achievement, etc. have to be ascertained experimentally.

There are two fundamental methods of establishing the validity of a test. They are, (1) logical analysis, and (2) empirical analysis.

By logical analysis the following types of validity are possible: Face validity: If the test appears or looks like a test to measure the quality to experts in the subject, it has face validity.

Logical validity: If the logical analysis of the content of the test shows that the items actually meausre the proposed entity and that the influence of vitiating factors is negligible, it has logical validity.

Empirical validities are based on statistical and experimental analysis of the tests. Most important are – (1) Contsruct validity: when the test correlates high with other tests which also measure the same qualities and which have established validities (eg., new intelligence test constructed should have high correlations with the Raven's Progressive matrices tests) or with ratings on intelligence obtained from a panel of expert observers. If a test correlates very highly with a similar (validated) test or with parallel forms of the same test, it is said to have congruent validity. Predictive validity: In this case, the criterion for establishing the validity of the test is its efficiency to forecast performance. A high score in a test of mechanical aptitude suggests that a candidate will perform well in the engineering studies or jobs, later. If the scores actually can predict success, it has predictive validity. A child with a high, I.Q., theoretically, should do well with his scholastic work. Obtained evidence by follow-up studies of individuals in the particular fields are correlated with the scores in the tests concerned. This yields predictive validity.

Factorial validity: This is obtained by the process of factor analysis. Factor analysis can show whether the test measures just one type of dimension or not.

See: Test, Standardized test

VALUES: Internalized beliefs considered worthy by the individual. Values have reference to social and humanitarian aspects of the individual's life. They are ideas with which the individual have identified and which have been accepted emotionally. That 'one should be honest in dealing with others', 'one should not exploit others', etc. are ideas that practically every person declares as important qualities of good character. But only very few have internalized these ideas as values. Their acceptance of the worth of the ideas lies deeper than at the cognitive level, it has its roots in the affective domain. So they are emotionally involved in them.

So, to behave in a way discordant with the value is painful, and so they avoid it and try to act according to the direction provided by the values. Value is a far stronger determinant of behavior than the knowledge one possess about an ethical principle.

Values that are related coalesce and produce a value system.

A well integrated personality, then, has a few complex value systems which determine the behaviour, inter-personal, social, etc. So one of the ultimate aims of education can be said to be the development of proper value systems in children.

See: Affective Domain, Education

VARIABLE: A quality (or trait) that varies in quantity; eg., body weight, intelligence, height, etc. The variables that are encountered in education and psychology are of two kinds: continuous and discrete. Intelligence and language abilities are continuous variables; i.e., the spread of the variable in the population is continuous, any value in the population is continuous, any value is possible between the maximum and minimum measures. Marital status and handedness are discrete variables: there can be only two types in the first example, married/unmarried and only three types in the second example, viz. right handed/left handed/ambidexterous. Intermediate categories (or fractional values) are not possible.

VARIANCE: The mean square deviation (S^2). It is the square of the standard deviation of a distribution. It is represented, by S^2 or s^2 and is given by the formula $s^2 = SX^2/N$: where SX^2 is the sum of deviation of each score from the mean, N : the total number of cases.

Variance is also a measure of variability and in many situations (in education research) analysis of variance (ANOVA) of distributions are undertaken to find out significant difference between two or more sets of observations (or groups).

See: Analysis of Variance

VEDIC EDUCATION: The education in India that prevailed around 2000 BC. One unique feature of Indian culture is its continuity, unlike that of most other early civilizations. So Vedic education (Aryan) can be considered as the precursor of the present system of education in India. The Vedic system continued up to about 800 BC. The most common type of the period was the gurukula system in which the pupils lived with the guru for 8 to 10 years. The pupil joined the gurukula usually between the ages 10 to 12. Academic education was restricted, first to the study of the Rigveda hymns of the Aryans. As the art of writing was not fully developed, all knowledge was transmitted orally. At the second stage, explanations and discussions were used for the in-depth study of the Vedas. The pupils attended to all types of work in the household. All children (usually less than ten) were treated alike. Study of Sanskrit literature and itihasas and puranas (like Ramayana) formed part of the curriculum along with astronomy, geometry, philosophy and elements of science. Hard physical labour and strict observance of celebacy helped the students to develop a strong body and a morally sound mind. The gurus were forbidden to accept any fees from the students but were entitled to receive guru-dakshina (offerings for the guru) at the end of the studentship. The basic fundamentals of modern education – development of total personality, preparation for a personally and socially useful life, individualization, can be traced back to this ancient system of education.

Chathurvarnya (four caste hierarchy) developed towards the end of this period (around 800 BC), and the system began to distengrate.

VERBAL SKILLS: The various proficiencies in the use of language. Literally it means the ability to use words. The verbal skills have mainly two components: cognitive and psychomotor (emotions, of course, also affect them); cognitive is concerned with the mental activity involved in speech and writing, and psychomotor is concerned with the expression, i.e., articulation, appropriate gesture, body movements, etc. in speech. As they are skills involving neuro-muscular coordination, they have to be developed, and the development is possible only by practice.

The most important verbal skills are, reading, speaking, reciting, writing and thinking.

See: Skill

VIDEO TEX: A computer device for displaying messages on a television screen delivered through the telephone line. This is also called view-data system. It was initiated in the United States. Messages are transmitted through the telephone line. Set as analogue signals which are converted into digital signals by an instrument and an adaptor. The view tex system may have thousands of pages of information containing data on weather forecasts, sports fixtures, travel and tourism, health information, entertainment, home education courses, etc. The items are displayed on the screen from which the user can select the desired item with a keypad.

VIEWLEX: An effective visual aid for young children. It is a simple viewer to look at a 35 mm film. The film can be manually wound to bring each frame in view, in conjunction with a tape recording. The film can be wound forward or backward. The tape recordings may also include questions, in addition.

VIHARA: The Buddhist centres of higher education that existed in ancient India. Those institutions flourished during the early centuries preceding the Christian era. The viharas were residential universities and those in Nalanda and Vikramasila were so famous during those days that, students sought admission to them from distant lands. Viharas were attached to monasteries.

VIRTUAL REALITY: In computer terminology, the environment simulated by the computer. The user can interact as in actual situation. It is often used in the training of airline pilots.

VISCEROTONIA: Personality type characterized by concern with eating. This classification is according to temperamental analysis. Viscerotonia is a cluster of traits the chief characteristics of which are: pleasure in eating, desire for comfort, lovability, craving for recognition and affection, easily moved by emotion and needing others' help when in difficulties (Viscera: Stomach).

VISWA-BHARATHI: The university founded by the great Indian poet, Rabindra Nath Tagore near Calcutta in 1922. It is a co-educational residential university of interenational repute. It has the following departments: Vidya-bhavana (school of research), Cheena-bhavana (school of Sino-Indian studies), Siksha-bhavana (College affiliated to Calcutta University), Kala-bhavana (department of fine arts), Sangeeth-bhavana (school of music), Sri-niketan (institute of rural reconstruction) and Silpa-bhavana (school of industries). It is an institution functioning on non-conventional lines with the declared object of brining the diverse cultures of the East into more intimate relationship with one another; approaching the science and culture of the west from the standpoint of their unity; and realising in common fellowship and humanitarian activity, the concord of the east and west.

See: Tagore Rabindranath

VOCATIONAL CHOICE: Selection of a job from among the various occupational openings. The choice of a vocation is most crucial in the life of an individual. His status in society, financial prospects, chances for professional growth and self expression, his friends and associates, etc., which are the determinants of his happiness and success in life, are dependent on his job. So this choice has to be made realistically. The job should be one in which he can succeed. To enable children to make such realistic choices of their vocation, (when they become adults), vocational guidance services are provided in the schools.

See: Guidance, Vocational Guidance

VOCATIONAL DEVELOPMENT: The pattern and sequence of development of vocational concepts in men according Donald. E. Super. The first stage, which corresponds with childhood, is the Fantasy stage when children have only vague and unrealistic ideas about the world of work. The second stage corresponds to adolescence – the stage of Tentative choice – when children have some notion about occupation but the range and depth of knowledge is limited. The third stage is the stage of Realistic choice, corresponding to early adulthood, when the persons have developed realistic ideas about the different occupations. As individuals develop at different rates, it is possible that an adult may remain at the tentative choice stage or even at the fantasy stage and make wrong decisions about their career.

Along with the development of vocational concepts, the individual also develops self-concepts. Distorted self-concept also may lead to wrong choices.

See: Self-concept

VOCATIONAL EDUCATION: Education for jobs, as a part of general education. The UNESCO definition (1974) is 'The comprehensive term embracing those aspects of the educational process involving in addition to general education, study of technologies and related sciences and the acquisition of practical skills, attitudes, understandings and knowledge relating to occupations in the various sectors of economic and social life'. Vocational education generally is an integral part of secondary education (and may begin at the upper primary stage). It may be a preparation for an occupation or field of occupation or as part of continuing education.

VOCATIONAL GUIDANCE: Career guidance given to students. In schools it is usually done by career masters. In the career cells facilities are provided for the collection of career pamphlets and career posters and other literature. Career masters disseminate career information, by career talks, career exhibitions, career conferences, etc. apart from giving individual counselling in deserving cases.

Universitities and colleges have provisions for vocational guidance services. The Employment Departments of the governments also have facilities for vocational guidance services.

See: Guidance

VON-RESTORFF EFFECT: The principle that a novel item is learned quickly irrespective of its position in the learning sequence. In serial learning a novel or unique item is quickly learned even if it occurs in the middle of the list. Letters 'K', 'P', etc. of the alphabet are easily learned if they are printed in attractive colours.

See: Serial learning

VYGOTSKY, L.S.: Russian psychologist and philogist. He made remarkable contributions to the theory of concept development. He showed the importance of language in concept formation and how an acquired concept is linked to its verbal equivalent (word). When the word is heard later (or recalled) the concept can be visualized.

See: Concept

W

WASH BACK: In Programmed Instruction it means Backward branching.

See: Programmed Instruction

WASHBURNE, CARLETON: The proponent of the 'Winnetka Plan' (Winnetka, in Chicago). He proposed a curriculum based on individual work in academic subjects and cooperative work in activities similar to those encountered outside the school. According to this plan, pupils worked at their own place, testing themselves at the end of each assignment. His important works were 'What is Progressive Education?' and a 'Living Philosophy of Education'.

WASTAGE: A term used to denote premature leaving of school (droppage). Droppage along with stagnation (due to detention or grade repetition) is a wastage both for the individual and the state. A child who drops out from school before completing the primary stage (five years of education) is likely to relapse into illiteracy. Literacy is a prerequisite for an enlightened citizenry which in turn is essential for the functioning of a successful democracy. Functional literacy is also essential for the individual to lead a successful life in modern society and protect himself from exploitation. The places provided in the school for the drop-outs, remain unutilized, and in terms of finance it is a colossal waste for the state. To bring back the drop-outs to non-formal education institutions, to make them functionally literate at a later stage means the incurring of additional expenditure for those children a second time. In an efficient educational setup, wastage and stagnation will be minimum.

WATSON, BROADUS: American psychologist (1878-1939) popularly known as the founder of the Behaviourist school of psychology. Watson wanted psychology to keep out mentalistic concepts like consciousness out of psychology and deal only with observable and quantifiable (measurable) behaviour in its realm. Psychology, he said, should use scientific methods to study behavioural phenomena, as in the case of other biological sciences. Starting from Pavlov's Classical Conditioning, he developed his own theories of behaviourism. He was able to explain practically most of the mental phenomena in behaviouristic terms. His books 'Psychology from the standpoint of the Behaviorist' (1919), 'Behavior' (1929) and 'Psychological care of Infant and Child' (1928) remain the basic text books on Behaviourism.

See: Behaviourism, Schools of Psychology

WEBER-FECHNER LAW: The law which states that the relationship between physical energy and sensation is logarithmic. When the intensity of a stimulus is low, even a small change in intensity becomes noticeable. For example: when light intensity is low a small change in intensity is noticed. But when the light is very bright, the change to become noticeable, it has to be large. This principle is seen operative, in other situations also. A small increase in wages of a low salaried person is easily recognized while such an increase in the higher salary grade will not be duly acknowledged.

WERTHEIMER, MAX: The founder of the Gestalt School of Psychology (1980-1943). Wertheimer was born in Prague. He was educated at Berlin, where he studied philosophy and psychology. Wertheimer, then moved to Frankfurt, where he started his pioneering work in psychology. Here he, first acquainted himself with Wolfang Kohler and then with Kurt Koffka. These three are known as the trio of Gestalt Psychology. The publication of his first paper, 'The Experimental studies on the perception of movement' (1912) was really the inauguration of Gestalt Psychology. Gestalts are wholes, the behaviour of which is not determined by that of their individual elements, whereas the part processes are themselves determined by the intrinsic nature of the whole. The main contributions of Gestalt Psychology were to the psychology of perception, thinking and problem solving. Wertheimer was the creative genius who produced the original theories of Gestalt psychology. Kohler conducted most of the experiments that helped to develop Gestalt theory of insight and problem solving. Most of the important books on Gestalt Psychology were written by Koffka. In 1933, Wertheimer and his family left Germany and went to the United States, where he lived till his death.

See: Gestalt, Schools of Psychology

WESCHESLER TEST: The Weschsler-Bellevue tests are intelligence tests for adults and children. The Welchsler test has an Adult Scale (WAIS) and an Inteiligence Scale for children (WISC). The Adult Scale contains both verbal and performance tests. In this test, instead of the I.Q., the norms are Deviation IQs for different age groups within the adult age range (i.e., 16+). The deviation I.Q. has a mean of 100 and S.D. of 15. Deviation I.Q. for raw score 129, at age 16, 40, 60 and 90 are given below:

Age	Raw Score is converted	Deviation IQ
16	129	115
40	129	114
60	129	121
80	129	136

WHITE COLLAR JOBS: Jobs that does not require manual work. The professionals and clericals are usually referred to as white collar workers. Manual workers are called Blue collar workers and their work, the blue collar job.

WHITEHEAD, A.N.: English philosopher mathematician and educationist (1861-1947). His 'Aims of Education' is regarded as a classic. He condemned the prevalent bookish education, and was against all dead knowledge and inert ideas. Mere accumulation of knowledge does not lead to power. Knowledge that is functional alone is important. Education should stimulate the child and guide his self-development. The student should gain generalized knowledge as well as specialized knowledge in one subject. Education should stimulate the child to think and he should experience the joy of discovery. A national system of education should have a literary, scientific and technical curriculum. He defined education as 'the art of utilization of knowledge'.

WHOLIST STRATEGY: The attitude taken in drawing inferences on the basis of all possible data. One has to draw a hypothesis only on the basis of considering all the available data. A person who adopts the wholistic strategy will only proceed on these lines, will take all pains to collect every bit of data considered pertinent, and will draw conclusions only after considering all the elements.

In concept formation also, holistic strategy leads to the formation of correct concepts. For forming generalizations, all relevant stimuli are to be considered. Otherwise, it could result in faulty generalizations and wrong concepts. If one does not care to consider all elements for formulation of generalizations he is said to follow Partist strategy (Partist strategy should be avoided).

WITHDRAWAL: 1. Terminating attendance voluntarily. The parent may withdraw his child from the school or the child himself may keep out and subsequently become a drop-out.

2. Tendency of individuals to keep aloof from other persons and social groups. Withdrawal tendency, if found in a person consistently over a period of time, is indicative of serious psychological problems. He appears sad and unhappy most of the time. Feelings of shame or guilt may be present in some cases, for which appropriate counselling will be effective. In deep seated trouble, psychiatric treatment may become necessary. Withdrawal (persistent) is an early sign of many major mental diseases.

See: Droppage

WITHDRAWAL SYMPTOMS: The sudden stoppage of addiction practices (drugs, liquors, etc.) produces undesirable overactivity of various systems and organs of the body. The symptoms that follow sudden withdrawal of drug abuse in an addict are: restlessness, uncontrollable flow of tears, nausea, vomitting, diarroheoea, irritability weight loss, etc. The personality of the victim seems disorganized. In severe cases hospital care will be needed.

WOOD–ABBOTT DESPATCH: Report of the commission on vocational education – in British India (1936-37). The report was prepared by A.A. Abbott and S.H. Wood of England at the request of the government. The commission recommended the following pattern for vocational education in India: Vocational schools of two types – Junior Vocational and Senior Vocational; Technical schools of two types: Junior Technical Schools and Senior Technical Schools and schools of Arts and Crafts. They also recommended the establishment of vocational training colleges, provisions for vocational guidance and publication of career pamphlets.

WOOD'S EDUCATION DESPATCH: The Indian Education Report, 1854. This comprehensive report, outlines the basic approach of the Britich Government towards the education of the natives. The objectives of the educational efforts of the government according to the report were: 'conferring upon the natives of India those vast moral and material blessings which flow from the general diffusion of useful knowledge... not only to produce intellectual fullness but also to raise the moral character... European knowledge will teach the natives the marvellous results of the employment of labour and capital and rouse them to emulate us in the development of the vast resources of their country... in the same time secure to us a large and more certain supply of many articles necessary for our manufacture.... and excessively consumed by all classes of our population ... "education should aim at the diffusion of the improved arts, science, philosophy and literature of Europe, in short, European knowledge... "English and vernacular languages of India together can be used as the media for the diffusion of European knowledge". The report suggested that in all schools in India there should be a sufficient number of school masters possessing the requisite qualification. Other suggestions were the creation of the departments of Public Instruction, establishment of graded schools all over the country, establishment of universities on the model of the University of London, with Senates, Chancellors, Vice-Chancellors and Fellows, giving grant-in-aid to private effort in education and the establishment of training schools and schools for females... The report also suggested that the educated Indian should be given employment in government service.

See: Sargent Report, Radhakrishnan Report, Mudaliar Report, Kothari Report

WORD PROCESSOR: A micro-computer system (including software), with a keyboard that enables the text to be composed, edited and stored in the computer. Any part of such stored material can be brought back for visual display. It can be also printed in hard copy or can be fed into any other system as needed.

WORK EXPERIENCE PROGRAMME: Providing work programmes for the student in the school. The student may be given opportunities for working part-time, in some of the work areas in the school – like library, noon-feeding service, campus beautification, etc. It may or may not be remunerative. The student gets work experience, along with his schooling.

Work experience programme may be also provided in the school as a part of the regular curriculum of the school, with the intention of developing basic work skills, proper attitude towards work, etc. Horticulture, Farming, Poultry, and the like can be introduced for work experience.

WUNDT, WILHELM: German psychologist (1832-1920). He established in Leipzig the first psychological laboratory (1879) in the world. The famous American psychologist Stanley Hall was a student under him in Leipzig.

X

X & Y THEORY (Mc Gregor's): Mc Gregor formulated this theory in 1970, drawing from Maslow's theory of hierarchy of human needs. He postulates two basic characteristics about human motivation.

Theory X: (1) People are usually lazy and very shy (2) Most people need coercion, control and threat, (3) Average person avoids responsibility and seeks direction, is not ambitious and prefers security to anything else. (4) Motivation occurs at physiological and security levels.

Theory Y: (1) For most people work is natural (2) If committed to clear objectives people will be self-directed. (3) Commitments to objectives is due to the reason they are linked to rewards (4) People usually desire to accept responsibility (5) Motivation happens at affiliation, esteem and self-actualization levels.

X-CHROMOSOME: The human sex-chromosome present in both spermatozoa (male germs cell) and ovum (female germ cell). Half the number of spermatozoa will contain 23 chromosomes of which the last one is the X-chromosome and the other half with 23 chromosomes of which the last is always an Y-chromosome. All the ova will have 23 chromosomes, of which the last will always be an X-chromosome. Fertilization of an ovum with a sperm cell with X-chromosome results in a female child while with a cell with Y-chromosome results in a male child. So it is the sperm cell that is the prime determinant of the sex of the child. That the sex-ratio in the population remains almost the same, also is due to this reason.

XENOPHOBIA: Mutual distrust and fear between races of people. This is a social phenomenon of prejudice and stereotyped attitudes are handed over traditionally to succeeding generations.

See: Phobias

XEROGRAPHY: Reprographic process that produces

multiple copies of original documents.

See: Electrostatic copying

XYZ GROUPING: A form of organization of class for instructional purposes. The class is divided into three groups according to the ability of pupils, usually high achieving group in X, low achieving group in Z and the average achievers in Y.

Y

Y-CHROMOSOME: The human Sex-chromosome present in the spermatozoa only. It is about 1/3 the size of the X-chromosome.

See: X-chromosome

YERKES-DODSON LAW: The principle that defines the relationship between the degree of arousal (motivation) and the difficulty of the task to be performed. The law states: "the optimum level of motivation declines as the difficulty of the task increases or there is an optimum level of arousal for every task and that the optimum is lower the more difficult the task". When the situation is least challenging the optimum level of arousal needed for performance of the task is very high and when the tasks is very complex the optimum level is very low. This law was enuciated by Yerkes and Dodson in 1908.

YOGA: The Indian system of physical and mental practices that are essential for preparing the individual for self-realisation. Yoga means union, and in Hindu philosophy it means the union of the individual soul (jeevatma) with the cosmic soul (Brahma or Parmatma). For this the body and mind have to be prepared, as an essential preliminary step. The Sage Pathanjali describes the yoga procedures and methods and its theory in his famous treatise in Sanskrit, 'Raja Yoga'. Yogasanas (yogic physical exercises), Pranayama (breathing exercises) and Dhyana (concentration or meditation) are the main procedures of Yoga practice.

The correct practice of yoga has been experimentally found to be effective in keeping the body and mind healthy and strong.

The system of therapeutical practices based on yoga (yoga therapy) is proved to be very effective in the treatment of various neurotic disorders like anxiety and depression.

YOGA THERAPY: The psychotherapeutic system based on Yoga. The Yoga practice of treatment draws heavily on the

Rajayoga treatise of Pathanjali. The basic assumption of this system is that man has the power to mobilize his mental energies and keep them under control so that he can lead a happy normal life. What happens to people in a complex society is that their mental energies get dissipated and they are at a loss to manage their affairs in the proper manner. So what the therapist has to do is to enable the person to master his abilities, mobilize his mental energies and coordinate his powers. This can be done by suitable practices prescribed in Yoga, like pranayama (breathing exercises) Yogasanas (Yogic exercises) dhyana (mental concentration relaxation, etc).

By regular practice under expert guidance, the symptoms (like anxiety, depression, etc) will disappear and the person achieves good mental health.

See: Yoga

YOUNG OFFENDER: A person below 18 years (minor) who has been convicted for a criminal offence. The term is equivalent to Juvenile delinquent.

Z

Z-SCORE: A derived score on a scale with a mean of zero and a standard deviation of 1.0. A raw score as such has very little meaning. For example: in a science test a boy obtained a score of 50, and in mathematics, 70. Can it be said that the performance of the student is better in mathematics? If we conclude from the magnitude of the scores, he is definitely better in mathematics. The mean of the science test was 30, with a standard deviation of 8 and that of the mathematics test were 60 and 10 respectively. The additional information indicates clearly that in the total distribution his position is better in science than in mathematics. To find out the real position of the raw score in the distribution, a 'standard score' is worked out. The basic standard score (from which practically all other standard scores are derived) is called the Z-score. It is given by the formula:

$$Z = \frac{x - m}{\sigma}$$

Where x is the raw score, m is the mean of the distribution s the standard deviation of the distribution and Z is the standard score corresponding to the raw score x.

Z score is the deviation from the mean expressed in terms of standard deviation. So, the standard score distribution has a mean of 0 and standard deviation of 1.0.

So in the example the standard scores corresponding to the raw scores in the two tests are:

Science: $\frac{(50 - 30)}{8} = 2.5$

Mathematics: $\frac{(70 - 60)}{10} = 1.0$

This means that in science the boy's position is 2.5 standard deviation (units) above the mean and so there is only approximately 1% of the scores above this value. In mathematics it is only one standard deviation above the mean so there are at least 15% of cases above this value. His performance in science is therefore far better than in mathematics.

Another advantage of the standard score is that, as the scores of the two distributions are converted into the same scale, they can be added. Raw score as such cannot be added as they belong to two different scales, i.e., with different means and standard deviations.

ZERO DEFECT: Fault free service–in Total Quality Management concept. According to Philip Crosby it is the commitment to success and elimination of failures. It assumes that the system works without any flaw. All failures are anticipated and precautionary steps taken to avoid their occurrence; in short, the systems works in the right way always.

See: Total Quality Management

ZERO TRANSFER: Learning of an activity that has no influence either positively or negatively on the learning of another activity. Learning of typewriting for example does not help or hinder learning of archery.

See: Transfer

ZIG ZAG BOOK: Scrambled text often used in Programmed Instruction. Text matter does not run continuously according to page number in scrambled texts. The pages have to be turned forward or backward independently one after another. The correct response to a frame will not be found immediately close to the frame, the learner has to look for it as indicated in the frame by turning the appropriate page either forward or backward.

See: Scrambled Text

ZOOPHOBIA: Irrational fear of animals, even harmless animals.

See: Phobias